STRINGED KEYBOARD INSTRUMENTS

FIRST EDITION IN GERMAN, 1955
BY URS GRAF-VERLAG, OLTEN, SWITZERLAND

TRANSLATED BY M. BOEHME-BROWN.

COLOR PHOTOGRAPHS AND PROCESS ENGRAVINGS
BY F. SCHWITTER LTD., BASEL
PRINTED AND BOUND BY WALTER-VERLAG, OLTEN
PRINTED IN SWITZERLAND · COPYRIGHT 1955

STRINGED KEYBOARD INSTRUMENTS

1440-1880

BY

FRANZ JOSEF HIRT

BOSTON BOOK AND ART SHOP 1968 [c1955]

BOSTON MASSACHUSETTS

DEDICATED TO DR. H. C. PAUL SACHER
FOUNDER OF SCHOLA CANTORUM BASILIENSIS
AND TO THE BERNISCHE MUSIKGESELLSCHAFT, BERNE,
IN RESPECT OF MY LONG COLLABORATION

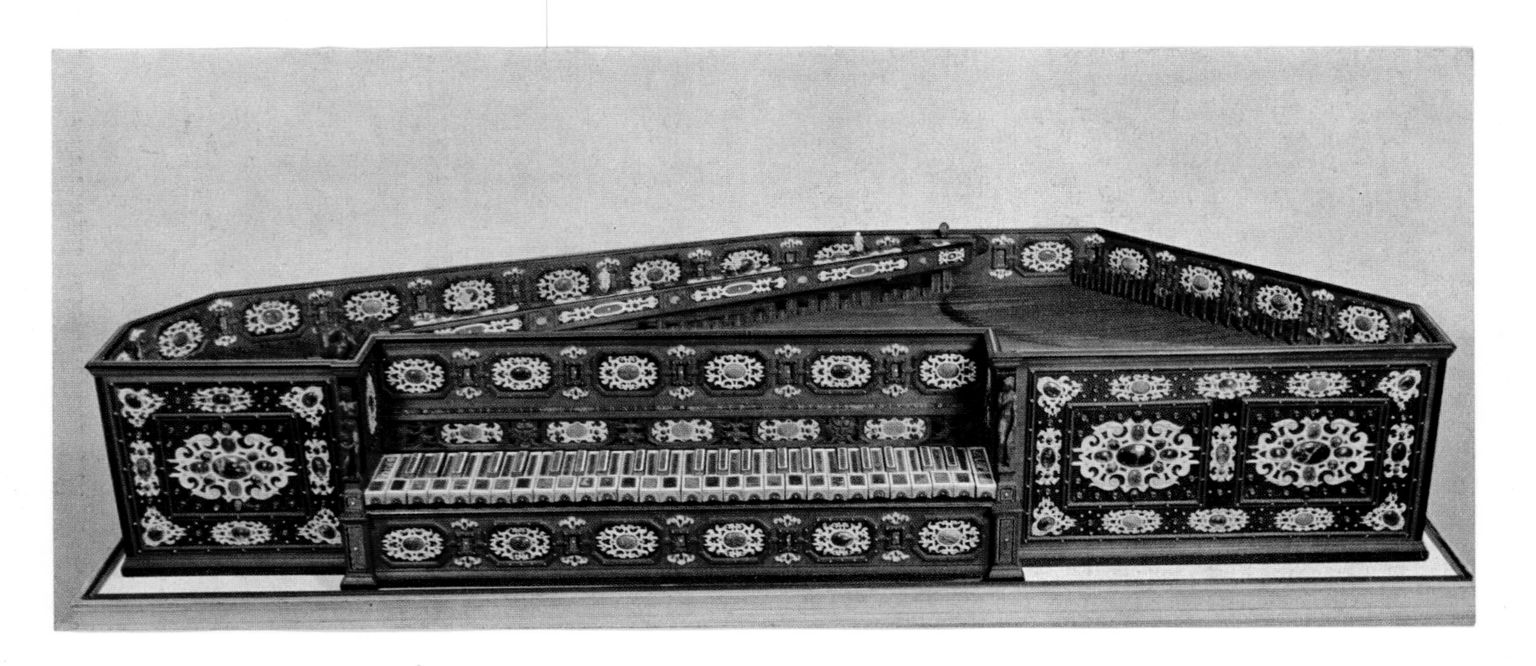

Virginal made by Annibale dei Rossi, Milan 1577. Victoria and Albert Museum, London (Description see p. 169)

We would like to offer our best thanks to Her Royal Highness Princess Wilhelmina of the Netherlands, to the Soviet Ministry of Foreign Affairs in Moscow, and to the various institutes and personalities mentioned hereafter, for their kind donation of valuable documents for illustration or permission to reproduce them:

Bamberg	Hanns Neupert, Museum of the History of Music
Boston	Museum of Fine Arts
Budapest	Hungarian National Museum of History
Chesam Bois	Philip James, Director of Art
Copenhagen	Museum of the History of Music
Göteborg	Museum
Hamburg	Museum für Kunst und Gewerbe
Holyoke	The Belle and William Skinner Collection of Old Musical Instruments
Icomb on Stow on the Wold	Dr. Rosamond Harding
Leipzig	Instrumentenmuseum der Universität
Lisboa	Dr. Ivo Cruz, Director of the Conservatório Nacional
Markneukirchen	Städtisches Gewerbemuseum
New York	Metropolitan Museum of Art
Oslo	Norsk Folke Museum
Paris	Erard
	Pleyel
Potsdam	Direktion der ehem. Staatlichen Schlösser und Gärten
Poznań	National Museum (by courtesy of the Polish Embassy in Berne)
Prague	Dr. V. Holzknecht, Director of the State Conservatory of Music
	National Museum
Salem	Essex Institute Museum
Stuttgart	Landesgewerbemuseum
	Kohlhammer-Verlag

The following Bureaus, Libraries, Museums and Private Collections have lent their kind support:

Eidgenössisches Politisches Departement, Bern
Her Royal Highness Princess Wilhelmina of the Netherlands
Soviet Ministry of Foreign Affairs, Moscow
State Department, Washington
British Embassy, Bern
United States Embassy, Bern
Norwegian Embassy, Bern
Polish Embassy, Bern
U.R.S.S. Embassy, Bern
British Council, London
Franklin Institute, Philadelphia
Schweizerische Landesbibliothek, Bern

Aarau	Museum Alt-Aarau, Schlössli
Aarburg	Museum der Historischen Vereinigung Alt-Aarburg
Altstätten	Historisches Museum
Amsterdam	Rijksmuseum
Ann Arbor	University of Michigan
Antwerp	Vleeshuis Museum
	J. A. Stellfeld Collection
Arbon	Historisches Museum
Arenenberg	Napoleonmuseum, Schloss
Bamberg	H. Neupert Museum of the History of Music
Barcelona	Museo de Música
Basel	Historisches Museum
	Schola Cantorum Basiliensis, Collection of Musical Instruments
Berlin	Institut für Musikforschung
Bern	Historisches Museum
Bischofszell	Ortsmuseum, Schloss
Bologna	Museo civico
Bonn	Beethovenhaus
Boston	Museum of Fine Arts
Bournemouth	K. Mummery Collection
Braunschweig	Städtisches Museum
Bremen	Focke-Museum
Bruges	Musée Gruuthuse
Bruxelles	Musée instrumental du Conservatoire Royal de Musique
Budapest	Hungarian National Museum of History
Bulle	Musée Gruyérien
Cambridge	Fitzwilliam Museum
Cardiff	Welsh Folk Museum
Chicago	Harding Museum
Chur	Rätisches Museum
Cincinnati	Art Museum
Clevedon	A.E. Leslie Spacie Collection
Copenhagen	Museum of the History of Music
	Claudius Collection
Dearborn (Mich.)	Henry Ford Museum
Delémont	Musée jurassien
Dereham	The Reverend I. N. Boston Collection
Dublin	National Museum of Ireland
Dundee	Albert Institute
Edinburgh	Royal Scottish Museum
Eisenach	Bachhaus
Exeter	Royal Albert Memorial Museum
Firenze	Museo degli Strumenti dell'Istituto Musicale Luigi Cherubini
Frankfurt a. M.	Historisches Museum
	Musikabteilung der Stadt- und Universitäts-bibliothek
Frauenfeld	Thurgauisches Museum
Fribourg	Musée d'Art et d'Histoire
Genève	Musée d'Art et d'Histoire
Glasgow	Art Gallery
Göteborg	Museum
Den Haag	Gemeente Museum
Hälsingborg	Museum
Halle a. d. Saale	Händelmuseum
Hamburg	Museum für Hamburgische Geschichte
	Museum für Kunst und Gewerbe
Hampstead	Fenton House
Haslemere	Norman Anderson Collection
Holyoke (Mass.)	The Belle Skinner Collection
Ipswich	Christchurch Mansion
Istanbul	Palais de Dolmabahçe
Keighley	Museum
Lausanne	Musée du Vieux Lausanne et Musée de Mon-Repos
Leicester	City Museum
Leipzig	Musikwissenschaftliches Institut und Instrumentenmuseum der Universität
Lichtensteig	Toggenburger Heimatmuseum
Lisboa	Conservatório Nacional
Liverpool	The Rushworth & Dreaper Collection
Le Locle	Musée Historique
London	Donaldson Museum (Royal College of Music)
	Horniman Museum
	London Museum
	Bethnal Green Museum
	Raymond Russell Collection
	Trinity College of Music
	Victoria and Albert Museum

Luzern	Städt. Sammlung alter Musikinstrumente, Tribschen
	Wagnermuseum, Tribschen
Manchester	Central Library
	Forsythe Brothers Collection
	Royal College of Music
Markneukirchen	Städtisches Gewerbemuseum
Milano	Museo Teatrale alla Scala
Modena	Museo civico
München	Bayerisches Nationalmuseum
	Deutsches Museum
	Städtische Musikinstrumentensammlung
Napoli	Museo storico musicale
Neuchâtel	Musée historique
New Haven	Yale University
New York	Metropolitan Museum of Art
Norwich	Castle Museum
Nürnberg	Germanisches Museum
	Rück Collection, partly also in Erlangen, University
Olten	Historisches Museum
Oslo	Norsk Folke Museum
Oxford	Ashmolean Museum
	Pitt Rivers Museum (University of Oxford)
Paris	Conservatoire des Arts et Métiers
	Musée de Cluny
	Musée instrumental du Conservatoire National de Musique
	Musée de l'Opéra
	Erard Collection
	Pleyel Collection
Peterborough	Museum
Philadelphia	University Museum
Potsdam	Direktion der ehem. Staatlichen Schlösser und Gärten
Poznań	National Museum
Prague	National Museum
	Villa Bertramka
Providence	Museum of Art
Rapperswil	Heimatmuseum
Salem (Mass.)	Essex Institute Museum
Salzburg	Carolino-Augusteum Museum
	Mozarteum
Sarnen	Heimatmuseum
Solothurn	Historisches Museum
Stockholm	Museum of the History of Music
Stuttgart	Württembergisches Landesmuseum
Taunton	Somerset County Museum
Thun	Historisches Museum, Schloss
Torino	Museo civico
Toronto	Royal Ontario Museum
Verona	Museo civico
Versailles	Château
Warrington	Municipal Museum
Washington	United States National Museum
Weimar	Goethehaus
	Lisztmuseum
Wien	Gesellschaft der Musikfreunde
	Historisches Museum der Stadt Wien
	Kunsthistorisches Museum, Collection of Old Musical Instruments
	Österreichisches Museum für angewandte Kunst
York	York Castle Museum
Yverdon	Musée du Vieil Yverdon
Zürich	Schweizerisches Landesmuseum

TABLE OF CONTENTS

INTRODUCTION

RENDO LIETI IN UN TEMPO GLI OCCHI EL CUORE
(Eyes' delight and heart's delight)

These words shining in delicate gold letters on the nameboard of a harpsichord by Vitus de Trasuntini of the year 1560 shall be the 'leitmotiv' of this book. The inner urge to its creation is the musician's joy in the keyboard instrument as such and in its beauty of outward form. Final and deciding factor was the World War I, the desire to place within reach of musicians and lovers of music a book containing beautiful pictures to form a complete survey of at least one field of western culture, to show its manifold facets of interest and pictures of those of its priceless treasures which have survived the terrors of destruction. My appeal to the world found an echo from all sides: from West and East, from North and South, from continent to continent came answers, all intent on the desired goal.

My book is dedicated primarily to 'Masterpieces of the keyboard instrument maker's art', to those treasures still preserved and accessible up to the present day. This being so, the earliest date indicated should be 1521, but it does not seem misplaced to go back still further to the year 1440, about which time Heinrich Arnold of Zwolle's description of a clavicymbalum keyed dulcimer appeared. With this date, in my opinion, we emerge from the 'mythical' into the strictly 'historical' age of the keyboard instrument, which prompts me to choose this point for the commencement of my considerations, setting as my furthest limit the year 1880. During this period the development of the stringed keyboard instrument *grosso modo* reached its highest point. My theme is, therefore, confined within the space of 440 years.

With a light heart I waive the responsibility of trusting myself to the somewhat thin and treacherous ice of so-called 'prehistorical' research on the origin and character of the earliest stringed keyboard instruments. I am glad to leave that to specialists, frankly confessing that as a player those questions do not interest me very much.

To ensure the book remaining of a reasonable size, and in view of the many important illustrations, the text hereto has had to be kept terse and somewhat formal in order to achieve descriptive completeness within given limits. The book has thus gained the character of a book of reference, which was always my intention. The material having been divided into several distinct parts facilitates reading, as I know from my own experience. That a certain uniformity of structure throughout the whole book has been the writer's aim will be obvious to the attentive reader.

The book is founded on the classics: Ernest Closson's 'Histoire du Piano', Rosamund Harding's admirable book on the Development of the Piano up to the year 1851, Hanns Neupert's writings about the Harpsichord and Clavichord, Tobias Norlind's 'Systematik der Musikinstrumente', Walter Pfeiffer's on the Hammer action and Curt Sachs's 'History of Musical Instruments'. Without a specialized knowledge of these works my book could hardly have been written.

To whom is the book directed? It is my hope that the magnificent illustrations, upon the choice and production of which the greatest care has been expended, will be a joy to many people. Between these pages pictures of the greatest treasures from all important collections of instruments in the Old and the New World appear for the first time collected together. I can also imagine the painter and the craftsman turning these pages with interest. For the piano builder the text, except for certain dates, will hardly bring much that is new. But the musician and the musical layman should find the answer to many questions in what I hope will prove to be the book's clear and concise method of presentation.

A book of pictures, such as this, usually requires an explanatory preface, but in this case the pictures practically speak for themselves. From the wealth of material before us a great many photographs stand out which elicit more than sheer interest in the instruments as such. They call forth visions of the history of music, of civilization, of politics and of world-culture in general. Such instruments, singled out for their connection with outstanding personalities, take precedence in our consideration. Thus, the photographs of these special examples speak an eloquent preface or introduction, the text which accompanies each one cooperating in the quite 'unsystematized' journey down through the centuries.

As a child I was always assailed by an indefinable feeling of fear on entering any strange Church. At the same time, a kind of magic took possession of me, drawing the half-reluctant boy, hesitating before the heavy, closed door, through into the all-enveloping grandeur of space. Was it caused by the solemn height and breadth of the interior, or was it born of a nervous dread of the rich tones of the organ which might suddenly break upon the air, or was it a sense of the Presence of God? Who can say? Certain it is that to this day I still feel something of that child-like awe when I play upon the instrument of Mozart, Beethoven, Chopin, Mendelssohn, Wagner or Liszt. My fingers touch the same keys, my ear hears the same tones as ... but, enough! These are very personal and intimate things which you, dear reader, may possibly experience in quite a different way.

The scene is laid in *Venice*, Mistress of the Mediterranean, center of Levantine commerce, at the summit of her glory and expansion. The year is 1491, the first maestro di cappella is chosen for the Church of San Marco when Venice enters the arena of musical history. In 1527 Adriaan Willaert was appointed maestro di cappella. Simultaneously from the churches of Northern Italy there sounds ever richer and more contrapuntal organ music. At the time of the organists of St. Mark's, Andrea and Giovanni Gabrieli and Claudio Merulos, the ricercare, fantasia, toccata, 'canzone alla Francese' became accepted forms. The first three of these, when not definitely intended as church music, were played upon the organ, the virginal or the harpsichord, whereas the 'canzone alla Francese', a form generally used for songs of a worldly character, was intended for the virginal or the harpsichord. In 1551, also in Venice, there appeared a collection of dances, published by Antonio Gardano called 'Intabolatura nova di varie sorte de balli da sonare per Arpichordi, Clavicembali, Spinette e Manochordi', a collection composed primarily for stringed keyboard instruments. What are these 'arpichordi, clavicembali, spinette e manochordi', what do they look like and how do they sound?

Virginals and harpsichords are generally built of cypress- or cedar-wood. For reasons of resonance the walls are extremely thin, the instrument itself resting in a richly decorated protective case, out of which it can be lifted. On the inner side of the lid there is usually a painting of some value. The edges, the jackrail and the cheekpieces are ornamented with little bone disks and the nameboard with arabesques or delicate ivory carving, or sometimes with a Latin motto. Occasionally this motto is to be found inside the lid. The nameboard shows the date when the instrument was built and the name of the maker. Over the soundhole on the soundboard, which is generally in cypress-wood, there is a delicately carved rose in wood. The keyboard, normally projecting, has keys in ebony or ivory, the faces of which are mostly shaped with the typical Gothic trefoil. On the sides we find protective laths which are characteristic of most of the early instruments. The compass of instruments at this time was mostly 4 octaves and a fifth, with a short bass-octave. The one-manual harpsichord is the most usual form. The tone of the single-strung (8') and later, (1514) of the double-strung (8', 8') instrument (the 4' stop was first introduced in 1582 but seldom used) is charming and silvery, its vibration awakening faint memories of the delicate beauty and transcendentalism of Fra Angelico's angels, bringing to life the slender, womanly grace of Botticelli's figures. Played on such instruments, the canzones by Gabrieli must have been as delicate as a silver-point etching.

Rome, Anno Domini 1547 Pope Paul III (Alexander Farnese) calls upon Michelangelo to complete the building of St. Peter's Church. From the Churches of San Giovanni in Laterano and Santa Maria Maggiore pious chorals are to be heard, for Rome now competes with Venice for first importance as a musical center in Italy. It is, therefore, not surprising that the first masterpieces of the instrument maker's art should see the light in Venice, the town of rich commerce and culture and also in Rome, center of Western Christianity. Here the first great masters worked, laying the foundation of that 'famous century' of Italian instrument-building. There were such great names as the Venetians Dominicus Pisaurensis, Johannes Antonio Baffo, Alexander and Vitus Trasuntinus, Benedetto Floriani, Johannes Celestini; whilst in Verona, in the Republic of Venice, there was Franciscus de Portalupis, in the Duchy of Milan Annibale and Ferrante de Rossi, in the Duchy of Modena, Alexander Pasi, and in Rome Hieronymus Bononiensis and Antonio Irena, all of whom were worthy to take their place amongst the great masters.

Clavichord, virginal, and harpsichord have after all always been luxury-instruments. Yet with that sure sense for proportion and line prevailing in the restraint of late Italian Renaissance decoration, even such a showy instrument as the spinet by Annibale de Rossi, constructed for the house of Trivulzio in Milan, even that virginal sparkling in the splendor of two thousand jewels does not appear ostentatious.

There is charm in the bewitching figure of the young player of a portative organ, in the hovering angels holding a lettered scroll on dark-blue ground on the two pedal-spinets of anonymous workmanship, and the clavicytherium, said to be the property of Pope Gregory XIII, with paintings of angels attributed to Fra Angelico, together with the restrained elegance of the instrument by Baffo and the brilliance of Rossi's bejewelled virginal, all combine to make up the wealth and versatility of a whole century of Italian culture and of Italian instrument-building.

There is, therefore, no doubt that the compositions, which were gradually developing from quite modest beginnings, were confronted with a beautiful and perfected instrument far beyond their demands.

Can Italy, the birthplace of the oldest remaining clavichords and virginals, perhaps also claim to be the first to produce keyboard instruments as such? Ambros[1] maintains that the clavichord originates in Italy, which statement has remained uncontested, leaving one to suppose that the same holds good for the virginals and harpsichords, though of this there is no actual proof.

The Italian 'cembalo' of the 17th century persists in its traditional double-stringed type; even the earlier single-stringed type, which practically abolishes the difference between virginal and harpsichord, has been to some extent preserved. The most frequent form is the single keyboard. Frescobaldi's works for the harpsichord and the 'Toccate e Correnti' by his pupil Michelangelo Rossi (1657), in spite of their complicated polyphony can be played with good effect on the instruments of this time. Yet a further advance along the path of strict polyphony must lead inevitably to *conflict between the composer's creative inspiration and the inadequacy of the instrument at his disposal.* What is the solution? The composer *confines himself to a more homophonic style of composition suitable to the nature of his instrument, a style generally characterized by great brilliance.*

The man standing at the crossroads of Italian harpsichord music at this fateful moment was Bernardo Pasquini (1637–1710), organist of Santa Maria Maggiore in Rome. He was Janus-faced, for his works belonged both to the past and the future.

At the turn of the 17th/18th centuries the change came at last to triple stringing (8′, 8′, 4′) and to the construction of two and even three manuals, thus distributing the three registers upon three keyboards and eliminating the use of stops.

The storm and passion for outward expression of the Baroque period gradually subsides, giving way to the curved and flowing lines of Rococo, the most feminine of all styles, which in its turn ebbs completely away into peaceful surfaces and straight lines, the stiff grace of Louis XVI style. And it is at this point that the Italian harpsichord, the most 'feminine' of all harpsichords, is shaped in an adequate style to be an adornment to any room.

It is the year 1839, the year after Chopin's '24 Préludes' and Berlioz's dramatic symphony 'Romeo and Juliet' appeared. Yet in idyllic Bergamo a man is still building spinets – a man for whom time has stood still. Was this spinet maker an oddity? Retrospect or presentiment?

[1] *Ambros*, Geschichte der Musik, Vol. II., Breslau 1864.

Retrospect or presentiment? I ask this question with regard to Cristofori's pianoforte. Was this surprisingly mature device (Stosszungenmechanik), so complete in its action and principle—the forerunner of our present piano—a creative stroke of genius and of technical invention, or the ripe fruit of an older tradition of which we know nothing certain? "This instrument (the dulcimer or 'Hackbrett' invented by Pantaleon Hebenstreit)," says Kuhnau,[1] "has the prerogative and quality over the harpsichord, that one can change the tone from *forte* to *piano*, wherein lies a great *momentum dulcedinis et gratiae musicae*." Cristofori, however, was certainly the first to achieve a serviceable form of hammer action capable of satisfying higher artistic demands. Thus his name will remain for ever connected with the history of the pianoforte, whether or not one will call him, as heretofore, the 'inventor' of the hammer action.

One thing is certain: the pianoforte was considered in Italy to be an oddity and was treated with indifference. Cristofori returned therefore, after 1726, to the making of harpsichords, dying in Florence in 1731, a disappointed and embittered man. A pupil of his, Ferrini, continued to build a few pianofortes and in 1732, in Florence, the first compositions for the new instrument were published by Ludovico Giustini, whilst Domenico Del Mela in Mugello, near Florence, constructed in 1739 the first Italian upright pianoforte. Were these the first of their kind? In any case, the experiment was in vain, for they remained unique examples, calling forth no single echo even in the land of their origin. Florence, the outpost in the South of the pianoforte, capitulated after 1739.

There were strange coincidences in these times; seven years after Cristofori's death in 1738, the last of the Medici family, in the person of the Florentine art-patron and maecenas of Cristofori, died and the Grand Duchy of Tuscany passed into the hands of Franz Stephan of Lothringen, husband of the Empress Maria Theresia of Austria. Italy renewed acquaintance with the rejected pianoforte by way of Germany and Vienna. And because, since 1780, the instrument had achieved popularity in the Emperor's town on the Danube, it became 'fashionable' in Italy. The fashion was to play upon these light, elegant Austrian pianos, with their sparkling 'Viennese action', those brilliant compositions which, in their virtuosity, so entirely suited the Italian taste. One realizes how much the Italians appreciated such instruments, which they must have imported, when one considers that it was not until the end of the 18th century that in Naples and Milan the first attempts were made to develop an Italian piano-building industry, beginning in the year 1840.

The existence of a valuable virginal-music, independent of that for the organ, in the last third of the 16th century and the first thirty years of the 17th century, points to a tradition of considerable duration in the matter of virginal-building and of virginal-playing in England. But to argue from this that England is the land of origin of the keyboard instrument is simply one more hypothesis for which there is no definite proof. It is, however, certain that in comparison with the very popular virginal, the clavichord could not compete at all. It seems that very soon Dutch virginals and harpsichords began to be imported on a large scale, for which Antwerp became the center from which England drew her supply. From the Dutch virginal the English virginal makers copied the square shape and general set-up; for instance, the soundboards decorated with paintings (fruit, flowers, birds), the decoration of the case with embossed parchment and the inside of the lid embellished by a painting.

1660. The bloody years of civil war being over, the English spinet- and harpsichord makers under Charles II (1660–1685) shook off continental influence: decoration of the case is rare and the whole shape alters. We are faced with the *English spinet*, which from now onwards presents a sharp contrast to the instruments of the European continent. James marks three distinct stages in the development of these successors of the virginal:

First period, 1660–1680. The instruments are mostly undecorated except for an occasional strap-hinge; their stands and bodies are made of oak.

[1] Mattheson: 'Critica Musica' for 8 Dec. 1717; letter from Kuhnau.

Second period, 1680–1715. The instruments of this period are generally made of walnut, the nameboard sometimes decorated with inlay. The best known makers of this time are Charles Haward, Stephen Keene, Charles Brackley, Thomas and John Hitchcock.
Third period, 1715 till (in my opinion) the end of the 18th century. General enlargement of the instrument, beautiful inlay work and increasing elegance of form. Makers: Joseph and John Harris, Baker Harris, and Joseph Mahoon. Some time previously the extent of the keyboard had been increased to five octaves, G_1 to g‴.
The harpsichord, which in the 18th century reached perfection, was first mentioned as early as 1492. The earliest English example in good preservation is the John Haward harpsichord, dated 1622, with a beautiful Renaissance stand. That man built in 1660 a harpsichord with four pedals ('pummels of wood'). Rather more than a hundred years later the Swiss Burkard Tschudi, London's famous harpsichord maker, took up Haward's invention once more, fitting his harpsichords from 1765 with the machine-stop and from 1769 onwards, with the 'Venetian Swell'-pedal, somewhat in the form of a Venetian blind. Later on, Tschudi's competitor, Jakob Kirkman, adopted the same idea in a modified form. Through an adjustable opening and closing of the whole harpsichord lid a similar swell-effect could be obtained. Whereas in the 17th century the woods used were mostly oak and walnut with beautifully engraved brass hinges, ivory natural-keys with ridged facing (Hitchcock style) and sharps in ebony being the only ornament, in the 18th century Tschudi and Kirkman worked chiefly in more valuable woods such as veneered mahogany, satinwood, etc., decorating the instruments with rich inlay. The original five-octave keyboard was increased by Tschudi in 1749 to five octaves and a fourth, i.e. from C_1 to F⁗, whilst retaining the usual trichord stringing (8′, 8′, 4′). To this were added 'lute' and 'buff' or 'harp' stop.
London, 5th July, 1765. "The famous harpsichord maker Burkard Thudi (sic), Swiss by birth, had the honor of building a harpsichord with two manuals for His Majesty the King of Prussia, which was much admired by all who saw it. As something very unusual it was noticed that Thudy had combined all the registers in one pedal, so that they can be used one after the other by pressure of the pedal, thus achieving the desired decrease and increase of tone, the dream of every player. Thudy had the excellent idea, moreover, of letting his unusual instrument be played for the first time by the most wonderful pianist of our time, namely by the famous nine-year-old musician Wolfgang Mozart, the astonishing little son of Mozart, the Salzburg organist. It was quite bewitching to hear the 14-year-old sister of the young virtuoso playing with amazing power the most difficult sonatas on one piano, while her brother accompanied her extempore on another piano. Both of them are wonders.'[1]
Frederick the Great, King of Prussia, was much pleased with this instrument and ordered two more harpsichords from Tschudi, probably as presents for his sister and brother, the extremely musical and talented Princess Anna Amalia and Prince Heinrich.[2] The instrument with the signature 'Burkat Tschudi fecit Londini 1766' with the maker's number 511 is still to be found in the New Palace at Potsdam. Though it originally stood in the Silver Salon—as shown in the photograph—it now stands in place of the second harpsichord with the number 512 (which is no longer in existence), in the music room at the New Palace.[3] As a sign of his appreciation Frederick sent the maker of these beautiful instruments a costly ring set with a picture of himself, a ring which Tschudi valued highly, leaving it in his will to the organ builder Schnetzler in London.
Charles Burney, English musicologist, whilst travelling in Europe in the years 1771 and 1772, describes his impressions in the form of a diary,[4] a musical Graf Keyserling of the 18th century. Whilst in Germany, he

1 'Salzburger Europäische Zeitung', 6 Aug. 1765 (No. 63).
2 Kinsky, Georg. Die Flügel Friedrichs des Grossen.
3 From information kindly supplied by Professor Dr. Kurth, Director of the Former State Palaces and Gardens, Potsdam, Sans Souci.
4 Burney, Charles, The present state of music in Germany, etc., London 1775. Edited by Percy A. Scholer, London 1959.

visited Potsdam, the King's residence. Let us accompany him as he enters, "the king's New Palace built since the last war. ... The apartments are fitted up with the utmost magnificence and taste. There is a suite of rooms appropriated to almost every branch of the royal family. Those of the king, of his sister Princess Amalia, and the Prince of Prussia, are the most splendid. In each of these apartments, there is a room dedicated to music, furnished with books, desks, a harpsichord, and with other instruments.

His majesty's concert room is ornamented with glasses of an immense size, and with sculpture, partly gilt, and partly of the most beautiful green varnish, by Martin of Paris; the whole furniture and ornaments of this room, are in the most refined and exquisite taste. There is a pianoforte made by Silbermann of Neuberg, beautifully varnished and embellished; and a tortoise shell desk for his majesty's use, most richly and elegantly inlaid with silver. ... In another apartment, there is a most magnificent harpsichord, made by Schudi, in England; the hinges, pedals, and frame are of silver, the case is inlaid, and the front is of tortoise shell; this instrument which cost 200 guineas, was sent to Hamburg by sea, and from thence to Potsdam, up the Elb and the Havel. ... And while I am on the subject of musical instruments, I must observe, that the Germans work much better out of their own country, than they do in it, if we may judge by the harpsichords of Kirkman and Shudi, (excuse me, Mr. Burney, Shudi is Swiss!) the pianofortes of Becker and the organs of Snetzler; which far surpass, in goodness, all the keyed instruments that I met with in my tour through Germany."

This opinion is astonishing when one remembers that in Germany at this time Gottfried Silbermann had been dead already 19 years and the organ builder Zacharias Hildebrand 15 years, whereas Gottfried Hildebrand, Hieronymus Albrecht and Johannes Albert Hass, Johann Heinrich II and Karl August Gräbner, also Johann Andreas Stein, were all at the height of their powers. Burney's statement either came 120 years too late or 30 years too early. If it had been said of Germany after 1648, when the Thirty Years' War had left the country completely impoverished, its economic life in town and country in ruins, his (Burney's) opinion would have been correct. It is certain that many valuable instruments must have been destroyed, that the making of harpsichords suffered a severe decrease in comparison with the much cheaper clavichord and one realizes that until the end of the 17th century no single instrument of any particular importance remained intact. All the more wonderful is the rise, during the 18th century, to a maximum of efficiency through the medium of just those craftsmen mentioned above, whose work was '*primus inter pares*'.

Had the clavichord of William Gruneberg in the Royal College in Manchester not been subsequently enlarged and altered, the unfretted five-octave instrument would have already been achieved in 1700. Curiously enough, the 'gebundene' (fretted) clavichord, with all its little advantages as well as its great disadvantages, was still in use until the turn of the century, such a famous craftsman as Hubert still building them in 1782.

In the richly fitted, sonorous instruments by Hieronymus Albrecht Hass and Christian Gottlob Hubert, German clavichord-building reached its highest point; and the unpretentious instruments of Gottfried Silbermann were worthy successors thereof.

This ideal instrument of a sentimental century was destined to achieve a literature of its own from about 1753 to 1800. In the rapturous and somewhat lacrymose mode of expression of those days it found extravagant praise. "The clavichord surpasses all others. Although by its very nature excluded from the public concert, it is all the more fitted to be the confidant of the recluse. Here, on the clavichord—if I have sensitivity and understanding enough—I can lend to the tone all manner of shades. I can decrease, vibrate, swell or let the tone die away completely. Here I can open my heart. I can dream, chase shadows and melt in ecstasy; here I can achieve the beauty of the infinitesimal." [1]

What riches of unlimited possibility belong to the German harpsichord of the 18th century! Let us compare the specification of some of these instruments:

[1] Reichardt, Mus. Almanach, 1782.

16′, 8′, 8′, 4′, 2′,	also one buff stop and one harp stop 8′ in the second manual, and one harp stop 16′ in the first manual; also manual coupler (1710? Johannes A. Hass) The true date must be much later, e.g. 1770 (Boalch).	
16′, 8′, 8′, 4′	buff stop	manual coupler (anonymus, mistakenly so-called 'Bach'-harpsichord)
– 8′, 8′, 8′, 4′	buff stop	manual coupler (1723, Hieronymus Albrecht Hass)
16′, 8′, 4′, 4′, 2′	the 2′ and 4′	worked by leather plectra (1734, Hieronymus Albrecht Hass)
16′, 8′, 4′, –′	buff stop	manual coupler (Johann Heinrich Gräbner II, 1774)
– 8′, 8′, 4′, –	buff stop	manual coupler (Johann Heinrich Gräbner I, 1722; Karl August Gräbner, 1782)

Development in instrument-building was on a grand scale as is seen by the fact that already in 1582 an inventory of instruments at the Court of Brandenburg mentions a stringed keyboard instrument with four stops, probably 8′, 8′, 8′, 4′; and in 1583 a Dresden inventory lists three examples of harpsichords, each with two manuals. This is an achievement which, as mentioned above, had been grievously delayed by the Thrirty Years' War. The keyboard compass at this time was usually five full octaves.

Like all continental instruments of that time the Hass harpsichords are known for their richly decorated cases, with paintings inside the lid and scattered flowers painted on the soundboard. Characteristic of them all is the covering of tortoise shell on the keys. The harpsichord by Silbermann in Eisenach with its dainty Rococo decoration is, however, an exception to the above and is in the style of all the Silbermann instruments, as also of the spinet and pianoforte by Johann Heinrich Silbermann of Strasbourg, the case showing a restrained elegance in late-Rococo style, with panelled lid, the rose on the soundboard having an 'S' within a triangle. Such panelled lids and a similar plain style is found in the instruments by Gräbner, as also in the pianoforte by Silbermann's pupil, Johann Andreas Stein of Augsburg.

The great fascination of the German harpsichords, particularly those of Silbermann, is what the organ builder Casparini calls their 'silvery voice', their 'gleaming metallic timbre' (Flade) which was also characteristic of the organs of those days and which Flade particularly stresses in his biography of Silbermann.

The 'pianoforte by the Neuberg Silbermann' mentioned by Burney has actually a very dramatic history. Let us turn back briefly to Florence, to the Court of Ferdinando de' Medici. In 1709, the curator of his instrument collection, Bartolomeo Cristofori, built his first pianoforte. And in 1711, the Marchese Maffei published in the 'Giornale dei Letterati di Venezia' a description of Cristofori's invention. Again in 1719, Maffei reprinted his report of 1711. In 1725, Mattheson, in his journal 'Critica musica', published a German translation of Maffei's description. In this way Cristofori's invention became known in Germany. In 1731, Gottfried Silbermann, in Freiberg near Dresden, built two pianos whose action is practically identical with the invention of Cristofori. It is therefore taken for granted that Silbermann knew of Cristofori's work, and that he copied it.

In 1717 Gottfried Schröter in Dresden invented a hammer action of which he made two distinct models; in one the hammer action works upwards and in the other, downwards. In the morning, between 8 and 9 o'clock on the 11th November 1721, Schröter takes his two models to the Royal Palace in Dresden, where he interests August I, King of Saxony, in his inventions. The King orders the construction of one of these models, but the finished instrument never materialized, nor were Schröter's models ever returned to him. This circumstance resulted in an uncomfortable situation and an argument about copyright. Who copied who's invention? Cristofori Schröter's, Schröter Cristofori's, Silbermann Schröter's or Cristofori's? The echo of this unpleasant quarrel is still to be heard in Adlung's 'Musica mechanica Organoedi', II part, p. 115 (published in 1768). What remains to us of the whole affair, which subsequent history has long ago explained satisfactorily, is the following passage on p. 116: "Of these instruments (pianofortes, author's note) Gottfried Silbermann had made two examples (the above mentioned two pianofortes, author's note). One of these the late organist Johann Sebastian Bach had inspected and played upon.[1] He praised the tone, which he admired. At the same time he criticized the instrument for being weak in the treble and having a heavy touch. This unfavorable remark Mr. Silbermann took very much amiss, for he could not bear to hear his workmanship criticized. For a long time he could not forgive Mr. Bach. And yet in his heart of hearts he knew Mr. Bach's criticism was not unjust. Therefore—and very much to his credit be it said—he refrained from making any further instrument on this method, giving his whole attention to improving and correcting the defect to which Mr. Bach had called attention. This demanded many years of work. And that this is true and the whole cause of the long delay I have no doubt, for Mr. Silbermann himself told me quite frankly all about it. After Mr. Silbermann had made many improvements, particularly in the action of the instrument, he sold one at last to the Prince's Court at Rudolstadt. ... Shortly after this, His Majesty the King of Prussia ordered one of these instruments and, on its finding his royal approval, several other examples from Mr. Silbermann. The tone of all these instruments showed plainly to anyone who like myself had seen the original instruments, how assiduously Mr. Silbermann must have worked. Mr. Silbermann had also the praiseworthy ambition to show one of these new examples of his work to the late organist Mr. Bach for his inspection, receiving his entire approval. Meanwhile, before Mr. Silbermann came forward with his new work, other clever makers had worked on other specifications of the same kind of instrument, though on rather different lines. How some of these turned out I cannot say, though the work of *Mr. C.E. Friederici*, a man well-known for combining great inventive faculty with the finest workmanship of this kind, seems to me to be specially worthy of mention." Such are the notes of the 'Composer to the Royal Court of Prussia', Johann Friedrich Agricola in Berlin (1720–1774), to be found in the works of Adlung.

I. G. Fischer, in the 'Nachrichten von dem berühmten Orgelbauer Silbermann'[2] (News of the famous organ builder Silbermann) gives the number of pianofortes sold to the King of Prussia as seven, for which, with the exception of the last one, he received 700 Talers each. Forkel[3] writes: "So much did the King admire the pianofortes of Silbermann of Freiberg that he proposed to buy them all. He brought the number of his purchases up to fifteen. They are now said to be all useless, standing about in different corners of the Royal Castles." Of these instruments after the World War I only the Silbermann pianoforte[4] in the music room at the Palace of Sans Souci remains. The second instrument on which Frederick the Great played a theme on 7th Mai 1747, on the occasion of his meeting with Johann Sebastian Bach, was destroyed by fire in the Stadtschloss at Potsdam in the year 1945. Bach himself sat down at the instrument "and to His Majesty's great pleasure extemporized on the King's theme." This theme Bach subsequently used as the basis of the 'Musikalisches Opfer' (Musical Offering: Canones diversi super Thema Regium).[5]

We must consider ourselves fortunate to have at least a picture of that instrument, as well as that of the historical Music Room of the Stadtschloss at Potsdam to bequeath to posterity.

1760. At this time Frederick II had already been four years at war with Russia, France and Austria. Alarmed by the ever-changing fortunes of war at Kolin, Rossbach, Leuthen, Hochkirch and Kunersdorf, twelve of Silbermann's pupils, amongst them Zumpe, Pohlmann, Ganer, Beyer, Becker and others moved to England, with whom Frederick was allied. 1760 saw the birth of the English 'square piano' made by Zumpe. When in

[1] 1735 or 1736 in Dresden.

[2] 'Freiberger gemeinnützige Nachrichten' 1800, p. 127.

[3] Forkel, Über Bachs Leben, Kunst und Kunstwerke, Leipzig 1802, p. 10.

[4] Reported by Prof. Dr. Kurth, Director of the former State Palaces and Gardens, Potsdam.

[5] Kinsky, Georg, Die Flügel Friedrichs des Grossen.

1763 peace was proclaimed between Frederick and Maria Theresia, a gallant gesture was made by the Prussian King in 1773, i.e. he presented the Austrian Empress with a harpsichord of Tschudi's making, finished with Tschudi's very newest invention, the so-called 'Venetian swell'. This was the new method of creating a crescendo with an operated opening similar in shape to a Venetian blind, which Tschudi had patented on the 13th December 1769. It was an attempt to retain the pompous, sonorous, somewhat penetrating timbre of the later English harpsichords, in the face of a progressive, fast-changing world and the rise of a new era in musical language.

Marie-Antoinette, daughter of Maria Theresia, would very likely not have heard the ringing tone of Tschudi's harpsichord, for since April 1770 she had been Queen of France, the wife of Louis XVI. The Austrian Emperor's daughter, who was a good musician, found at her disposal, standing in the Music Room at the Petit Trianon, the spinet by Pascal Taskin (1778) and the first square piano by Sébastien Erard. The former, with its charming, somewhat sweet tone, was the tender reflection of a finished and vanishing epoch, whilst the latter, though of a weaker tone, was capable of more vivid and passionate utterance. Indeed, with the sound of Erard's first square piano a new musical era was born. The new instrument sounded strange to the ear, for the French had known little of the clavichord, nor had it achieved any general popularity owing to the dynamic effect of the new pianoforte. This was in direct contrast to the reactions of the Germans or to that of their southern neighbors, the Spaniards. The clavecin exactly expresses the French style, its qualities are '*la netteté, la précision, la clarté*'.

Pascal Taskin, an adept pupil and successor of his master, François-Etienne Blanchet, curator of the collection of instruments at the Court of Versailles since 1781, repaired and in some cases altered the beautiful harpsichords of the end of the 17th and beginning of the 18th centuries. But not only on the soundboards of French instruments do we find the typical burnt-in inscription 'refait par Pascal Taskin à Paris', for both Blanchet and Taskin devoted their greatest care and skill to the remodelling and preservation of the old Dutch instruments, particularly those of Ruckers. These latter, apart from a few exceptions, are mostly of the splendid finish typical of the 18th century. From generation to generation these instruments were considered valuable heirlooms. If repairs such as a new stand or a new case were necessary, these were decorated by the most famous French painters with scenes, or with decorative designs: for instance by Claude III Audran (1658–1734), Antoine Watteau (1648–1721), François Boucher (1703–1770). The decoration of some of the instruments is in any case to be attributed to the above masters, and the shapes of these instruments, partaking of the ostentatious Louis XV and Louis XVI style, are nevertheless in perfect taste. As is the case with all continental instruments, and the French are no exception to this rule, the same conditions prevail: beautiful paintings on the lid, richly decorative cases and tasteful ornamentation of the jackrail.

Till the end of the 18th century the soundboards show the same type of finish, a fragile rose is usual and dainty scattered flowers painted either in oil-color or in gouache-paints. In this respect, however, the Strasbourg master-maker, Johann Heinrich Silbermann, is an exception, for his instruments dispense with all decorative painting, relying for their great attraction solely on elegance of form and on their own speciality, i.e. the panelled lid and the parchment rose formed of three Silbermann 'S's.

Triple-stringing (8′, 8′, 4′) in the large two-manual harpsichords, with a compass of five octaves (Dumont), were usual since 1697. Tibaut, whose instrument shows such perfect inlaid work is a fitting and worthy introduction to the 'Great Century' of the French harpsichord. Mention should also be made of the use, since 1679 (Tibaut harpsichord) of leather plectra by the French harpsichord makers. These were used before Taskin did so, already in 1752 by Richard, to obtain a telling contrast between the finer, more brilliant quill plectra, 'jeu de plumes', and the softer tone caused by leather plectra, 'jeu de buffle'. The clavecin was heard for the last time in a French concert hall in 1815.

We now come to the earliest *Dutch* instruments, which first appear on French soil decorated in the French manner. Let us betake ourselves to Antwerp and see them in their original form. The earliest plucked keyboard instrument in preservation is a virginal of the year 1548 made by Joes Karest of Cologne.

The Flemish virginal of the 16th century is very attractive in form, and its influence on England's virginal-building is obvious. On the other hand the English spinet of the 18th century may well have been what inspired Albert Delin in Tournai to build spinets.
Dutch harpsichord-building was in its prime in the years between 1590 and 1790. Through the work of the Ruckers, the 'Steinways of the 17th century', as also of Couchet and Britsen, Antwerp became the center of European harpsichord- and virginal-building. The chief characteristic of the Ruckers' instruments is their decoration of the inside walls with yellow paper printed in arabesques (black ornament with a pattern of sea-horses), a wallpaper introduced in 1600 by Patin. And on the lid, unless ornamented with a painting, there is generally a Latin motto. The same can be said of his virginals and also of the various instruments made by Britsen. The soundboards are decorated with guasch-paintings (scattered flowers, birds, harlequins, fruit, insects) and with a bronzed rose made of lead showing an angel playing a harp, wherein also appeared the different makers' initials, 'H.R.' (Hans Ruckers), 'J.R.' (Johannes Ruckers), 'A.R.' (Andreas Ruckers). The spinet by Delin, dated 1765, with the initials 'A.D.' in the bronzed lead rose and with its meagrely decorated soundboard still carries on the Ruckers tradition well into the middle of the 18th century.
The instruments rest upon a stand and are not mounted firmly upon legs of their own. Double- and triple stringing (8′, 8′, 4′) is the usual form and another characteristic of all good Dutch instruments is the presence of the maker's signature.
At this time the ornamentation of the harpsichords was undertaken by the most famous painters of the day: Paul Bril (1554–1626), Pieter Bruegel (called 'Höllenbruegel', 1564–1637), Jan Bruegel (called 'Sammetbruegel', 1568–1625), Peter Paul Rubens (1577–1640), Franz Francke (1581–1643), Anton van Dyck (1599–1641), David Teniers (1610–1690), Phil. Schey (1626). The Ruckers' instruments possess a soft, sweet timbre almost Italian in quality, whereas the other Dutch instruments were less silvery in tone.
The Dutch instruments still maintained their great reputation in the 18th century, but the decoration had become simpler. Until about 1750 they retained their beautiful paintings, the compass of the keyboard being five octaves except for Delin's spinets with its compass of four octaves and a third. Master-builders became also fewer, being reduced to the names Jakobus van der Elsche, Albert Delin, Johann Daniel Dulcken and Johannes Petrus Bull.
Till about 1530, the predominating instrument was the clavichord, which is first represented on a Dutch relief-carving in wood in the Amsterdam Rijksmuseum. After this time the construction of the clavichord became increasingly rare. Improvements on the simple form of the clavichord were introduced by the painters P. Meulener (1602–1654) and Dirk Stoop (1602–1686).
The early pianoforte of the 18th century retains in its outlines the form and also the style of decoration of the older instruments. The clavichord became the square piano and the harpsichord the Grand Pianoforte. Whilst the Silbermann technique, in the hands of Zumpe and the other eleven 'apostles' of German instrument-making emigrated to London, there to work out a simplified form (Stossmechanik) in building Square Pianos, in Augsburg, Johann Andreas Stein, pupil of the Strasbourg Silbermann, worked at improving the method of the developed German action (Prellzungenmechanik). This latter, in its improved form—the Hammerkapsel—was the creation of the Silbermanns. In 1770 the goal was reached: the Prellzunge—counterpart in its resilience to the Stosszunge—was discovered. Stein's action achieved immediate popularity in Germany, being called the 'developed German action', but on reaching Vienna it was named the 'Viennese action'. "The German action may be played upon with ease by the weakest hand. It allows the performer to impart to his execution every possible degree of light and shade, speaks clearly and promptly, has a rounded, fluty tone and does not impede rapidity of execution by requiring too great an effort." (Hummel.) [1]
The technical equality of the two different actions has now been achieved.

[1] Hummel, J.N. Ausführliche Anleitung zum Pianofortespiel, 1828.

In 1776, in London, Tschudi's son-in-law and successor John Broadwood, his assistant Robert Stodart and the Dutchman Americus Backers combined together to work out an improvement on the Silbermann alias Cristofori method. They dispense with the intermediate lever, or under-hammer, and the jack (Stosszunge) now acts directly in a notch of the butt (Hammernuss). A regulating screw (Stellschraube) and button were added for controlling the escapement. Thus the so-called 'English grand action' came into being. "One must give the 'English action' its due and concede that it has great strength and richness of tone. These instruments do not allow of the same degree of force as the Viennese, for the keys are considerably heavier to the touch. Also they fall much deeper, so that the release of the hammer repeatedly struck cannot function fast enough. At first one is ill at ease, because especially in runs one tends to press the keys right down. On the other hand the singing quality of these instruments, through their richness of tone, has a charm entirely of its own." (Hummel.) The regulating screw controlling the hammer's escapement was introduced after 1794 also by Stein/Streicher in Vienna as an addition to his *Prellzungenmechanik* (Viennese action).

Paris 1786. A lull before the storm! Must not he, Sébastien Erard, son of a simple cabinetmaker in Strasbourg, have seemed to the man in the street to be a deserter, a traitor, one who had identified himself with the detested aristocracy? Were not his square pianos for ever connected with the memory of the Duchess of Villeroi? Did she not show favor to the talented young instrument builder, fitting out a workshop for him in her palace, placing everything at his disposal for the development of his genius? Should the Paris Churches ever ring the alarm, sound the tocsin of revolution, would not his business, perhaps even his very life, be in danger? His powerful genius, his tireless industry, constituted a definite call to give France first place in the history of piano-building. His life belonged to France, not to himself, not to a dying epoch. He dared no longer identify himself with the Royal house, to sink with it into a certain grave. His brother Jean-Baptiste was not 'suspect', not 'compromised'. He would be able to carry on the workshop in the rue de Bourbon, steering it with a firm hand through the coming storm. Could one not make a virtue of necessity and open a branch workshop in London, the world's center of piano-building? He had made his decision. Erard left Paris, a Paris on the very verge of eruption, and arrived in London.

1789. Outbreak of the Revolution! The royal family forsook Versailles never more to return. On this tragic autumn afternoon of the 5th October, in the elegant music room at the Petit Trianon the Queen's piano stood mutely forlorn. Over the white ivory keys of the Taskin spinet, slowly spread the sinister black death-shadow of the guillotine (10th October 1793). *1792.* The little square piano by Wolber, with its small, thin little voice, does its very best to support the fiery song by Rouget de Lisle: 'Allons enfants de la Patrie.' It is an aggressive melody, though with a swing of its own. Six years later fate decrees the writing of its counterpart in the Canton of Bern, the weighty, rythmic 'March of Bern'. Muted thunder of canon from Neuenegg and from Grauholz (5th March 1798) reawaken historical memories.

Paris was the town fated to see great political and social upheaval. But in Vienna the scene was laid for a revolution of another order, a revolution in the style of piano-playing bringing with it a complete change in the instrument itself.

Mozart's concert grand pianoforte was the expression of perfect harmony between the instrument itself and the composer's work of art. For Beethoven, however, protagonist of a new era, the instrument became the bed of Procrustes. Hedged in as he was by its limited compass, Beethoven was often forced to alter the repeats in his sonatas because the performance was impossible on the instrument at hand. How often had he discussed with his friends, Streicher and his wife, how they could increase the volume of tone which no longer satisfied his vision of sound-possibility. Nor was Broadwood of London spared from similar criticisms on the part of Beethoven. To what straits the gulf between his creative genius far in advance of his time, and the inadequate instruments at his disposal had brought him can be seen in the report of the London harp builder Johann Stumpff in the year 1824, after his visit to Beethoven in Vienna. Beethoven of course complains bitterly to Stumpff about the *inadequacy of the piano which allows of no powerful or effective performance* and shows him his Broadwood piano (see illustration). "What a sight presented itself," wrote Stumpff.

"There was no sound left in the treble, and broken strings lay tangled together like a bush struck down in a thunderstorm."[1] Was the 'thunderstorm' the Sonata for the piano in B op. 106 (1818–19) or the opening of the C minor Sonata, op. 111 (1822)? The Broadwood instrument of 1817 with its five iron braces was not equal to the demands of such dramatic and sonorous subjects. After Beethoven the revolutionary, upward curve was carried further forward by his pupil Karl Czerny, an excellent player and pedagogue, who was Franz Liszt's teacher, and was furthered by the latter's demoniacal technique and powerful tone.

Composition for the piano having reached an almost orchestral fullness and power demanded a new style of playing which, even at that time, must have been based on the modern principle of arm-technique. This latter, however, presupposes an instrument which resembled its forerunners only in its outward form. The birth of the new instrument took place gradually and painfully. In the same year (1824) that disaster overtook Beethoven's Broadwood piano, Erard's new seven-octave concert-grand with a compass from C_1 to c'''', suffered a similar fate in a Paris concert room. We read: "Young Liszt played the piano-concerto in B minor by Hummel on a seven-octave piano. Unable to stand the immense strain put upon it, the piano unfortunately lost pitch. It was necessary to break off in the middle of a piece in order, as nearly as possible, to tune the strings half a tone higher and to replace those that were broken. Did this demand on the instrument originate in the musicians who thereby thought to achieve new effects, or did it rather come from the makers themselves, seeking to show off their instruments and attract buyers?"

Liszt's round of triumphs from concert to concert was the death warrant of the pianoforte. The number of pianos put 'out of commission' grew with every concert given. They belong to the 'heroic' epoch of piano history, like those tattered banners of famous regiments of the Battle of Waterloo (1815).

Meanwhile, English and French piano-building was striving to enter new fields of construction. Inventions came and went, were patented and abandoned, both in the same year. From this untenable situation some outlet had to be found; an instrument had to be constructed which would not fail the artist at the crucial moment. The musician had to be able to rely upon both the construction of the instrument as well as upon the fullness of its tone to fill concert halls of ever-increasing dimensions and as a soloist to be able to hold his own above the growing size of orchestras: he had to have an instrument capable of satisfying the demands of modern pianoforte compositions. America, with its highly developed piano-industry was to show European instrument makers new methods.

In the English colonies of North America, particularly in Philadelphia, New York and Boston, the spinet and the harpsichord had been in use since the middle of the 18th century, added to which, since 1775, the first American square pianos appeared in Philadelphia.

In 1799, while the battles of the North American War of Independence were raging, a British merchantman, with a 'London made' pianoforte on board, bound for New York, crossed the Atlantic. In 1783, by the Peace of Versailles, England recognized the independence of the thirteen United States. Since 1789, the importation of London instruments to Boston gradually became superfluous, for in 1791 the work of Benjamin Crehore made Boston the second most important city with regard to the piano industry. Philadelphia forestalled Boston by about two years through the presence there of the piano maker Charles Albrecht.

The motto of the American instrument maker was: great strength of tone with maximum carrying-power, but without losing the singing-quality, whilst making use of every possible new scientific theory.

Already in 1800, Isaak Hawkins of Philadelphia patented an upright piano, the soundboard set in a metal frame, also reinforced behind with metal, and with a metal wrestplank. And in 1825 Babcock in Boston constructed *Square Pianos* for the first time, *the frames of which consisted of cast iron all in one piece.* Encased in this 'armour-plating' the instruments were equal to all demands of modern times. What matter if their slender line of outward form be sacrificed? Pleyel, the foremost piano maker of Europe, was the first in that same year to avail himself of the new American invention. Goll, native of Zürich, the progressive piano

[1] Closson, Ernest, Histoire du Piano, p. 104.

maker in Vienna, in 1826 was the next to follow suit, and after him, in 1831, William Allen of London. Into the vast halls of the Great Exhibition of London in 1851 came the first American pianos (Chickering, Nunns & Clark, Conrad Meyer) and in 1867, supplemented now by the brilliant work of Steinway, even more examples of the American piano industry landed in France for the Paris Exhibition. With their cast iron armor as improved upon by Chickering and Steinway, and with their cross stringing they broke down the last resistance of the piano industry, conquering in a victorious but peaceful offensive the whole of Europe. After the year 1867 the American system and American-made pianos undoubtedly held first place. It was not until after the Franco-German War of 1870/71 that the piano industry of the now unified German Empire found in their own Bechstein and Blüthner protagonists to combat this state of affairs and to effect a balance.

Strange phenomenon! Why should increase in tone-volume run parallel with *loss of good taste?*

Almost from its first appearance in Germany the newly-born square piano coveted the addition of the harp- and lute stops. Being already an instrument capable of tone-modulation, that which lies in the hand of every player, this addition was certainly superfluous, the instrument needed only two: the damper (loud) and the soft-pedals. The 18th century, however, focussed as it was on mechanical gadgets, consistently following the direction first taken by Dalitz, was destined to see the birth of other curiosities. Bohemia seems to have been fertile soil for these strange productions of an inventor's skill gone astray and of inventions devoid of good taste. About the year 1795 Vincenz Blaha, doctor of medicine and philosophy, built a two-manual claviorganum fitted with Janissary music (triangle, cymbals, half-moon, big drum) arranged behind a silk curtain and set in motion by the foot. Already early in the 19th century the use of the Janissary music in Austrian and German pianos had made itself disagreeably felt, even first-class firms like Streicher building them into their instruments. This was against their better judgement, as is seen by a letter of Andreas Streicher of December 8th 1802, where he speaks of these 'alterations' being simply 'tricks' which he categorically rejects, at the same time remarking that the piano maker finds himself forced to construct them *to satisfy public demand.* In her book about the Piano, Rosamund Harding goes deeply into the question of this fashion and gives the necessary historical details. At the time of the Turkish War (1663–1699) the Turkish musical instruments became the great fashion and were introduced into most of the famous European regiments, for instance in England, Germany, Prussia, Austria, France and Russia. The Empress Catherine II of Russia celebrated the peace with Turkey to the sound of Janissary music. Frederick the Great and the Court at Vienna both had Turkish bands. Turkish influences even crept into musical composition of the time, as, for instance, in the chorus of Scythians in Gluck's 'Iphigenia in Tauris', Mozart's 'Abduction from the Seraglio' and 'Rondo alla Turca', and Schubert's opera 'Des Teufels Lustschloss'. Even in organ-building the cymbal stop (Weingarten 1750) and kettledrum and cymbals (Danzig, Katharinenkirche) were in use.

Is it any wonder, therefore, to hear the above mentioned Rondo alla Turca played by German and Austrian pianos complete with banging of drums and tinkling of bells, little nigger-boys in bright turbans clashing tiny cymbals with their miniature arms all worked by clever mechanism? (Pyramid-piano by Schlimbach.) Heart, what moro do you desire? England with her soberness and France with her good taste have never favored these harmless gadgets so reminiscent of gipsy fairgrounds. But such curiosities of cultural history can still be found fairly frequently in collections of musical instruments.

But something even better was yet to come: in 1796 the brothers Still made an instrument for an inventor of the name of Kunz which had 230 strings, 360 organ-pipes, 150 different novelties, two manuals and 25 pedals.[1] In 1795, in London, the so-called 'bookcase piano' by the piano maker Stodart introduced the notorious series of 'practical' pianos. Yet one must confess that the Good Spirit of the classical past stood godfather to the upright grand. As an instrument it even earned the praise of Haydn. After 1812 desk-pianos (Oh Erard!) and chest-of-drawers pianos made their appearance; even pianos which with one touch could

[1] Hertz, Eva, Johann Andreas Stein, Würzburg 1947, p. 42.

become tea-tables! As the last phrase of Beethoven's Fugue, op. 110, died away the piano-lid was closed and the whole instrument transformed into a playground for gaily-rolling billiard balls. And in France, of all places, a bed was made with a built-in piano which began to play as one lay down. "If music is the food of love, give me excess." (Shakespeare.) The year 1830 saw the beginning of imitation. Form, which had become heavy and clumsy, in shame-faced modesty was covered with a layer of imitation mother-of-pearl, horn or tortoise shell. The naturals of the keyboard were made of imitation ivory. In general the great piano firms were innocent of this shoddy elegance, but in the building of fancy instruments new influences were making themselves felt: New-Gothic, New-Baroque, New-Rococo. In a musical concert given by Mr. and Mrs. Neureich, Liszt's 13th Hungarian Rhapsody was played in great style on a Louis XV Pianoforte. 'Period of no taste, with styles of all periods.' Looking back one is tempted to say that the disappearance of the tapering leg to the instrument and the appearance of the first lathe-cut, round piano-leg was the 'mene, mene, tekel, upharsin' of good taste.

When the Streichers, together with Nannette's brother Matthäus Andreas, moved from Augsburg to Vienna, it meant that the center of piano industry moved from Germany to the Austrian capital. The Napoleonic campaigns had, amongst other consequences, caused such a decline in *German* piano industry, that in the statistics of the year 1816 piano-building is no longer listed as an independent industry but simply included under the heading of fine mechanics. The German piano maker was powerless against the overwhelming competition of English and French production.

The year 1835 saw the production of the first pianino (cottage piano) bringing renewed significance to the industry of North- and Middle-Germany. Then came the second All-German Industries Exhibition of 1844 in Berlin, which gave a great impulse to trade. In spite of this the piano industry did not rise above the level of good mediocrity and cannot be compared with the best products of other countries. At the time of the IV Industries Exhibition in Munich the experts' criticism was that "the German piano makers seem, for the most part, to be hurrying to catch up with their colleagues in England and France, but that the incentive to construct more beautiful, and if possible, even more perfect instruments, is not as active as it is in the neighboring countries. The wonderfully low price of many instruments is not, as is the case with the foreign products, a sign of simpler and undecorated construction, but is far more likely to denote careless, badly finished work which, although for the moment the buyer is satisfied, will revenge itself on the maker in the long run."[1] From about 1862 onwards a measure of balance in comparison with foreign production was achieved, but it was not until after the Franco-German war in 1870/71 that equality in the world market was reached.

I am reminded again of Burney's words that the German piano maker constructs much better pianos when living abroad than he does in his own country. This proved to be true in the first half of the 19th century when firms of good name, even some firms of world-renown, owed their fame to the genius of their German founders.

Austria's piano-building was now centered in Vienna. Its variety was great, from the clear, firm tone of the Walter-pianos, so full of character, to the more weighty and sonorous timbre of the instruments by Matthäus Andreas and Carl Stein and of those also by Nannette Streicher and the mellow, floating, almost tomantic sound of Conrad Graf's building. Later, in the 80's, the Streicher pianos with their clear nobility of tone and the fantastic, almost cloying sweetness of the pianos by Bösendorfer, were all eminently suited to the special atmosphere of Vienna's musicality. Whilst in France, England and North America the problem of how to increase the tone and general solidity of the instruments and the perfecting of the action (Erard) as such, and specially of the further development of the cottage-piano was given first consideration, Austria and Germany were concentrating all their attention on the improvement of the upright grand piano. The rather cold and

[1] Schafhäutl, Emil, Die Pianofortebaukunst der Deutschen, München 1855, p. 1018.

prosaic Empire-style became warmer in the Viennese and South-German manner of building: the shape had more charm, the bronze decoration was daintier, the caryatides, sphinxes and chimerical figures supporting the instruments, as well as the lion's-claw feet, were more imaginative. A typical instrument of the Biedermeier period, which confined itself to Germany and Austria, was the *Lyraflügel*, the embodiment of the simple comfort and unobtrusive beauty which characterized both furniture and house-decoration of that middle-class era.

The oldest English square pianos were still built on quite ugly stands and were dreary and unimaginative. One exception was the delightful instrument by Goulding, D'Almaine and Potter. It was built in the Hepplewhite style and was quite unique. It is the only English instrument I know of after 1680, where the sides of the case are richly decorated with paintings as well as the inside of the lid. The fact that the instrument stands on slender legs and is graceful in shape is specially remarkable.

This is the last trace of those years of culture when England's best decorative artists and her great makers of beautiful furniture such as Robert Adam (1728–1793), Hepplewhite (Heppelwhite style: 1760–1765) and Thomas Sheraton (1751–1806) made their influence felt in the outward form of instrument-building.

In 1796 Broadwood produced a pianoforte in Sheraton style in which the beautiful design of that master of marquetry was eventually ruined by the addition of two wooden pedals in the finished product. But in general the English piano remained true to the good tradition of its forerunner, the harpsichord.

I have already mentioned Stodart's 'bookcase piano'. The invention of the maker Southwell, called the 'cabinet piano', from the aesthetic point of view, was a mistaken attempt to produce an upright piano constructed with vertical stringing. The total height, being based on the necessary length of the vertically-strung bass-string, left a large upper-structure covered in with stretched silk, heavy and awkward-looking. It is a sign of the increasing bad taste of those times that this instrument remained popular still about 1860, at which time the method of oblique- and cross stringing had long been in use, so that this huge monstrosity was no longer called for. On the continent these dreadful things, to the best of my knowledge, were never built at all. France turned her attention to producing cottage-pianos and Germany and Austria built beautiful pyramid-, giraffe- and lyra-pianofortes.

The first cottage-pianos are, from the standpoint of beauty, very satisfying, without, however, quite attaining the elegance and suitability of the 'piano droit' by Blanchet and Roller, or that of Pleyel, not to mention the graceful virtuosity of Pape's clever solution of the sound-and form-problem in his 'piano-console', the prototype (?) of our modern cottage-piano. The tone of the English pianoforte is very brilliant and carrying, though rather dry and hard. The Broadwood piano is sometimes called the 'English Erard' and the Clementi/Collard piano the 'English Pleyel'. Till about 1873 the leading piano makers were to be found in England and France.

In the second half of the 18th century the French square pianos and pianofortes still retained the ornate decoration of the Rococo period verging on the Classical: paintings inside the lid, costly inlay, richly decorated soundboards. The Taskin pianoforte of 1790 added to all this beauty the traditionally lovely rose over the soundhole. Johann Heinrich Silbermann's piano was finished with the panelled lid and the Silbermann rose which we connect with all products of the Silbermann school. Erard, who returned to Paris in 1796, contributed his famous piano, finished in 1808 for Louis Napoleon, King of Holland. This gorgeous instrument is the most perfect embodiment of Empire style, inspired by Napoleon, 'French Consul for life', and adopted by the two famous court architects Ch. Percier and P. Fontaine. The name 'Empire' style came into being after Napoleon became Emperor (2nd December 1804) and was the accepted representative style at all the courts of Europe. As an example of good taste Pape's square piano of 1840 stands out at the time of Louis-Philippe (1830–1840) when a general descent from the ornate style was setting in. The same can be said of his beautiful pianino of 1850 with its lovely superimposed bronzes and the five enamelled medallions in Sèvres porcelain. After 1850 there arose that conventional, ordinary series of pianos and *pianinos* to which the French piano industry lent at least a certain accent of nobility and warmth through the extravagant use of

rosewood and mahogany, in welcome contrast to the usual, uniformly ugly black instruments, wearing as it were the shroud of dead beauty, which characterized the majority of the products at that time.
The tone of the Erard piano of those days with its straight stringing is rich and clear and of great fullness whilst the cross-strung Pleyel is transparent and sweet and of a certain womanly charm.
As already mentioned above, until about 1873 the French piano industry took the lead before all others.

Steinway's motto:

«Geselle ist, wer was kann;
Meister ist, wer was ersann;
Lehrling ist jedermann.»

Who knows his trade is a journeyman;
A master is he that invents the plan;
An apprentice, each and every man.[1]

Let us now turn briefly to those countries which, although not destined to take the lead in the development of the piano, have nevertheless produced works of great qualitative excellence, which cannot be overlooked in the history of that instrument.

Iberian peninsula

Spain. In a Spanish inventory of instruments made in the year 1480 is found the first mention of a clavichord, or 'manicordio'. In his work 'Musica practica' which appeared in 1482, Ramis de Pareja speaks of the great popularity of this instrument, which suffered no decrease till the beginning of the 19th century. Its rather hard and carrying tone, though capable of modulation, is closely related to that of the Vihuela and Guitar, the national instruments dear to the Spanish heart. Five instruments have survived, four of which are 18th century and the fifth from the 19th century (1809). Three of these are unfretted, one is partly so, and the fifth is fretted. The compass varies from three octaves and a sixth to four octaves and a fourth, with single- and double stringing.
In comparison with the clavichord the harpsichord could not hold its own. It was not until the 18th century that the harpsichord also found its admirers and became very popular. In the same manner as the Italian instruments the Spanish harpsichord was housed in a protective case. In the years 1800 to 1805 there originated in Barcelona the earliest known examples of square pianos built by Swiss makers.

Portugal. 15th to 18th centuries. Clavichords, most of which were the work of Portuguese makers, were popular in all classes of the population and particularly at Court. Although, as early as 1555, Bermudo favored the building of fret-free clavichords, Portugal, in contrast to Spain, gave preference to the fretted form of instrument until after the beginning of the 18th century. From this period three instruments have survived, of which all three are fretted. The last was built in 1796. Two of them are double-strung and one is single-strung with a compass varying from three octaves and a seventh to five octaves (1796). The harpsichords, however, were mostly imported ones and not of great value. They were usually single-manualled and either single- or double-strung (8′ or 8′, 8′). Purchasers of such instruments were limited to the aristocrats, rich business people or high Church dignitaries. In the Lisbon Museum of Musical Instruments is to be seen the only remaining example, to my knowledge, of a Portuguese harpsichord. It was about the year 1760 (?) that the first pianoforte is said to have been built, the work of Manuel Antunes in Lisbon.

[1] Steinway Motto: English translation by courtesy of Messrs Steinway & Sons. New York, London, Hamburg.

Denmark, Norway, Sweden and Soviet Russia

As early as 1469, on a fresco in the Tirps Church, Upland, is to be seen a clavichord, but although a most popular instrument in Denmark, Norway and Sweden, the clavichord did not reach perfection until the second half of the 18th country. Still preserved are instruments by Jansen (1757), Moss (Norway), Georg Moshack (1763, Copenhagen), Pehr Lundborg (1772–1788) and Pehr Lindholm (1780–1813), both in Stockholm. It seems that both in Denmark and Norway the harpsichord was little known, that is to say I know of no makers of plucked keyboard instruments. It was in 1770 that the square piano first appeared in both of these countries. In Sweden the two best-known makers of plucked keyboard instruments were Gottlieb Rosenau of Stockholm and Gustav Wolthersson in Göteborg. The beautiful harpsichord by Rosenau (1786) as also the clavichords by Lundborg and Lindholm of the same date, are witnesses to the high achievements and artistic perfection of Swedish instrument-building at that time. The earliest examples still extant are the square pianos built by the Swedish maker Peter Kraft in 1788.

In Russia, the Soviet Union of today, clavichords were first produced in 1740. Harpsichords were uncommon in comparison with the widely-known and popular clavichord and, in the last years of the 18th century, the harpsichord disappeared from practical musical life, along with the clavichord, for in 1771 the making of pianofortes begann in Russia, surperseding in a surprisingly short time the production of the older instruments.

The pianoforte had indeed successfully asserted itself in the whole of northern Europe by the year 1780.

Belgium, Switzerland

Belgium. In 1769 the pianoforte was played for the first time in Liège. The earliest examples of square pianos still in preservation date from 1785 and 1789. After 1831 the production of *pianinos* began.

Switzerland. The earliest (?) extant, though unsigned clavichord dates from the year 1723. In the second half of the 18th century spinets and harpsichords were produced in Basel, Bern, Fribourg, Neuchâtel and probably also in Zürich. The earliest square pianos bear dates of the last quarter of the 18th century. But before 1825 the pianoforte-industry in Switzerland was of little importance. Nearly all instruments were imported from abroad, more especially from Germany. The year 1848 saw the almost complete breakdown of the industry in German Switzerland owing to the extensive import of Viennese and Stuttgart pianos, and in Western Switzerland through importation of French instruments. More than 50% of all the instruments in Switzerland at that time were of foreign origin. On the other hand the export of Swiss instruments was rendered extremely difficult, owing to high export duties.

The year 1854 sees a great rise in piano-building in Zürich, with increased exportation to Germany and Holland. In 1880 we find no fewer than 259 piano makers at work in Switzerland. Of these the Canton of Zürich claims 155, the Canton of Bern 30, Geneva 19, St. Gallen 18, Neuchâtel 9 and the remaining 37 are distributed over the rest of the country. At this time Swiss instrument-building stood very high in the eyes of the world; her pianos were to be found in Holland, Belgium, Russia, Sweden, Norway, England, France, Spain, America, Australia and the East Indies. It must be mentioned here in passing that since 1850 the upright grand piano and the square piano were gradually dying out in Europe. North America saw the longest popularity of the square piano (till after 1880) and the latest beginnings of a piano industry, compared with Europe, starting as late as 1860.

The downfall in North America of the square piano was destined to take a strange form. The Congress of Piano-Makers in Atlantic City in 1903 decided to buy up every available square piano for the price of a few hundred thousand dollars. This enormous number of instruments was piled up pyramid-high on the hill at Chelsea, fifty feet in height, one upon another, and burnt.

Now we have reached the end of our journey through the centuries. Sound and form change. But unchanging is the spirit which gives birth, whether consciously or unconsciously, to any true work of art. The thought to which the virginal of Andreas Ruckers in 1620 gave visible expression, is written in invisible letters on every instrument:

OMNIS SPIRITUS LAUDET DOMINUM.

The introduction gives a clear definition of the purpose and scope of this book. Just as it is the task of the artist interpreting a composition to act as an intermediary between a musical work of art and the audience, the pianist likewise may be allowed to awake the interest of the reader in the instruments and the beauty of their shapes. Particular care has therefore been taken in the choice of the abundant illustrations. The explanations accompanying them were not originally intended as a kind of history of the stringed keyboard instruments from 1440 to 1880. Concentration on the essential has been attempted, so as not to burden the reader with too much technical detail. It is therefore far beyond the author's aim to give an exhaustive survey of the technical side of stringed keyboard instrument construction; he particularly wants to stress this point. Those wishing to become better acquainted with the matter would do well to consult the excellent specialized works mentioned in the introduction; the ample bibliography may also serve the purpose.

The instrument makers of former times liked to put a motto on their instruments. So too I wish to add a motto as a preliminary to this book. Bearing in mind the imperfection of all human endeavor, it reads as follows:

IN MAGNIS ET VOLUISSE SAT EST
(Propertius)

PART I

STRINGED KEYBOARD INSTRUMENTS OF RELIC VALUE

NOTE: As far as possible, our description of the illustrations refers to the corresponding catalogue notes. Where there has been no official catalogue [1], the text is based on the information received by the author from curators and officials of the various museums. Some of the descriptions are the author's personal notes whilst viewing the instrument in question.
It is therefore inevitable that the following descriptions, though uniform in their method of presentation, are not all of equal value.

[1] See Bibliography: Bamberg, Bargagna, Berlin, Bessaraboff, Bierdimpfl, Bologna, Breslau, Broadwood, Chouquet, Copenhagen, Donaldson, Eisenach, Engel, Epstein, Fett, Geiringer, Göteborg, Guarinoni, Hälsingborg, Hammerich, Josten, Kastner, Kinsky, London, Mahillon, Morris, Neuchâtel, Rushworth & Dreaper, Sachs, Santagato, Schlosser, Schroeder, Simoni, Skinner, Stanley, Stiehl, Svanberg, Tribschen, Watson, Willson, Wood.

UPRIGHT HARPSICHORD (Clavicytherium)

Italy

An unsigned instrument:
SHAPE: case cabinet-shaped, painted blue with gold ornamentation, the pedestal with a border of arabesques, carved and gilded. To right and left of each of the doors, slender columns with gilded socles and capitals. On each door are angels in flowing garments with golden wings and haloes. One angel in crimson robes and dark-blue cloak is blowing a trumpet, the other, robed in gold with red and green cloak is playing the rebec. The carved and gilded beam above the columns is finished with an ornate blue and gold shield bearing the papal insignia in color on a black ground. The stand of the instrument is in gilt and of a later date.
KEYBOARD: compass E/C to f″ (2 octaves and a fourth). Short bass-octave. Naturals of light-brown wood, carved and gilded facings. Sharps colored black.
INTERIOR: on the soundboard, two small, Gothic, carved wooden roses of different size framed in gilded parchment.
MEASUREMENT: total height 3 ft 2 in., width 2 ft 4 in., depth 12 in.
AT HOLYOKE: The Belle Skinner Collection. Cat. No. 7.

The instrument is said to have belonged to *Pope Gregory XIII* (b. 1502, d. 1585; Pope 1572–1585). The painting on the doors is attributed to *Fra Giovanni da Fiesole* (*Fra Angelico*, b. 1387, d. 1455).

5

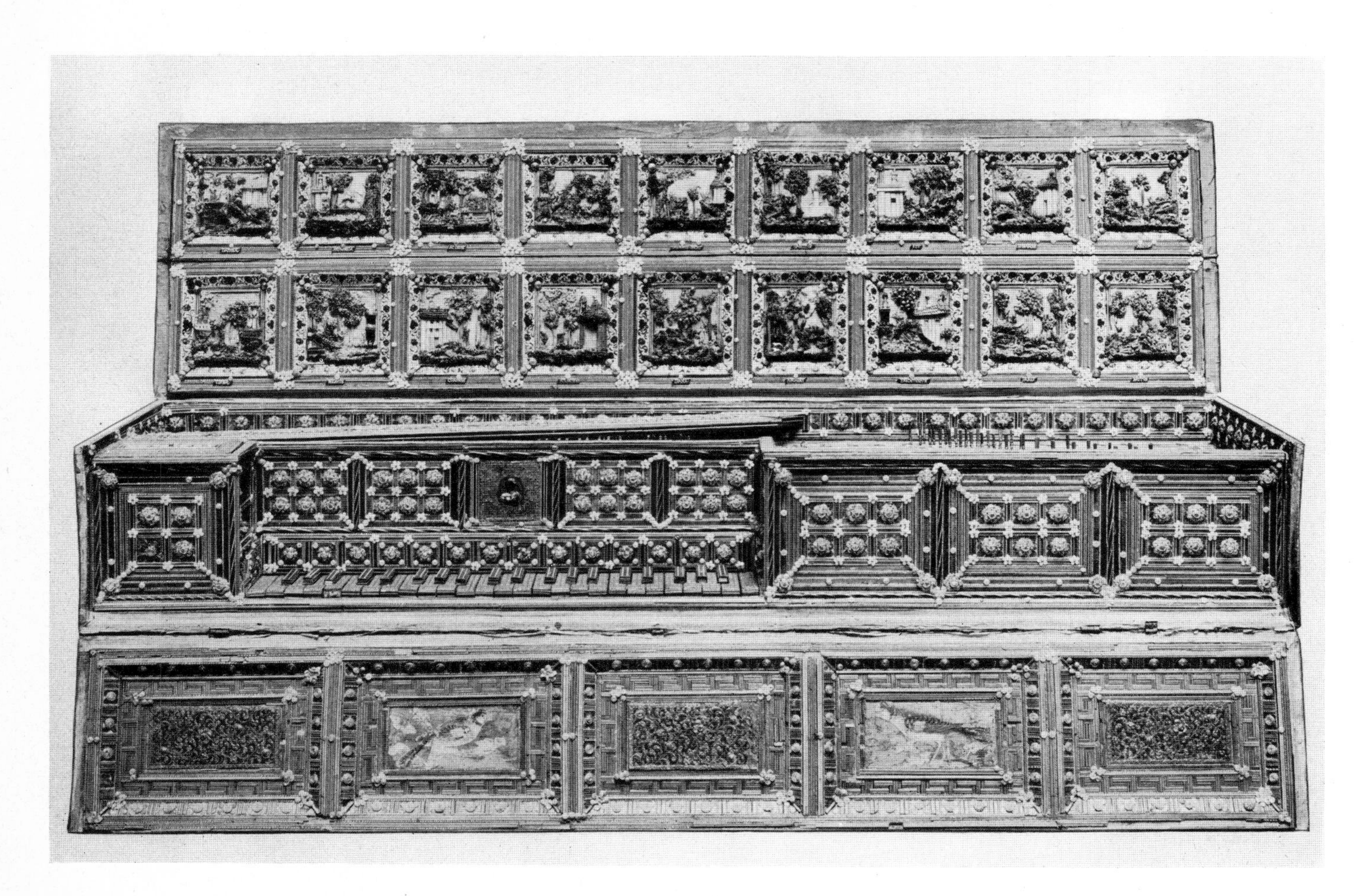

VIRGINAL

Italy (about 1570)

UNSIGNED.
SHAPE: the instrument fits into a case covered in crimson Genoese velvet edged with a striped yellow silk border. The inside of the lid has flowers and trailing vines in gold painted on a blue ground sprinkled with gold. The hexagonal instrument is of cypress-wood and is richly decorated with delicate blue and red arabesques on a gold ground. The front is subdivided into panels. The front panel to the left of the keyboard shows the coat of arms of the King of England, as designed by Queen Elizabeth I. On the other front panel to the right of the keyboard her device: on a tree-stump a crowned silver falcon holding in its claw a golden scepter.
KEYBOARD: projected. Compass E/C–c''' four octaves. Short bass-octave. Naturals covered with ebony. Sharps in ivory inlaid with silver and rare woods.
MEASUREMENT: the whole case, height 5 ft 5 in., width 1 ft 11 in., depth 8 1/2 in. The instrument case itself: length 5 ft 3 in., width 16 in., depth 7 in.
IN LONDON, Victoria and Albert Museum. Cat. No. 19, 1887.

The instrument is possibly the work of *Benedetto Floriani*, a famous spinet maker well-known in Venice in 1571. There is a great resemblance with the spinet No. 33 in the Museum of Instruments in Leipzig.

VIRGINAL

Flemish or Italian (about 1600)

UNSIGNED.
SHAPE: case made of pinewood encrusted with colored reliefs in Murano-glass.
KEYBOARD: compass E/C to c''' (4 octaves). Short bass-octave.
MEASUREMENT: length 4 ft 11 1/2 in.
IN LONDON, Victoria and Albert Museum, No. 402, 1872.

Reputed to have been the property of *Princess Elizabeth, daughter of James I of England, and Queen of Bohemia* (b. 1595, d. 1662).

DOUBLE MANUAL HARPSICHORD

Johannes Ruckers—Flemish, Antwerp 1612

SIGNATURE: Ruckers' rose over soundhole on the soundboard with the initials 'J.R.'
SHAPE: the instrument is specially remarkable for the paintings by famous Dutch masters. Inside of lid (p. 10): landscape by Jan Breughel the elder, the so-called 'Sammetbreughel' (1568 to 1625); group on the left in the picture showing Apollo and Marsyas is by Hendrik van Balen (1575–1632); Inside of front lid: scene from Orpheus, Orpheus amongst wild beasts, by Paul Bril (1554–1626).
KEYBOARD: compass of both manuals F_1 to f‴ (5 octaves, owing to later extension).
INTERIOR: the soundboard is decorated by Frans Francken (the younger?), 1581–1643, with garlands of flowers in gouache-painting. Over the soundhole, Ruckers' rose.
STRINGING: originally trichord, probably 8′, 8′, 4′.
ACTION: originally three rows of jacks.
IN PARIS, Musée instrumental du Conservatoire National de Musique. Cat. No. 327.

This magnificent instrument was originally ordered by *Maria de' Medici* for *Elizabeth of France*, eldest daughter of Henry IV of France and future wife of Philip IV, King of Spain. The instrument stood in the Escorial at first and after the death of Queen Elizabeth it became the property of her daughter, *Princess Maria Theresia*. When she married Louis XIV of France the instrument was moved to the Court of Versailles where it came to rest in the salon of her ladies in waiting. After Maria Theresia's death this instrument by Ruckers graced the Salon of *Madame de Maintenon* in Versailles, later being moved to the lovely Pavillon in Saint-Cyr when Madame de Maintenon became Superintendant of the Maison Royale de Saint-Cyr.

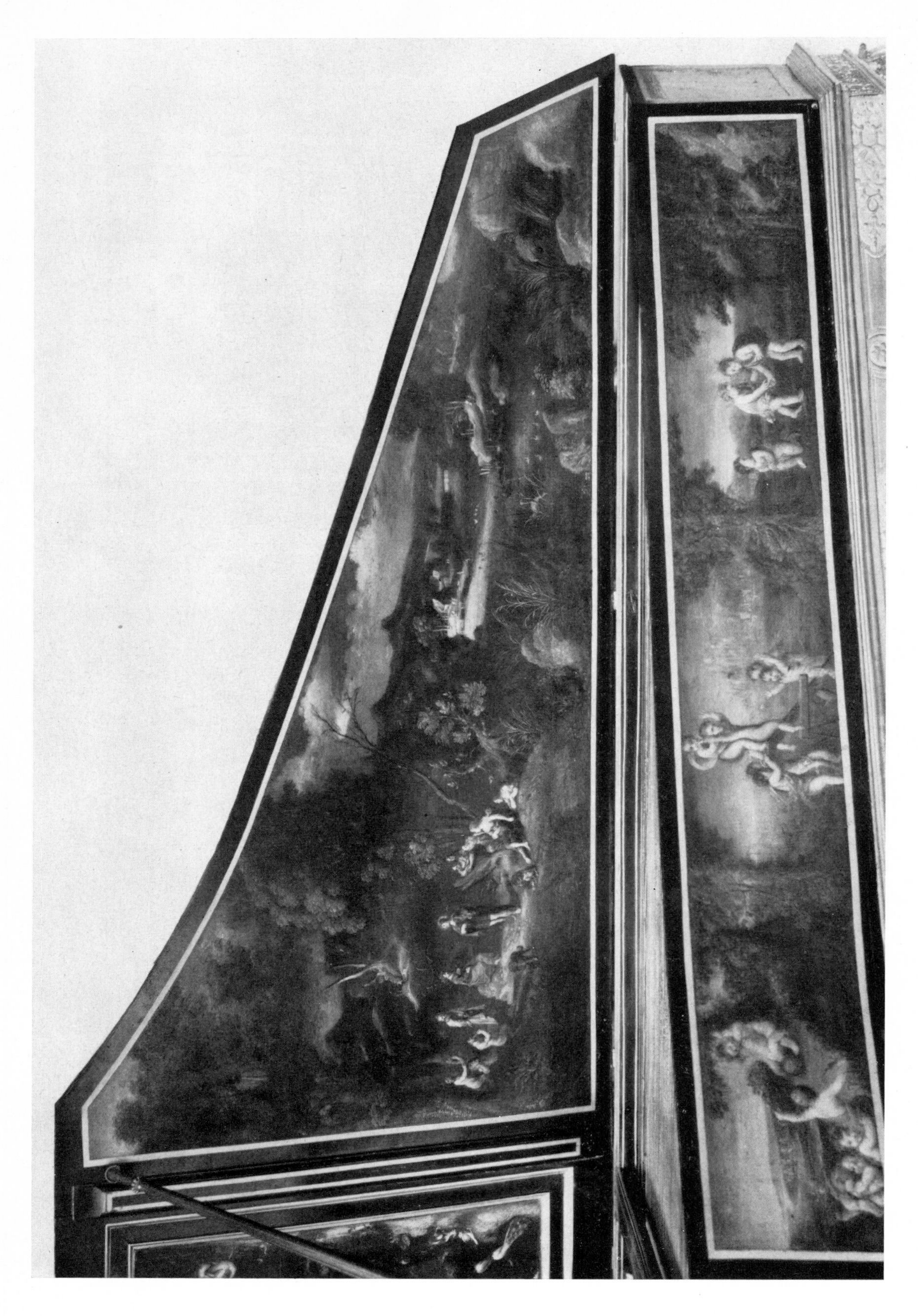

Page 9: Inside of front lid.
Page 10: Inside of lid.

HARPSICHORD

Andreas Ruckers the Elder—Flemish, Antwerp 1640

SIGNATURE: inscription on the paper of the nameboard partly illegible:—'A(NDRE)AS (RUCKER)S 1640.' Another signature lower down, on the wood of the nameboard just above the keys reads: 'ANDREAS RUCKERS, ME FECIT. ANTVERPIAE.'
SHAPE: the case is lined inside with the yellow paper printed with black Renaissance ornamentation, which is characteristic of the instruments by Ruckers. The inside surface of the lid bears the inscription '1640/ MUSICA LETITIAE / COMES MEDICINA DOLORUM'; and on the inside of the front lid: 'CONCORDIA / MUSIS / AMICA.' To the left of the player is a little built-in box for the tuning key.
KEYBOARD: compass C to d''' (4 octaves and a second).
INTERIOR: soundboard painted with scattered flowers and birds, the date repeated in red figures. The soundhole has a rose—a kneeling angel with a harp, flanked by the initials 'A.R.'—which is framed round by a garland of painted flowers.
STRINGING: double-strung 8', 4'.
ACTION: two rows of jacks.
STOPS: two side stops.
MEASUREMENT: length 6 ft, width 2 ft 5 1/2 in., height of case 9 1/2 in. (without stand); extreme height 3 ft (with stand).
AT HOLYOKE, The Belle Skinner Collection, Cat. No. 20.

This instrument is said to have been played upon by *Georg Friedrich Händel* (according to writing in faded ink on the underside of the case; see catalogue of The Belle Skinner Collection, pp. 20 seqq).

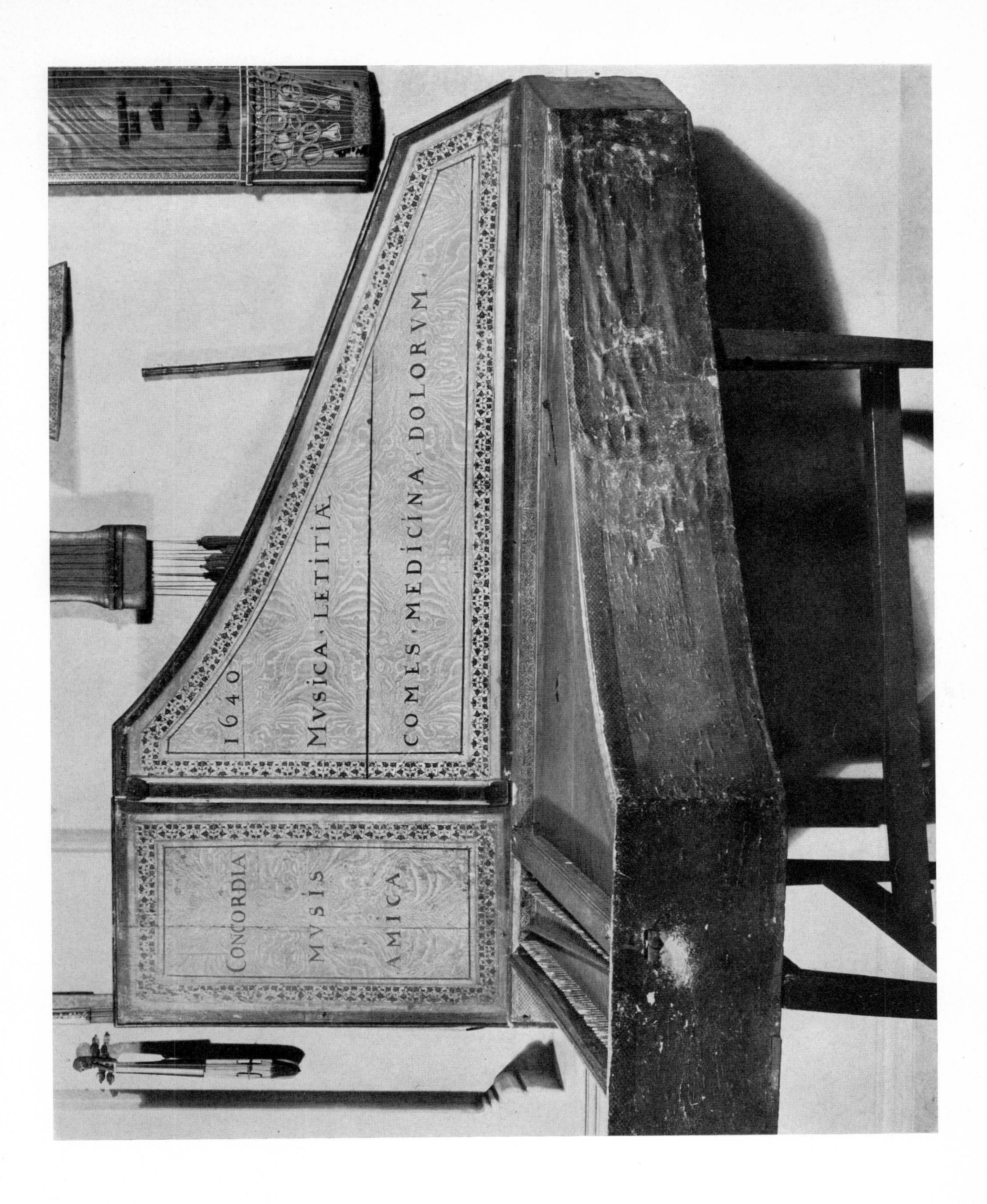
1640
MVSICA · LETITIÆ
COMES · MEDICINA · DOLORVM ·
CONCORDIA
MVSIS
AMICA

DOUBLE MANUAL HARPSICHORD

Andreas Ruckers the Younger—Flemish, Antwerp 1651

SIGNATURE: over the soundhole Ruckers' characteristic rose: angel with a harp and the initials 'A. R.'
SHAPE: the black-lacquered case made of pinewood is decorated inside with flowers painted in gold and a Latin motto, all on a red ground. The inscription on the inside of the lid reads: 'SIC TRANSIT GLORIA MUNDI' and 'MUSICA DONUM DEI.'
KEYBOARD: two manuals. Compass of both manuals G_1 to f''' (four octaves and a seventh). G sharp is missing. Keys modern.
INTERIOR: the soundboard is ornamented with paintings of dainty leaves and flowers and of monkeys playing musical instruments. The soundhole is finished with the above mentioned Ruckers' rose.
STRINGING: triple-strung 8′, 8′, 4′. To the lower manual 8′, 8′, 4′, upper manual 8′.
STOPS: originally side stops, now fitted with two hand stops in the nameboard, coupling the rows of jacks of both the 8 ft registers of the lower keyboard.
MEASUREMENT: height 3 ft., length 6 ft 8 in., width 3 ft.
IN LONDON, Victoria and Albert Museum, 1079–1868.

The instrument probably belonged originally to *Georg Friedrich Händel* (1685–1759).

UPRIGHT HARPSICHORD (Clavicytherium)

Martinus Kaiser—Germany, 17th century

SIGNATURE: 'Martinus Kaiser / Ser. Electoris / Palatini / Instrumentorum Opifex / et huius modi / Inventor.'
SHAPE: case ornamented in beautiful Boule, with ebony, tortoise shell, ivory and mother-of-pearl inlay and richly gilded.
KEYBOARD: naturals, tortoise shell, sharps, covered with mother-of-pearl. Compass G_1 to c''' (without $G_1\#$).
STRINGING: bichord: 8', 8'.
MEASUREMENT: breadth 101 cm, depth 50 cm, height 283 cm.
IN VIENNA, Kunsthistorisches Museum, Collection of old musical instruments. Inv. No. 377 (8801).

Formerly the property of *Emperor Leopold I* (b. 1640, d. 1705), German Emperor 1658–1705.

DOUBLE-STRING SPINET

Bartolomeo Cristofori—Italy, Florence 1693

SIGNATURE: inscription to the right of the keyboard inside a little compartment reads: 'BARTHOLOMAEUS CHRISTOPHORI PATAVINUS / FACIEBAT FLORENTIAE / MDCXCIII.'
SHAPE: the instrument itself is inside an outer case on a stand with four slightly curved legs. The instrument body, made of cypress-wood, richly decorated with elaborate ebony inlay.
KEYBOARD: compass C–c''' (4 octaves). Naturals faced with beautiful carving, the keys covered with box-wood with ebony inlay; sharps, ebony, veined with cypress-wood.
INTERIOR: on the soundboard, a beautiful rose of carved cypress-wood.
STRINGING: double-strung.
ACTION: by pulling the whole keyboard forward by means of 2 levers set into the cheekpieces, only *one* row of jacks can function, i.e. only *one* string is plucked.
MEASUREMENT: breadth 184 cm, depth 73 cm, height 78 cm (with stand).
IN LEIPZIG, Instrumentenmuseum der Universität. Heyer Cat. No. 53.

This instrument was built for *Ferdinand de' Medici* (d. 1713), son of Cosimo III, Grand Duke of Tuscany (1670–1723).

GRAND PIANOFORTE

Gottfried Silbermann—Germany, Freiberg 1747
(see p. 22 above)

Originally in the Stadtschloss, Potsdam. Destroyed by fire in 1945.

It was upon this instrument, on 7th May 1747, that *Frederick the Great* played a theme to *Johann Sebastian Bach* (1685–1750). Bach himself sat down at the instrument "and to his Majesty's great pleasure extemporized on the King's theme" (L. Mitzler's Bach-Nekrolog vom Jahre 1754). This same theme Bach subsequently used as the basis of his 'Musical Offering' (Canones diversi super Thema Regium). See Georg Kinsky's book: Die Flügel Friedrichs des Grossen. The above instrument was standing in the Stadtschloss when the whole palace was destroyed by fire.

DOUBLE MANUAL HARPSICHORD

Burkat Tschudi—England, London, 1766

(see p. 21)

This instrument has the maker's number 511 inscribed in it and is probably of the same specification as No. 496. Stand and pedals are modern.
It stood in the Musiksalon, Neues Palais, Potsdam.

Frederick the Great ordered two pianos by Tschudi for his sister, Princess Anna Amalia, and his brother Prince Heinrich. Those instruments were numbered 511 and 512. No. 512 has not survived.

DOUBLE MANUAL HARPSICHORD

Burkat Tschudi—England, London 1765

SIGNATURE: maker's name inlaid on nameboard: 'Burkat Tschudi Fecit Londini 1765.'
SHAPE: the instrument bears the number 496. Case made in finely polished mahogany; outside, inside and also on the inside of the lid the ornamentation is of inlaid veining in light-colored maple-wood and dark striping of mahogany arranged in squares, the hinges of ornate bronze. The upper and lower edges are framed in a supperimposed gilt. The four spindle-shaped turned legs are joined to form a stand and end in griffins' claws holding a golden ball.
KEYBOARD: two manuals. Compass of both manuals C_1 to f''' (5 octaves and a fourth).
The keyboard is in Hitchcock style; naturals, ivory with ridged facings. Skunktail sharps.
STRAINING: trichord 8', 8', 4'.
STOPS: five front stops work the coupling, in and out, of the different registers. There is also a lute stop, a buff stop and a pedal-('Machine') to disconnect two strings whilst playing.
MEASUREMENT: breadth 103 cm, depth 270 cm, height 96 cm.
IN THE CASTLE AT WROCLAW (BRESLAU), Cat. No. 21.

This instrument was made for *Frederick the Great*, King of Prussia, and in the summer of 1765 was first played by the nine-year-old *Wolfgang Amadeus Mozart* when he was staying in London. During the World War II it was moved from its original place in the Schlossmuseum in Wroclaw, for greater safety, to an unknown destination.

GRAND PIANOFORTE

Gottfried Silbermann—Germany, Freiberg (1746)

AT POTSDAM, Schloss Sans Souci, Musiksalon.
Formerly the property of *Frederick II (the Great)*, King of Prussia (b. 1712, d. 1786).
SHAPE: case of oak.
KEYBOARD: compass F_1 to d''' (4 octaves plus a sixth). Black naturals, white sharps.
INTERIOR: rose on the soundboard.
MEASUREMENT: breadth 93 cm, depth 230 cm, height 94 cm.

Frederick the Great playing the flute
After a drawing by Adolph Menzel

DOUBLE MANUAL HARPSICHORD

Burkat Shudi (Tschudi) and John Broadwood—England, London, 1773

SIGNATURE: inscription on nameboard: 'Burkat Shudi and Johannes Broadwood, No. 691, Londini fecerunt 1773, Patent.'
SHAPE: case of mahogany. The nameboard shows fine inlay work portraying musical instruments.
KEYBOARD: two manuals; compass of both manuals C_1 to f''' (5 octaves and a fourth). White naturals, black sharps.
STRINGING: triple-strung 8', 8', 4'. Lower manual 8', 8', 4' three rows of jacks; upper manual has both 8' of the lower manual, one row of jacks, which connects the first 8' and the second 8' of the lower manual.
STOPS: five front stops, three left and two right with the following names and functions (left to right): lute (8' of upper manual, plucking point at a spot very near the bridge); octave (4' of lower manual); harp (a leather strip is pressed against the 8' string of the lower manual); 8' lower manual; 8' upper manual. Two pedals: the left pedal connects the lute stop of the upper manual and the harp stop of the lower manual after previously setting the stop button inside the case to the left of the keyboard; the right pedal serves the so-called 'Venetian swell', an invention which Tschudi patented on 13th December 1769 though he had been already using it for three years. It was a movable mechanism shaped somewhat like a Venetian blind built in above the stringing through the opening and closing of which crescendo and diminuendo were achieved. Our picture shows the instrument with the swell open.
MEASUREMENT: width 104 cm, depth 270 cm, height 97 cm.
IN BRUSSELS, Musée instrumental du Conservatoire Royal de Musique. Cat. No. 1604.

Frederick the Great, King of Prussia, presented this instrument to the *Empress Maria Theresia of Austria* (b. 1717, d. 1788).

Illustration opposite: Burkat Tschudi with his first wife and his sons Josua and Burkat; about 1744, artist unknown.

DOUBLE MANUAL HARPSICHORD

Burkat Shudi and John Broadwood—England, London 1775

SIGNATURE: inscription on nameboard: 'Burkat Shudi and Johannes Broadwood No. 762 Londini fecerunt 1775.'
This instrument has the same shape and disposition as that of No. 691 by Shudi and Broadwood.
MEASUREMENT: width 104 cm, depth 271 cm, height 95 cm.
IN VIENNA, Kunsthistorisches Museum, Collection of old musical instruments. Loaned by the Gesellschaft der Musikfreunde, Vienna.

It is said that the instrument was formerly the property of *Joseph Haydn* (1732–1809).

SQUARE PIANO

Johann Schantz—Austria, Vienna (last decade of 18th century)

SIGNATURE: 'Johann Schantz Bürgerlicher Instrumentenmacher auf der Wien beym Weissen Ochsen Nr. 62 in Wien.'
SHAPE: simple case on four tapering legs.
KEYBOARD: compass F_1 to f''' (five octaves), naturals black, sharps white.
STRINGING: bichord.
ACTION: English action (Einfache Stosszungenmechanik).
STOPS: divided dampers adjustable by an iron lever.
MEASUREMENT: width 102 cm, depth 43 cm, height 77 cm.
IN VIENNA, Kunsthistorisches Museum, Collection of old musical instruments. Loaned by the Gesellschaft der Musikfreunde, Vienna.

Formerly the property of *Joseph Haydn.*

GRAND PIANOFORTE

Johann Jacob Könnicke—Austria, Vienna 1796

SIGNATURE: inscription on nameboard: 'Joh. Jakob Könnicke, Instrumentenmacher in Wien, 1796.'
SHAPE: mahogany case, on three legs. Sides of keyboard and nameboard decorated. Legs probably not original.
KEYBOARD: compass F_1 to g''' (five octaves and a second); black naturals, white sharps.
ACTION: Viennese action.
STOPS: one knee lever; damping.
MEASUREMENT: length 98 cm, depth 213 cm, height 86 cm.
IN VIENNA, Städtische Sammlungen.

Formerly the property of *Joseph Haydn.*

CLAVICHORD

(about 1768)

UNSIGNED.
KEYBOARD: compass C–d‴ (four octaves and a second).
IN PARIS, Musée instrumental du Conservatoire National de Musique. Cat. No. 334.

Formerly the property of *André Grétry* (1742–1813).

VIRGINAL

Italy (second half of 17th century)

UNSIGNED.
SHAPE: the case is richly decorated with cupids, flowers, a coat of arms and ornaments. On the inside of the lid is a painting by Fra Gioacchino 1667 (Venetian school): Judith showing the Hebrews the head of Holofernes. On the nameboard is the following inscription: 'INDOCTA MANUS NOLI ME TANGERE.'
KEYBOARD: compass E/C to c‴ (four octaves). Short bass-octave.
INTERIOR: beautiful rose over soundhole in soundboard.
MEASUREMENT: width 152 cm, depth 50 cm, height with stand 91 cm, without stand 21.5 cm.
IN MILAN, Museo Teatrale alla Scala, Cat. No. 67.

This instrument is said to have belonged to *Domenico Cimarosa* (1749–1801), but there is no guarantee for the truth of this assumption.

DOUBLE MANUAL HARPSICHORD

Johann Heinrich Gräbner—Germany, Dresden 1722

SIGNATURE: written label: 'Johann Heinrich Gräbner / kgl. Hof-Orgelmacher und Organist / an der Frauenkirche / fecit Dresden anno 1722.'
SHAPE: this handsome instrument is mounted now upon a carved gilded stand.
KEYBOARD: fitted with a transposing-adjustment; two manuals. The transposition raises the scale half a tone. Compass E_1 to e''' (five octaves), after transposition F_1–f'''. Naturals in ebony, sharps of ivory.
STRINGING: trichord. On the lower manual 8', 8'; upper manual 4', also coupler.
MEASUREMENT: width 100 cm, depth 260 cm.
IN PRAGUE, at the Villa Bertramka, where Mozart lived with the family Dušek while he was in Prague.

Mozart played the instrument in the palace of the Duke Nostiz in the autumn of 1787. This is the sole remaining piano by *J. H. Gräbner* (see Georg Kinsky's book: Mozartinstrumente, p. 15).

The Mozart Family

Oil painting by de la Croce, 1780/81; Salzburg, Mozart-Museum.

SQUARE PIANO

UNSIGNED.
SHAPE: plain oak case.
KEYBOARD: compass F_1 to f''' (five octaves); naturals in black, sharps white.
MEASUREMENT: width 176 cm, depth 53 cm, height 80 cm.
IN VIENNA, Historisches Museum der Stadt Wien, possibly lost during the war.

Formerly the possession of *W. A. Mozart*. Later the instrument was acquired by Caroline v. Sayn-Wittgenstein and presented to *Franz Liszt*. From 1848 till 1861 it stood in the Musiksaal on the second floor of the Altenburg in Weimar beside the Alexandre/Erard organ. See Kinsky's book 'Mozartinstrumente'.

FRET-FREE CLAVICHORD

Germany (second half 18th century)

UNSIGNED.
KEYBOARD: compass F_1 to f''' (5 octaves); naturals black ebony, sharps covered in ivory.
MEASUREMENT: width 138 cm, depth 45 cm, height 76 cm.
IN SALZBURG, Internationale Stiftung Mozarteum, Mozart-Museum.

Property of *Wolfgang Amadeus Mozart* (1756–1791).

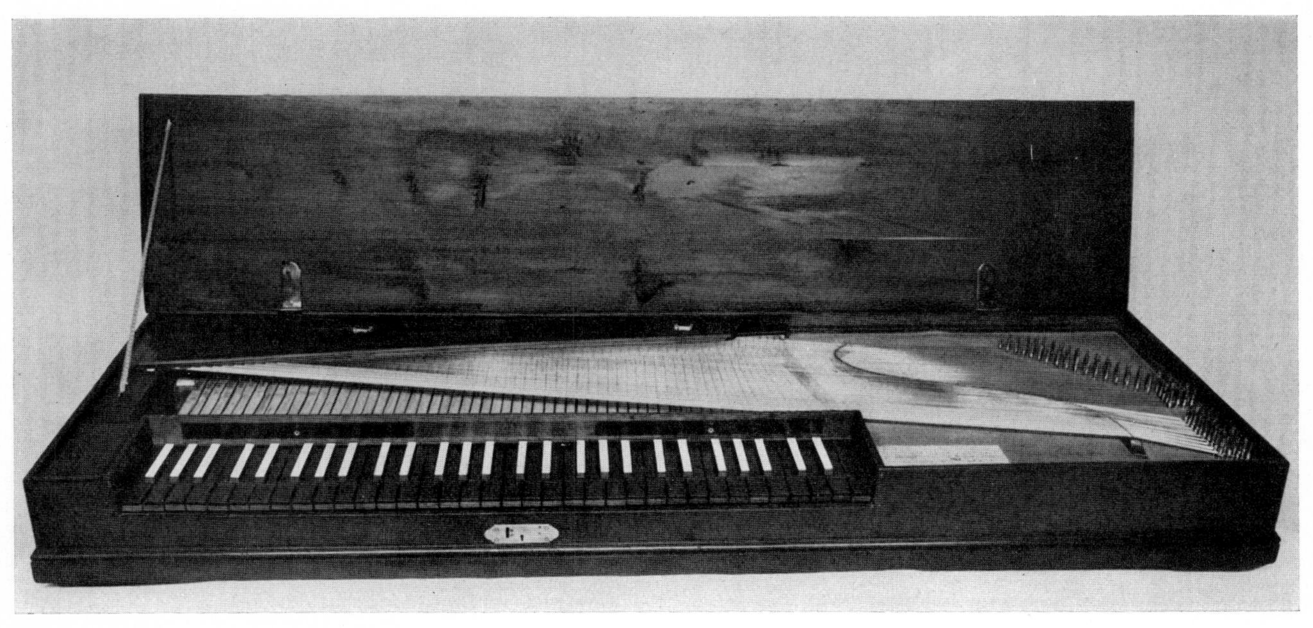

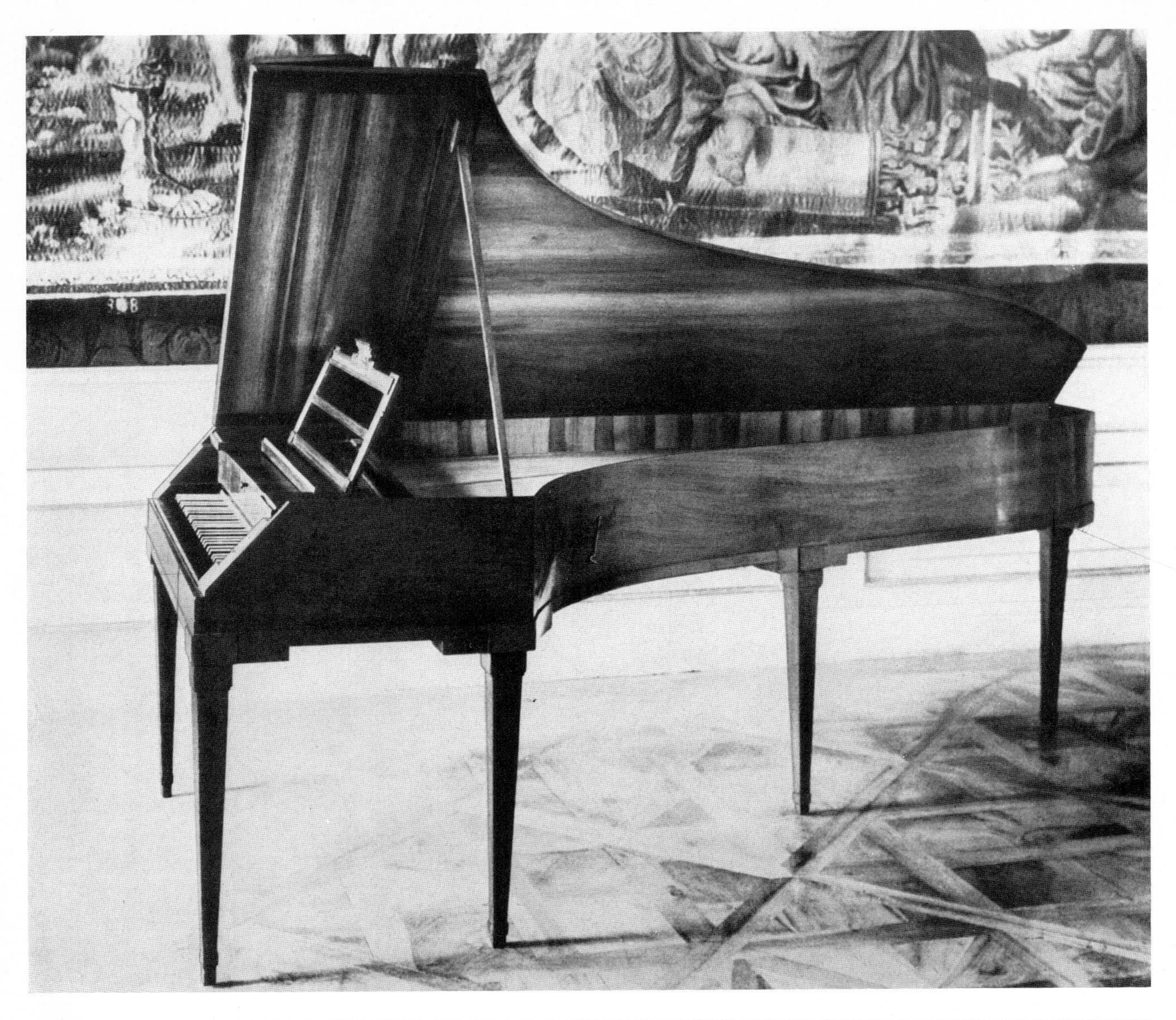

CONCERT GRAND PIANOFORTE

(Anton Walter—Austria, Vienna?)

UNSIGNED.
SHAPE: polished walnut case of a reddish yellow, stands on five tapered legs.
KEYBOARD: compass F_1 to f‴ (5 octaves); naturals ebony, sharps covered with bone.
STRINGING: bichord.
ACTION: Viennese action.
STOPS: two knee levers; divided dampers; one front button stop; piano.
MEASUREMENT: width 99 cm, depth 224 cm, height 86.5 cm.
IN SALZBURG, Internationale Stiftung Mozarteum, Mozart-Museum.

Concert piano belonging to *Wolfgang Amadeus Mozart*. According to information from his son Karl, Mozart used this instrument continuously till the end of his life.
The instrument was originally built at Mozart's expressed wish with a pedal-keyboard which has been lost. The tone is till clear and strong in the forte, soft and sweet in the piano, and its action light and brilliant, the ideal instrument for the interpretation of Mozart's piano compositions.

SPINET

Pascal Taskin—France, Paris 1778

SIGNATURE: inscription in crimson letters on the nameboard, 'FAIT PAR PASCAL TASKIN A PARIS 1778.'
SHAPE: irregularly shaped case painted with ivory-colored Vernis-Martin paint, and with gilded edges. The inside of the instrument is completely covered with birds, flowers and musical emblems painted in delicate colors, and framed in a design of flowers. The inside of the lid shows a scene from La Fontaine's Fables: Renard the Fox in the trap, surrounded by trees, birds, musical instruments and different colored insects all painted in brilliant colors and with the greatest care. The same designs are to be found on the nameboard where two flaming hearts are intertwined with flowering vines. The instrument stands upon four fluted tapering legs. The fluting is gilded, the legs covered to match the case with Vernis-Martin paint.
KEYBOARDS: compass E_1 to f''' (5 octaves and one semitone); naturals black, sharps white.
INTERIOR: the soundboard has no soundhole, but there is a large painted bunch of roses and cornflowers amongst which the initials 'P. T.', the maker's initials, are beautifully interwoven, with the date 1778 below.
MEASUREMENT: width 3 ft 6 1/2 in., depth 1 ft 4 in. to 2 ft, extreme height 2 ft 6 3/4 in.
AT HOLYOKE, The Belle Skinner Collection, Cat. No. 17.

Probably at one time property of *Queen Marie-Antoinette* of France (b. 1755, beheaded 1793). A plausible reason for this assumption is given in detail in The Belle Skinner Catalogue, pp. 47–50. This beautiful instrument is in perfect condition for playing and has an exceptionally sweet tone.

FAIT PAR PASCAL TASKIN A PARIS 1778

SQUARE PIANO

Johannes Wolber—France, Paris 1790

SIGNATURE: inscription on nameboard: 'Johannes Wolber à Paris rue Argenteuil No. 17.'
KEYBOARD: compass F_1–f''' (five octaves).
IN PARIS, Musée instrumental du Conservatoire National de Musique, Cat. No. E. 1722.

At one time the property of *Marie-Joseph Chénier* (b. 1764, d. 1811). On this instrument, in the year 1792, *Rouget de Lisle* (b. 1760, d. 1836) played the Marseillaise for the first time in Paris.

GRAND PIANOFORTE

Erard Frères—France, Paris 1803

SIGNATURE: inscription on nameboard: 'Erard Frères / Rue du Mail No. 37 à Paris 1803.'
SHAPE: mahogany case on three legs.
KEYBOARD: compass F_1 to c'''' (five octaves and a fifth), naturals covered with ivory, ebony sharps.
INTERIOR: four small iron braces.
STRINGING: trichord.
ACTION: English action (Stosszungenmechanik).
STOPS: four wooden pedals: keyboard glide, piano, damping and lute.
MEASUREMENT: width 109 cm, depth 222 cm, height 93 cm.
IN VIENNA, Kunsthistorisches Museum, Collection of old musical instruments. Loaned by the Landesmuseum Linz.

The property of *Ludwig van Beethoven* (1770–1827) from 1803 to 1816: presented to the composer by *Sébastien Erard* (Summer 1803).

Silhouette of Beethoven, sixteen years old, by Neesen

GRAND PIANOFORTE

John Broadwood & Sons—England, London 1817

SIGNATURE: maker's name on nameboard: 'John Broadwood & Sons / Makers to His Majesty and the Princesses / Great Pulteney Street, Golden Square / London.'
SHAPE: case in red-brown mahogany with brown and copper-colored marquetry. The instrument has the maker's number 7362.
Inscriptions: above the maker's name: 'BEETHOVEN.' Also the following: 'Hoc instrumentum est Thomae Broadwood Londini donum propter ingenium illustrissimi Beethoven.'
KEYBOARD: compass C_1 to c''' (six octaves); naturals covered in ivory, and ebony sharps.
STRINGING: steel strings, trichord throughout.
ACTION: English Grand Action.
STOPS: lyre with two wooden pedals: Keyboard glide, separated damping (the pedal on the right is divided, the right half lifts the damper in the treble, the left half lifts the dampers in the bass).
MEASUREMENT: width 115 cm, depth 247 cm, height 92 cm.
IN BUDAPEST, Hungarian National Museum of History. Inv. No. 41,1887.

On the 27th December 1817 this instrument was despatched by *Thomas Broadwood* from London to Vienna, as a present to *Beethoven*. In the year 1824 Beethoven was visited by the harp-builder Johann Stumpff of London. Beethoven complained bitterly to Stumpff about the inadequacy of pianos which allow of no powerful and effective performance and showed him his Broadwood piano. "What a sight presented itself," wrote Stumpff. "There was no sound left in the treble, and broken strings lay tangled together like a bush struck down in a thunderstorm."[1]

[1] Closson, Ernest, Histoire du Piano, p. 104.

GRAND PIANOFORTE

Conrad Graf—Austria, Vienna (about 1823/25)

SIGNATURE: maker's name 'Conrad Graf / Kaiserl. kön. Hof-Fortepianomacher / Wien / nächst der Carls-Kirche im Mondschein No. 102.'
SHAPE: plain mahogany case.
KEYBOARD: compass C_1 to f'''' (six octaves and a fourth); ivory naturals; sharps probably ebony.
STRINGING: from C_1 to C# trichord, from D to f'''' quadruple stringing.
ACTION: Viennese action.
STOPS: three pedals, keyboard glide, piano (by inserting a strip of felt between hammer and strings), and damping.
MEASUREMENT: width 122 cm, depth 245 cm, height 87 1/2 cm.
IN BONN, Beethoven House: Inv. No. Mö 2.

Conrad Graf: ".... made by myself for Beethoven a few years before his death." (From the certificate of authenticity of 26th June 1849.) On the front of the damper rail is to be seen the inscription 'L. VAN BEETHOFEN.' "Above the keyboard and the hammers there was a sort of souffleur's box to catch the sound, made like a bent soundboard in soft, thin wood. The idea was to direct the waves of sound from the instrument to the ear of the player in a more concentrated form." (See Gerh. v. Breuning's book: 'Aus dem Schwarzspanierhaus', pp. 58/59.) The piano, 'put at the disposal of Beethoven', was taken back by the maker, Conrad Graf, after Beethoven's death in 1827 and sold to the Wimmer family, bookseller in Vienna. After the marriage of his daughter, Lotte Wimmer, with Pastor J. Widmann, of the Reformed Church, the piano was moved to Liestal, Canton of Basel, in Switzerland, where it later became the property of his son, the poet Joseph Victor Widmann, who eventually sold the instrument in August 1889 to the Beethoven House in Bonn. For the above details about the Beethoven piano by Conrad Graf, I am indebted to kind information from Dr. E. A. Ballin, Director of the Beethoven Archives in Bonn.

GRAF
WIEN

GRAND PIANOFORTE

Erard frères—France, Paris 1808

SIGNATURE: inscription on the soundboard: 'Erard frères à Paris 1808.'
SHAPE: this magnificent instrument is numbered 234. The case is in mahogany with three legs shaped like columns with Corinthian capitals. On the sides are bronze ornamentations and medallions. The nameboard is adorned with figures of animals in gold on a dark blue ground with the inscription: 'Antoine Ascalon fecit 1808.' The whole is in Empire style.
KEYBOARD: compass F_1 to c'''' (five octaves and a fifth); white naturals, black sharps.
STRINGING: triple stringing.
ACTION: repetition action with damper above the strings (over-damper).
STOPS: four pedals; from left to right: lute (by pressure of felt-strip on strings), damping, piano (by insertion of felt between hammer head and strings), keyboard glide. One knee lever: bassoon (by pressing roll of paper against strings).
IN AMSTERDAM, City castle.

The instrument was built for *Louis Bonaparte* (b. 1778, d. 1846), King of Holland (1806–1810), brother of the Emperor Napoleon I.
In the archives of the House of Erard there is the following entry under the factory-number 234: 'Nr. 234 livré au Roy d'Hollande par Herman le 26 août 1808' (according to kind information from the House of Erard).

GRAND PIANOFORTE

Erard frères—France, Paris 1808

IN AMSTERDAM, City castle front view.

Sébastien Erard
by Jacques-Louis David (1811)
(Paris, Erard Collection)

SQUARE PIANO

Erard frères—France, Paris 1808

SIGNATURE: inscription on nameboard: 'Erard frères / Rue du Mail No. 13 à Paris 1808.'
Maker's number 7488.
KEYBOARD: compass F_1 to f''' (five octaves); white naturals, black sharps.
STRINGING: double-strung.
IN PARIS, Musée instrumental du Conservatoire National de Musique, Cat. No. 339.

Formerly the property of *Ferdinand Herold* (1791–1833).
At this instrument the following operas were composed: 'L'Illusion' (1829), 'Zampa' (1831), 'Le pré aux Clercs' (1832).

SQUARE PIANO

Henri Pape—France, Paris 1817

SIGNATURE: inscription on nameboard: 'Pape / Facteur de Pianos / Cour des Fontaines / à Paris.'
KEYBOARD: compass F_1 to f'''' (six octaves). Modern covering of keys.
IN PARIS, Musée instrumental du Conservatoire National de Musique. Cat. No. 341.

Once the property of *Luigi Cherubini* (baptized 1760, d. 1842).
At this instrument Cherubini composed during the last 25 years of his life (1817–1842).

GRAND PIANOFORTE

Joseph Brodmann—Austria, Vienna (about 1812)

SIGNATURE: 'Brodmann/in Wien.'
SHAPE: case in light colored walnut in plain, clear-cut lines, with square legs; a black lyre on the rail connecting the two front legs.
KEYBOARD: compass F_1 to f'''' (six octaves); naturals covered with bone, sharps made of pear-wood covered in ebony.
STRINGING: triple-strung.
ACTION: Viennese action.
STOPS: four pedals: keyboard glide, bassoon, piano and damping; knee lever.
MEASUREMENT: width 119 cm, depth 228 cm, height 89 cm.
IN BERLIN, Institut für Musikforschung, Cat. No. 312.

Carl Maria von Weber (1786–1826) bought this instrument in 1812, when he was at the height of his reputation.

SQUARE PIANO

Walter & Sohn—Austria, Vienna (1820/25)

SIGNATURE: inscription on the nameboard: 'Walter & Sohn / Wien.'
SHAPE: plain case on four legs.
KEYBOARD: compass F_1 to f'''' (six octaves); white naturals, black sharps.
STRINGING: E_1 to B_1 single, double to b, and from c onwards triple stringing.
ACTION: Viennese action.
STOPS: two pedals: damping, piano (insertion of leather strip).
MEASUREMENT: width 165 cm, depth 76 cm, height 84 cm.
IN VIENNA, Kunsthistorisches Museum, Collection of old musical instruments. Loaned by the Gesellschaft der Musikfreunde, Vienna.

This instrument was originally owned by the painter Wilhelm August Rieder, in whose house it was often played upon by *Franz Schubert* (1797–1828).

GRAND PIANOFORTE

John Broadwood & Sons—England, London 1820

SIGNATURE: maker's name: 'John Broadwood & Sons / Makers to His Majesty and the Princesses / Great Pulteney Street, Golden Square / London.'
SHAPE: mahogany case. The separate pieces of the wood are inlaid and divided by an inlaid black line. The bases of the legs ornamented with conventional leaf-pattern. Three small brass hinges to the cover in the shape of a lyre. Stamped on the wrestplank is the maker's number 8525. Also on the wrestplank, on the right-hand side, the date A.D. 1820 has been cut.
KEYBOARD: compass F_1 to f'''' (six octaves). Naturals covered with ivory, ebony sharps.
INTERIOR: two metal braces.
STRINGING: trichord all through; for the 16 deepest notes brass strings, and for the remainer steel strings have been used.
ACTION: English Grand Action. In the bass the hammers are covered with felt, in the upper register with soft leather.
STOPS: lyre with two wooden pedals: keyboard glide, divided damping (the right pedal is divided).
MEASUREMENT: width 116 cm, depth 225 cm, height 91 cm.
IN FRANKFURT AM MAIN, Stadt- und Universitätsbibliothek.

Formerly owned by *Felix Mendelssohn-Bartholdy* (1809–1847).
The instrument now belongs to the 'Manskopf'sches Museum für Musik- und Theatergeschichte in Frankfurt a.M.'

GRAND PIANOFORTE

Nannette Streicher—Austria, Vienna 1820/21

SIGNATURE: maker's name: 'Nannette Streicher, née Stein, Vienne.'
SHAPE: the instrument is numbered 1563. Cherry-wood case. Above the soundboard, halfway between the stringing and the lid of the instrument, there is a dust-cover made of Bohemian pinewood 4 mm thick, fastened with hooks to little wooden, leather-covered blocks stuck to the inside walls of the case.
KEYBOARD: compass F_1 to f'''' (six octaves). Bone-covered naturals, ebony sharps.
INTERIOR: wooden string-plate: two very narrow iron braces between wrestplank and edge of plate underneath the strings.
ACTION: Viennese action.
STOPS: lyre with four pedals; damping, keyboard glide, harp and bassoon.
IN WEIMAR, Goethehaus.

On the 14th July 1821 this instrument was delivered at *Johann Wolfgang von Goethe's* house in Weimar. (Goethe, b. 1749, d. 1832.) In September 1822, May 1825 and May 1830 it was played upon by *Felix Mendelssohn*. Excerpt from Mendelsson's letter to his parents dated 20th November 1821 (?): "I play here much more than at home, seldom less than four hours, sometimes six and occasionally even for eight hours at a time. Every afternoon Goethe opens the Streicher instrument with the words: 'I have not heard you at all today, make a little noise for me.' Then he comes and sits beside me and when I have finished (I generally improvise) I either ask for a kiss or else I just take one."
Clara Wieck played upon it early in October 1831. And it was on the 24th April 1830 that Goethe heard *Wilhelmine Schroeder-Devrient*, accompanied on this same instrument, sing his ballad, the Erlkönig, which Schubert had just set to music.
See Georg Kinsky's article: 'Der Streicherflügel im Weimarer Goethehaus und andere Musikinstrumente aus dem Goethekreis', in the 'Instrument Maker's Magazine' (Zeitschrift für Instrumentenbau).

GRAND PIANOFORTE

John Broadwood & Sons—England, London 1820

View of interior

In Frankfurt am Main, Stadt- und Universitätsbibliothek.

SQUARE PIANO

Johann Wilhelm Freudenthaler—France, Paris 1823

Signature: inscription on nameboard: 'Freudenthaler / Breveté de S.A.R. Mr. le Duc d'Orléans / Rue Montmartre No. 164 à Paris.'
Keyboard: compass F_1 to c'''' (five octaves and a fifth).
In Paris, Musée instrumental du Conservatoire National de Musique, Cat. No. 342.

Formerly owned by *François-Adrien Boieldieu* (1775–1834).
At this instrument he composed, amongst other things, the opera 'La Dame blanche'.

GRAND PIANOFORTE

A. Tischner—Russia, Leningrad (St. Petersburg), (second quarter of 19th century)

SHAPE: mahogany case, bronze ornaments, on three turned, round legs.
KEYBOARD: compass C_1 to f'''' (six octaves and a fourth).
STOPS: two pedals fastened to a lyre.
IN LENINGRAD, State Institute for Scientific Research in Music and the Theatre.

Property of *Michail I. Glinka* (1804–1857) from 1824 till 1856.

UPRIGHT PIANOFORTE

Erard—France, Paris 1834

SHAPE: the instrument, which is built of elm is ornately decorated with inlay in mahogany and rosewood in the form of Greek palm-leaves, and a frieze of laurel, with Etruscan vases and emblems of music. The maker's number is 13279.
KEYBOARD: compass F_1 to f'''' (six octaves). Naturals covered in ivory, sharps ebony.
STRINGING: trichord.
ACTION: English action (Stosszungenmechanik) with over-damper, 'mécanique à baïonnette'.
STOPS: two pedals: damping (by shortening the hammer action).
MEASUREMENT: width 155 cm, height 107 cm.
IN PARIS, Musée de l'Opéra.

Property of *Gaspero Spontini* (1774–1851).
In the records of the House of Erard there is the following remark under the entry 'Piano Erard Nr. 13.279':

'Piano vertical 3 cordes Etrusque	le 20/6 1834	Donné par Monsieur Erard à Monsieur Spontini, son beau-frère.'

On the front of the instrument a copper plate bearing the inscription: 'Piano ayant appartenu à G. Spontini / offert par Madame Erard / à l'Académie Nationale de Musique 1er octobre 1879.' (Information by courtesy of the Firm Erard.)

GRAND PIANOFORTE

Conrad Graf—Austria, Vienna 1839

SIGNATURE: inscription on nameboard: 'Conrad Graf / Kaiserl. kön. Hof-Fortepianomacher / Wien / nächst der Carls-Kirche im Mondschein Nr. 102.' Besides this, on the upper-side of the wrestplank and on the key-bed there is a double eagle stamped in with the words: '2616/Werk/des/Conr. Graf/in Wien.'
SHAPE: case made of rosewood, standing on three delicately turned legs.
KEYBOARD: compass C_1 to g'''' (six octaves and a fifth). White naturals, black sharps.
INTERIOR: over the strings there is a so-called dust-cover which can be removed.
STRINGING: deepest octave double, the remaining octaves with treble stringing.
ACTION: Viennese action.
STOPS: lyre with four pedals: keyboard glide piano, piano (by shorter or longer insertion of a felt strip above the hammer), and damping.
MEASUREMENT: width 126 cm, depth 237 cm, height 89 cm.
IN VIENNA, Kunsthistorisches Museum, Collection of old musical instruments. Loaned by the Gesellschaft der Musikfreunde, Vienna.

This instrument was a wedding present from Conrad Graf to *Clara Wieck* in 1840 and remained in *Robert Schumann's* (1810–1856) house until his death, when *Johannes Brahms* presented it, after 1873, to the Gesellschaft der Musikfreunde in Vienna.

GRAND PIANOFORTE

Ignace Pleyel and Co.—France, Paris 1839

SIGNATURE: maker's name: 'Ignace Pleyel et Comp[ie] / Facteur du Roi / Paris.'
SHAPE: the case is veneered in mahogany and stands on three round, turned legs. On the right-hand side of the instrument there are three bronze appliqués. The manufacturer's number is 7267.
KEYBOARD: projected. Compass C_1 to g'''' (six octaves and a fifth). White naturals, black sharps.
INTERIOR: five iron braces from hitch-pin block to wrestplank.
STRINGING: single to triple stringing.
ACTION: 'mécanique simple échappement' (repetition action).
STOPS: lyre with two pedals: keyboard glide and damping.
MEASUREMENT: width 127 cm, depth 219 cm, height 90 cm.
IN PARIS, Pleyel Collection.

Formerly owned by *Frédéric Chopin* (1810–1849).
At this instrument he composed the Préludes op. 28 (1838), the g-minor Nocturne op. 37 No. 1 (1840), the Funeral March from the b-minor Sonata op. 35, and the f-minor Fantasia op. 49 (1840/41).

GRAND PIANOFORTE

Erard—France, Paris 1840

SIGNATURE: on the lid: 'Par Brevet D'Invention / Erard / à Paris.' And on the soundboard appear the words: 'Par Brevet D'Invention / Erard / à Paris No. 14932.'
SHAPE: case made of rosewood with inlay in maple and rosewood. There are three hexagonal feet, shaped conically and with capitals. Above the strings is a soundboard which can be lifted open.
KEYBOARD: compass C_1–f'''' (six octaves and a fourth).
INTERIOR: iron hitch-pin block with five iron braces.
STRINGING: C_1 to E_1 double (steel strings covered in copper wire); F_1–C♯ triple (steel strings covered with iron wire), the remainder triple string.
ACTION: double escapement action, under-damper.
STOPS: two pedals on a loose lyre: keyboard glide and damping.
MEASUREMENT: width 116.5 cm, depth 194.5 cm.
IN ERLANGEN, Rück Collection.

In the records of the Rück Collection there is documentary evidence that the piano was formerly in *M. Schlesinger's* house, the Music Publisher, in Paris. "Every Wednesday the musicians and writers of Paris met and much music ensued, many famous musicians of that time playing on the Erard. Amongst others who frequented the house were Alary, Cherubini, Hiller, Liszt, Mendelssohn, Meyerbeer, Viardot-Garcia, Paganini, Ries, Rossini, Rubinstein, Spontini, Beriot, and Wagner. The latter lived in the house for a year. Chopin, who was delicate and did not care to sit at long dinners, would soon slip away to the music-room, where he would sit down to the piano, take my mother (the five-year-old child) on his knee and teach her to play. He composed lovely pieces for her, things suitable for her little fingers. Listeners on many occasions were George Sand, Alexandre Dumas, Flaubert, and others. In 1855 the Schlesingers left Paris, moving to Baden-Baden and taking their Erard with them. At that time Baden-Baden was also a center for celebrities so that their house No. 1 Schlossberg was often visited by both resident artists and those passing through. Mme Viardot-Garcia had her School of Music in Baden-Baden: she and her pupils often sang at the house of my grandparents, and Alexandre Dumas, Turgenev, Liszt, Rubinstein, George Sand and others were frequent guests."
For these details we are indebted to Frau Helene Horsfall née Foucault, M. Schlesinger's granddaughter by adoption.

GRAND PIANOFORTE

Erard—France, Paris (about 1858?)

SIGNATURE: 'Erard'.
SHAPE: case covered with mahogany veneer, on three six-sided legs. On the soundboard is to be seen the following inscription: 'Par Brevet d'Invention Erard à Paris'; to the left of the maker's name the words: 'Siegfried, Schluss', and to the right: 'Tristan, Schluss'.
KEYBOARD: projected. Compass A_2 to a'''' (seven octaves). Ivory-covered naturals, ebony sharps.
INTERIOR: iron hitch-pin block with six iron braces.
STRINGING: straight stringing, single- and triple-strung.
ACTION: double escapement action with under-damping.
STOPS: lyre with two pedals: keyboard glide and damping.
MEASUREMENT: width 135 cm, depth 252 cm, height 95 cm.
AT TRIBSCHEN NEAR LUCERNE, Wagner Museum. Cat. No. 125. Lent by Frau Winifred Wagner and her four children.

This piano arrived on 3rd May 1858 at Wagner's Asyl in Zürich-Enge as a present to *Richard Wagner* (1813–1883) from Madame Pierre Erard.
It was upon this instrument that the II and III Acts of 'Tristan und Isolde' were played for the first time. The piano accompanied Wagner to Venice, stood for five months in the year 1859 in the Hotel 'Schweizerhof', Lucern and then followed him to Paris, Vienna, Munich, Tribschen and eventually to Bayreuth.

G. VERDI

Hochgeehrter Herr,

Abermals schulde ich Ihnen
vielen und besonderen Dank.
Der neue Steinway Flügel
ist ein grossartiges Meisterstück an
Kraft, Wohlklang, singenden Eigenschaften
und vollkommenen harmonischen Effecten
welche selbst meinen alten, schon
claviermüden Fingern Entzücken
gewähren. Immerwährender Erfolg
bleibt ein schönes Attribut
der weltberühmten Firma
Steinway. —
In Ihrem Brief, hochgeehrter Herr
erwähnen Sie einige Neuerungen
am Flügel z. B. dass der klingende
Körper aus einem einzigen Stücke
gebogen ist und dass ein Theil der
Saiten, welche bis dahin todt lagen,
nun Theil daran nimmt und als besondere
Töne in die Grundtöne eingreift und
ihr Nutzen wird besonders durch
den Namen des Erfinders garantirt.
Meine Unkenntniss des Mecha-
nismus der Clavier-Construction
eingestehend, kann ich nur das
prächtige Resultat in Kraft
und Vollkommenheit bewundern.

Bezüglich auf den Gebrauch
Ihres so willkommenen tonhaltenden
Pedals mit den ausgehaltenen Tönen sende
ich Ihnen beiliegend 2 Beispiele
„Danse des Sylphes" von Berlioz,
und No 3 meiner „Consolations".
Heute schreib ich nur die ein-
führenden Takte beider Sachen,
nebst der Bemerkung, dass,
wenn es Ihnen genehm ist, ich die ganze
Transcription vollständig,
mit genauer Anpassung an Ihr
tonhaltendes Pedal vollenden will.

Hochachtungsvoll,
und verbindlichst
dankend
November 83 – Weimar F. Liszt

Berlioz Partitur habe ich heute nicht zu Händen, und citire das Sylphentanz Motif aus dem Gedächtniss. Wenn Sie es aber wünschen, hochgeehrter Herr Steinway, transcribire ich gerne mit Einrichtung des getheilten Pedals, das ganze Stück, und gleichfalls die Nummer 3 meiner Consolations. —

Das genannte Pedal darf nicht, meines Erachtens zu häufig gebraucht werden, wird aber von vortrefflichem Effecte sein, vorzüglich in etwas ruhigen piano Stellen.

F. Liszt

November 83 – Weimar.

Steinway & Sons

C. BECHSTEIN
BERLIN.

GRAND PIANOFORTE

Erard—France, Paris (about 1870)
(see p. 78)

SIGNATURE: inscription on the inside of the lid 'Erard'.
SHAPE: rosewood case on three six-sided legs. The instrument is numbered 38932.
KEYBOARD: compass A_2 to a'''' (seven octaves). Ivory-covered naturals, ebony sharps.
INTERIOR: iron string-plate with six iron braces.
STRINGING: straight side stringing; single to triple stringing.
ACTION: double escapement action with under-damping.
STOPS: lyre with two pedals: keyboard glide and damping.
MEASUREMENT: width 135 cm, depth 252 cm, height 96 cm.
IN MILAN, Museo Teatrale alla Scala. Cat. No. 42.

Formerly owned by *Giuseppe Verdi* (1813–1901).

GRAND PIANOFORTE

Steinway & Sons—U.S.A., New York 1882
(see p. 81)

SIGNATURE: 'Steinway & Sons / Patent Grand / New York & Hamburg.'
SHAPE: the instrument, which stands on three heavy, compact-looking round legs, bears the number 49382.
KEYBOARD: compass A_2 to a'''' (seven octaves). Ivory-covered naturals, ebony sharps.
INTERIOR: complete cast iron frame.
STRINGING: single to triple stringing, over-strung.
ACTION: Steinway's repetition action, Pat. 30th Nov. 1875; over-damping.
STOPS: lyre with three pedals: keyboard glide, sustaining pedal, damping.
MEASUREMENT: width 139 cm, depth 222 cm, height 100 cm.
IN MILAN, Museo Teatrale alla Scala. Cat. No. 38.

Formerly the property of *Franz Liszt* (1811–1886).

GRAND PIANOFORTE

Carl Bechstein—Germany, Berlin (about 1880)
(see also p. 82)

SIGNATURE: 'C. Bechstein / Hof-Lieferant Sr. Maj. des Kaisers und Königs / Berlin.'
SHAPE: rosewood case, black, on three round legs. Numbered 18899.
KEYBOARD: compass A_2 to c''''' (seven octaves and a third). Ivory-covered naturals, ebony sharps.
INTERIOR: complete wrought iron frame. Inscription on soundboard: 'Pianofortefabrik C. Bechstein, Hofl. S. Majestät des Kaisers und Königs, S. Hoheit des Prinzen Fr. Carl von Preussen etc., Berlin.'
STRINGING: over-strung; single to triple stringing.
ACTION: repetition action.
STOPS: lyre with two pedals: keyboard glide and damping.
MEASUREMENT: width 156 cm, depth 264 cm, height 98 cm.
IN WEIMAR, Liszt Museum. Cat. No. 127.

Formerly the property of *Franz Liszt* (1811–1886).

Liszt at the piano

(photograph by Held, Weimar)

GRAND PIANOFORTE

Carl Michael Schröder—Russia, Leningrad (St. Petersburg), second half of 19th century

In Leningrad, State Institute for Scientific Research in Music and the Theatre.

Belonged formerly to *Alexander P. Borodin* (1833–1887).

PART II

KEYBOARD, STRINGING, FRAME AND ACTION

Bibliography: *Kinsky*, Georg. Kurze Oktaven auf besaiteten Tasteninstrumenten (Short octaves on stringed keyboard instruments). A Contribution to the history of the piano. Zeitschrift für Musikwissenschaft. 2nd year (1919/20), p. 65. *Marcuse*, Sybil, Transposing Keyboards on extant Flemish Harpsichords.

KEYBOARD

1. The word 'CLAVIER' comes from the Latin 'clavis', signifying a key. In the action of the organ the key, when pressed down, opens the slide or orifice directing the stream of air to the pipes.
The expression 'Palmulen' for the keys is more unusual: 'palma' means the palm of the hand and 'palmula' the little hand. Relatively often one sees the word 'Tangenten' used, which is derived from the Latin 'tangere', meaning 'to touch'. This word is, however, still used in connection with the clavichord to signify the small, *spade-shaped* piece of iron or brass which is let into the back end of the key. The word most in use is 'Tastatur' (keyboard): 'Taste' comes from the Italian word 'tasto', meaning 'touch'.

2. The SHORT-OCTAVE: Until about 1500 'F' was the lowest bass-note. With the increase of the bass compass to 'C' at the beginning of the 16th century the short-octave came into use, i.e. the seldom used notes C♯, D♯, F♯ and G♯ were dispensed with; F♯ and G♯ were replaced by D and E which gave the following set of notes:

D E B♭
C F G A B c

The usual E-note is therefore C.
Since 1610 the short C-octave was divided: through the '*Brechung*' (split keys) of D and E the notes F♯ and G♯ were replaced giving the following order of notes:

F♯ G♯
D E B♭
C F G A B c

At the same time the compass of the bass was increased to include G as follows:

B_1, C, C♯, D, D♯, E (sound)
G_1, C, A_1, D, B_1, E

This order of notes was called the short G-octave.

3. COMPASS: early times till approximately 1500 — 2½ to 4 octaves
1500 till approximately 1550 — 4 octaves, C to c'''
1550 till approximately 1600 — 4½ octaves, C to f'''
1600 till approximately 1700 — 4½ octaves to 5 octaves

Up till this time only the short bass-octave had been in use. Thomas Hitchcock increased the keyboard compass about the year 1690 and Nicholas Dumont in 1697, to five full octaves: G_1 to g''', and F_1 to f''' respectively. This increase in the compass, especially by renovation of valuable old Flemish instruments of the 17th century, was called in France during the 18th century 'mettre à ravalement', and those increased to five octaves were said to be 'mettre à grand ravalement'.

1700 till approximately 1765 —	5 octaves	F_1 to f'''
1765 till approximately 1794 —	5 octaves and a 4th	C_1 to f'''
1794 till approximately 1804 —	6 octaves	C_1 to c''''
1800	6 octaves	F_1 to f''''
1804 till approximately 1824 —	6 octaves and a 4th	C_1 to f''''
1824 till approximately 1880 —	7 octaves	C_1 to c'''''
1880 till approx. present day —	7 octaves and a 3rd	A_2 to c'''''

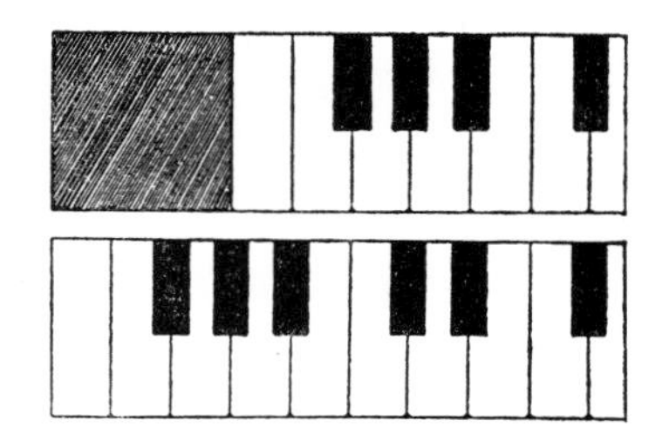
(Copied from Marcuse, p. 416)

4. Transposition keyboard: In the two-manual harpsichord the pitch of the lower manual was generally a 4th lower in pitch than that of the upper manual. The usual compass of the upper keyboard was usually four octaves and a short bass-octave: E/C to c''', and the lower keyboard had $4\,^1/_2$ octaves, E/C to f'''.

It was shortly after 1642 that this disposition of notes was discontinued and the transposition keyboard (lower manual) became the *Registermanual.* The earliest instrument known of today which has two manuals dates from about 1560 and is of Italian origin; it is formed like two harpsichords one above another in the shape of a *Hackbrett* (see 'upright harpsichords'). A Dresden inventory of musical instruments of the year 1593 also mentions three double manual harpsichords.

In the Italian harpsichords and clavichords, the German Querspinette and the English spinets the keyboard is generally projecting, otherwise mostly recessed. In the pianoforte industry, Erard was the first to make the now universally accepted projected keyboard with its own folding cover (1808).

5. Keys

Sharps stained dark Naturals boxwood	Italy, 16th and 17th centuries
Sharps stained black Naturals yellow lemon-wood	Italy, 17th and 18th centuries
Sharps ebony-covered Naturals boxwood	Italy, 16th to 18th century Germany, 15th to 19th century
Sharps stained black Naturals bone-covered	Netherlands, 16th to 18th century Spain, 18th century
Sharps ebony-covered Naturals ivory-covered	Italy, 16th to 18th century Germany, 16th to 17th century Sweden and England, 18th century; in general since beginning of 19th century
Sharps rosewood Naturals boxwood	Italy and Portugal, 18th century
Sharps oak Naturals bone-covered	Netherlands, 17th century
Sharps bone-covered Naturals ebony-covered	France, end 17th to end 18th century; England, 18th century (exceptional); Germany and Austria, 18th century
Sharps ivory-covered Naturals ebony-covered	Italy, 16th to 18th century; England, end of 17th to end of 18th century; Germany, France, Netherlands and Sweden, 18th century
Sharps ivory-covered Naturals tortoise shell-covered	Germany, 18th century
Sharps tortoise shell-covered Naturals ivory-covered	Germany, 18th century
Sharps covered with mother-of-pearl Naturals ebony-covered	Spain

The above details have to do with keys made of the most ordinary materials. Woods much in use were willow and pear, the sharps sometimes ornamented with inlaid ivory or veined with silver, the key-faces arcaded with half-circles or shaped with Gothic trefoil arches.

STRINGS

MATERIALS USED: *Plucked keyboard instruments:* sheep's gut, copper, silver, gold; for the bass notes, brass or steel and for the middle and treble notes, steel.
CLAVICHORDS: brass, iron, steel.
EARLY PIANOFORTES: similar stringing as that of the plucked keyboard instruments and clavichords.
The first to introduce the covering of the bass-strings with brass or copper wire was Sainte Colombe, a Frenchman, in the year 1675.
STRINGING: *Harpsichords* can be single- and up to quintuple-strung, clavichords from double- to quadruple-strung. The early pianofortes are single-strung (J.M. Schmahl) or double-strung, since 1790 (Erard, square piano) triple- and quadruple-strung (Conrad Graf, 1812).
In the 19th century, around 1830 or so, German and French patents were taken out for instruments strung with groups of five and even six strings. In modern piano-building single-, double- and triple stringing prevails.
STRAIGHT STRINGING: The disposition of the strings was originally straight: horizontal for square pianos and pianos, vertical for upright grands and cottage pianos. In upright instruments this called for a considerable height of the case, for the shortening beyond a certain minimum of the string's length led to unsatisfactory tone.
OBLIQUE STRINGING: A reduction in the height without prejudicing the sound could be achieved by carrying the same length of string obliquely from the left-hand upper end of the instrument down to the right.
SEMI-OBLIQUE STRINGING: This form of wiring was used in the second quarter of the 19th century.
CROSS STRINGING: This involves crossing the bass strings over the middle and treble notes.

The ideal of piano-building in the 18th and early 19th century was to retain the silvery tone of the plucked instrument.[1] The length and thickness of harpsichord strings standardized the measurement for piano strings, which were kept as thin[2] as possible.
Strings of weaker material meant weaker and looser tension. This, in its turn, needed no metal reinforcement of the frame-construction, enabling the whole case to be built of wood.
The beginning of the 19th century, however, saw the first appearance of the piano as a solo-instrument in larger concert halls and theatres. Now began the struggle against the sonority of augmented orchestras and the departure from moderation and clear-cut classical style in music. The Romantic era dawned, necessitating an instrument less personal in character with a powerful, carrying tone, one that was equal to every require-

[1] Very instructive is the report on this subject of experiments carried out in the Siemens Werk Research Laboratories by Trendelenburg, Thienhaus and Franz with the insertion of an electrical sound-filter, the so-called Octave-sieve, for recording the tone volume of the clavichord, harpsichord and the modern piano. The resulting graph (Oszillogramme) proved clearly how rich in overtones is the tone of the harpsichord in comparison with the overtone poverty of a modern pianoforte.—*Meyer and Buchmann*, in 'Die Klangfarben der Musikinstrumente', give the following comparisons:

Teiltonzahl =	Clavichord	Harpsichord	Early Pianoforte	Modern Grand Piano
für c 128 Hertz	38	33	23	14
c^1 256 Hertz	18	19	12	6–9
c^2 512 Hertz	15	10	9	4–5
c^3 1024 Hertz	4	9	5	2

[2] Normal thickness of harpsichord c′-string: 0,235 mm.

ment. This implied the *use of stronger, thicker and more tightly strung strings,*[1] in consequence of which the *hammers had to be heavier*[2] in order to set such strings in vibration. Hereto a stronger soundboard[3] was necessary, capable of carrying the increased tension. For at the bridge a certain component of the string tension works downwards on the soundboard. Owing to the thicker strings, *soft hammers* and thicker soundboards, a great loss in overtones was observable. Better radiation of the deep tones necessitated an enlargement of the soundboard surface, whereby the whole timbre of the tone became darker and fuller. One can therefore understand that in stringed keyboard instruments with increasing tone volume, the moment of spectral tone division necessitates deeper tone frequencies. The tone development mentioned above shows a definite advance towards increased volume which, in those days, could only be achieved by mechanical means. It was unavoidable that this entailed a considerable alteration in tone color, namely a loss of overtones. To instrument makers this change in tonal color, may have been partly desired and partly taken as a necessary evil.[4] In any case, by the use of mechanical means the development in tone volume was very closely connected with the development of tonal color. One can say that the power of the concert grand piano as such has now reached its zenith as far as mechanical and acoustic properties go: the rest lies today in the efficiency of the pianist.

The development of the stringed keyboard instrument has shown how closely allied are its tone color and its dynamics, namely its greatest obtainable volume of tone. It is, however, quite possible today, with the help of an electro-acoustic transmitter to achieve considerable increase in tone volume and dynamic without change of tone color. It is especially conceivable that the brilliant, ringing tone of the harpsichord, which is so rich in overtones, could be adapted in the above manner to the needs of present-day concerts. (Trendelenburg, Thienhaus, Franz.[5])

That the revival of the clavichord and harpsichord demands, as a first essential, a return to a tonality historically genuine in the rendering of early keyboard music, will be obvious to the reader of the foregoing facts. The modern reconstruction of the old pianos of Mozart's time by Neupert, Bamberg and Rück of Nürnberg can be considered a praiseworthy and promising step in this direction. One cannot imagine present-day musical life without the clavichord and harpsichord, yet it will astonish a later generation to remember that we played the music of Haydn, Mozart, Schubert and Mendelssohn on the same powerful, steel-plated concert-grands upon which we also performed the works of Liszt, Brahms, Franck, Reger, Debussy and the Moderns.

Those who have either played upon or listened to the Mozart piano in the Mozarteum in Salzburg, the beautiful Erard of 1808 in the City castle in Amsterdam, the Conrad Graf and the Streicher pianos in the Rück Collection in Erlangen, will agree that this is not simply exaggerated historical pedantry. Nowhere is the theory of 'progress' more out of place than in the art of musical instrument-building, for, in conformity with the times, each epoch has produced the perfect instrument.

[1] Thickness of modern pianoforte c′-string: 1 mm.

[2] See 'Covering of hammer heads', by Pfeiffer.

[3] In old plucked keyboard instruments and clavichords the average thickness of soundboards was 4 mm, those of the modern pianoforte being 8–10 mm (Sachs).

[4] Tyndall, an English expert in acoustics, writes: "*Pure tone without any overtones would be like pure water, weak and tasteless;*" Siegfried Hansing, an authority on piano-building, is of a different opinion: "It is obvious that we are not looking for overtones in the tone of the piano: indeed these can only be considered to be a disagreeable accessory. Our aim is to obtain the pure body-tone ... In contrast to Tyndall's assertion, *overtones are like a greasy soup, repulsive and indigestible.*" (Hansing, Das Pianoforte in seinen akustischen Anlagen, new edition 1950).

[5] *Trendelenburg. Thienhaus, Franz,* Zur Klangwirkung von Clavichord, Cembalo und Flügel. Akustische Zeitschrift, 5th year, vol. 6, Leipzig 1940.

TABLE OF DATES

France

- 1440 Heinrich Arnold of Zwolle mentions stringed keyboard instruments with single- and double stringing.
- 1675 Introduction of wrapped strings by Sainte Colombe.
- 1790 Erard increases stringing resistance by using thicker strings and builds square pianos with trichord stringing.
- 1800 Hillebrand of Nantes first uses cross stringing for square pianos.
- 1828 Pape patents the method of cross stringing in his piano-console (French Pat. No. 5833).
- 1843 Herz patents oblique stringing for grand piano (French Pat. No. 12375).
- 1848 Montal patents demi-oblique stringing for square- and upright pianos (French Pat. No. 3711).

Germany

- 1511 Virdung's first mention of use of steel strings in clavichord-building.
- 1745 Friederici's first use of oblique stringing for pyramid piano.
- 1833 Friedrich Greiner patents cross stringing for grand piano (Bavarian patent).
- 1850 Founding of first cast steel piano-string factory (Poehlmann in Franconia).

England

- 1790 Broadwood strengthens stringing by use of thicker strings.
- 1802 Loud uses oblique stringing for upright pianos (Engl. Pat. No. 2591).
- 1821 Collard first uses aliquot stringing (Engl. Pat. No. 4542).
- 1834 Introduction of cast steel strings (Webster, Birmingham), instead of the usual iron or brass.
- 1835 Fischer makes first use of cross stringing in England (Engl. Pat. No. 6835).

U.S.A.

- 1830 Babcock introduces cross stringing.

Austria

- 1834 Kaspar Lorenz and Samuel Meiszner use cross stringing (Austrian patent).

Belgium

- 1847 J. Vogelsangs of Brussels makes use of cross stringing (Belg. order No. 2901).

- 1867 Since the Great Exhibition of Paris, cross stringing becomes general.

FRAMEWORK

The early pianofortes were originally constructed entirely of wood, in the same manner as the plucked keyboard instrument, and clavichords. With the increasing tension and pull of thicker strings following on the demand for greater volume of tone and durability of material, it was soon obvious that the old wooden case was too weak to stand the strain.

The danger of a collapse led to a gradual introduction of metal reinforcement of the framework. After many trials, some unsuccessful, some more unsatisfactory, this development culminated in the invention and use of the cast iron frame, an ironplate in which wrestplank, hitch-pin block[1] and the connecting iron braces form a complete whole, with strength to resist the powerful tension of the strings. The introduction of the cast iron frame was at first opposed by piano builders on the grounds that it was too massive and of a coarse-grained material which brought with it a deterioration of tone, but properly constructed, modern cast iron frames made of the best material are now free from all disadvantages.

At this point it is necessary to mention the agraffes (brass studs) and the 'Druckstab', named also capo tasto bar. The agraffes are small metal studs bored with as many holes as there are unison strings, fixed to the wrest-pin block. The capo tasto is a metal bridge through which the upper treble strings were passed. The aim of both these inventions is to fix the strings firmly and to increase their resistance to the impact of the hammers, thus achieving greater brilliance and power of tone.

TABLE OF DATES

Germany

1739 Schröter's model of a tangent action already made use of an iron bar pressing on the strings, an invention which Erard returns to in 1838 ('basse harmonique').

1839 Jakob Becker patents the iron frame for grand pianos and square pianos (Bavarian patent).

1839 Ibach's first concert-grand piano has no metal reinforcement.

England

1799 Joseph Smith patents the invention of iron bracing for pianofortes and square pianos (Engl. Pat. No. 2345).
First use of iron reinforcement in frame constructions which, up to this time, had been exclusively of wood.

1820 Thom and Allen patent 'compensation frame' (Engl. Pat. No. 4431), a system of solid or tubular steel or copper stanchions between hitch-pin block and wrestplank for grand pianos, square- and upright pianos.

1820 At this time, according to Stodart, the string-tension of a six-octave piano had increased to 13 000 lbs (5900 kg).

1821 Hervé, a workman at Broadwood's, invents metal hitch-pin block and wrestplank.

1827 Broadwood patents the 'Composite iron Resistance Frame', which connects the iron hitch-pin block with the wrestplank[2] by four iron braces, for grand pianos (Engl. Pat. No. 5485).

1831 William Allen of London patents the complete cast iron frame, called 'Cast-Iron grooved Frame', all in one piece, for grand pianos, square- and upright pianos (Engl. Pat. No. 6140).

[1] American: straining-pin block.

[2] American: turning-pin block or turning rail.

U.S.A.

1800 Isaak Hawkins, Philadelphia, patents his portable grand pianoforte, in which the soundboard is framed in metal and braced behind with metal rods. The wrestplank is also of metal (Engl. Pat. No. 2446).

1825 Babcock of Boston builds the first square pianos with a complete iron frame: 'Cast Iron Frame', American patent.

1840 Chickering of Boston patents the improved cast iron frame for square pianos (American Pat. No. 1802).

1843 Chickering patents the cast iron frame, for grand pianos (American. Pat. No. 3238).

1866 Steinway patents cast iron frame for pianinos.

1867 Universal acceptation of the cast iron frame at the Great Paris Exhibition.

France

1808 Erard builds grand pianos and square pianos with metal bracing (Engl. Pat. 3170) and patents the agraffe (Engl. Pat. 3170).

1822 Erard makes use of and patents the 'Compensation Frame' for grand-, square- and upright pianos (French Pat. No. 2170).

1822 Erard abandons the use of the Compensation Frame, substituting instead six iron stays in frame construction of grand pianos (French Pat. No. 3512).

1825 Pleyel is the first piano builder on the continent to use the American cast iron frame for his grand pianos and square pianos (French Pat. No. 1808).

1838 Erard's invention of the 'barre harmonique' (French Pat. No. 9572).

1840 Erard uses cast iron frame for grand-, square- and upright pianos (Engl. Pat. No. 8643).

Austria

1826 Johann Jakob Goll, a Zurich piano maker working in Vienna with the title 'Instrument and Pianomaker to the Austrian Emperor', uses the cast iron frame in the years 1822–1825.

1808 Wachtl and Bleyer in Vienna estimate the string-tension of their pianos at 90 cwt (4500 kg).

1820 Stodart pianos with six octave compass having a tension of 13 000 lbs (5900 kg),

1850 a double-strung square piano 10 000 kg and a grand piano 14 000 kg.

1880 String-tension of the average piano corresponds to a weight of 17 000 to 18 000 kg (increased today to 20 000 kg).

ACTION*

A string can be made to vibrate by stroking (friction), by plucking or by means of a hammer. According to the manner of tone production, one can divide stringed keyboard instruments as follows:

A those with friction action: Geigenwerk
B those with plucking action: spinets, virginals, harpsichords
C those with hammer action: clavichords (tangent action)
Tangentenflügel (tangent [hammer] action)
pianofortes (hammer action)

A. STROKE ACTION OR FRICTION

ACTION OF THE GEIGENWERK: The stroke on the string is brought about by five or six little wheels connected to a fly-wheel, which drives them with a string and several rollers round its axis at a definite speed. The edges of these little wheels are covered with parchment, with rosin applied to it. The fly-wheel is set in motion by a foot-pedal.

B. PLUCKING ACTION

1. VIRGINALS, SPINETS, HARPSICHORDS

The plucking of the string is done by rows of jacks resting loosely on the far end of the keys. By pressing the key down the jack rises, plucking the string with a plectrum, fixed to its upper end, thus setting the string in vibration.

"A slot is cut in the upper part of each jack, and let into this is a small upright strip of wood, about one inch in height, called the tongue. Projecting from this tongue at right angles, and just below the adjacent string, is the plectrum, a small wedge of hard leather, or a strip of quill, about one eighth of an inch in length, which actually plucks the string. The tongue is pivoted on a pin inserted laterally through it, so that the upper part can be pressed back and away from the string, though it is normally kept upright by a small spring at the back, usually made of hog's bristle.

When a key is depressed, the jack rises, and the plectrum plucks the string as it passes. When the key is released the jack falls back with it; but, when the plectrum reaches the string on its descent, the pivoted tongue is

* *Bibliography: Closson*, Ernest, History of the Piano, pp. 121–132. *Harding*, Rosamund, A History of the Pianoforte; *Hansing*, Siegfried, Das Pianoforte in seinen akustischen Anlagen, pp. 150–191. *Josten*, Hanns, Württembergisches Landesgewerbemuseum. Catalogue of Musical Instruments, pp. 102–116. *Le Cerf et Labande*, Les traités d'Henri Arnout de Zwolle, pp. 3–5. *Neupert*, Hanns, Das Klavichord, pp. 18–22; ditto, Das Cembalo, pp. 7–10, 84–88. *Pfeiffer*, Walter, Vom Hammer. *Sachs*, Curt, Die modernen Musikinstrumente, p. 159; ditto, Das Klavier, pp. 4, 7, 14, 21, 28–32. Russell, Raymond, The Harpsichord and Clavichord.

forced back, and this simple escapement allows the plectrum to repass the string without plucking it again. The hog's bristle spring then returns the tongue to its upright position, and finally the damper touches the string and silences it." (Raymond Russell, The Harpsichord and Clavichord, p. 14.)

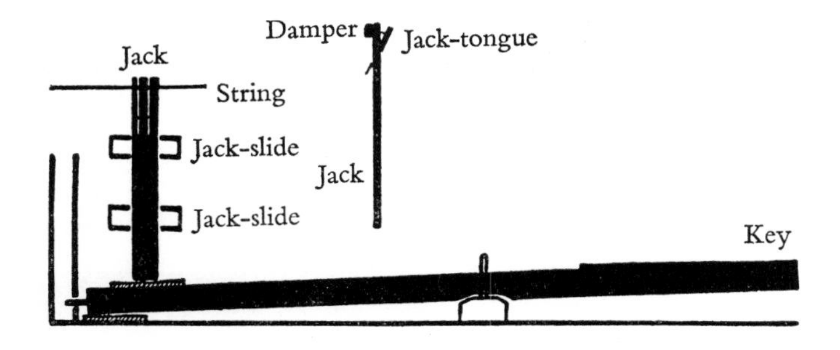

Fig. 1: Quill Plucking Action (copied from Sachs: Das Klavier, p. 15)

Different types of jacks

1. *Jacks lying horizontally:* rising vertically, as in harpsichords.
2. *Jacks standing perpendicularly*, from back to front, as in the upright harpsichord, and plucking above the keyboard by using wooden or metal angle levers *('stickers'[1])* connecting the key with the jack. After plucking the string the jack is forced back into position by leverage of a wire spring.

Material of plectra

Until 1650 leather plectra were used and later on a small quill, especially those cut from raven feathers. Whilst in England in the first half of the 18th century the instrument makers made use of metal plectra, the French builders favored a return to leather in the year 1760. The leather, compared with the brittle quill, is of almost indefinite durability. According to Arnold Dolmetsch, the leather plectrum yields a purer and more mellow tone than the quill, the timbre of which is certainly more brilliant but also somewhat shriller.

II. CLAVIHARP ACTION (DIETZ)

The string was plucked by hooked brass pieces fixed to wire-pins which were let into the back of the key, the release of the key making them slide across the strings.

C. HAMMER ACTIONS

That tone production by tapping a string is one of the oldest forms and that it certainly is the original way of producing vibrations in keyboard instrument-building, has now been proved without a doubt by the translation from the Latin into French of the Latin MSS. No. 7295 in the Paris National Library by G. Le Cerf and E. R. Labande[2]. This book was published as a facsimile of the Latin manuscript with excellent annota-

[1] American: abstracts.

[2] *Le Cerf et Labande*, Les traités d'Henri Arnout de Zwolle et de divers anonymes. Paris 1932.

tion, causing a great sensation. The author of the manuscript, Heinrich Arnold[1], describes four different actions, the Latin word used being 'forpices'. On studying the rather fragmentary descriptions and their accompanying drawings of the first three of these types of action, one is still uncertain whether they are plucking or hammer action. (Sachs interprets the words 'percutere' and 'ictus' as clearly indicating the latter type[2].) The description, however, of the fourth type of mechanism is so clear that Galpin, with its help, was able to reconstruct both mechanism and instrument, believing it to be the *Eschaquier*.

I. CLAVICHORD ACTION
(Tangent action)

Originally the string was struck by a small upright wooden-wedge fixed on the far end of the key, later on by a narrow spatulate piece of iron or brass called the tangent.

By depression of the key the tangent pressed on the string from below, simultaneously dividing it and also causing it to vibrate. To stop sympathetic vibration of the upper, or 'dead' part of the string, lying between the place of the tangent's impact and the wrest-pin, a strip of cloth twisted between the strings, or the pressure of a felt-covered strip of wood is used.

In contrast to the hammer action, the tangent does not leave the string until the key is released.

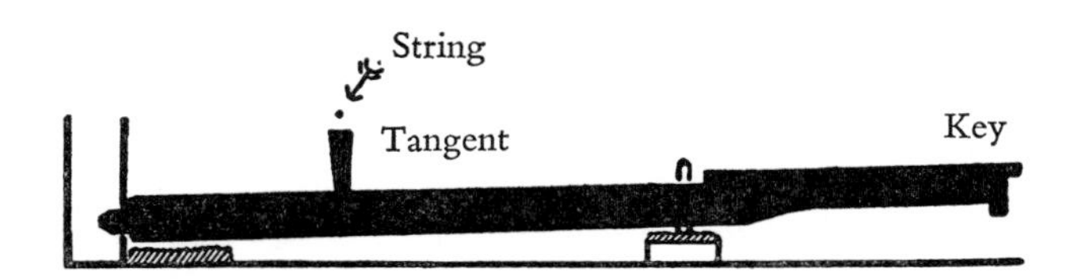

Fig. 2: Clavichord Action (copied from Sachs: Das Klavier, p. 3)

II. TANGENT (HAMMER) ACTION

The string is struck by means of upright pieces of leather-covered wood set in guides and fixed to the far end of the keys, called tangents.

A *Stösser* (jack) fixed to the key-end, together with an intermediate lever (or under-hammer), moves the tangent on depressing the key, pushing it against the string. Following the stroke, the tangent falls back into position and is caught by the intermediate lever (description of tangent action by Schmahl, 1795).

[1] Heinrich *Arnold,* native of the town of Zwolle in Holland, the date of whose birth is unknown, probably studied at first at the University of Zwolle, passing later to the University of Paris, where Jean *Fusoris* (1365–1436) was one amongst his teachers. Here he developed his outstanding abilities becoming an all-round, highly gifted Renaissance personality: doctor, astronomer, astrologer, clock- and astronomical instrument maker as well as a famous authority on organ-building and musicology. In his capacity as a doctor he was first employed by Philip the Good, Duke of Burgundy, at Dijon (1432–1554), later at the courts of Louis XI and Charles VII in Paris, where, in 1466, he died of the pest, the epidemic which he, as an astrologer, had prophesied. Arnold was buried in the Church of St-Etienne in Dijon. Arnold's Treatise is the *earliest textbook on the construction of all types of stringed keyboard instruments* and his works, written in 1440, are of incalculable value. They bring research on this subject for the first time out of the vague region of hypothesis and conjecture onto the firm foundation of actual fact.

[2] *Sachs,* Curt, The History of Musical Instruments, London 1942, p. 338. According to Arnold this mechanism could be used for *all types of keyboard instruments.*

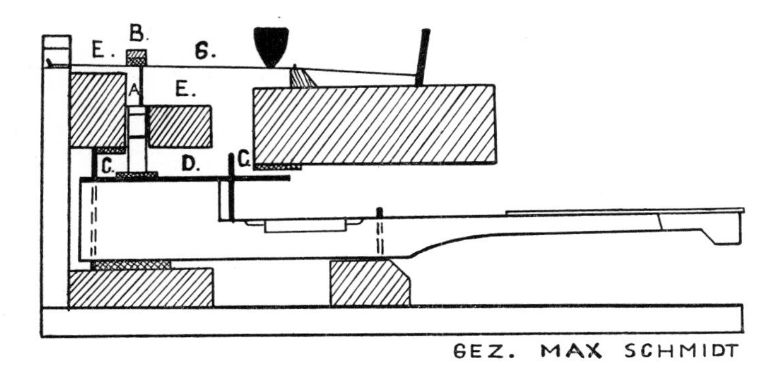

Fig. 3: Tangent piano action by Schröter, 1739 (after a design by Rosamund Harding)
A = hammer, B = damper, C = guide-pins for lever D, E = blocks between which the jack-shaped upright hammer is suspended, F = iron bar (capo tasto), G = string.

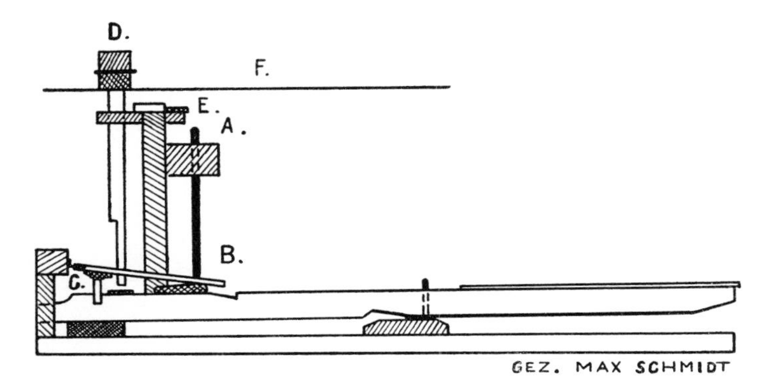

Fig. 4: Tangent Action by Christoph Friedrich Schmahl, Regensburg 1795 (after a design by Rosamund Harding).
A = tangent, B = intermediate lever, C = jack, D = damper, E = piano stop, F = string.

A mechanism compounded of the tangent action and the Prellmechanik is described in 1440 by Heinrich Arnold von Zwolle, the first generally known tangent (hammer) action. In this case the string was struck by means of lead-weighted, wooden tangents rising vertically, fitted with crosswise metal cramps at the upper end and fixed loosely upright in guides at the far end of the key.
By depressing the key, which hits a *Prelleiste*, the tangent is forced against the string, after which it falls back of its own weight even before the key is released. No kind of dampers are used.

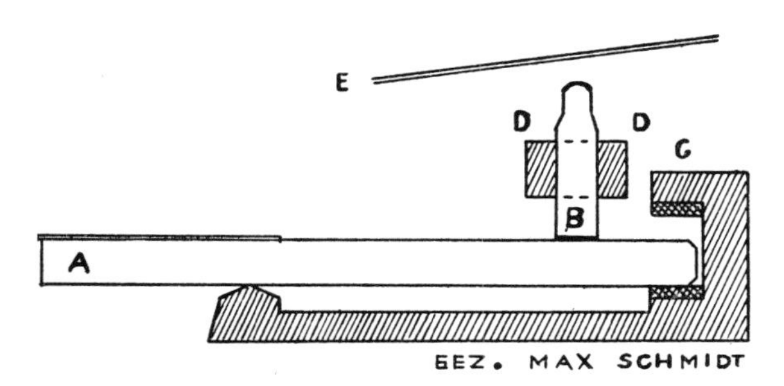

Fig. 5: Tangent Action by Heinrich Arnold von Zwolle (see: Grove's Dictionary of Music, 1940, Plate XIV)
A = key, B = tangent, C = Prelleiste, D = tangent slide, E = string

Schröter's mechanism of 1739 with its use of *Stosser* and intermediate lever as a connection between key and *tangent-hammer* is founded on the same principle as the early one described by Heinrich Arnold with its

loosely fixed automatically moving tangent-hammer. The only difference between the two is that the jack-shaped hammer is not fitted to the back of the key: it is hung loosely between two small wooden blocks above the intermediate lever. And in Späth/Schmahl's mechanism the tangent-hammer is fitted loosely on the intermediate lever: thus the last phase and final perfection has been achieved of a mechanism 340 years old, dating back to the year 1440.
This achievement seems, however, in course of time to have been overlooked, for otherwise it is hard to understand the groping, immature experiment carried out by Marius (1716) embodying the antiquated principle of a clavichord tangent altered to resemble a hammer-head which lacked the freedom to fall back automatically into position.

TABLE OF DATES

1440 Tangent-hammer standing at back of key (Heinrich Arnold's description).
1716 Marius, Paris (French Pat. No. 172, 173, 174, 175).
1739 Schröter, Dresden, with spring-jack.
1759 Weltmann, Paris; 'clavecin à maillet' (harpsichord pianoforte).
1780 Späth and Schmahl, Regensburg.

III. HAMMER ACTIONS

Walter Pfeiffer differentiates between four kinds of hammer action: *Prell-*, *Stoss-*, *Zug-* and *Gelenkgetriebe*.
Prell- and *Stossmechanik* are in use up to the present day, our modern pianos and grand pianofortes being all built on the principle of the *Stossmechanik*.
I will try, in a few words, to compare the *Prell-* and *Stossmechanik*, only briefly mentioning *Zug-* and *Gelenkgetriebe*.
My description is founded on Pfeiffer's work 'Vom Hammer' and his technical expressions I shall also make use of to a great extent. Interested readers are warmly recommended to read this book which is wonderfully clear and extremely readable.
In the *Prellmechanik* the hammer lies on the key. When the key is pressed down, the end of the shank is jerked up against a ledge behind it.
In the '*Stossmechanik*', the hammer is separate from the key and is hinged in a hammer-rail[1] either in front or rather further back; the hammer-head lies either directly on the key or else on a hammer-rest. The impulse to the hammer is an upward push. The gradual development of both mechanisms is a series of progressions from the uncertain to the certain in achieving perfect hammer-escapement. "Escapement means freeing the hammer for the stroke and for its automatic return to position, whereby complete release is effected." (Pfeiffer.)

1. 'Prellmechanik'

The string is struck, in primitive actions, by a hammer lying on the key or set into a 'Kapsel' in developed actions. This 'Kapsel' is a wood or metal fork screwed on almost at the far end of the key. The hammer-head points towards the front of the instrument. The end of the hammer-shank, called the hammer-beak, runs under the 'Prelleiste', which crosses the whole keyboard above the back of the keys.
By pressing down the key, the hammer-beak strikes against the 'Prelleiste', throwing the hammer against the string, which then falls back after the stroke, and on releasing the key, into its original position. In place of the 'Prelleiste', Johann Andreas Stein (1770) introduced a 'Prellzunge', or tongue, behind each key, "gelenkig in eine Leiste eingeachste Prellzungen" (Pfeiffer): movable tongues fitted into a ledge behind each key.

[1] American: hammer-beam.

DEVELOPMENT OF STOSS- AND PRELLMECHANIK
(English and German Action)

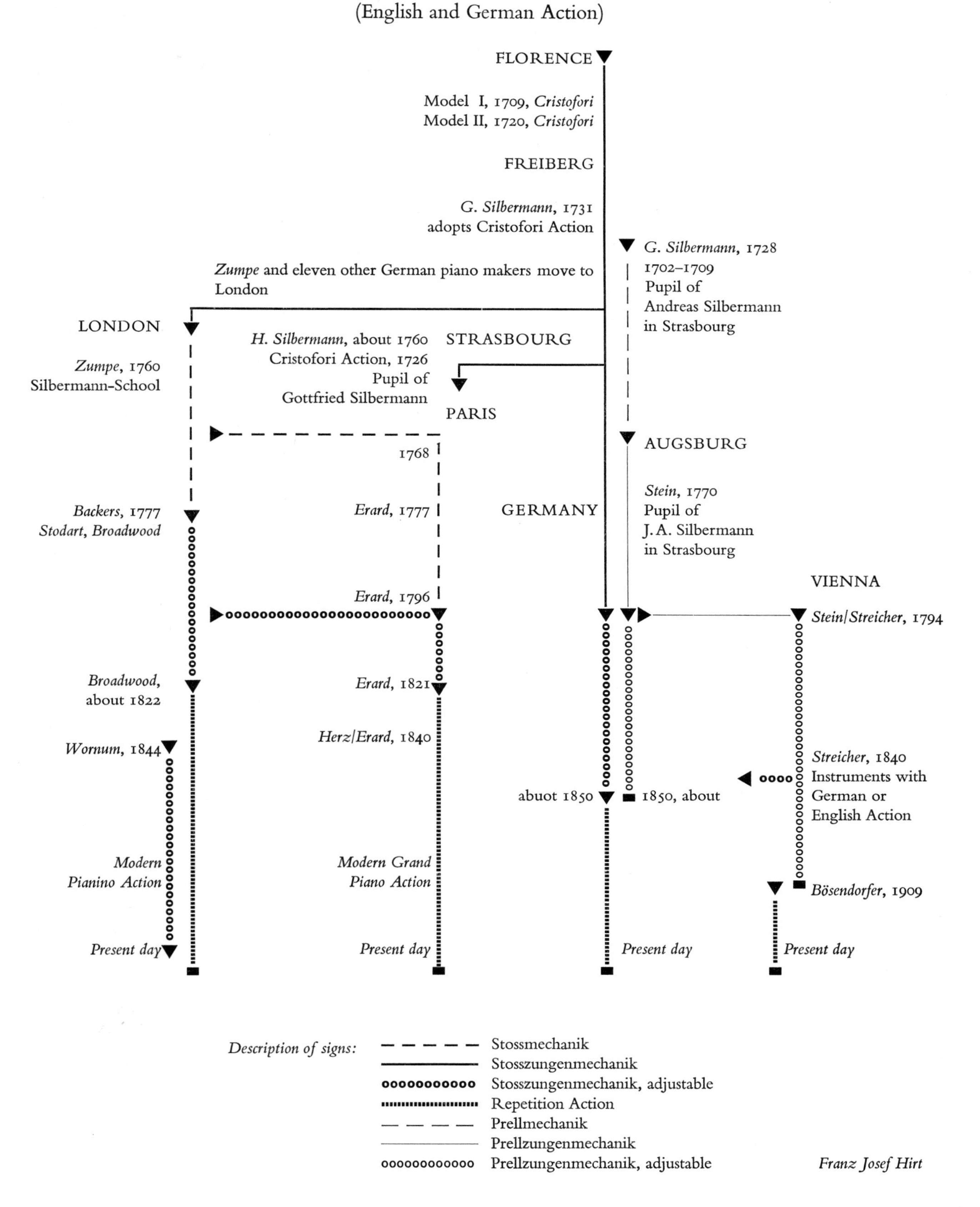

The hammer-beak (Hammerschnabel) pressed the 'Prellzunge' backwards, leaving it to spring back to its original position after the hammer had struck the string ('Prellzungenmechanik'). Originally there was no check.

After 1794, Stein/Streicher in Vienna added a regulating screw to the 'Prellzungenmechanik', to control the escapement (Viennese action).

Fig. 6: Prellmechanik without escapement (primitive German action)
(copied from Sachs: Das Klavier, p. 28)

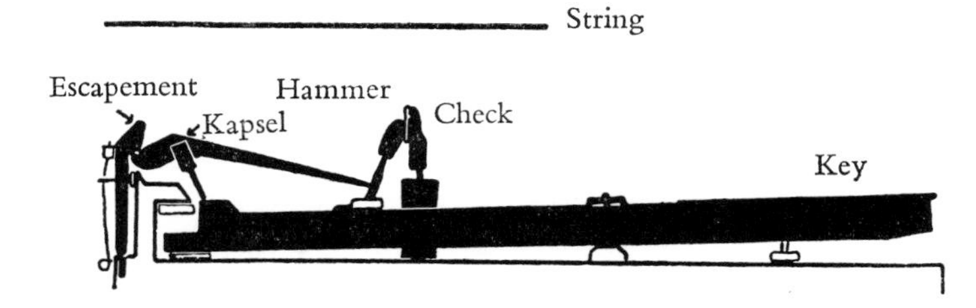

Fig. 7: Prellmechanik with escapement ('Prellzungenmechanik', developed German action)
(copied from Sachs: Das Klavier, p. 30)

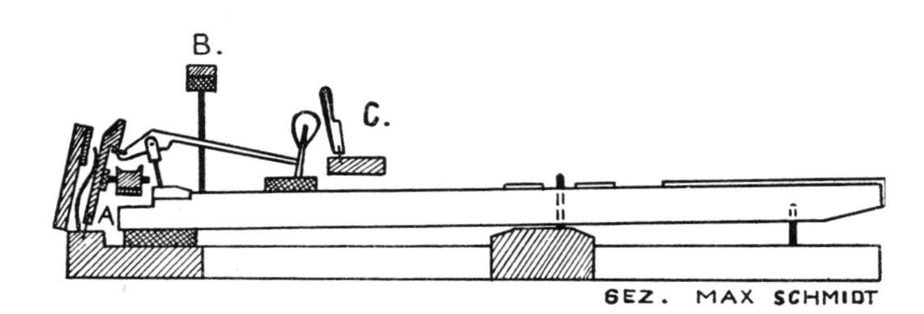

Fig. 8: Prellmechanik with adjustable escapement by Streicher 1829. (Viennese action)
A = regulating screw, B = damper, C = check

2. 'Stossmechanik'

In primitive actions the impulse to the hammer is either brought about by the key itself, or by means of a rigid jack set into the back of the key or in some cases by a spring pusher, rather like a hopper-jack[1] fitted loosely upright at the far end of the key. In each case the point of impact is the so-called hammer-butt ('Hammernuss'). Escapement takes place at the simultaneous striking of the hammer and the retreat of the jack. In the case of these simple forms there is no check[2]. In Cristofori's action the oldest known form of 'Stosszungenmechanik', a pliable, springy 'hopper' let into the back of the key takes the place of the rigid jack. Here escapement is brought about by the sideways slide of the hopper past the end of the hammer-butt.

[1] American: jack flyer, also fly lever and flyer, also repeating spring tongue and pusher or lifter (after Rosamond Harding).
[2] American: back catch.

After the stroke the hopper springs back to its original position whilst the returning hammer is caught on the check attached to the far end of each key.
In all these cases there is room to introduce a 'Treiber' or intermediate lever horizontally, between the key and the hammer.
Consequently, in the 'Stosszungenmechanik', the jack slides past the head of the 'Treiber' or intermediate lever. The London pianoforte makers, Bakers/Broadwood/Stodart, in 1776, added still something more to the regulation of the 'Stosszunge' by the introduction of a 'Stellschraube', or regulating screw which controls the hammer-escapement: this was 'Stosszungenmechanik with controlled escapement'.

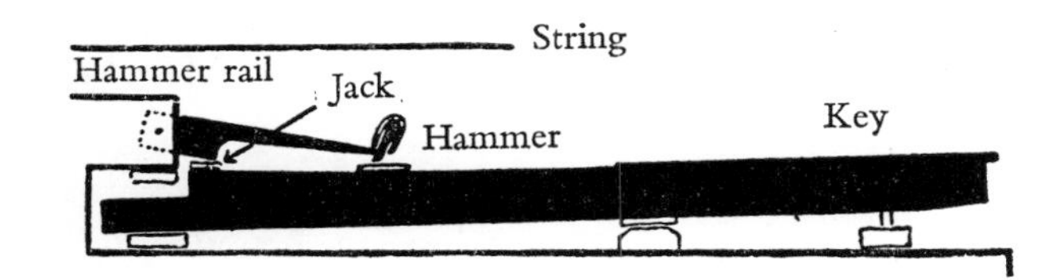

Fig. 9: Stossmechanik without escapement (primitive Anglo-German action)

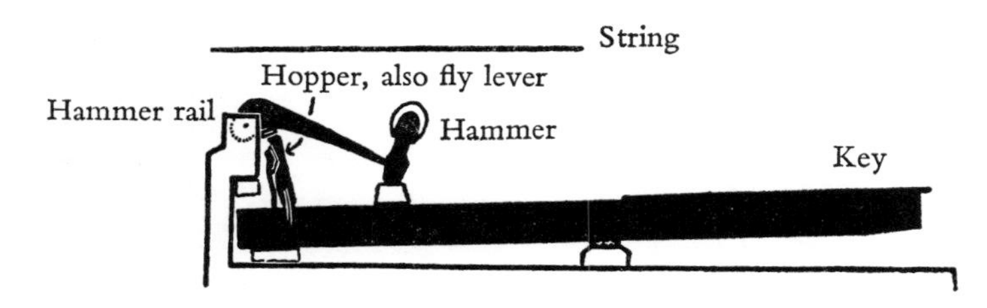

Fig. 10: Stossmechanik with escapement ('Stosszungenmechanik', developed Anglo-German action)

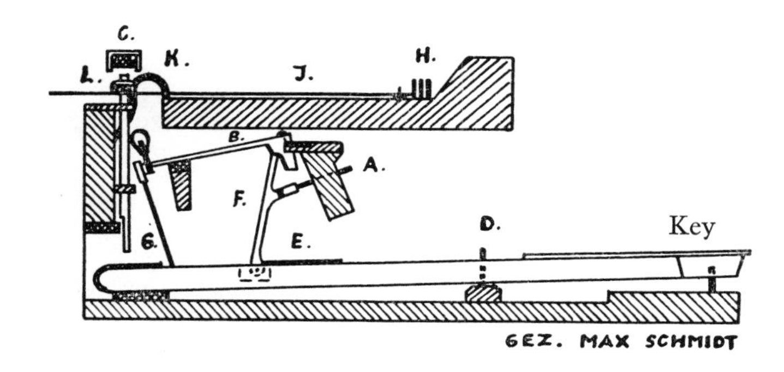

Fig. 11: English Grand Action by John Broadwood and Sons, 1795 (after a design by Rosamond Harding)
A = regulating screw, B = screw, on withdrawing which the hammer can be removed, C = damper-rail to prevent dampers springing up, D = pivot, E = spring, F = escapement, G = check, H = wrest-pin, J = string, K = iron bar, L = damper.

It was in 1821 that Erard in Paris invented the 'mécanique à double échappement', our modern 'repetition action with double escapement', which is now the working-principle of most piano makers. On pressing down the key a movable jack, fixed to the key, lifts a whole unit consisting of the intermediate lever, hopper and repetition lever. The hopper, its lower end fitted into the intermediate lever and its head loosely movable into the repetition lever, transmits the movement to the hammer, resting on the hammer-rest and attached to a hammer-rail, and throws it against the string. A specially shaped pin acts as a safeguard, guiding the hammer at the moment of striking. The impact of the horizontal, movable arm of the hopper against the escapement pilot (set-off button) which is attached to the hammer-rail, causes the hopper, just before the

actual stroke, to slide past the roll of the hammer-shank loosening its hold on the hammer itself, which now goes alone with the extra strength of its sudden release. After the stroke, the returning hammer is caught by a metal screw let into the hammer-butt and held against the repetition lever in readiness for a renewed attack by the hopper as long as the key is not completely raised. The least movement of the finger on the latter causes immediate return of the hopper under the roll of the hammer-shank, thus ensuring rapid repetition of touch consequent on the proximity of hammer to string.
The hammer returns to its original position only when the finger is removed from the key (description of Erard repetition action, 1822 model).
Pfeiffer has given the very suitable name of 'Kurzhubgetriebe' to repetition action.
Henri Herz, in 1840, somewhat simplified the Erard repetition action with double escapement, which, except for slight alteration, is used almost exclusively today. The same can be said for Wornum's pianino action, 1842 model. Except for variation in shape, in placing of dampers, differences in the form of escapement and use of repetition spring (first used in 1878 by Brinsmead, London, in improved form by Langer & Co, Berlin), the type of piano mechanism has altered also very little since 1842. Amongst the countless instruments which have contributed to history, the following merit special mention for their present-day significance:

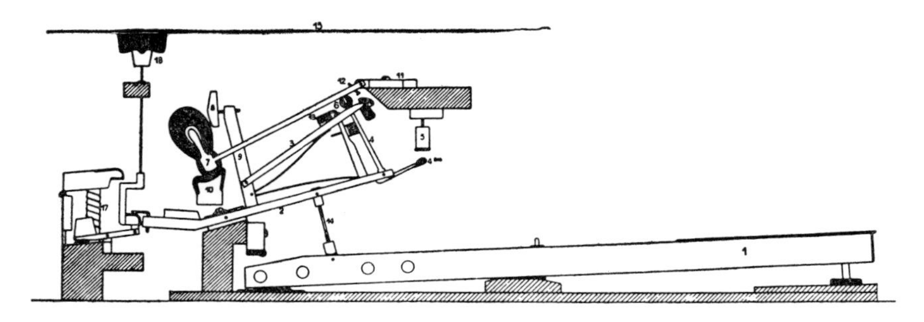

Fig. 12: Repetition Action with double escapement by Erard, 1822 model.
1 = key, 2 = intermediate lever, 3 = escapement, 4 = jack, 4bis = projection on jack, 5 = escapement pilot, 6 = hammer-shank head, 7 = hammer-head, 8 = check, 9 = check shank, 10 = hammer rest, 11 = hammer fork, 12 = repetition screw, 13 = regulating button (regulating the height of escapement), 14 = hopper regulator (to guide the hammer), 15 = string, 16 = damper, 17 = pedal spring.

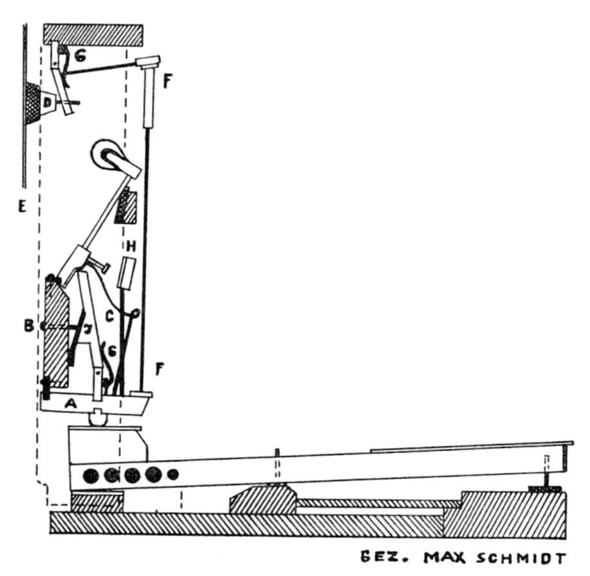

Fig. 13: English Action with adjustable escapement, by Wornum, 1842/45. ('Upright tape-check-action'.)
A = whippon, B = screw regulation, C = leather tape connecting hammer-butt with wire on whippon accelerating return of hammer, D = damper (over-damping), E = string, F = damper lifter or wire, G = spring, H = check, J = hopper.

Wornum's Pianino mechanism, 1842 model (so-called 'Tape-Check Action').

The string is struck by a forward movement of a hammer attached to a hammer-rail resting on a hammer-rest. By depressing the key, the 'Winkelstosszunge' (angle-jack attached to the hammer-rail) which stands on a whippon, or sort of 'see-saw', catches the hammer on the hammer-butt, throwing it against the string. Controlled by a regulating screw the hammer, just before the impact, is released for the blow and for the subsequent return to position. The whippon, by its own weight, tightens a little tape-end connecting the hammer-butt with a short end of wire on the whippon itself and accelerates the return of the hammer to its original position. A balance-check fixed to the hammer-butt comes to rest on the check in the whippon allowing the hammer to glide slowly back on to the hammer-rest.

The German action and the English action have been employed in several different forms:

1. *lying horizontally:* a) up-striking; b) down-striking (only with primitive Prellmechanik and Stossmechanik);
2. *standing vertically:* a) striking from the front above the keyboard (with Stoss- or Stosszungenmechanik; sometimes using stickers, long wooden rods connecting jack and hammer); b) from back to front, striking above the keyboard (Stosszungenmechanik);
3. *hanging:* from the front, striking below the keyboard; the hammer is set into a butt which is screwed onto a hanging side-arm of the key (Prellzungenmechanik).

The expressions 'vorderständig' and 'hinterständig' in connection with the hammer-rail were, I believe, first used by Curt Sachs and need brief explanation:
'vorderständig' = standing in front, i.e. before the hammer's point of impact;
'hinterständig' = standing behind, i.e. behind the hammer's point of impact.
The placing of the hammer-rail or Prelleiste determines the direction in which the hammer-head is pointing. Thus the hammer-head is either
a) behind, facing the back of the instrument or
b) in front, facing in the opposite direction to the key, towards the front of the instrument.
Position a) is conditional on the hammer-rail or 'Prelleiste' standing in front of the hammer's point of impact, and position b) on the hammer-rail or 'Prelleiste' standing behind it.

For the reader's further information I will add a survey of the definition 'Prell'- and 'Stossmechanik' from various prominent authors.

Prellmechanik

Harding's definition: German action, Prellmechanik (primitive);
Kinsky's definition: Prellmechanik;
Sachs's definition: Prellmechanik (1923): German Prellmechanik without escapement (1940).

Prellzungenmechanik

Harding's definition: German action; German action (developed);
Kinsky's definition: German action;
Sachs's definition: German action (1923); German Prellmechanik with escapement (1940).

Stossmechanik with 'hinterständige' hammer-rail, 'standing behind'

Harding's definition: 'Primitive Anglo-German Action' without escapement;
Sachs's definition: Stossmechanik (1923), German Stossmechanik without escapement (1940).

Stosszungenmechanik with hammer-rail behind

Harding's definition: 'Developed Anglo-German Action' with escapement;
Sachs's definition: English action (1923); German action with escapement (1940).

Stossmechanik with 'vorderständige' hammer-rail or hammer-rail in front

Harding's definition: Stossmechanik;
Sachs's definition: Stossmechanik (1922).

Stosszungenmechanik with hammer-rail in front

Harding's definition: Stosszungenmechanik or English Action; Cristofori Action;
Kinsky's definition: English action;
Sachs's definition: English action or Stosszungenmechanik.

Rosamund Harding, however, reminds us that the so-called English Action or Stosszungenmechanik *is in no way identical with the 'English Grand Action'* for grand pianos, in which there is no intermediate lever (Treiber), the hopper acting directly on the hammer-butt; a divergence from the Cristofori mechanism. The somewhat perplexing and contradictory nature of these differing definitions will not escape the reader.
Accepting the unmistakably proved by Pfeiffer that there is no mechanism 'without' escapement, I should like to propose the use of the more precise definition '... with or without escapement *appliance*' if we are to carry on the traditional classification at all.

From the point of view of escapement *mechanism*, not of the escapement 'as such', Prell- and Stossmechanik can be summarized retrospectively as follows:

a) without escapement appliance

Prellmechanik
characteristic:
the one-piece Prelleiste;

Stossmechanik
characteristic:
the rigid jack (Stösser).

b) with escapement appliance

Prellzungenmechanik
characteristic:
division of one-piece Prelleiste into a row of loose 'Prellzungen'.

Stosszungenmechanik
characteristic:
instead of a rigid jack a loosely moving (Stosszunge) 'hopper'

c) with adjustable escapement
(regulating screw or button)

Prellzungenmechanik

Stosszungenmechanik:
all repetition actions (called in German 'Kurzhub-getriebe').

3. Down-striking action ('Zugmechanik')

In the down-striking action hammers are above the strings: the stroke takes place from above by hammers fitted into a sheath (or Kapsel). On pressing down the key, the spring-hammer, placed on the back arm of the key itself, "pulls the Schnabel or 'beak' of the two-armed hammer down, throwing the other part of the double unit, i.e. the hammer end, against the strings. At that moment the hammer is released by an adjustable spring for the stroke—after the blow has fallen the spring pulls the hammer-unit back to its original position" (Pfeiffer: Vom Hammer, p. 33). A check is present.

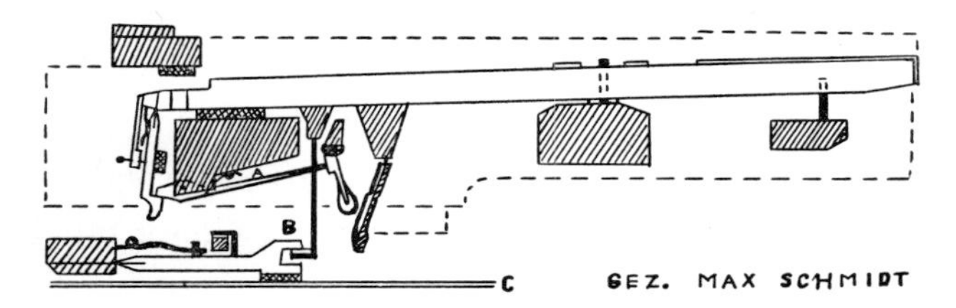

Fig. 14: Down-striking action, by Nannette Streicher, 1825 (after a design by Rosamund Harding).
A = spring, B = damper, C = string.

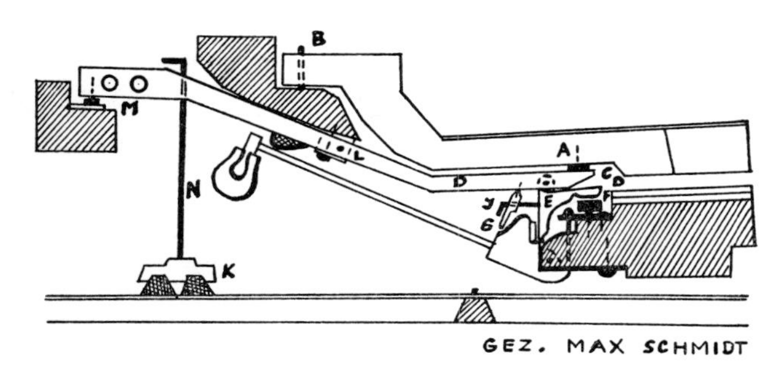

Fig. 15: Down-striking action ('Zugmechanik'), by Pape, 1839 (from the patent).
A = key, B = lever, C = hopper, D = intermediate lever, E = spring hammer, F = regulating screw, G = movable check, J = hook, K, N = dampers, M = screw.

Research has been going on for many years to find a satisfactory down-striking action. The fact that this mechanism was built *under* the soundboard, the hammers striking against the strings through an opening in the soundboard itself, was considered to be a constructional weakness and prejudicial to the tone. By directing the hammer's blow on the string *from above* and towards the soundboard, it was hoped to correct these supposed deficiencies.

In the sketches by Marius, in the year 1716 submitted to the 'Académie des Sciences de Paris' and patented, there is a model of a 'Clavecin' with down-striking hammers (French Pat. 173, 1716). Schröter also mentions, in 1738, a down-striking mechanism invented by himself. But it was not until the year 1823 that Streicher in Vienna, built a really serviceable down-striking mechanism and patented it under the name 'Patent-Pianoforte' action. In the years between 1823 and 1850 many well-known piano makers in Austria, France, England and America brought out patents for down-striking mechanisms, as for example Nannette Streicher, Mathias Müller and Wilhelm Leschen in Vienna, Pape, Kriegelstein and Arnaud, Wölfel and Wirth in Paris.

But these apparent advantages were offset by serious constructional disadvantages. The down-striking action, already in itself so complicated, entirely precluded the possibility of rapid repetition. All trials and experiments to overcome this were in vain, success being denied even to such a technical genius as Pape himself.

Just as unpractical proved to be the invention of the piano maker Hans Jakob Goll of Zurich, who, ignoring the technical problem of the down-striking action, built the *soundboard above the strings* in his 1822 patent, bringing the hammer-stroke towards the soundboard in order to achieve the desired improvement in tone. And this invention of Goll's was adopted by Henri Herz, Robert Wornum and Claude Montal, who built their instruments accordingly.

There was, however, a great disadvantage to this position of the soundboard, i.e. that to replace a string, the whole upper part inside the instrument had to be lifted out, a grave defect which, like many other inventions in the history of piano-building, proved to be prejudicial to its survival.
In the first half of the 19th century the down-striking action was of considerable importance, but since about 1860 it has hardly ever been used and is today only of historical interest.

4. 'Gelenkmechanik'

This mechanism consists in eliminating the hammer's freedom to strike and then fall back; its movement right up to the string and its subsequent return being determined by a guide fitted into the hammer itself and forming a so-called 'Gelenkhebel'.
This action includes adjustable escapement and it was able to hold its own until the middle of the 19th century. Its principle, however, entirely dispensed with that main characteristic of hammer action as such, i.e. the hammer's free swing, depriving the hammer of free movement, a principle which in the long run proved to be impracticable.

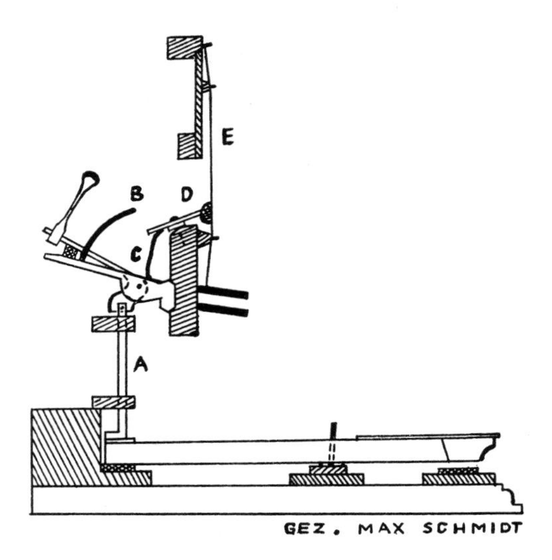

Fig. 16: Upright Pianoforte Action (Gelenkmechanik'), by Domenico del Mela, 1739 (after a design by Rosamund Harding). A = sticker, B = one of two guide wires, C = cord, D = damper, E = string.

DAMPERS

The dampers on the strings can act either *together* or *separately*.
A COMPLETE MUTING of strings is achieved by pressure against the strings of a thin wooden rail covered either with cloth or wool.
A PARTIAL MUTING can be arranged in several ways:

1. *by separate units moving vertically* (up-striking action)

In plucked instruments muting is caused by one or two soft pieces of felt stuck into the upper end of the jack.
Kastendämpfung—section-dampers—are characteristic of the German action, whereby the dampers which stand loosely on the key sink vertically within a narrow box on a removable guide resembling the jackrail of a harpsichord.

Cristofori used wooden tangents covered at the upper end with felt standing loosely upon the back end of the key. On releasing the key these tangents fell either from above or rose from below, to press on and between the strings. The system of muting in modern pianos follows the same principle, but in place of the old wooden tangents several folds of soft felt on wire uprights are used which are:

a) *either* fitted into a double arm lever standing behind the end of the key and connected to the far end of the intermediate lever by a hook. By pressing down the key the sinking of the back of the key draws the damper away from the strings, and by releasing the key the damper returns automatically to its original position *below* the string. This is called the *under-damper;*

b) *or* the wire uprights are fitted into the single-arm lever behind the end of the key and the damper felts lie above the strings. On pressing down the key the rising back end of the key raises the damper from the strings; release of the key sends damper back to its original position. This system is called the *over-damper.*

Both systems include a pedal, the connecting rod of which works the lever attached to the dampers.

2. *by single- or double-armed damper lever* (down-striking action, 'Zugmechanik')

On pressing down the key or the pedal (collective action) the felt-covered dampers which are either fitted into one arm, or else into one long rail, are raised from the strings. On releasing the key or the pedal, the dampers, falling from above, cover the strings (this is in over-damper action), or else the damper rises from below (in under-damper action).

Also in upright pianos and grand pianos one discriminates between damper action from above or below according to whether the string is damped above or below the hammer's point of impact.

In France, the pianino action is named after the form and disposition of the damper. The older form of over-damping is called 'mécanique à baïonnette', because the damper is fixed at the upper end of a wire-upright like a bayonet, the newer form of under-damping being named 'mécanique à lame'.

The type of under-damping first made use of in 1800 by Isaak Hawkins has proved to be more satisfactory and is still used in modern pianinos.

COVERING OF HAMMER-HEADS

According to Maffei's description the hammer-heads in Cristofori's action (1709) were covered with leather, probably a fine buckskin. In the instrument of Cristofori of the year 1720, the hammers are not the originals. In this respect, however, we can gain more knowledge from the Cristofori piano of the year 1726. Here the hammers are not of wood but are made of parchment strips formed into a ring and covered with leather at the striking point. These are fixed to the hammer-shank on little squares of wood. This same characteristic form of hammer-head is to be found in the instruments by Gottfried and Heinrich Silbermann, showing that Gottfried Silbermann had studied Cristofori's invention and had taken it as his model. Sheep's leather or soft deerskin was most generally used: the latter being still popular in Germany in 1856. Previously, experiments were made in England in using flannel, but being less durable it made an unsatisfactory covering. The modern felt covering was first used in Paris in 1826. During all this time the hammer-heads increased gradually in size and weight, in respect to which Pfeiffer publishes the following details:[1]

[1] *Pfeiffer,* Walter: Vom Hammer, p. 117.

Place of origin	Weight in grammes of hammer-head Bass First hammer	Treble Last hammer
Cristofori 1726	1	0,5
Stein 1773	1	0,45
Mahr 1807	0,4	0,2
Erard about 1850	4	2
Kützing about 1860	4	2
Modern hammer-head, Average 1943	8,4	4,1

Pfeiffer (pp. 116, 117) illustrates the increasing size of hammers in the following table:

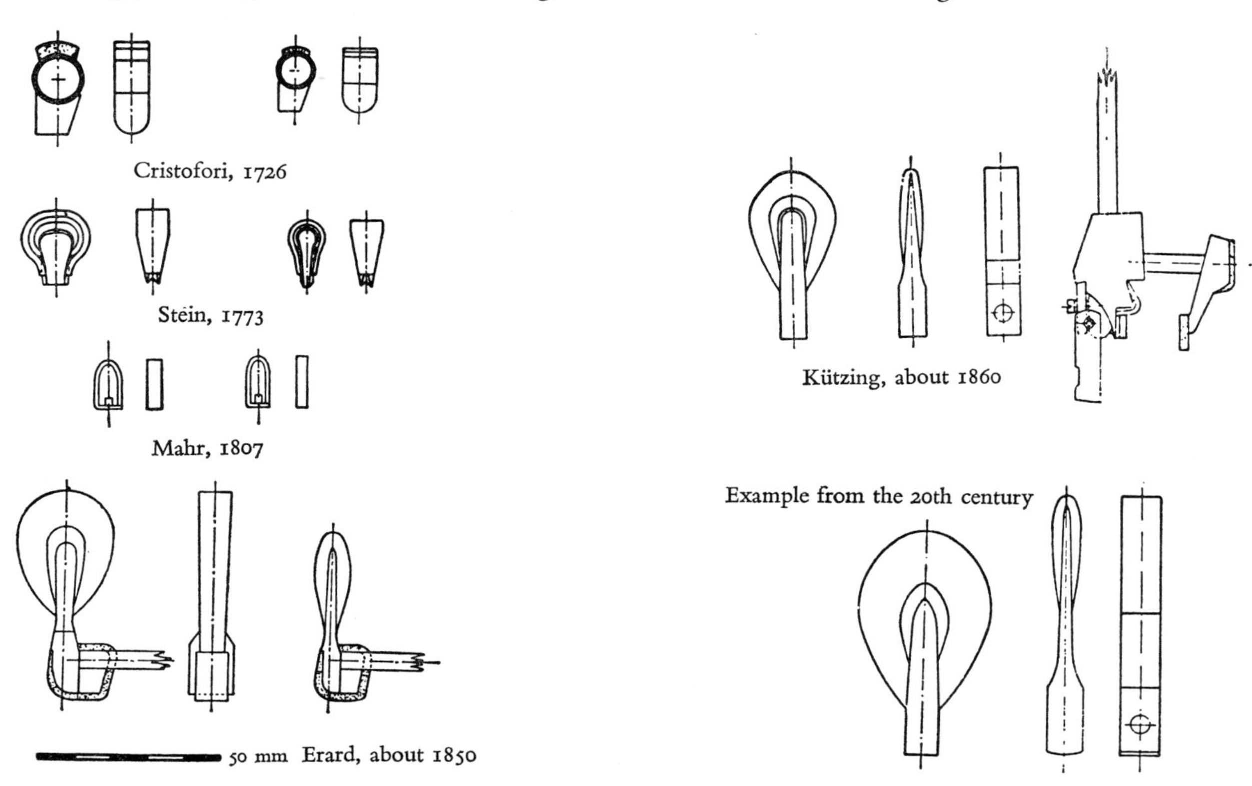

Here we may mention another peculiarity of 18th century square piano-building, i.e. the use of double hammers of which the one head was uncovered whilst the other was covered with leather. The tone issuing from the former had the timbre of a harpsichord, the leather-covered hammer producing the usual piano tone.

TABLE OF DATES

1. Prellmechaniken or German Actions

a) without escapement
(primitive German Action)

1728 G. Silbermann, with 'Kapsel'.

b) with escapement
('Prellzungenmechanik', developed German Action)

1770 J. A. Stein, Augsburg.

1800 M. Müller, Vienna, upright. First 'Tape-Check Action', forerunner of Wornum.

19th century, first half. Ehrlich, Bamberg (suspended).

c) with adjustable escapement
('Prellzungen', Viennese Action)

1794 Stein/Streicher, in Vienna.
1840 Streicher gradually changes from Viennese to English Action.
1904 Bösendorfer finally stops manufacture of grand pianos with Viennese Action.

2. STOSSMECHANIK

a) without escapement
(Stossmechanik)

1735 anonymous, upright.
1742 Söcher, with rigid jack.
1760 Zumpe, with rigid jack.
1770 Schmahl, with spring-jack.
1778 Zumpe, with under-hammer, or intermediate lever.
1798 Southwell upright, with stickers ('Sticker Action').

b) with escapement
('Stosszungenmechanik', English Action).

1709 Cristofori, with intermediate lever.
1745 Friederici, upright.
1775 J. G. Wagner, Dresden, without intermediate lever.
1825 Schleip, Berlin, upright.

c) with adjustable escapement

1776 Backers/Broadwood/Stodart, without intermediate lever, 'English Grand Action'.
1787 Landreth, London, upright. Impact of hammer coming forward from behind (Engl. Pat. No. 1596).
1800 Hawkins, Philadelphia, upright, without intermediate lever, jacks fixed to key, for upright pianos (Engl. Pat. No. 2446).
1807 Southwell, upright with intermediate lever and stickers, for upright pianos (Engl. Pat. No. 3029).
1808 Erard, first repetition action with double escapement ('mécanisme à étrier'), for grand pianos and square pianos (Engl. Pat. No. 3170). This form of construction proved to be a failure.
1821 Erard, repetition action with double escapement, for grand pianos (Engl. Pat. No. 4631).
1840 Erard/Herz, modified repetition action with double escapement: the modern grand piano action (Engl. Pat. No. 8643).
1842 Wornum, 'Tape-Check Action' for cottage pianos (Engl. Pat. No. 9262): the modern pianino action.

3. DOWN-STRIKING ACTION

1716 Marius, Paris (French Pat. No. 173).
1717 Schröter, Dresden, without escapement.
1783 Hillebrand, Nantes, for square pianos.
1820 Pether, London; Prellmechanik without escapement. Impact of hammer against a Prellleiste above the hammers; for square pianos.
1823 Johann Streicher, Vienna, 'Zugmechanik' (in which the hammer is returned by spring) (Austrian patent).
1860 By this time the down-striking action is already antiquated.

4. 'GELENKMECHANIK'

1739 Del Mela, Italy, without escapement.

1842 Foundation of first factory for manufacture of piano action parts by I. C. Isermann, Hamburg.
1844 Founding of Schwander's factory for piano action parts in Paris, in partnership with Herrburger from 1865 onwards.

Explanations to pp. 115–118

p. 115 'Prellmechanik' with 'Kapseln'; square piano by Gottfried Silbermann, 1749

Fig. 1 before the stroke
Fig. 2 after the stroke

p. 116 'Méchanique à double échappement' by Erard, about 1890 (Grand Pianoforte action with under-damping)

Fig. 3 before the stroke
Fig. 4 after the stroke

p. 117 Repetition action by Schwander/Herrburger, modern (Grand Pianoforte action with over-damping)

Fig. 5 before the stroke
Fig. 6 after the stroke

p. 118 Modern Pianino action (with under-damping)

Fig. 7 before the stroke
Fig. 8 after the stroke

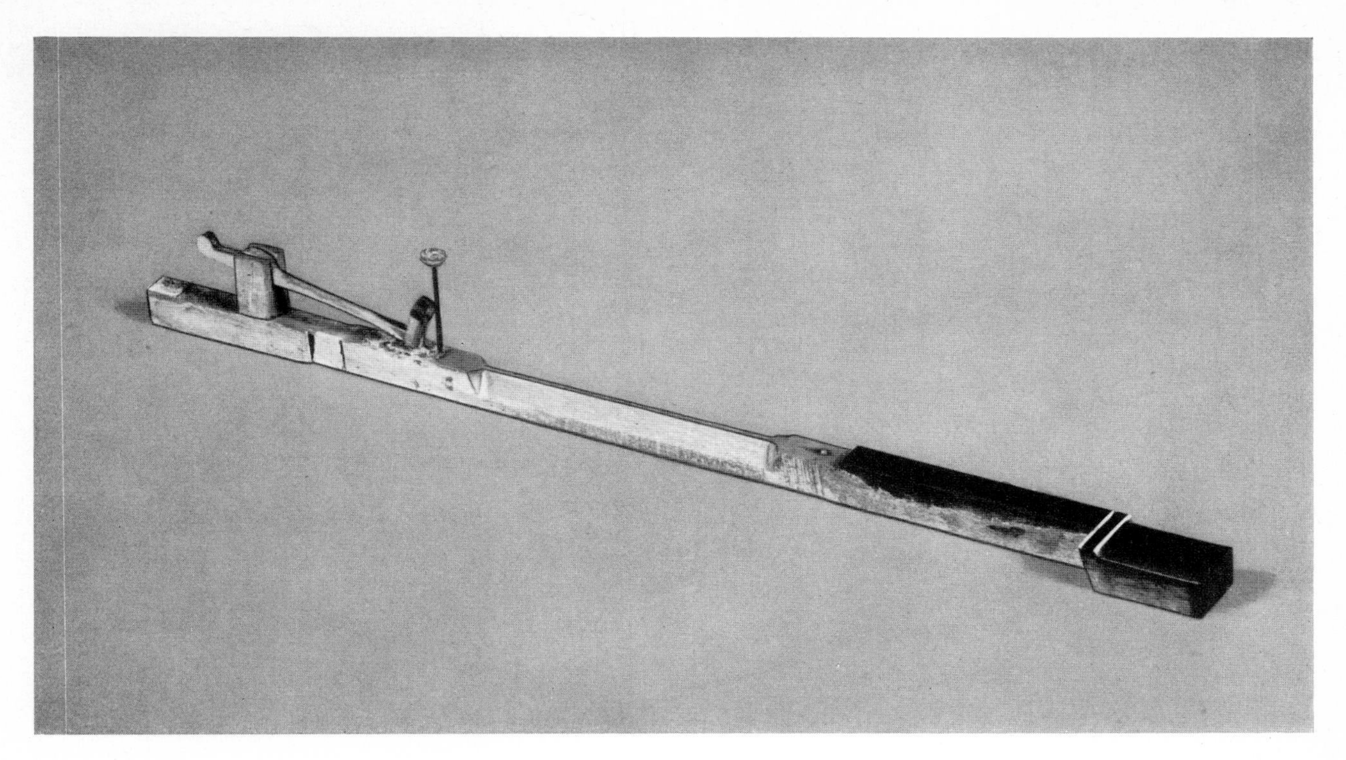

Fig. 1

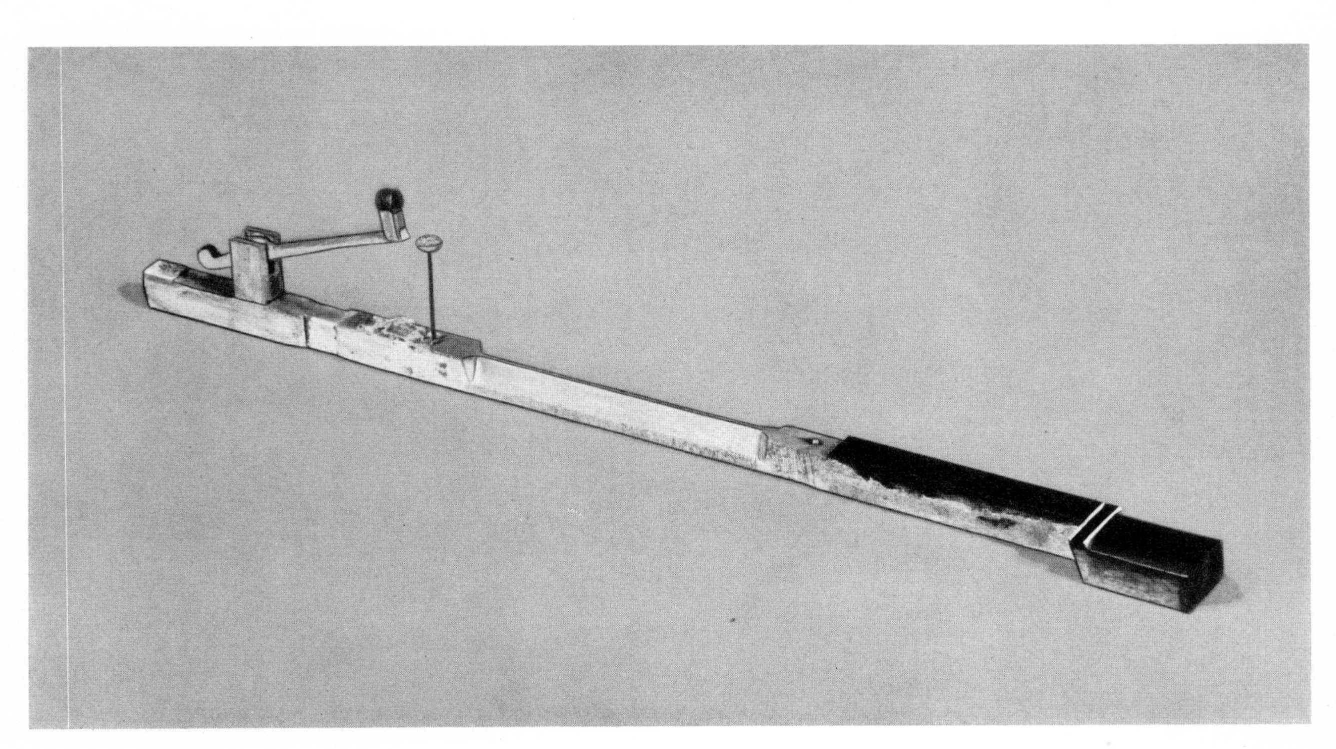

Fig. 2

Fig. 3

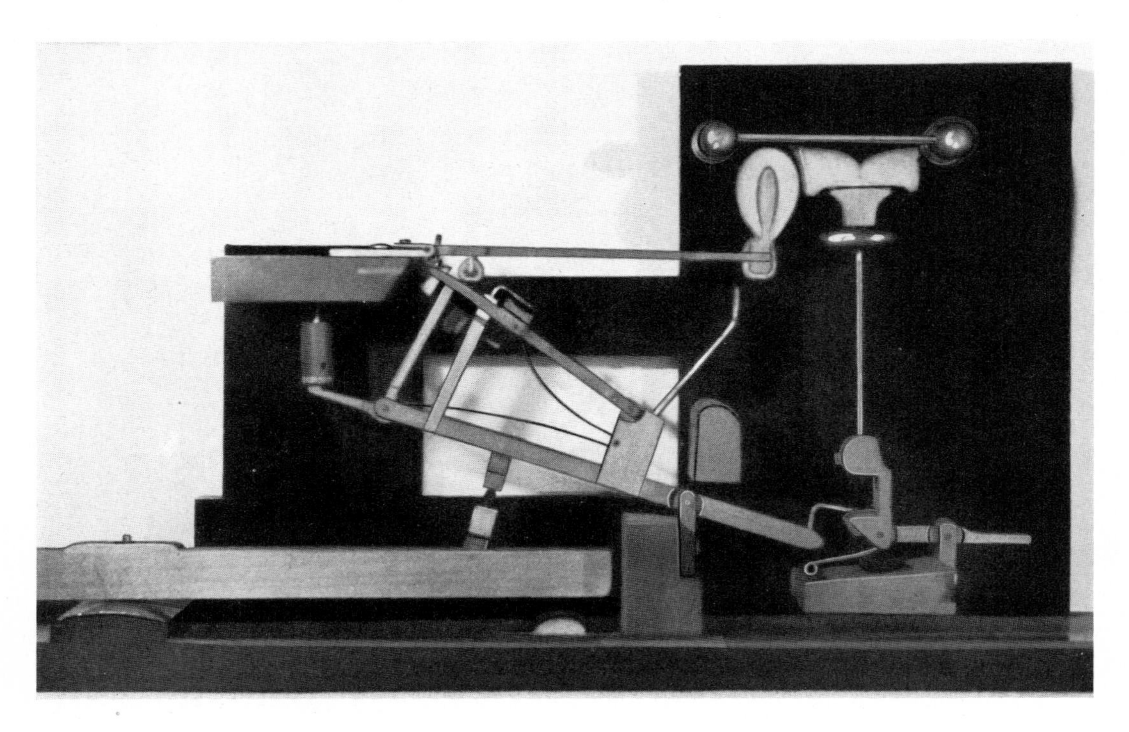

Fig. 4

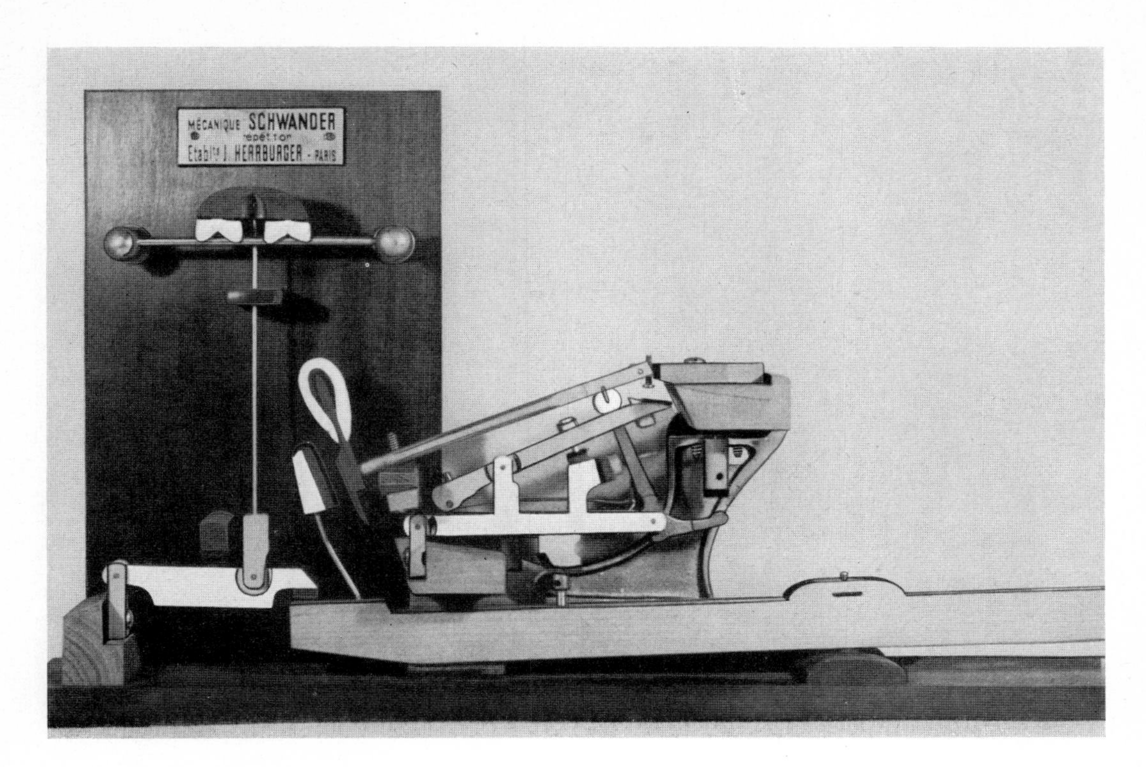
MÉCANIQUE SCHWANDER
répétition
Etablts J. HERRBURGER - PARIS

Fig. 5

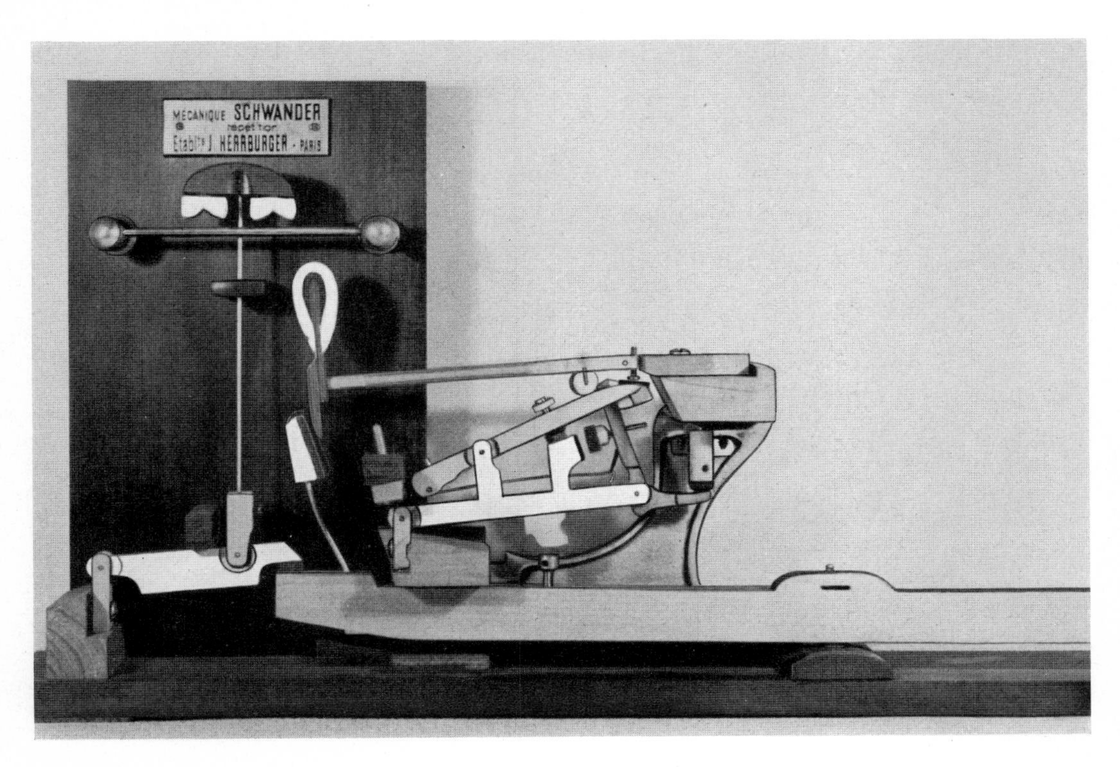
MÉCANIQUE SCHWANDER
répétition
Etablts J. HERRBURGER - PARIS

Fig. 6

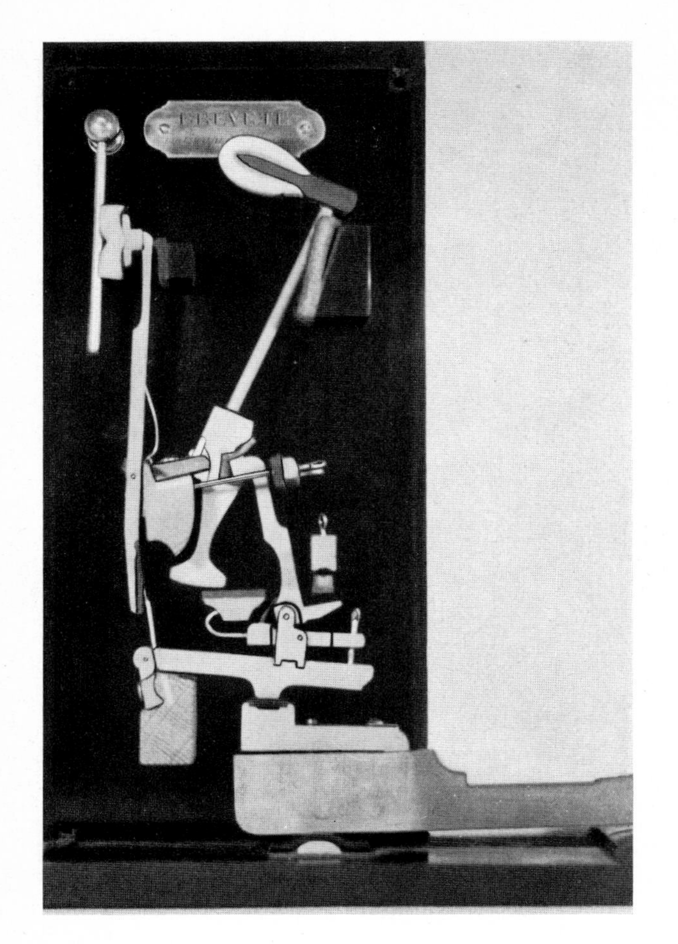

Fig. 7

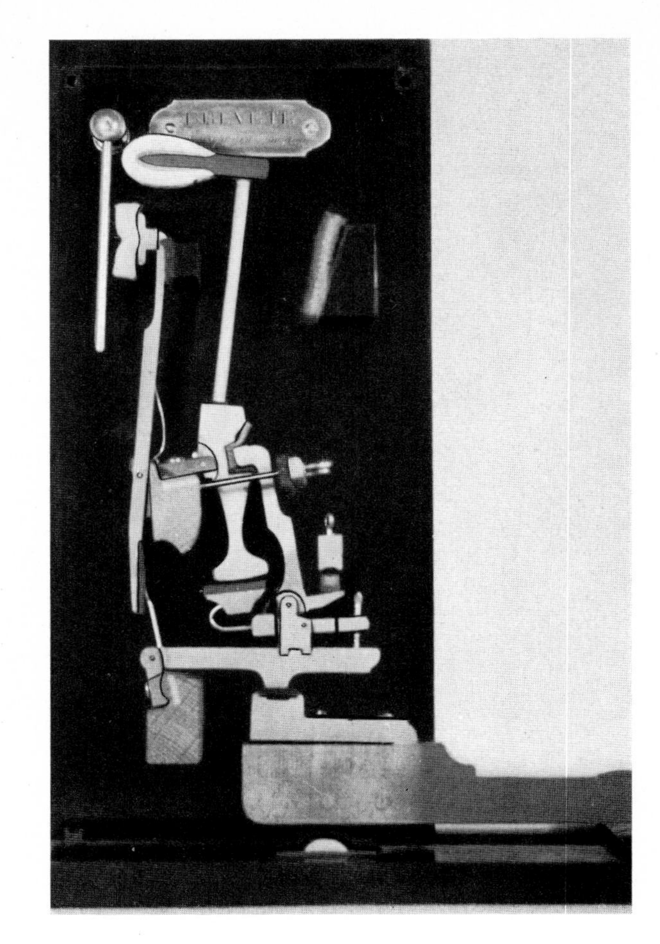

Fig. 8

REGISTER

The word 'register' is used in organ-building to denote a group of pipes of similar construction and tone-color.

Early in the history of piano-building the need arose to be able to alter and enrich the tone. The great similarity between the plucked keyboard instrument and the organ made this easy to do by using several strings whose rows of jacks could be pulled in and out of position to achieve contrasts of tone.

In contrast to the multi-stringing of pianofortes, plucked instruments were not only single-strung in the normal 8′[1], but also an octave higher in the 4′-tone and respectively deeper in the 16′, though the latter register was seldom constructed. There were also quadruple-strung instruments with a second 8′ register producing a complete contrast in tone to that of the first 8′.

Not only by variation of string groups and their multiple combination, but through the material of which the plectra was made, the choice of plucking position on the string, as well as by differing string thicknesses, gradations of tone color were effected. The 18th century created a still further enrichment of tone by introducing the lute stop.

Tschudi's 'Venetian swell', patented in 1769, shaped somewhat like a Venetian blind, introduced for the first time an incompatible element into harpsichord-building. This step, symptom of the great decline in musical taste after 1750 and a vain attempt to readjust the harpsichord to a time of advancing and unreconcilable demands, marked the beginning of a development whose final achievements bordered on grave lack of good taste. Already in 1765, early piano construction (Dalitz!), following on the decline of the demand for plucked instrument-building, was seized by the urge to produce those later instruments overloaded with different tone effects, to which they gave the name 'variations' (stops) and then developed them ad absurdum.

Although the pianoforte was capable of every shade of expression demanded by this new craze for effect, builders imagined themselves bound to produce these trivialities. Not to mention the bad taste of having cymbals, bells and Turkish music stops, there were stops for basoon—jeu de luth—and harp substitutes produced by pressure on the strings of parchment rolls, brushes, strips of cloth or felt, brass hooks and so on, sounding thin and poor, sometimes even ludicrous. It was therefore not surprising that of all these variations only two or three have survived in modern piano-building, i.e. *damping* (raising the dampers the so-called 'loud pedal'), *Verschiebung* (shifting the keyboard by mechanism to the right to strike only two strings), and a *sostenuto* pedal in Steinway pianos.

To be able to find one's way in the maze of these variations and their manifold names, they have been listed according to similarity in their mechanism. This idea originated, as far as I know, in Rosamund Harding's excellent book. By including the clavichord, harpsichord and a few other additions the list has become still more complete.

The connection and disconnection of the rows of jacks in the harpsichord, the working of the various changes in timbre in harpsichord, clavichord and piano, is all done by stops. These are moved either by hand, with the knee or with the foot, as the following outline will illustrate:

[1] Term used formerly in organ-building, corresponding to the length of pipe C.

I. HAND STOPS

1. *Side stops*, or levers, by piercing the right sidewall of the case. Earliest form, till about 1700 and still used in Holland during the 18th century. Require usually a helper, their use by the player alone being impossible without interruption of the performance. These were used in harpsichords and pianos.
2. *Inside stops*, inside the case lying on the wrestplank, worked by a lever: in harpsichords, clavichords, and pianos.
3. *Front stops*, by piercing the nameboard: used in harpsichords, clavichords and pianofortes. All these stops were worked by pushing or pulling.

II. KNEE STOPS

since 1765

1. *Knee levers*, with vertical action.
2. *Knee levers*, to work sideways.

III. PEDALS

Pedals worked by the foot
Harpsichords and pianos

Lastly, the *manual coupler* should be mentioned. By pushing back either the upper or the lower manual both could be connected, so that whilst playing on the lower keyboard the keys of the upper were automatically set in motion.

Summary of 'Veränderungen' or variations					
No.	*Tone character changed by*	*Name of stop*	*Instrument*	*Country*	*Epoch*
1	shortening radius of hammer stroke and lifting keyboard	'Piano'	Clavichord	Germany	
2	leather plectra	'Peau de buffle'	Harpsichord	France	1760
3	use of a specially broad tangent, half of which is leather-covered. Sliding keyboard allows alternate use of plain or covered half of tangent	'Laute'	Clavichord	Germany	
4	plucking string at a point very close to bridge	'Laute' 'Oboe'	Harpsichord	England Germany	middle of 18th century, Tschudi
5	pressure on strings of felt- or cloth-covered strip of wood	'Laute' 'Flageolet'	Harpsichord Piano-harp	Germany France Belgium	1813 till end of 19th century
6	pressure near bridge on strings of felt- or cloth-covered strip of wood	'Piano'	Clavichord	Germany	
7	a) pressure of strip of leather on string b) pressure on strings of wooden strip covered with doeskin	'Harp' 'Buff stop' 'Piano'	Harpsichord Piano-harp	England France/ Belgium	18th century 1813 till end of 19th century
8	Inserting sideways leather-covered strip of wood against *one* string in a unison	'Buff stop'	Square piano	England	1786, patented by John Geib
9	pressure of wooden strip covered with parchment against strings from lowest bass-note up to c′, e′ or f′	'Fagotto' 'Pédale de Basson' 'Fagoth' 'Bassoon' Claviharp	Harpsichord Harpsichord Pianoforte Claviharp	Italy France Austria Germany England France	1813 till end of 19th century
10	strip of wood covered with wool or fringed silk pressed against strings	'Laute' 'Harfenzug'	Tangent piano Pianoforte	Germany Germany	1780–1810
11	piece of wood lined with leather, hair or silk fringe pressed against strings along the bridge	'Sordine' or 'Mute'	Square piano	England	
12	pressure on strings of broad strip of cloth- or leather-covered wood lying directly in front of hitch-pin block	'Laute'	Pianoforte	Germany	

No.	*Tone character changed by*	*Name of stop*	*Instrument*	*Country*	*Epoch*
13	varied lengths of tongue-shaped pieces of leather or cloth fixed to strip of wood interposed between tangent or hammer and the strings	'Laute' 'Piano' 'Pianissimo' 'Piano' 'Piano' 'Jeu de buffle' 'Jeu céleste'	Clavichord Tangent piano Pianoforte Pianoforte Pianoforte Pianoforte Pianoforte Pianoforte	Germany Germany Germany Germany England France France France	about 1780–1810
14	insertion of leather strip under *one* string of the unison; by sliding the keyboard the hammer strikes only the muted string	'Harp' 'Harpe'	Square piano Square piano	England France	1790, patented by Hancock 1808, patented by Erard
15	leather tongues on a strip of wood, to front edges of which are glued pieces of bone or ivory, inserted between hammer and strings	'Cembalo' 'Harpsichord stop'	Pianoforte Square piano	Germany England	first used in 1745 by G. Silbermann patented by Bury in 1788
16	pressing from below, to right of point of impact, small brass pieces or metal jacks on the strings	'Pantaleonzug'	Clavichord	Germany	
17	pressure of small brass hooks from below against the strings	'Harfenzug'	Harpsichord	Germany	mentioned in 1619 by Praetorius
18	playing with closed cover and open swell, called 'Fortepiano durch einen Tritt'	'Piano'	Clavichord	Germany	mentioned in 1749 by Adlung
19	use of mechanism resembling a Venetian blind lying over the strings, or by opening and closing portion of lid, worked by a foot pedal	'Venetian Swell' 'Schweller' 'Schwebung' 'Grand Forté' 'Swell'	Harpsichord Pianoforte especially in Square pianos	England Germany France England	patented in 1769 by Tschudi introduced in 1776 in Germany by Friederici
20	damper mechanism: a) *separated:* lifting *bass* damper or *middle-register* damper, or b) *simultaneous:* bass and middle-register together, by collective stop	'Forte' 'Forte' (called after its function, 'damping')	Pianoforte Tangent piano Piano-harp	Italy and all countries Modern damping Germany France Belgium	1709 Cristofori; separated damping still in use till 1830 1780–1810 by Schmahl 1813 till end of 19th century
21	sliding keyboard a) from front to back b) sideways, the hammer striking three, two or one string	'Pianozug' 'Una Corda' 'Keyboard shift' 'Harmonica'	Clavichords (multi-strung) Pianoforte Pianoforte Pianoforte	Germany Italy England France and all countries	 first in 1720 by Cristofori

No.	*Tone character changed by*	*Name of stop*	*Instrument*	*Country*	*Epoch*
22	striking *under* side of soundboard in square pianos and pianofortes, and against the *back* of soundboard in upright pianos, with a large leather-padded hammer	'Drum' 'Grosse Trommel' 'Schlagzeug' 'Bodenschlag' 'Tambour guerrier'	Pianoforte	England Germany Austria France	patented in 1797 by Rolfe and Davies
23	three small metal semicircles, producing different notes, struck with a metal beater	'Bells' 'Glocken' 'Triangel' 'Triangle'	Pianoforte	England Germany Austria France	
24	two or three thin brass strips which are knocked against the bass strings	'Cymbal'	Pianoforte	Germany Austria France	
22 23 24	a pedal which coupled drum, bells and cymbal	'Janissary music' 'Janitscharenmusik' 'Türkische Musik' 'Pédale de Musique turque'	Pianoforte	England Austria Germany France	patented in 1799 by Smith
25	shortening radius of hammer stroke	'Piano'	Pianinos		
26	the lifting of a flat bar lying across ends of keys which keeps certain dampers from falling back till pressure on key is released, through remaining dampers are unaffected	'Sostenuto pédale' 'Sustaining pedal'	Pianoforte	France USA	invented in 1862 by Montal patented in 1874 by Steinway
27	octave coupling		Pianoforte	France	patented in 1812 by Erard
		'Octave Coupler'	Pianoforte	England	patented in 1816 by Kirkman
		'Oktavzug'		Austria	patented in 1824 by Streicher
				Germany	patented in 1831 by Kisselstein
		'Octave Coupler'		USA	patented by Oliver and Jackson
28	Transposition by:				
	a) lifting the jacks onto neighboring keys		Spinet	Netherlands	17th century
	b) sliding the keyboard (inwards or sideways)		Harpsichord	Germany	mentioned in 1619 by Praetorius
			Clavichord	Italy	mentioned in 1760 by Burney
			Square piano	Germany	by Schmahl, 1770
			Pyramid piano	Germany	1780
	c) removable keyboard		Square piano	England	patented in 1801 by Ryley
	d) with special construction		Cabinet piano	France	patented in 1813 by Erard
	e) with a double keyboard		Square piano	England	patented in 1844 by Hewitt
	f) with an adjustable frame which moves the stringing		Pianoforte	England	patented in 1846 by Woolley

Italy

1514 For Pope Leo V, a Venetian organ builder makes a 'clavicembalo grande con do registri'. It is uncertain whether the word 'registri' refers to two strings (bichord stringing) or two register-stops.

1538 Introduction of 8′ and 4′ registers ('instrumento in ottava').

1576 Franco Ungaro (Franciscus Patavinus), a Venetian instrument maker, builds plucked keyboard instruments with three stops, probably 8′, 8′, 4′.[1]

Germany

1582 An inventory of instruments at the Court of Brandenburg mentions a stringed keyboard instrument with four stops, probably 8′, 8′, 8′, 4′.[1]

1765 Dalitz constructs for the first time square pianos with so-called 'Veränderungen' (variations).

1774 Joh. Gottlob Wagner builds square pianos with pedals.

England

1769 Tschudi patents the 'Venetian swell', a device for producing crescendo for harpsichords (Engl. Pat. No. 947).

1783 Broadwood patents loud and soft pedals (Engl. Pat. No. 1379).

France

1741 Niels Brelin builds upright harpsichords with eight pedal-stops.

1765 Berger, in Grenoble, builds first harpsichords and spinets with knee-stops, 'registre mû par le genou' (mechanism for producing a crescendo).

Before 1776 Erard constructs a 'clavecin' with pedals.

1862 Invention of sustaining-pedal by Montal, Paris.

U.S.A.

1874 Steinway, New York, patents sostenuto-pedal.

[1] *Sachs*, Curt, History of Musical Instruments, p. 341.

PART III

STRINGED KEYBOARD INSTRUMENTS IN SYSTEMATIC ORDER

Bibliography: Norlind, Tobias, Systematik der Saiteninstrumente, vol. 2: Geschichte des Klavieres.
The plot of this Part III follows in broad outline the principles of Norlind.

ESCHAQUIER

(also called eschequier, eschiquier, eschaquier d'Angleterre, exaquier, exaquir, exacherium, escaque—or Schachbrett). Of this mediaeval instrument whose secret has remained undiscovered, there are, except for a few meagre details (see following dates, etc.) no detailed descriptions, no picture, and no examples in existence. Consequently it would be outside the bounds of this book to examine more closely into the hypotheses of the experts on this subject.

TABLE OF DATES

1340 Guillaume de Machault, in a detailed inventory in 'Li temps pascour' does not yet mention the Eschaquier.

1360 King Edward III of England presents his prisoner King John of France with an 'eschequier' made by a certain Jehan Perrot.[1]

1377 Mention of the 'eschaquir d'Engleterre' by Guillaume de Machault in the poem 'La Prise d'Alexandrie'.[1]

1378 Mention of the 'eschequier' in verses by Eugène Deschamps.[1]

1388[2] King John of Aragon, in a letter, asks his brother-in-law, Philippe the Bold, to send him an 'instrument semblant d'orguens qui sona ab cordis' and an organist 'abte de tocar exaquier(e) los 'petits orguens'.[3]

1404 Mention in the 'Minneregeln' of a 'Schachbrett' by Eberhard Cersne of Minden.[1]

1511[4] The Duke of Lothringen buys an 'instrument, faisant l'echiquier, orgues, espinette et fluctes'.[1]

1560 Antonius Arena mentions the 'exacherium' as a dance-instrument.

WOOD USED IN PIANO-BUILDING

Germany, Austria, Switzerland and Northern Countries: walnut, pine, birch, cherry, spruce, oak, maple, fir, hornbeam, copperbeech, pear, alder, rosewood, mahogany.—Veneered: walnut, cherry, rosewood, mahogany.

Netherlands and Belgium: oak, spruce, walnut, stone-pine, Scotch fir and mahogany.—Veneering: mahogany.

France: walnut, poplar, cypress (rare), mahogany, rosewood. Veneering: walnut, mahogany, rosewood.

England: walnut, oak, mahogany, rosewood.—Veneering: mahogany, rosewood.

[1] *Pirro*, André, Les Clavecinistes, pp. 5–7.

[2] A stringed keyboard instrument ('qui sona ab cordis'), resembling a small portable organ ('semblant d'orguens'), judging by its shape would be the 'upright Harpsichord' mentioned as early as 1450, i.e. the clavicytherium (Sachs).

[3] *Sachs*, Curt, The History of Musical Instruments, p. 336.

[4] The instrument consists of a small organ ('Orgues, fluctes'), a spinet and an 'eschicquier'. Apart from the wind-produced tone of the organ there remains for the 'eschicquier', as a contrast to the tone of the spinet's plucking action, only the tangent action of a clavichord, or a kind of hammer action (the tangent[hammer]action of the clavichord described by Arnold von Zwolle?). The mechanism of the 'eschicquier' cannot however have been that of the clavichord (tangent action), for already in 1404 Eberhard Cersne of Minden, in his 'Minneregeln', differentiates between the 'Clavichordium' and the 'Schachbrett', describing them separately. The only remaining alternative is therefore hammer action. Nor is there any question of its being similar to the Dulce Melos with its hammer action described by Arnold of Zwolle, for the literature of that time makes a careful distinction between the 'bons eschecquiers et doucemelles'.—As we have already seen, (under 'Hammer action' and 'Tangent[hammer]action') the vertically rising tangent mechanism of those times cannot be compared in any way with the rotary movement of modern hammer mechanism, nor is it comparable with that of the upright piano set at an angle of 90%. Obviously the latter mechanism has no connection with that of the stringed keyboard instrument 'semblant d'orguens qui sona ab cordis'. (See article 'Chekker' by F.W. Galpin in Grove's Dictionary of Music and Musicians', 4th edition, 1940, pp. 118, 119.)

Italy: willow, pine, cypress, cedar, ebony.—Veneered: walnut, cherry.
Spain: walnut, pine, cedar.
Portugal: pine, walnut.

The *soundboard* in clavichords, spinets, and harpsichords was generally made of fir, cypress or cedar-wood.

A. STRINGED KEYBOARD INSTRUMENTS WITH STROKE ACTION

GEIGENCLAVICYMBEL
(Hans Hayden model, 1610)

SHAPE: harpsichord.
KEYBOARD: as in a harpsichord.
INTERIOR: ditto.
STRINGING: material: in the bass, thick brass or steel strings wound with parchment; in the treble, strong steel strings without parchment.
ACTION: stroke action (friction).
STOPS: none.

TABLE OF DATES

About 1610 Hans Hayden, Nürnberg, builds the first Geigenclavicymbel ('Nürnbergisch Geigenwerck').
1625 Geigenclavicymbel by Raymundo Truchado, a Spaniard.
1664 'Arched Viall' in England.
1708 Cuisinié's 'Clavecin vielle' in France.
1709 'Klaviergambe' by Gleichmann.
1742 Le Voir, of Paris, improves upon the mechanical friction action.
1754 Hohlfeld's 'Bogenflügel' substitutes the violin-bow by 'circular horsehair close under the stringing mechanically controlled by key-pressure to continuously stroke the strings' (Neupert).

B. STRINGED KEYBOARD INSTRUMENTS WITH PLUCKING ACTION

I. Plucked keyboard instruments

A. *lying horizontally:*

1. Virginal
   a) Spinettino or octave virginal
   b) Spinet
   c) Querspinettino
   d) Double-strung spinet
   e) Double-keyboard spinet
   f) Double-keyboard spinettino
   g) Spinet with split keys
   h) Double virginal
   i) Spinet with pedals
2. Harpsichord
   a) Harpsichord-virginal
   b) Clavecin brisé
   c) Harpsichord with pedal
3. 'Lautenclavicymbel'

B. *Standing vertically:*

Upright harpsichord (Clavicytherium)

II. Plucked keyboard instruments combined with organ

1. Regal spinet
2. Organ-spinet
3. Organ-harpsichord

III. Pianoforte combined with plucked keyboard instrument

1. Pianoforte combined with spinet
2. Pianoforte combined with harpsichord

IV. Mechanical plucked keyboard instruments

1. Mechanical spinet
2. Mechanical harpsichord-organ

Bibliography: Neupert, Hanns, Das Cembalo; also his article 'Cembalo' in Die Musik in Geschichte und Gegenwart, vol. 2, col. 954. *Norlind,* Tobias, Systematik der Saiteninstrumente, vol. 2: Geschichte des Klavieres. *Sachs,* Curt, History of Musical Instruments.

I. PLUCKED KEYBOARD INSTRUMENTS

A. LYING HORIZONTALLY

1. VIRGINAL

built after 1500, first description in Virdung's 'Musica getutscht und auszgezogen', Basel 1511

DESIGNATION: German: Spinett, Symphonia; English: virginal; French: épinette; Italian: spinetta, spinetta da tavola.
ETYMOLOGY: spinetta from 'spina', a thorn; figuratively a quill; virginal from 'virga' or little stick = the jack.
SHAPE: the Italian virginal is pentagonal and built of cypress- or cedar-wood. For reasons of resonance the instrument itself is made of exceedingly thin wood. It therefore needs the protection of a strong outer case from which it can be lifted when in use.
The Flemish and the English virginal are made of stone-pine and are rectangular in shape. Both the above types, like the clavichord, were originally built as portable instruments without supports; later they were given stands and since about 1750 were mounted firmly on legs.
KEYBOARD: in Italian virginals this was projected; naturals made of boxwood or covered with ivory, sharps of boxwood or ebony.
The *Flemish virginals* had a recessed keyboard; naturals covered with bone, sometimes with ivory, sharps coloured black or else made of ebony. In general this type had only one manual, two manuals was an exception; it was also rare to find one with pedal connecting the bass.
INTERIOR: the strings, fastened to wrest-pins on the wrestplank (right-hand side), lie parallel with the key-board, pass over two bridges, both on the soundboard, to be wound round the hitch-pins in the hitch-pin block on the left. A soundhole in the soundboard serves to project the tone.
In Italian virginals the wrest-pins are placed straight, with an arched bridge, whilst in Flemish instruments the pins stand irregularly and the bridge is angular. The *rose* used as an ornament over the soundhole is in carved wood in the Italian instruments, but Flemish instruments have a metal rose. Another Flemish characteristic is the decoration of the soundboard with flowers, birds, etc. in gouache-painting.
STRINGING: generally single, occasionally double stringing.
ACTION: quill plectra.
STOPS: in double-strung instruments: either by pulling out or pushing in the keyboard, or by means of front stops in the nameboard, one row of jacks can be put out of action, leaving only the *one* row to pluck the corresponding 8′- or 4′-strings.

1a SPINETTINO OR OCTAVE VIRGINAL
beginning 16th till about middle 18th century

Designation: German: Oktavspinett, Kleininstrument; English: octave virginal; French: petite épinette; Italian: spinettino, spinettina, ottavino.
Shape: rectangular, sometimes of irregular form, but laid in a rectangular case. These were originally portable instruments which were laid on any ordinary spinet to be used as an upper manual in 4′-pitch. Since about 1650 it had become an independent instrument on a little stand and by the beginning of the 18th century was mounted on legs of its own.
Keyboard: recessed or projected, on the broad side of the instrument, generally one manual, seldom two.
Interior: resembling an virginal. The triangular octave virginal had frontal stringing, as in a spinet.
Stringing: single-strung in 4′-pitch (octave virginal), or else a fifth higher (Quint-spinettino).
Action: quill plectra.
Stops: none.

1b SPINET
found in Italy (since 1610), England (1660 till end of 18th century), and Germany

Designation: German: Querspinett; English: spinet; Italian: spinetta traversa.
Shape: wing-shaped instrument. The right side bent in the shape of an ‘S’.
Keyboard: projected, on the long side of the case, generally one manual, occasionally double-manual.
Interior: the strings fastened to wrest-pins on the wrestplank (which is placed above the keyboard along the whole length of the nameboard) run oblique, at an acute angle to the keyboard, to the right flank where they pass over two bridges (one on the wrestplank, the other on the soundboard), to the hitch-pins on the hitch-pin block.
Stringing: mostly single-strung; double and triple stringing are an exception (18th century).
Action: quill- or leather plectra.
Stops: front stops on double-strung instrument by Harris (England 1757).

1c QUERSPINETTINO
second half of 17th century

Shape: rectangular, right side broader or curved.
Keyboard: on the broad side of the case, taking up the entire front.
Interior: resembling the spinet.
Stringing: single-strung.
Action: quill plectra.
Stops: none.

1d DOUBLE-STRUNG SPINET
ascertained 1623–1757

Stringing: two 8′-strings. The second set of strings is sometimes in 4′-pitch. As the main characteristic of the spinet is its single stringing, these instruments really belong to the order of harpsichords. They have nothing in common with the spinet except the outward form.

The same can be said for the

1e DOUBLE-KEYBOARD SPINET
ascertained 1610 till the first half of 18th century;

and the

1f DOUBLE-KEYBOARD SPINETTINO
ascertained 1677,

an elegant copy of a double-manual harpsichord, which is more or less of a plaything, as for both manuals there is only one set of strings.

1g SPINET WITH SPLIT KEYS
ascertained 1726

1h DOUBLE VIRGINAL
about 1580 to 1623

By the addition of a removable octave virginal on the right of the keyboard, two separate instruments are combined in one.

1i SPINET WITH PEDALS

Six or eight pedals are connected in the lowest octave to the keys of the manual by means of strings or wires. These are drawn through holes in the keybed and fixed to the underside of the keys, making it possible to lower the keys of the manual whilst playing with both hands.

2. HARPSICHORD

DESIGNATION: German: Klavizimbel, Kielflügel, Flügel; English: harpsichord; French: clavecin; Italian: (clavi)cembalo, gravicembalo, arpicordo, cembalone.
ETYMOLOGY: 'cembalo' comes from the word cymbal or dulcimer. A dulcimer to which keys ('claves') have been added, becomes a 'clavicembalo'.
SHAPE: triangular with the treble side curved inwards. Formerly this instrument had no stand but in later years it was mounted firmly on legs. In Italy and Spain a showy case was made to receive the instrument and Italian harpsichords are strengthened generally with protective wooden slats on the sides.
KEYBOARD: can be recessed or else projected and is on the short side of the instrument, with either single or double manual.
INTERIOR: the strings, fastened on wrest-pins on the wrestplank in front, are brought round the bridge on the soundboard—sometimes also round the bridge-pins sloping obliquely from the bridge on the soundboard—and are then wound round the hitch-pins on the treble side. The 4′- and 16′-strings are passed over special bridges and fastened to an opposite bridge which has the same function as a hitch-pin block, the 4′-strings

below and the 16′-strings *above* the 8′-strings. Formerly in bichord instruments, the strings were not laid side by side but one above another, so that the plucking could be done by a single plectrum. Of course this meant that the two strings were not plucked simultaneously, but one after the other.
Above the row of jacks is a jackrail to keep them in place whilst playing and a soundhole in the soundboard, generally decorated with a rose, projects the tone.
STRINGS: material: for the bass notes brass strings were used, which later on were wrapped with brass, copper or silver-plated copper wire; and steel strings in the middle and treble.
STRINGING: unichord to quintuple-chord; in the latter case two strings for the 8′-tone and three for the 4′-, 16′- (rarely) and the 2′-pitch (very rarely).
ACTION: quill- or leather plectra. To each set of strings there is a special set of jacks; except in the case of the double-strung instruments of early times with the strings one above another (see 'Interior', above). The timbre of the tone produced is largely determined by the choice of the plucking point.
STOPS: side stops, side levers and, in later times, inside-levers, frontal stops and pedals, connecting and disconnecting the respective jacks, permit single or combined sounding of the strings and determine the changes in tone-volume and tone-color, two and sometimes even three manuals making quick changes possible from one set of strings to another. On harpsichords with three manuals the different stops are divided: the lower manual plays the 8′-register, the middle manual the 8′- and 4′- and the upper manual only the 4′. By this arrangement stops were rendered superfluous.
For details about other stops, for instance the lute and harp, see under heading 'Stops'.
COUPLERS: a further enrichment of tone can be achieved on double-manualled instruments by pushing back the lower or the upper manual, or by the use of a stop, thus connecting the upper and lower manuals.

2a HARPSICHORD VIRGINAL

beginning of 17th century till 1735

This is on the same principle as the double virginal except that the octave virginal is placed on the treble side of the harpsichord.

2b CLAVECIN-BRISÉ

patented by Marius in 1700—till 1715

a folding, three-piece portable harpsichord which, when closed, resembles a rectangular box.

2c HARPSICHORD WITH PEDAL

ascertained 1667

Same principle as pedal-spinet.
This very primitive form is not to be confused with the

CEMBALO-PEDAL

which has a complete pedal-keyboard with strings on which the manual instrument stands. In modern copies (Neupert) the usual 16′- and also 8′- and 4′-registers are added.

3. 'LAUTEN-CLAVICYMBEL'

This instrument combines lute and theorbo (bass lute) in one instrument and is fitted with gut strings strung as in a harpsichord. In 1740 the organ-builder Zacharias Hildebrand built to a specification given to him by J. S. Bach a 'Lauten-clavicymbel' which had two sets of gut strings and one 4′-set of brass strings. They were one-, two- or even three-manualled.

B. STANDING VERTICALLY

UPRIGHT HARPSICHORD
middle of 15th till end of 18th century

DESIGNATION: German: Clavicytherium; English: upright harpsichord; French: clavecin vertical; Italian: cembalo verticale, spinetta verticale, claviciterio.
SHAPE: upright harpsichord shape.
KEYBOARD: recessed or projected, on the broad side of the instrument; one manual.
INTERIOR: resembling that of a harpsichord.
STRINGING: material as in a harpsichord, originally single-strung, since beginning of 17th century sometimes double-strung, with 8′, 8′.
ACTION: quill plucking action set vertically.
STOPS: shifter (in double-strung instruments).

II. ORGAN SPINETS AND HARPSICHORDS
second half of 15th till end of 18th century

1. REGAL SPINET

2. ORGAN-SPINET

3. ORGAN-HARPSICHORD

The combination of a harpsichord and a small organ is mentioned as early as 1460 by Paulus Paulirinus. In 1480 the name 'Claviorganum' appears for the first time in Spain. Curt Sachs, however, draws attention to the fact that by this name a combined instrument was not meant but a fairly large house-organ.[1]

[1] *Sachs*, Curt, History of Musical Instruments, p. 342.

The organ-mechanism was built into the lower part of the instrument consisting of either reed-stops (Regal) or else of only one or two flute-registers with partly closed, partly open wooden pipes, sometimes also of a combination of read- and flute-stops. A bellows worked by a foot pedal supplied the air. By means of knee or foot pedals connected to a valve, the organ-mechanism can be connected or disconnected at will, playing on either piano or organ alone. Norlind also mentions instruments made for great buildings "where organs of monumental size were combined with one or more harpsichords." The organ-harpsichords were the most popular being built up to the end of the 18th century.

III. PIANOFORTE COMBINED WITH PLUCKED KEYBOARD INSTRUMENT

1. PIANOFORTE COMBINED WITH SPINET (1788)

2. PIANOFORTE COMBINED WITH HARPSICHORD (1777)

Both instruments were so arranged that by means of a stop or a foot pedal each could be played separately.

IV. MECHANICAL PLUCKED KEYBOARD INSTRUMENTS

second half 16th century till 1800

1. AUTOMATIC SPINET

2. AUTOMATIC CLAVIORGANUM

In spinet automats the jacks are set in motion by pins projecting from a cylinder. This type of instrument was in great favor in the 17th century and was later added to by combining a harpsichord with an organ. In Norway harpsichord-organs were still being built in 1800.

1404 First mention in a Low German poem, the 'Minneregeln' by Eberhard Cersne of Minden, of the 'Clavicymbolum'.

1409 First picture in 'Les très belles heures du Duc de Berry' of a keyboard instrument in the shape of a harpsichord.

1440 Treatise by Heinrich Arnold of Zwolle. Description and sketches of stringed keyboard instruments of the period, excepting the eschaquier.

1450 approx. First description of an upright harpsichord.

1461 The harpsichord mentioned in a letter from the instrument maker Tantini for the first time in Italy.

1480 First representation of an upright harpsichord sculptured on the altar at Kefermarkt in Austria.

1492 Earliest mention of the harpsichord in England.

1521 Oldest harpsichord still in existence, by Hieronymus Bononiensis, Italy. Double-stringed instrument.

1523 Oldest surviving virginal by Franciscus de Portalupes, Verona.

1548 Earliest Dutch harpsichord in existence, a spinet by Joes Karest.

1579 Oldest remaining claviorganum, by Ludowic Theewes.

1598 Mention in two letters from Hippolito Cricca of two keyboard instruments with organ mechanism, 'Pian e Forte con l'orghano di sotto'.
Plucked or hammer action? (see also under pianoforte dates).

16th century, end. Dutch harpsichord manufacture gathers importance through work of Hans Ruckers and his sons, in Antwerp.

17th century. The supremacy amongst harpsichord makers of Ruckers, Couchet and Britsen make Antwerp the center of European harpsichord manufacture. Importance of Italian manufacture waning.

1622 Oldest existent harpsichord by John Haward.

1718 Johann Christoph Fleischer builds the 'Lautenclavicymbel' and the 'Theorbenflügel'.

1739 Johann Gottlieb Clemm builds in Philadelphia the first American spinet.

18th century. England, France and Germany leading in harpsichord manufacture: the importance of Holland's harpsichord building gradually decreasing and Italian manufacture, except for Cristofori, insignificant.

1782 Karl August Gräbner, Dresden, builds the last German harpsichord.

1792 Vincenzio Sodi builds the last Italian harpsichord.

1795 Last use in England, on a public occasion, of the harpsichord at the traditional performance of the 'King's Birthday Ode' in St. James' Palace.

1798 The Paris Conservatoire awards the 'Prix de Clavecin' for the last time.

1805 Himmel performs publicly in Berlin for the last time on a harpsichord.

1809 Kirkman in London builds the last English harpsichord.

1815 Last appearance of harpsichord in a French concert hall.

1816 Harpsichord appears for last time in Italy in a performance of Rossini's 'Barber of Seville'.

1839 Alessandro Riva, in Bergamo, builds the last spinet.

C. STRINGED KEYBOARD INSTRUMENTS WITH STROKE ACTION

with Tangent Action: Clavichords
with Hammer Action: Pianofortes

I. Clavichords

1. Clavichord
   a) 'gebunden', or fretted
   b) 'bundfrei', or unfretted
2. Cembal d'amour
3. Clavichord with pedal

II. Organ-clavichord

Bibliography: Neupert, Hanns, Das Clavichord. Also his article 'Clavichord' in Die Musik in Geschichte und Gegenwart, vol. 2, col. 1467. *Norlind*, Tobias, Systematik der Saiteninstrumente, vol. 2, Geschichte des Klavieres. *Sachs*, Curt, History of Musical Instruments. *Harding*, Rosamond, A History of the Pianoforte.

I. CLAVICHORDS

1. THE CLAVICHORD

second half 14th century till after 1812

Designation: German: Clavichord, since 1600 also 'Clavier'; English: clavichord; French: manicorde, manicordion, clavicorde; Italian: clavicordio, monocordo, manicordo.
Etymology: the word comes from the Latin 'clavis' meaning a key, actually a 'key' in the sense that the keyboard-keys are shaped like a mediaeval house-key, and 'corda' meaning a string. This instrument was originally single-strung, developing later to polychord with a keyboard.
Shape: mostly rectangular, occasionally pentagonal or blunt hexagonal, or trapezoid or oval in form. These were built originally as portable instruments or table clavichords without any stand, stands being added in later years and firm stands with legs not until 1740. In front, on the player's left, there is a little built-in box to take the tuning-key and reserve strings and since the 18th century a drawer has been added on the right, to hold music.
Keyboard: the keyboard is on the broad side of the case, either recessed or projected, generally only one manual, very rarely, in later times, two manuals. Originally the naturals were mostly light in color and the sharps were dark. Later on, however, dark naturals and white sharps became general, subsequently the naturals were covered with ivory and the sharps with ebony.
The woods used were box, cypress, lemon, ebony; bone, ivory, tortoise shell or even more valuable material for the covering.
Interior: the strings were fastened to pins on the wrestplank at the right-hand side and run parallel to the keyboard to hitch-pins on the hitch-pin block at the left.
Originally all the strings were of a uniform length, thickness and tension, but later on variations were made in length and thickness. Those instruments of the former type were called monochords and those of the latter were named clavichords (after Ramis de Pareja, 1482). In early times the wrest-pins were always placed in a double row and running straight. Later on, on account of an increased number of strings they stood in four rows and in broken order.
In Italy, in 16th century instruments, two, three or four bridges were constructed on the soundboard, one for each group of strings, which was called the 'Italian mensur'. The increasing number of strings, however, soon necessitated the use of one complete bridge across the whole stringing. At first this was in a straight line, later zig-zagged or curved and finally became a bridge in the form of an 'S', which was called the 'German mensur'.
The soundboard which is made of pinewood or cypress has a soundhole or else an opening at one side to let the sound escape. These soundholes are often decorated with a beautiful rose cut in wood, paper, parchment or metal.
Stringing: material: bass-strings brass, in later times wrapped with copper wire; middle and treble strings in brass, iron or steel.
Method of stringing: generally double, seldom triple- or quadruple-strung. In the latter case two string-unisons were used for the 8'- and the two others for the 4'-tone. And these octave-strings were brought over a special bridge. The whole acoustical layout (soundboard, bridge and strings) was situated in one third of the body of the instrument on the right-hand side.
Action: tangent action (see 'clavichord action').
Stops: in these clavichords fitted with stops the interior and the frontal stops were in use, also lute, piano and Pantaleon-stop. The remaining two thirds of the interior was taken up by the keyboard and the action.

a) FRETTED CLAVICHORDS

beginning 15th century till about 1800

The tangent, having the double function of being sound-producer as well as wedge-shaped bridge dividing the string, it follows that strings can produce different notes according to the point at which they are stopped. This made it possible to play on one set of strings with several neighboring keys which, like the frets on a lute, touch the strings with their tangents at different points: consequently a larger number of keys could correspond to a smaller number of strings. This enabled an instrument to be built lighter and cheaper and because of its resemblance to the frets on a lute it earned the name 'fretted' or 'Bundklavier'. This string combination had however the disadvantage of excluding certain harmonies, as of two simultaneously produced notes on one string, only the top note was audible.
Through the construction later on of

b) UNFRETTED CLAVICHORDS

1700 till about 1812

in which each tangent had its special string, the number of keys corresponding to that of the strings, the above mentioned limitation of harmonies was corrected.

2. CEMBAL D'AMOUR

invented in 1721 by Gottfried Silbermann

STRINGING: "By lengthening the string to the left a double length is achieved which the tangent strikes at the center of the whole length, enabling both halves to sound, the left half having its own bridge on a second soundboard." [1]

3. CLAVICHORD WITH PEDAL

1467 till beginning 19th century

KEYBOARD: pedal-boards were added, originally only connected to the deepest manual keys. Later on they were separately strung in 16′-tone. By placing two clavichords one above another and adding pedal boards a useful double-manualled practice instrument for organists was produced.

II. ORGAN CLAVICHORD

16th century till end of 18th century

A combination of clavichord and small organ.

[1] *Neupert*, Hanns, Das Clavichord, p. 30.

Italy is, in all probability, the land of origin of the clavichord.[1]

1404 First mention of the 'Clavicordium' in a Low German poem, the 'Minneregeln' by Eberhard Cersne of Minden.

15th century, first half. Representation of a clavichord in a wood-carving in the Cathedral Church of St. Mary's, Shrewsbury, England.

1440 First detailed description of clavichord by Heinrich Arnold of Zwolle, based on an earlier treatise by a certain Baudecet of Reims. Picture of a clavichord in the 'Weimarer Wunderbuch', Germany. Shortly after 1440 is to be noted a representation in a Dutch wood-carving of a clavichord, now in the Rijksmuseum, Amsterdam.

15th century, second half. The Erlanger treatise 'Pro clavichordiis faciendis' mentions a clavichord with 2 1/2 octaves.

1459/63 The pedal-clavichord first mentioned by Paulus Paulirinus.

1467 First picture appears of pedal-clavichord in Hugo von Reutlingen's manuscript 'Flores musicae'.

1469 First representation of clavichord in Sweden in a fresco in the Tirps Church in Upland.

1477 England builds clavichords.

1480 In a Spanish inventory, a clavichord under the name 'manicordio' is listed.

1482 The Spaniard Remis de Pareja mentions in his work 'Musica pratica' the clavichord as being a popular musical instrument in Spain and Italy.

1497 France builds clavichords.

1723 Invention by Gottfried Silbermann of the 'Cembal d'amour'.

1740 Clavichord building begins in Russia.

1744 H. A. Hass, Hamburg, builds triple-strung clavichords.

1780? Fret-free clavichord by Johann Wilhelm Gruneberg, Germany. Keyboard compass: over five octaves (F_1 to g‴).

1812 Clavichords no longer in use.

[1] *Ambros*, Geschichte der Musik, Breslau 1864.

PIANOFORTES

I. Pianofortes

A. *Lying horizontally:*

1. Grand Pianoforte
   a) Pedal-pianoforte
2. Square Piano
   a) harp-shaped; Querflügel
   b) small pianos: Orphica, sewing table piano
   c) as pieces of furniture: writing-table, chest of drawers, tea-table pianos
   d) Square Piano with pedals

B. *Standing vertically:*

1. Upright Grand Pianofortes
   a) with doors: harpsichord-shaped; Pyramid
   b) in the form of a bookcase
   c) without doors: Pyramid, Giraffe, Lyre
2. Upright Square Pianos
   Piano sloping backwards; Square Pianoforte turned upwards on its side
3. Upright Pianos
   a) with high upper framework: Cabinet-Pianoforte
   b) with upper framework of medium height: Ditanaklasis; Portable Grand Pianoforte; Pianino
   c) with low upper framework: Cottage Piano; Piccolo Pianoforte; Piano droit
   d) without upper framework: Piano console; Pianino

II. Pianofortes combined with organ

A. *Lying horizontally:*

1. Grand Pianoforte-Organ
2. Square Piano-Organ

III. Pianofortes with Harmonium

A. *Lying horizontally:*

1. Grand Pianoforte-Harmonium

B. *Standing vertically:*

1. Cabinet-Pianoforte-Harmonium
2. Pyramid-Harmonium
3. Giraffe-Harmonium
4. Pianino-Harmonium

IV. Pianoforte combined with harpsichord

see under: plucked keyboard instruments

V. Automatic pianofortes combined with organ

I. PIANOFORTES

A. LYING HORIZONTALLY

I. GRAND PIANOFORTE
from 1709 till present day

DESIGNATION: German: Flügel; English: grand piano; French: piano à queue; Italian: pianoforte a coda.
SHAPE: till about 1820 the grand piano took the traditional harpsichord form with slender tapering legs. With the increasing compass of the keyboard and the introduction of metal frames the instrument gradually attained to its present form.
KEYBOARD: formerly recessed, since 1808 (Erard) projecting, with its own folding cover.
INTERIOR: the strings in frontal arrangement are fixed to wrest-pins[1] on the wrestplank[2] made of hardwood (beechwood), passed through agraffes, or metal studs, round the bridgepins on the soundboard and wound round hitch-pins on the hitch-pin block. The year 1800 saw the first introduction of metal reinforcement in framework construction which up to this time had relied exclusively on wood, and from 1825 (Pleyel, French Pat. 1808) onwards the change gradually took place in favor of one-piece iron framework.
The case with its strong wooden stays formerly bore the whole weight of the strings' tension. Since the introduction of the iron frame this burden has been lifted.
STRINGING: material: bass-strings of steel wrapped with copper; middle register and treble made of drawn steel wire.
METHOD OF STRINGING: unichord, bichord, trichord, sometimes quadruplechord (Conrad Graf, Vienna). Originally straight stringing, since 1859 (Steinway) overstrung.
ACTION: English action, German action, down-striking action (Zugmechanik), repetition action with double escapement.
STOPS: originally hand stops, later on knee levers and lastly pedals, the latter on a pedal-rod fastened to wires, later on being replaced by a solid lyre-shaped mounting.
The number of pedals varied until 1850 between one and six, according to the country of origin. The modern piano has now only three: soft, loud and sustaining pedal.

1a PEDAL PIANOFORTES
18th century till beginning of 19th century

having the addition of a pedal-board with corresponding stringing.

2. SQUARE PIANOS
1742 till 1880 in Europe, till 1903 in America

DESIGNATION: German: Tafelklavier; English; square piano; French: piano carré; Italian: pianoforte da tavola.

[1] American: turning pins.
[2] American: turning block or turning rail.

SHAPE: from the clavichord the square piano inherited the traditional oblong table shape, the recessed keyboard on the broad side of the instrument and the little built-in box to hold reserve strings, etc. The beginning of the 19th century with its growing number of strings, increasing keyboard compass and the introduction of iron framework (1820) demands an instrument of greater size and resistance. When the use of cast iron framework became general (1820) and the keyboard compass increased to seven octaves, the square piano took up almost as much space as a grand piano without having such beauty of tone. It retained its popularity in America longer than in any other country.
KEYBOARD: recessed, without a separate cover: this meant uncovering the whole instrument in order to play.
INTERIOR: in early examples the disposition of strings and soundboard was similar to that of a clavichord. Later on, in 1783, Broadwood introduced an alteration, placing the wrestplank and wrest-pins to the back of the instrument, considerably improving its tone. This was changed again halfway through the 19th century to frontal stringing, as in the construction of pianofortes.
STRINGING: material: at first thin brass strings, later on the bass strings covered with copper wire; middle register and treble, drawn steel wire.
METHOD OF STRINGING: single- and double-strung, after 1820 single- to triple-strung. From 1828 onwards gradual introduction of cross stringing.
ACTION: Prellmachanik or German action (primitive); Stossmechanik without escapement; Prellzungenmechanik or German action (developed); Stosszungenmechanik or English action.
STOPS: first hand stops, later knee levers and ultimately pedals suspended on a rod held in place by wires. In later times the pedals were firmly mounted in shape on a lyre, varying in number from one to six.

2a HARP-SHAPED SQUARE PIANOS AND QUERFLÜGEL
the former from 1770–1790, the latter from 1782 till after 1810

SHAPE: harp-shaped.
KEYBOARD: recessed, on the long side of instrument.
STRINGING: single to triple stringing.
ACTION:Stossmechanik; later with English or developed German action.
STOPS: front stops, later with knee levers.
The harp-shaped square pianos by the maker Schmahl are often transposable by means of a shifting keyboard. They have from three to five front stops.

2b SMALL PIANOS
1795–1850

a) ORPHICA
1795–1830

SHAPE: the instrument could be slung across the shoulders on a strap and played standing.
KEYBOARD: three to three and a half octaves in compass; the keys themselves are only about half the size of normal piano keys.
STRINGING: single-strung.
ACTION: Viennese action.
This instrument which could be used out-of-doors was consequently called the 'week-end piano' by the English.

b) Sewing table piano
first half of 19th century

Shape: fitted as a sewing table, with mirror and drawer to keep music in, etc.
Keyboard: to be pulled forward. Compass, generally, of three octaves.
Stringing: single-, or double-strung.
Action: Developed German action.

2c PIANOS AS PIECES OF FURNITURE
1812–1860

These were a combination of an instrument and a piece of furniture generally taking the form of 'piano-secrétaires' or chest of drawers; even tea-table pianos, billiard table pianos and travelling pianos are witnesses to the particular tendency of those times, which now appears unintelligible. These strange mixtures produced pretty, even sometimes distinctive pieces of furniture, but cannot be said to have created serviceable instruments.

2d SQUARE PIANO WITH PEDALS
about 1780

These pianos have the addition of a pedal-board with strings to correspond.

B. STANDING VERTICALLY

1. UPRIGHT GRAND PIANOFORTES
from 1735 and in use until about 1850

Norlind divides the upright pianos into three outstanding groups; cabinet pianos with doors, cabinet pianos, and upright pianos without doors. Let us follow up these groups:

Designation and shape:
a) *with doors:* 1735, shape of harpsichord. 2. Pyramid, 1745–1760, triangular case tapering upwards. After 1760 no more upright grand pianos were built in Germany. The return of the pyramid piano dates from 1804 from the workshops of Wachtl and Bleyer, in Vienna.
b) '*in the form of a bookcase*', 1795 to 1815: William Stodart in London invented a 'bookcase-piano' built into a rectangular case. On the right side of the instrument were shelves to hold books of music. Height: 245 to 275 cm. Stodart's upright grand piano was also constructed by Viennese and German makers from 1804 till about 1850 in modified forms, as a 'double bookcase-piano' and as an 'aufrecht stehendes Querpianoforte', considerably lower in height.

c) *without doors: Pyramid,* 1804 till about 1850. Triangular case, flat sides, tapering upwards, the top blunt and generally crowned with a vase or urn. The front is pierced, backed with silk. Invented by Wachtl, Bleyer and Seuffert in Vienna in 1804 (Sachs).
Giraffe, popular till about 1850. Norlind names two types: the standing giraffe, the bass side straight, the treble curved or oblique ending at the top with curves or scrolls: and the *lying giraffe* in the form of a couchant harp (1810 to 1830).
The upright pianoforte by Domenico del Mela in 1739 is the unique example at that time of the upright giraffe piano. It was not until 1805 that this instrument can be said to have been developed by the Viennese makers Wachtl, Bleyer and Seuffert. The invention of the lying giraffe can also be attributed to the above mentioned makers (1810). Both types were frequently constructed in Northern Europe till about 1830/50. After this time their popularity waned, the demand entirely ceasing by the beginning of the 20th century.
The only exception to the above is the double-giraffe piano, which was properly speaking a bookcase-piano, made by Nordquist in 1826.
Lyre, 1824 till about 1850: in the shape of an antique lyre, the case hollowed out at the sides, gilded and with imitation lyre-string and rods backed with silk. Invented in Berlin in 1824 by J.L. Schleip, this lyre-shaped piano was manufactured almost exclusively by Berlin piano makers till about 1850. It was the last form of the upright grand pianoforte.
A small-sized lyre-piano was produced by J. A. Westermann, probably about the same period (1825).
KEYBOARD: originally recessed, projected in later models.
INTERIOR: resembling an ordinary piano.
STRINGING: bichord and trichord, mostly straight strung; upright pianos and lyre-pianos, sometimes oblique.
ACTION: Stossmechanik ('stehend' and 'hängend'), English, German (primitive and developed).
STOPS: originally hand stops (Friederici 1745); after 1795 upright grand-, giraffe- and pyramid-pianos had from two to six foot-pedals, the couchant giraffe- and lyre-pianos having also knee levers.

2. UPRIGHT SQUARE PIANOS
1798 to 1811

DESIGNATION AND SHAPE: with broad side of case resting on a stand and vertical front; patented by Southwell, 1798.
'Piano with case sloping backwards': broad side resting on stand, front sloping backwards. Height 137.2 cm. Patented by William Southwell, 4th March, 1811 (Engl. Pat. No. 3403).
'Square pianoforte turned upwards on its side: similar to Southwell's model of 1798. Height of upper part about 76 cm. Patented in 1811 by Frederick William Collard (Engl. Pat. No. 3481).
KEYBOARD: projected and with its own folding cover.
INTERIOR: same as in square piano: tuned from the side. The 'Piano sloping backwards' has an oblique soundboard.
STRINGING: method and material similar to the square piano. Collard's 'Piano sloping backwards' is strung obliquely.
ACTION: Stossmechanik or English action. The hammer strikes from the front, the damping of the strings from behind.
STOPS: pedals.

3. UPRIGHT PIANOS

1800 to present time

SHAPE: the case is rectangular with keyboard in the middle, thus dividing the instrument into two parts, lower and upper framework. According to the method of construction the height of the latter varies, sometimes it is suppressed.

DESIGNATION:

a) with high upper framework (French: piano vertical), 1802–1806; piano patented by Thomas Loud in 1802; height 190.5 cm (Engl. Pat. No. 2591).

'*Cabinet-Pianoforte*' (French: piano vertical), 1807–1860; invented and patented in 1807 by William Southwell, Dublin; upper framework open, filled in with piece of stretched cloth; height: between 180 and 235 cm, according to maker (Engl. Pat. No. 3029).

b) with upper framework of medium height (French: pianino), 1800 to present time. '*Ditanaklasis*', invented in 1800 by Mathias Müller in Vienna. Models I and II both with deeply recessed center; model I for two players sitting opposite each other; model II for one player. Height: model I: center 154 cm, sides 184 cm; model II: center 153.4 cm.

'*Portable Grand Pianoforte*', patented by Isaak Hawkins, Philadelphia, in 1800; total height 138 cm (Engl. Pat. No. 2446).

The pianino, from about 1850 to present time.

c) with low upper framework, 1811–1860.

'*Cottage piano*', patented by Robert Wornum 26th March 1811 (Engl. Pat. No. 3419). Second model of same, 1813, called at first 'Harmonic' changed later to 'cottage piano'; height 120 cm.

'*Piccolo pianoforte*', patented 1826 by Robert Wornum; height: 98 cm, later (in 1838) 117 cm (Engl. Pat. No. 5384).

'*Piano droit*', invented by Blanchet and Roller, Paris, 1827. Case undersized, sides in lyre-shaped curves with semicircular opening under the keyboard; height 120 cm.

d) without upper framework, 1828 till about 1850/60.

'*Piano console*', invented 1828 by Henri Pape, Paris: height: 100 cm (French Pat. No. 5833).

KEYBOARD: projected, the whole can be carried by the console legs, sometimes constructed to fold.

INTERIOR: in *vertical strung* instruments the frame stands the opposite way to that of a piano, i.e. the wrestplank is above, the upper end of it, below.

In *obliquely strung* instruments the wrestplank is also above, but the hitch-pin block, similar to square pianos, is placed at one side. Use of iron frames, metallic stays, metal hitch-pin block and metal wrestplank began in 1800: first cast iron frame used by Babcock in 1825.

STRINGING: material: the same as in the Grand Piano. Method: from single to triple stringing;

a) *vertical strung:* Ditanaklasis, Portable Grand Pianoforte, Cabinet Pianoforte, Cottage Piano, Piano vertical, the early Pianino.

In all these instruments the bass strings reach down to the floor.

b) *diagonal (oblique):* Piano droit, Cottage Piano (Model II).

c) *cross-strung:* Piano console, Pianino.

ACTION: mostly 'stehende' English action, rarely with 'stehend' developed German action.

STOPS: knee levers, pedals.

Comparative measurements of pianos

Kleinklavier	height: 105 cm or more
	height: 105 cm or less*
Stutzklavier	height: 106–120 cm
Klavier	height: 121–135 cm
Konzertklavier	height: 136 cm or more
	height: 144–150 cm*
Kleinflügel	length: 140 cm or more
	length: 141 cm or less*
Kleiner Stutzflügel	length: 145–165 cm
	length: 141–160 cm*
Stutzflügel	length: 165–180 cm
	length: 161–180 cm*
Kammermusikflügel	length: 185–210 cm
	length: 181–210 cm*
Konzertflügel	length: 215 cm or more
Kammerkonzertflügel	length: 211–250 cm*
Konzertflügel	length: 251–290 cm*

Information taken from 'Zeitschrift für Instrumentenbau', 59th year, p. 210.
* Information according to *Pfeiffer* in 'Von Flügel- und Klavierbezeichnungen'.

II. PIANOFORTES COMBINED WITH ORGAN

1. GRAND PIANOFORTE-ORGAN

1770 till about 1800

2. SQUARE PIANO-ORGAN

1785 till 1800

Both types are a combination of pianoforte with a smaller or larger organ-mechanism. The piano-organ is the successor of the harpsichord-organ, the square-organ that of the spinet-organ.

III. PIANOFORTE COMBINED WITH HARMONIUM

1. GRAND PIANOFORTE-HARMONIUM

1834–1900

2. CABINET PIANO-HARMONIUM

1820

3. PIANINO-HARMONIUM

1836 till beginning of 20th century

These three variations are a combination of pianoforte and harmonium.

IV. PIANOFORTE COMBINED WITH HARPSICHORD

see under: plucked keyboard instruments

V. MECHANICAL PIANOFORTES COMBINED WITH ORGAN

AUTOMATIC PIANO-ORGANS

1820

1598 Two letters from Hippolito Cricca, called Paliarino, to Alphonse II, Duke of Modena, mention two keyboard instruments with organ attachment, which he calls 'Pian e Forte con l'orghano di sotto'.

1673 Athanasius Kirchner describes, in his 'Phonurgia nova', a universal instrument built by Michael Todini, a Savoyard, combining an organ, an upright harpsichord (archicymbalum) and three 'Clavicymbali' in dulcimer form. The stroke of the three latter is made by very small hammers (marculi) (?).

1709 Cristofori, Florence, builds pianofortes.

1711 Father Wood, an English monk in Rome, builds the first English pianoforte.

1711 Cristofori's invention described by Marchese Maffei in 'Giornale dei Letterati di Venezia'.

1717 Independently of Cristofori, Gottlieb Schröter of Dresden invents a hammer action. Construction of two models, one with up-striking, the other with down-striking action.

1719 Maffei reprints his original report of 1711.

1720 Oldest surviving pianoforte by Cristofori.

1725 Mattheson publishes, in his paper 'Critica musica', a German translation of Maffei's report, thereby making Cristofori's invention known in Germany.

1731 Gottfried Silbermann, in Freiberg near Dresden, builds two pianofortes.

1732 Dodici sonate per piano e forte, by Lodovico Giustini, Florence, 1732, in which *precise instructions for expression are given for the first time.*

1735 First upright pianoforte? (Date contested by Kinsky: accepted as authentic by Rosamund Harding.)

1736 Gottfried Silbermann shows J. S. Bach two of his pianos. Bach's criticism.

1738 Hammer action beginning to be accepted.

1739 Domenico del Mela di Gagliano builds the first Italian upright pianoforte.

1744 Square piano by Johann Söcher in Sonthofen (Allgäu). Oldest surviving square piano.

1745 Christian Ernst Friederici in Gera builds the first pyramid pianoforte.

1747 J.S. Bach, in Potsdam, plays upon the improved Silbermann pianoforte in the presence of Frederick the Great, praising the instrument.

1752 Johann Joachim Quantz, in his 'Anleitung, die Flöte traversière zu spielen', mentions the pianoforte with appreciative words.

1755 William Mason, poet and composer, after a journey through Germany, brings back to England a small pianoforte bought in Hamburg.

1757 'Sonate für Klavicymbel oder Hammerklavier' by Johann Christoph Friedrich Bach: first German composition for the pianoforte.

1759 Philipp E. Bach, in his 'Versuch über die wahre Art, das Clavier zu spielen', mentions the pianoforte as being the equal of the clavichord.

1759 Weltmann, Paris, exhibits to the French Academy of Science his 'clavecin à maillet', a combination of pianoforte, harpsichord and a small organ fitted with a chime of bells.

1760 Arrival in London of Zumpe and eleven other German piano makers, mostly Silbermann's pupils. Commencement of square piano-building in England.

1760 Manuel Antunes builds the first pianoforte in Portugal.

1762 Oldest known square piano by Zumpe.

1766 Construction of first English pianoforte.

1767, 16th May. Announcement of a concert in London: 'At a concert in Covent Garden Theatre, for the accompaniment of songs Dibdin will use a new instrument called a Piano-Forte'.
First appearance in a concert hall of the pianoforte.

1767 Mention of pianoforte in Adlung's 'Musica Mechanica Organoedi'.

1768 Mlle Lechantre plays for the first time in Paris on 8th September at a 'concert spiritual', with little success, on a pianoforte.

1769 Pianoforte played for first time in Belgium, at Liège.

1770 Earliest French square piano in existence, by W. K. Mercken. Johann Matthäus Schmahl

in Ulm builds square pianos in shape of a harp with transposing keyboard.
Introduction of square piano in Sweden.
Clementi composes his three pianoforte sonatas, op. 2.

1771 Pianoforte manufacture begins in Russia.

1771 On 22nd April in Paris, Mlle Branche and Romain de Brasser perform for the first time the 'Ariettes choisies mises en sonates pour le Clavecin ou le Piano-Forté'; and for the second time the 'Trois sonates pour le Clavecin ou Forté-Piano'. After composing his C-minor Sonata No. 20 (Peters No. 18), Haydn now writes exclusively for the pianoforte.

1773 A pianoforte is used at a concert in New York.

1774 Josephus Merlin builds a grand pianoforte, a combination of pianoforte and harpsichord (Engl. Pat. No. 1081).

1775 John Brent (Johann Behrent) exhibits the first American square piano in Philadelphia.

1777 Stodart in London, builds the first 'Grand Piano', a combination of pianoforte and harpsichord (Engl. Pat. No. 1172).
Erard's first square piano.

1779/88 Importation of London pianos to Boston.

1780 Square piano popular all over Europe.

1783 Broadwood patents improved square piano. Old method of clavichord side-stringing becomes obsolete. Broadwood's first Grand Pianoforte.

1786 Pianoforte used for the first time in America, in a Philadelphia concert hall. First American composition for pianoforte: 'Sonata Piano Forte' by Reinagle.

1788 Oldest surviving Swedish square piano, by Peter Kraft of Stockholm.

1789 Oldest remaining Belgian square piano, by Winand. Southwell experiments with the idea of building a 'Pianino'.
Charles Albrecht builds square pianos in Philadelphia.
Oldest remaining American square piano.

1795 Stodart's bookcase-pianoforte patented, which is praised by Haydn.

1796 Erard's first grand piano.

1800 The first upright pianos: by Hawkins, Philadelphia, and Math. Müller, in Vienna.

1800 Through the work of Benjamin Crehore, Boston takes second place to Philadelphia as center of the early North American piano manufacture.

1804 Pyramid and Giraffe pianos, by Wachtl, Bleyer and Seuffert, in Vienna.

1807 Invention by Southwell of 'Cabinet-Piano' (Engl. Pat. No. 3029).

1811 The year of the earliest cottage-pianos: Southwell, Collard, Wornum.

1824 Lyre-piano: Schleip, Berlin. Gradual withdrawal of pyramid pianos.

1827 First Pianinos in France (Pleyel, Blanchet & Roller).

1830 ditto, in Switzerland (Flohr).

1831 ditto, in Belgium (Lichtenthal).

1835 ditto, in Germany. Growing importance of piano manufacture in North- and Middle Germany.

1850 onwards. Gradual withdrawal of square pianos and upright pianos in Europe.

1860 North America builds pianinos.

1880 End of the square piano in America.

D. CLAVIHARP AND 'TANGENTENFLÜGEL'

1. HARP PLAYED WITH KEYS

from 1665 to end of 19th century

This is a harp fitted with a keyboard, the strings being plucked mechanically.

I. CLAVIHARP (DIETZ MODEL)

in use from 1813–1890

DESIGNATION: German: Klavierharfe; English: harp played with keys; French: claviharpe.
SHAPE: pedestal shaped like a column, with S-shaped harp-neck; unprotected strings like a harp, Similar in shape to a Giraffe-piano.
KEYBOARD: on the long side.
STRINGING: material: bass, steel strings wrapped with copper wire; middle and treble registers: steel strings.
METHOD OF STRINGING: monochord.
ACTION: tone produced by little brass hooks.
STOPS: from two to four foot-pedals: bassoon, loud, flageolet, piano.

TABLE OF DATES

1637 Mersenne mentions 'une nouvelle forme d'épinette dont on verse en Italie'. (Reference to the claviharp?)

1655 First mention of the piano-harp in an inventory of the Archduke Siegmund Franz, of Innsbruck.

1681 Johann Kurtz in Calw, Württemberg, builds claviharps.

1781 Jean-Antoine Berger in Grenoble builds claviharps.

1798 William Southwell, London, invents 'a harp played with keys'.

1813 Claviharp by Johann Christian Dietz, Paris.

1813 Clavilyra built by John Bateman, London.

1830 c. Mussard in Lausanne builds claviharps.

1841 Euphonicon, by John Steward, London.

1890 Invention of 'Calderarpa', by Caldera and Racca, Italy.

1890 c. Christian Dietz III builds the last 'Klavierharfe' (claviharp).

1891 Piano-harp by Ignatz Lutz, Vienna.

2. WITH TANGENT ACTION

Tangent-pianos are an intermediate of clavichord and pianoforte, in which the tone is produced by wooden jacks thrown against the string. All those stringed keyboard instruments can be said to belong to the original form which are fitted with the tangent (hammer) action described by Heinrich Arnold in 1440 ('Quartus Modus forpicum'). See also under 'Hammer action'.

I. With Tangent Action

a) *rectangular in shape*

1. Heinrich Arnold's 'clavicordium qui sonaret ut dulce melos'.
2. Dulce Melos.

b) *harpsichord shape*

3. Heinrich Arnold's 'clavicymbalum'.
4. Tangentenflügel.

II. Tangentenflügel with Organ

5. Tangentenflügel fitted with organ mechanism.

1. HEINRICH ARNOLD'S 'CLAVICORDIUM QUI SONARET UT DULCE MELOS'
recorded in 1440

SHAPE: rectangular.
KEYBOARD: on the broad side of the case. Compass: three octaves.
INTERIOR: the strings, tuneable from the side, are fixed to wrest-pins on the wrestplank at the right, run parallel to the keyboard over two bridges to the hitch-pin block on the left.
STRINGING: single-strung, thirty-six strings.
ACTION: tangent action (Heinrich Arnold's 'Quartus Modus forpicum').

2. DULCE MELOS
from 1400 to about 1550

DESIGNATION: Latin: dulce melos; German: Hackbrett; English: dulcimer; French: tympanon, doucemelle, dulcemer; Italian: salterio tedesco.
SHAPE: rectangular.
KEYBOARD: on the broad side of the case.
INTERIOR: the strings, tuneable from the side, are fixed to wrest-pins on the wrestplank at the right, run parallel to the keyboard to the hitch-pin block at the left. The twelve semitones of an octave correspond to twelve pairs of strings, i.e. one pair to each tone. These are brought over four bridges halving the length of each string and lying between the different octaves. By this means on each pair of strings both the upper and the lower octave of each note is produced. For example, the three keys, c, c′, c″ play the same c′-pair of strings, the corresponding three c♯-keys play the c♯-pair of strings, and so on.
STRINGING: bichord.
ACTION: tangent hammer action.

TABLE OF DATES

1440 First description by Heinrich Arnold of Zwolle, of a dulcimer (Dulce Melos) with a keyboard.
1491 Jehan de Avranches plays before Charles VIII on a 'doulcemer'.[1]
1503 An inventory of furniture of Queen Isabelle the Catholic mentions a 'doulcemer'.[1]
1506 A 'doulce mère' is played before the Duke of Lothringen.

[1] *Pirro*, André, Les Clavecinistes, p. 14.

3. HEINRICH ARNOLD'S 'CLAVICYMBALUM'

harpsichord-shaped, tangent hammer action

1440

4. TANGENTENFLÜGEL BY SCHMAHL

1780–1810

SHAPE: like a grand piano.
KEYBOARD: one manual.
STRINGING: bichord.
ACTION: tangent action.
STOPS: hand stops, knee lever; loud, piano, pianissimo.

5. TANGENTENFLÜGEL COMBINED WITH ORGAN

end of 18th century

TABLE OF DATES

1440 First description, with a sketch, of tangent hammer action by Heinrich Arnold von Zwolle. Arnold bases his information on a book by a certain Baudecet, a harpist of Reims, who lived at the beginning of the 15th century.

1708 Cuisinié's 'Clavecin vielle' is played by little tangents, or 'maillets'.

1716 Marius, Paris, invents a tangent hammer action: 'Clavecins à maillets'. He constructs four models:
1) triple stringing: the hammer strikes the string like a clavichord-tangent.
2) triple stringing.
   a) down-striking.
   b) up-striking.
3) triple stringing: upright piano.
4) double stringing: pianoforte shape. Combination of harpsichord and pianoforte.

The models—engravings—were laid before the French Academy and patented. But these models were never manufactured and fourty-three years elapsed before the word 'pianoforte' occurs again in the records of the French Academy.

1739 Schröter of Dresden builds a model of tangent action with a spring jack.

1780 First manufacture of tangent action pianos by Späth and Schmahl in Regensburg.

1812 c. Tangent action obsolete.

PART IV

STRINGED KEYBOARD INSTRUMENTS

'GEIGENWERK'

Hans Hayden—Germany, Nürnberg

After an illustration in Praetorius Theatrum instrumentorum seu sciagraphia, Syntagma musicum, Vol. 2, supplement Wolfenbüttel 1620.

'GEIGENWERK'

Fray Raymundo Truchado—Spain 1625

SIGNATURE: on the inside, left: 'FRAY RAYMUNDO TRUCHADO INVENTOR 1625.'
SHAPE: the outside of the wing-shaped case is covered in crimson velvet. On the treble side is the former owner's coat of arms in silk and gold embroidery. The inside of the cover is ornamented with two oil-paintings; left: tritons abducting a nymph whom Cupid is piercing with an arrow; on the right: a park landscape with a palace in the background. The hinges, the lock and the handle still show signs of previous gilding. One can judge from the magnificence of this instrument that it must have been the property of some distinguished personality whose identity has unfortunately not been traced.
KEYBOARD: recessed. Its height from the floor is only 34 cm, so that the player could only use the instrument whilst sitting on the floor in the oriental manner. When one remembers the strong Moorish influences at work in Spain, this is not surprising. Compass E/C to c''' (four octaves). Short bass-octave.
INTERIOR: the 45 gutstrings in frontal position are fixed to pins on the wrestplank and run horizontally to the keyboard passing over four curved, disc-shaped bridges to hitch-pins on the treble side. The hitch-pin block follows the same curve as the bridges. Painted flowers and leaves adorn the soundboard and the rose is in carved wood.
STRINGING: single stringing.
ACTION: the tone is produced by four discs let into the soundboard, crossing it vertically and protruding about one third above its surface. These are set in motion by a turning-handle. The edges of these discs are covered with cloth. By revolving the first disc on the left the first nine strings are set in vibration; the second disc works strings number ten to twenty; the third disc, the strings twenty-one to thirty-two and the fourth disc corresponds to the last thirteen strings. A full circuit of the first disc corresponds to 2 1/2 circuits of the fourth, or treble-disc. By depressing the keys, movable metal pins fixed in a curved cross-rail between wrestplank and the rotating discs and connected to the keys, press the corresponding strings against the revolving discs and friction, like that of a violin bow, is caused.
IN BRUSSELS, Musée instrumental du Conservatoire Royal de Musique. Cat. No. 2485.

FRAY RAYMVNDO TRVCHADO:INVENTOR:1625

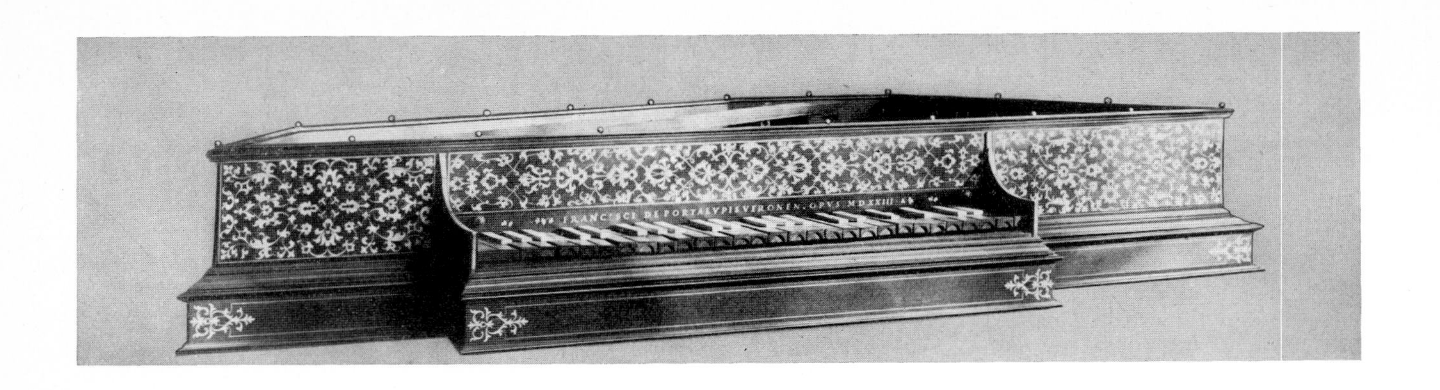
FRANCISCI DE PORTALVPIS VERONEN. OPVS MDXXIII

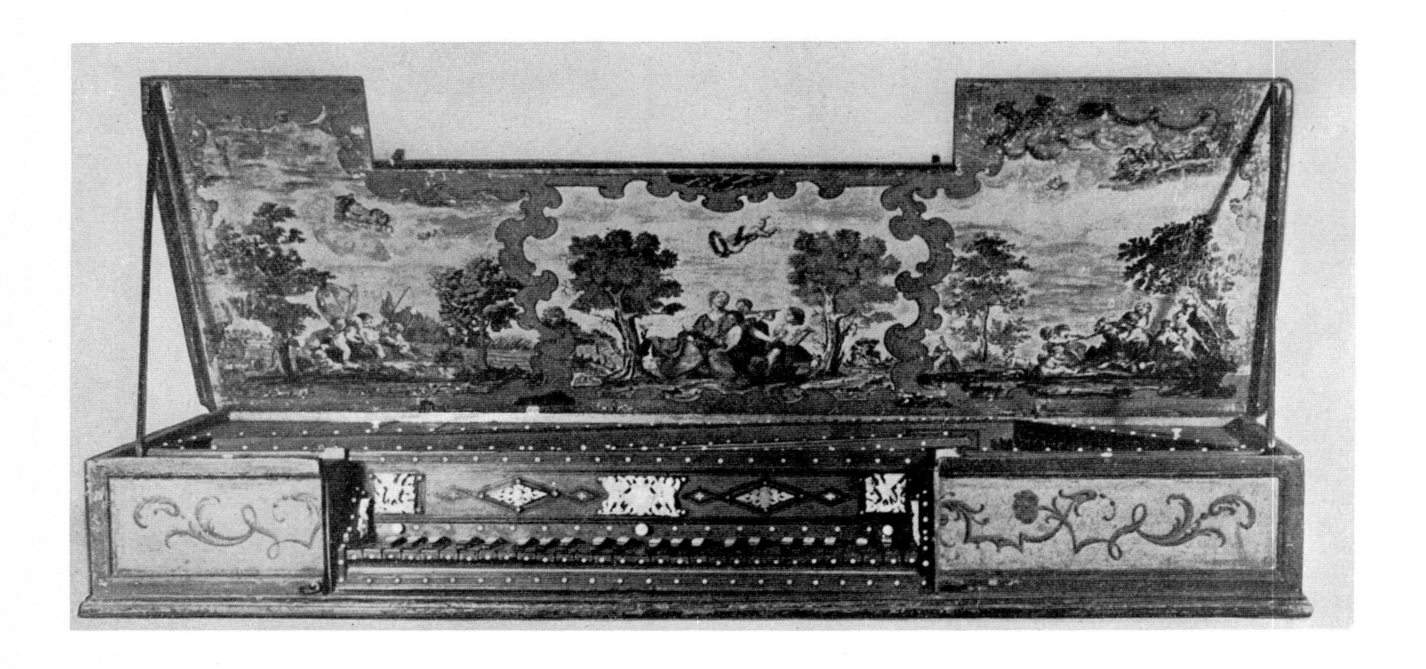

VIRGINAL

Franciscus de Portalupis—Italy, Verona 1523

SIGNATURE: on the nameboard: 'FRANCISCI DE PORTALUPIS VERON: OPUS MDXXIII.'
SHAPE: pentagonal case in ebony, the sides and nameboard elaborately inlaid with ivory. The top edge of the case is studded with little bone discs.
KEYBOARD: projected. Compass E/C to f''' (four octaves and a fourth). Short bass-octave. Black naturals, sharps covered with white bone.
INTERIOR: rose partly disfigured.
IN PARIS, Musée instrumental du Conservatoire National de Musique. Cat. No. 313.

This is the oldest spinet in existence.

VIRGINAL

Antonius Patavini—Italy, Padua 1550

SIGNATURE: 'ANTONI PATAVINI OPUS MDXXXXX.'
SHAPE: the instrument is contained in a rectangular case which makes it look like a virginal. This case was probably given to it in the 17th century at a time when the virginal was very popular. The lid of the case has been stuck over with painted paper depicting various scenes. The outer walls of the case are ornamented with delicately carved ivory figures, that in the center being the coat of arms of the Bembi family, a patrician Venetian family, the original owners of the instrument.
KEYBOARD: projected. Compass E/C to f''' (four octaves and a fourth). Short bass-octave. Boxwood naturals, sharps made of ebony with ivory ornaments.
INTERIOR: a Gothic rose on the soundboard.
MEASUREMENT: width 146 cm, depth 50 cm.
IN BRUSSELS, Musée instrumental du Conservatoire Royal de Musique. Cat. No. 272.

VIRGINAL

Marcus Jadra—Italy 1552

SHAPE: the top edge of the case and the cheekpieces ornamented with little bone studs.
KEYBOARD: projected. Compass E/C to f''' (four octaves and a fourth). Short bass-octave.
INTERIOR: a very beautiful rose over the soundhole of the soundboard.
AT OXFORD, Pitt Rivers Museum. Oxford University.

VIRGINAL

Domenicus Venetus—Italy, Venice 1566

Signature: on the nameboard: 'Domenicus Venetus 1566.'
Shape: the instrument is of irregular nonagonal shape set in an outer case which has designs in wood-inlay and metal mounts. The nameboard is inlaid with wood and burnt into it are black ornamental designs. In the center is a shield (two figures holding a coat of arms with the initials CB) and in Latin the words: 'Unicuiq(e) Probo Patet Praeclara Bentivoli Domus', in English: 'to every honest man the House of Bentivogli stands open.' This spinet was built for the Dukes Bentivoglio in Bologna, which is to be seen by the motto and their coat of arms: it stood in the Palace Bentivoglio in Bologna. On the inside of the cover is a valuable oil-painting of Apollo with the nine Muses in a colored framing of vignettes, fabulous animals, women's heads, ornaments, etc. The left-hand lower corner and right-hand upper corner of the case are filled in to form boxes, each with a lid. The instrument itself is of cypress-wood. The stand is modern, a copy of an old design.
Keyboard: recessed. Compass E/C to f''' (four octaves and a fourth). Short bass-octave. Naturals covered with boxwood, sharps black.
Interior: magnificent rose on the soundboard in delicate chased work.
Action: leather plectra.
Measurement: breadth 125 cm.
In Nürnberg, Rück Collection.

VIRGINAL

Johannes Antonius Baffo—Italy, Venice 1570

Signature: on the jackrail: 'Johannes Antonius Baffo Venetus mdlxx.'
Shape: the case, irregular pentagonal in shape is inlaid with a design of leaves in different colored woods, whilst the top edge, the jackrail and the cheekpieces are studded with little bone buttons. The stand is modern.
Keyboard: projected. Compass E/C to f''' (four octaves and a fourth). Naturals white, sharps black. Short bass-octave.
Measurement: breadth 162 cm.
In Paris, Musée de Cluny. Cat. No. 1112.

SPINET

Italy—17th century

UNSIGNED.
SHAPE: the case is decorated with charming paintings on a gold ground. The center of the nameboard is a beautiful medallion in engraved amber, the stand ornately carved and with coat of arms of the House of Orléans.
KEYBOARD: Compass C to c''' (four octaves). Inlaid keys.
IN PARIS, Musée instrumental du Conservatoire National de Musique. Cat. No. 321.

VIRGINAL

Annibale Dei Rossi—Italy, Milan 1577

SIGNATURE: on the nameboard: 'ANNIBALIS DE ROXIS MEDIOLANENSIS MDLXXVII.'
SHAPE: the case of this unique instrument is inlaid with ivory and with about 2000 precious stones: pearls, emeralds, rubies, sapphires, turquoise, amethysts, agates, garnets, etc. This extravagantly decorated instrument was built for a member of the well-known Milanese family Trivulzio, famous for their great collections of works of art.
KEYBOARD: elaborately decorated. Compass E/C to f''' (four octaves and a fourth). Short bass-octave. The faces of the naturals carved in half-moon design.
MEASUREMENT: length 4 ft 10 in., width 1 ft 10 in., depth 11 1/2 in.
IN LONDON, Victoria and Albert Museum. 809–1869.

This instrument was bought from a French private owner for the sum of £ 1200.

See colored frontispiece, p. V

VIRGINAL

Italy—17th century

UNSIGNED.
SHAPE: case in cedar-wood. The outside is ornamented with wonderfully fine carving of leaves.
KEYBOARD: projected. Compass E/C to f''' (four octaves and a fourth). Short bass-octave. The original keys have unfortunately not survived.
MEASUREMENT: length 150 cm.
IN BRUSSELS, Musée instrumental du Conservatoire Royal de Musique. Cat. No. 1579.

SPINET

Italy, Venice (first half of 18th century)

UNSIGNED.
SHAPE: this magnificent table-shaped instrument is completely covered with gilded and painted ornament in relief, on a yellow background. In sixteen panels are small landscapes, three of these paintings on the outside of the cover being on canvas, the rest painted directly on the instrument itself. Flower-paintings also decorate the inside of the lid (two vases, a basket of fruit and flowers).
KEYBOARD: Compass four and a half octaves. Short bass-octave. Yellow boxwood naturals, black sharps.
MEASUREMENT: length 162 cm, depth 54 cm.
IN COPENHAGEN, Claudius Collection. Cat. No. 60.

It is not unlikely that this lovely instrument is the work of Petrus Centamin, a Venetian spinet maker. It has a remarkable resemblance to a spinet of the year 1711 by Centamin in the Deutsches Museum in Munich (Inv. No. 9231).

VIRGINAL

Joes Karest aus Köln—Flemish, Antwerp 1548

SIGNATURE: signed on the nameboard: 'JOES KAREST DE COLONIA.'
SHAPE: the outer walls of the case are inscribed. 'LAUDATE DOMINUM IN CORDIS ET ORGANO, LAUDATE EUM IN SYMBALIS BENE SONANTIBUS.'
The date, 1548, is above in a kind of shield with three crowns arranged in a triangle.
KEYBOARD: the case is trapezoid in shape, the keyboard placed on the long side, parallel to the stringing. Compass E/C to c''' (four octaves). Short bass-octave.
INTERIOR: on the inside of the framework, in yellow lettering on a blue ground are the words: 'OMNIS SPIRITUS LAUDET DOMINUM IN CORDIS ET ORGANO.'
The soundboard has two soundholes, one circular, the other oblong, the short side of which is formed of two triangles.
MEASUREMENT: length 147 cm, depth 48 cm.
IN BRUSSELS, Musée instrumental du Conservatoire Royal de Musique. Cat. No. 1587.

The oldest existing Flemish spinet.

DOMI NVM
LAVDA
OES·KARES DECOLONIA
·CORDIS·ET·

MVSICA·DISPARIVM·DVLCIS·CONCORDIA·VOCVM
PELLO·LEVO·PLACO·TRISTIA·CORDA·DEOS
ORGANO
LAVDATE

VIRGINAL

Flemish 1568

UNSIGNED.
SHAPE: case in walnut with elaborately carved weapon trophies and groups of musical instruments. The lid which has a blue ground, is ornamented inside in the center with a medallion portraying a scene from the Orpheus Saga and with carved and gilded scrollwork and a Latin motto in gold lettering. On front lid and jackrail, similar gold lettering. The outside of the lid shows a bold, curved design with flower-motifs and an oval medallion in the center containing the coat of arms of Wilhelm, Duke of Cleven, Berg and Jülich (1516–1592). On the outer walls of the case are carved reliefs of an animal's head bearing in its mouth a metal ring with which to carry the instrument.
KEYBOARD: recessed. Compass four octaves. Short bass-octave, naturals of pale boxwood, black sharps.
MEASUREMENT: length 5 ft 7 in., width 2 ft 4 in., height 16 in.
IN LONDON, Victoria and Albert Museum. Cat. 447–1896.

VIRGINAL

Johannes Grauwels—Flemish, Antwerp (about 1580)

SIGNATURE: on the jackrail: 'JOHANNES GRAUWELS FECIT.'
SHAPE: the very beautiful painting on the inside of the lid is attributed to Peter Breughel the elder, and portrays a Flemish 'Kermess' Festival.
KEYBOARD: recessed. Compass: E/C to a'' (three octaves and a sixth). Short bass-octave.
INTERIOR: soundboard ornamented with paintings.
MEASUREMENT: length 153 cm, depth 45 cm.
IN BRUSSELS, Musée instrumental du Conservatoire Royal de Musique. Cat. No. 2929.

DVLCI SONVM REFICIT
TRISTA CORDA MEJOS

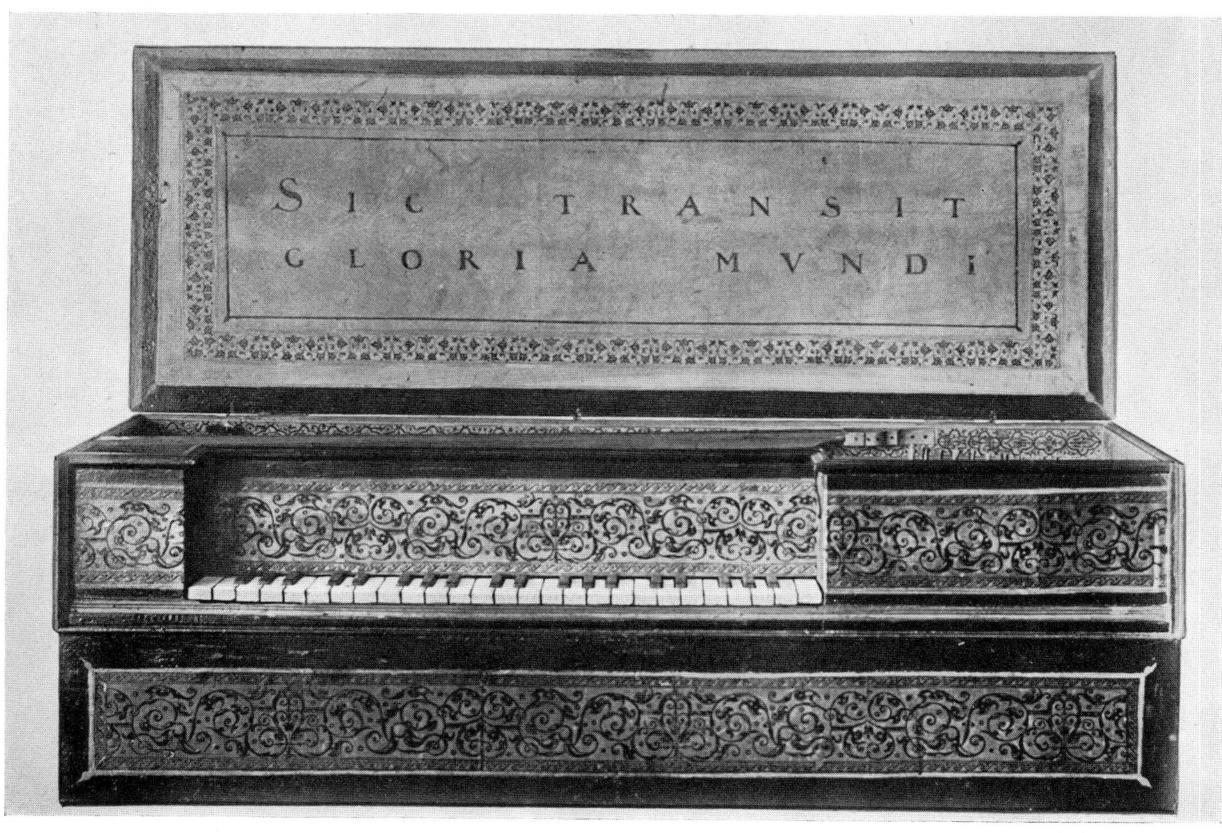
SIC TRANSIT
GLORIA MVNDI

VIRGINAL

Hans Ruckers—Flemish, Antwerp 1610

SIGNATURE: inscription on jackrail: 'HANS RUCKERS ME FECIT ANTVERPIAE 1610.'
SHAPE: square, pinewood case painted green. The lid and the keyboard cover which folds open, downwards, both hang from iron rings after the manner of those times. Inside of lid, nameboard, cheekpieces and the entire front are all decorated with the original parchment patterned with sea horses (Patin's invention in 1600). The inside of the lid bears the inscription: 'DULCI SONUM REFICIT TRISTA CORDA MEJOS.' The parchment covering of nameboard and cheekpieces is most ancient and valuable. The instrument has an arcaded and carved stand in antique style.
KEYBOARD: recessed. Compass not original C to f''' (four octaves and a fourth). Actual compass (short G-octave) G to c''''; the instrument is tuned one fifth above normal 'a'. Naturals covered in ebony, sharps in bone.
INTERIOR: the jackrail runs obliquely from left-front to the right at the back: it is deeply fluted on both sides and rests on beautifully shaped holders. The pinewood soundboard is ornamented with scattered flowers and has the well-known Ruckers' rose, original and untouched, of a kneeling angel playing a harp and the initials 'H.R.'
MEASUREMENT: length 135 cm, depth 50 cm, height with stand 92 cm.
AT HALLE AN DER SAALE, Museum in Händel's Birthplace.

VIRGINAL

Andreas Ruckers—Flemish, Antwerp 1620

SIGNATURE: inscription on the jackrail: 'ANDREAS RUCKERS ME FECIT ANTVERPIAE.'
SHAPE: the instrument bears the maker's number, 30. The rectangular case, the front which flaps downwards, the inside of the lid, nameboard and cheekpieces are all decorated with antique printed parchment. On the lid, inside, are the words: 'SIC TRANSIT GLORIA MUNDI.' The stand is of more recent date.
KEYBOARD: compass: E/C to c''' (four octaves), bass-octave short. White naturals, black sharps.
INTERIOR: a Ruckers' rose on soundboard with the initials 'A.R.'
IN WASHINGTON, Smithsonian Institution, United States National Museum, Cat. No. 303, 543.

VIRGINAL

Gabriel Townsend—England, 1641

SIGNATURE: 'Gabriell Townsend fecit 1641.'
SHAPE: the case is ornamented with embossed and gilded parchment appliqués showing the coat of arms of England and the letters ER (Elisabeth Regina). The painting inside the lid is a naïve representation of Orpheus with his lute amongst wild animals.
KEYBOARD: recessed. Compass: C to e''' (four octaves and a third).
INTERIOR: soundboard painted with flowers and birds. Rose made of chased and gilded parchment.
MEASUREMENT: length 176 cm, depth 54 cm, height 89 cm.
IN BRUSSELS, Musée instrumental du Conservatoire Royal de Musique. Cat. No. 1591.

Earliest surviving English virginal.

VIRGINAL

Adam Leversidge—England, London 1666

SIGNATURE: on the jackrail: 'Adamus Leuersidge Londini fecit 1666.'
SHAPE: this charmingly decorated instrument is in a case made of dark oak, on which the beautiful original hinges and lock are still preserved. Every part of the interior is also richly ornamented. Bands of embossed and gilded parchment frame the front and sides. Inside the lid is a painting of the 'Mall' in St. James's Park, London, with a distant view of Arlington House. In the background of the picture are to be seen groups of trees and a lake animated by little boats whilst the foreground is enlivened with figures of courtiers in colorful clothing, ruffles and feathered hats, the ladies in costumes of the 'Restoration period', all strolling in the shade of the trees. On the front lid, which flaps downwards, is another English landscape.
KEYBOARD: compass B/G to f''' (four octaves and a seventh). Short bass-octave.
INTERIOR: gilded jackrail. Soundboard ornamented with flowers. The lovely carved rose is entwined in a wreath of tulips.
MEASUREMENT: width 5 ft 6 1/4 in., depth 1 ft 8 1/2 in., height 3 ft (with stand).
AT HOLYOKE, The Belle Skinner Collection. Cat. No. 13.

According to inscription inside the nameboard the instrument was restored by Arnold Dolmetsch of Chickering & Sons, Boston.

OCTAVE VIRGINAL

Philippe Denis—France, Paris 1672

SIGNATURE: inscription on jackrail: 'PHILIPPE DENIS A PARIS 1672.'
SHAPE: the case of this lovely instrument is decorated in Chinese style with paintings in gold on a ground of black lacquer, also the nameboard.
KEYBOARD: compass B_1 to c''' (four octaves and one note). 4'-pitch. (Presumably short G-octave.) Black naturals, white sharps.
INTERIOR: soundboard and jackrail ornamented with painted flowers. Delicate rose.
IN PARIS, Musée instrumental du Conservatoire National de Musique. Cat. No. 322.

SPINET

France or Italy, 1731

UNSIGNED.
SHAPE: this rectangular spinet, probably of Italian origin, is said to have been renovated in France in the time of Louis XVI. The inside and outside of case are in dark blue lacquer, the latter painted with colored arabesques. The sides show baskets of flowers and arabesques with birds' and griffins' heads flanked by gilded flambeaux. On the front are garlanded flowers and Spanish lilac. Jackrail, nameboard and cheekpieces are also adorned with garlands and flowers-sprays framed in a gold line. On the top are painted musical emblems: lyre, viola and shawm surrounded with sprays of Spanish lilac in natural colors. Inside the cover is a Netherlands landscape: in the foreground a lake with sailing-boat and a scarlet-coated man standing on the shore. On the left are moss-covered rocks and a tall tree, in the middle distance, hills and meadows; and on the right are trees, bushes, and a ruined castle. The stand is of more recent date.
KEYBOARD: compass C to c''' (four octaves without C#). Ebony naturals, sharps covered with bone. The lowest and the highest key bear the date 1731.
INTERIOR: soundboard patterned with flowers; simple rose, deeply recessed.
MEASUREMENT: width 2 ft 11 in., depth 1 ft 5 5/8 in., height 2 ft 8 1/4 in. (with stand).
AT HOLYOKE, The Belle Skinner Collection. Cat. No. 16.

OCTAVE VIRGINAL

Aloysius Ventura—Italy, Venice 1533

SIGNATURE: inside edges of case inlaid with bone upon which is the following inscription: 'OPUS HOC FECIT ALOYSIUS VENTURA VENETIA QUI NOVATUR IN LOCO NUNCUPATO 1533.'
SHAPE: the case, rectangular in shape, is entirely covered with black leather and stands on four small, round knob-shaped feet. Inside of lid, nameboard, edge of medallion, inside lid and the case itself are all ornamented with little bone discs. The medallion, also of leather, has a painting of an angel with two doves.
KEYBOARD: compass b to c''' (three octaves and a second; 4'-pitch). Naturals covered with bone, key-faces carved; sharps stained brown, with inlay.
INTERIOR: pretty rose on soundboard.
ACTION: originally probably leather plectra, replaced by little pieces of bone.
MEASUREMENT: length 84 cm, depth 38.5 cm, height 13.5 cm.
AT THE HAGUE, Gemeente Museum. No. 1235.

OCTAVE VIRGINAL

Italy (16th century)

UNSIGNED.
SHAPE: triangular case without lid, with colored flower ornamentation on a pale blue ground.
KEYBOARD: projected. Compass E/C to c''' (four octaves). Short bass-octave. 4'-pitch.
INTERIOR: beautiful sunk rose on soundboard.
MEASUREMENT: length 2 ft 7 1/2 in., height 5 1/2 in.
IN LONDON, Horniman Museum.

ALOYSIUS VENTURA. VENETIA: QUI

OCTAVE VIRGINAL

Italy (end of 16th century)

SHAPE: the instrument is in a beautifully painted case. The painting on inside of cover represents a ship in full sail, sea-gods, dancers andmusical instruments. The painting is attributed to Federigo Zucchero, though without guarantee. On the nameboard are charming figures done in gilt etching.
KEYBOARD: compass E/C to c''' (four octaves). Short bass-octave. 4'-pitch. White naturals, black sharps.
STRINGING: one string for each note.
MEASUREMENT: length 2 ft 3 1/2 in., width 17 in.
IN LONDON, Victoria and Albert Museum. 218–1870.

OCTAVE VIRGINAL

Jacobus Bagninius—Italy, Lucca 1613

SIGNATURE: 'JACOBUS BAGNINIUS FECIT LUCENSIS ANNO 1613.'
SHAPE: the pentagonal instrument has a case whose outer walls are painted bright red with scrolled ornaments. A medallion on outside of lid represents Cupid, whilst the inside is a large sea-scape, and a coat of arms surrounded by scrolled ornamentation.
KEYBOARD: compass E/C to c''' (four octaves). 4'-pitch. Short bass-octave. Naturals of yellow-brown wood, sharps black.
INTERIOR: rose on soundboard.
MEASUREMENT: length of case 84 cm, depth 46 cm, height 20 cm.
IN COPENHAGEN, Claudius Collection. Cat. No. 54.

OCTAVE SPINET

Joseph Mae de Coninus (Italy?) 1707

SIGNATURE: 'Joseph Mae de Coninus MDCCVII.'
SHAPE: trapezoid in shape, of cedar-wood, in a painted case. Large painting inside of lid, on three square legs connected by a rail.
KEYBOARD: compass B_1 to c''' (four octaves and a second). 4'-pitch. Boxwood naturals, imitation ebony sharps.
INTERIOR: spruce soundboard with parchment rose.
MEASUREMENT: length 98 cm, depth 62 cm, height 98 cm.
IN MUNICH, Deutsches Museum. Inv. No. 19434.

OCTAVE VIRGINAL

Netherlands (17th century)

UNSIGNED.

SHAPE: rectangular case on four gilded knob-shaped feet. The whole is of pinewood, veneered and decorated throughout with inlay in many-colored woods: the inlay (plants, scrollwork, musical instruments, etc.), evidently derived from some piece of Italian furniture.

KEYBOARD: recessed. Compass E/C to a'' (without g♯, 3 octaves and a sixth). Short bass-octave. Bone naturals, ebony sharps with notches. 4'-pitch.

INTERIOR: pine soundboard with scattered ornaments: on the jackrail the inscription 'SIC TRANSIT GLORIA MUNDI' points to Dutch origin, yet the parchment rose appears to be Italian.

STRINGING: strings run towards front right-hand side.

ACTION: divided transposition—stops right and left of keyboard—moved the jacks to such a degree that they were lifted to the neighboring keys.

MEASUREMENT: length 104 cm, depth 39 cm, height 25 cm.

IN BERLIN, Institut für Musikforschung. Cat. No. 2217.

OCTAVE SPINET

France (beginning 18th century)

UNSIGNED.
SHAPE: the instrument stands high, like a little piano, on a Rococo stand. The whole is in poplar-wood with Chinese ornamentation in gilt on a red lacquer ground.
KEYBOARD: compass C to c''' without C# (four octaves). Ebony naturals, bone sharps: all the keys have been renovated, though retaining the original material. 4'-pitch.
INTERIOR: the soundboard is divided into three parts, occupying front, upper and back of raised centerpiece; some of the strings run across the whole width of the upper part, the bass-strings across another part, and in the third, the treble strings. The bridges are straight except for slight irregularities.
MEASUREMENT: length 83 cm, depth 33 cm, height 87 cm.
IN BERLIN, Institut für Musikforschung. Cat. No. 2213.

ENGLISH SPINET

Johannes Player—England (about 1680)

SIGNATURE: inscription on nameboard: 'JOHANNES PLAYER FECIT.'
SHAPE: wing-shaped harp. Case and stand of oak.
KEYBOARD: compass G_1 to c''' (four octaves and a fourth). Short bass-octave. Bottom two sharps split.
MEASUREMENT: length 4 ft 10 in., depth 6 1/2 in., width 1 ft 6 1/2 in.
IN LONDON, Victoria and Albert Museum. 466–1882.

ENGLISH SPINET

Joseph Mahoon—England, London 1747 (?)

SIGNATURE: inscription on nameboard: 'Joseph Mahoon, London.'
SHAPE: case in walnut, wing-shaped.
KEYBOARD: compass G_1 to g''' (five octaves). Black naturals, white sharps.
IN WASHINGTON, Smithsonian Institution. United States National Museum. Cat. No. 96,636.

ENGLISH SPINET

Baker Harris—England, London (about 1750)

SIGNATURE: inscription on nameboard: 'BAKER HARRIS FECIT.'
SHAPE: case harp-shaped with mahogany inlay, on a stand. Brass hinges on top of the lid.
KEYBOARD: compass E to g''' (four octaves and a third). Ivory-covered naturals with carved faces, ebony sharps.
INTERIOR: soundboard of spruce.
MEASUREMENT: length 56 cm, depth 112 cm, height 14.5 cm.
IN BOSTON, Museum of Fine Arts. Cat. No. 297.

BAKER HARRIS

Ioseph Maria Gozzini Opus Fecit Anno MDCCXXVI

SPINET

Johann Heinrich Silbermann—France, Strasbourg (middle of 18th century)

UNSIGNED.
SHAPE: the walnut case stands on four slender, curved legs which are fixed to the instrument. Panels form the lid, which has brass hinges. The instrument is remarkable for its exquisite finish and elegance.
KEYBOARD: compass F_1 to f‴ (five octaves). Black naturals, white sharps.
INTERIOR: spruce soundboard with beautiful parchment rose in the famous Silbermann motive, the three 'S's.
MEASUREMENT: breadth 65 cm, length 191 cm.
IN BASEL, Kirschgartenmuseum (Historisches Museum). Cat. No. 226.

SPINET

Joseph Maria Gozzini—? 1726

SIGNATURE: inscription on nameboard: 'Joseph Maria Gozzini Opus fecit Anno MDCCXXVI.'
SHAPE: this beautiful and unusual instrument is octagonal, a very strange shape for a spinet, and stands on eight legs. The lid and sides are colored red: in panels framed in gold are paintings of flower-bouquets. In the center of cover is a flap which when hinged back forms a music-stand.
KEYBOARD: compass E/C to c‴ (four octaves). Short bass-octave. Naturals in yellow wood, black sharps.
INTERIOR: rose on soundboard.
STRINGING: double stringing: 8′, 8′, which can be played either singly or together with coupler.
MEASUREMENT: length 152 cm, depth 72 1/2 cm, height 65 cm.
IN COPENHAGEN, Claudius Collection. Cat. No. 59.

SPINET

Gottfried Silbermann—Germany, Freiburg 1723

SIGNATURE: inscription written in ink on a paper label on left side of soundboard: 'G. Silbermann 1723.'
SHAPE: walnut case on three curved legs.
KEYBOARD: compass G_1 to f''' (four octaves and a seventh). Black naturals, white bone-covered sharps.
STRINGING: double stringing.
ACTION: a push stop to the right of player connects or disconnects the jack with the second string.
MEASUREMENT: length 67 cm, depth 175 cm, height 74 cm.
IN GÖTEBORG, Museum. Cat. No. 145.

OCTAVE SPINET

Israel Gellinger—Germany, Frankfurt am Main 1677

SIGNATURE: inscription on front edge of wrestplank: 'Israel Gellinger Frankfurt am Mayn 1677.'
SHAPE: cypress-wood pentagonal case in the shape of a lying harp.
KEYBOARD: two manuals. Compass of both: f to d''' (two octaves and a sixth, each). f# and g# are left out. Ivory-covered naturals, the key-faces having appliqué of embossed paper; sharps stained black. 4'-pitch.
INTERIOR: soundboard decorated with flowers. The rose formerly over the soundhole has disappeared.
ACTION: leather plectra.
MEASUREMENT: length 48 1/2 cm, depth 40 1/2 cm, height 12 1/2 cm.
IN LEIPZIG, Instrumentenmuseum der Universität. Heyer Cat. No. 52.

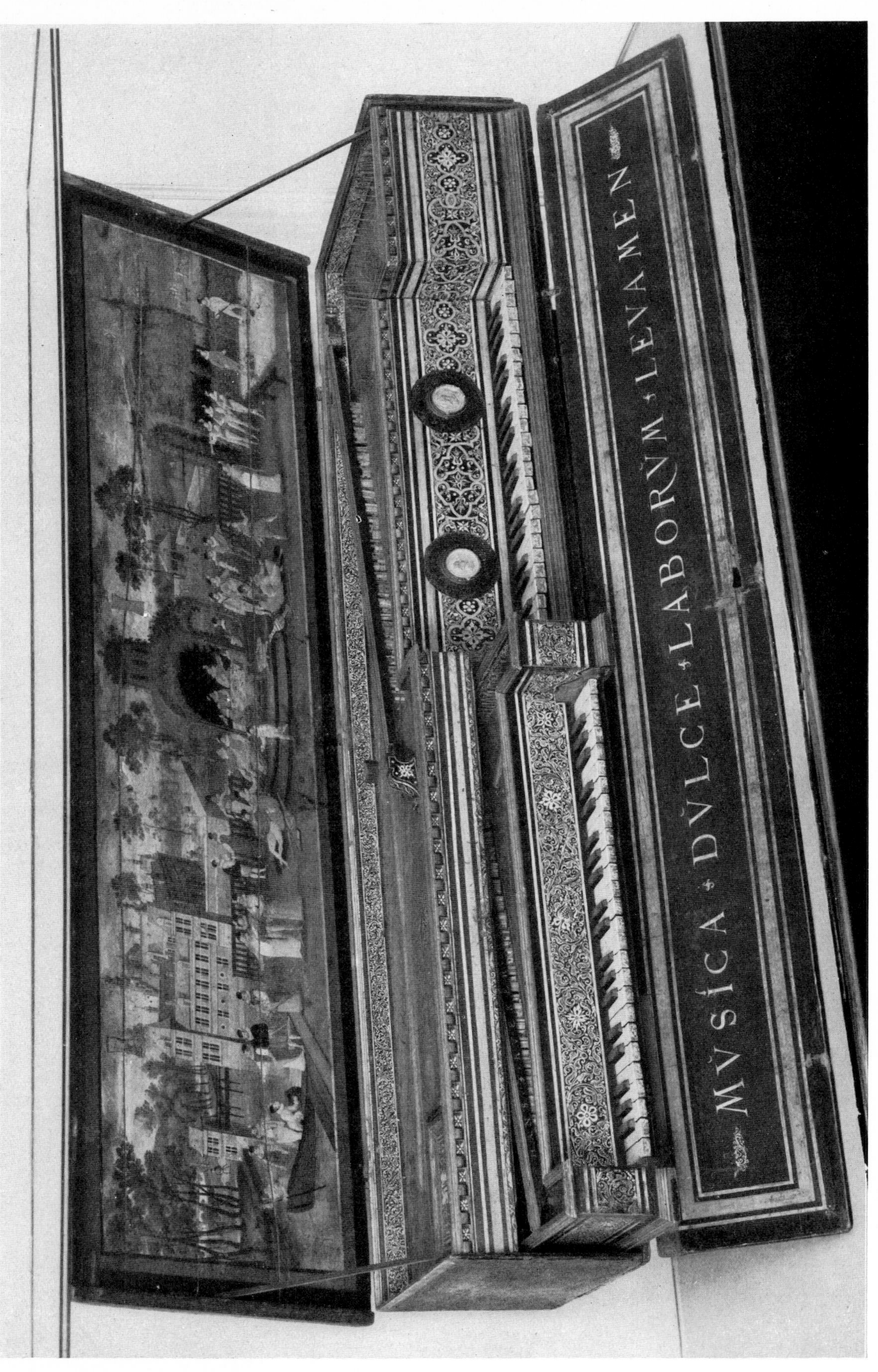
MVSICA DVLCE LABORVM LEVAMEN

DOUBLE VIRGINAL

Hans Ruckers—Flemisch, Antwerp 1581

SIGNATURE: 'HANS RUCKERS ME FECIT, 1581.'
SHAPE: oblong. Outside of case undecorated; painted on lid within, a fête champêtre of the 16th century. Over keyboard of larger instrument, plaster medallions of Philip II of Spain and his fourth wife, Doña Ana of Austria. On the front board: 'MUSICA DULCE LABORUM LEVAMEN.'
KEYBOARD: two keyboards side by side, the smaller octave instrument to the left removable: compass on both C to c''' (four octaves). Short bass-octave. Natural keys.
INTERIOR: on larger instrument H.R. rose, on smaller a geometrical rose. Soundboard painted with flowers.
IN NEW YORK, Metropolitan Museum of Art, Acc. No. 29.90 (see Grove's Dictionary, vol. 7, p. 305), London 1954.

DOUBLE KEYBOARD VIRGINAL

Hans Ruckers—Flemish, Antwerp 1610

SIGNATURE: inscription on nameboard: 'Hans Ruckers / me fecit Antverpiae / 1610.'
SHAPE: faded remains of green ornamentation on a gold ground still recognizable on outside of case. The raised and built-in octave virginal is of later date.
KEYBOARD: compass of lower manual C to f''' (four octaves and a fourth). Compass of upper manual identical. White naturals, black sharps.
INTERIOR: Ruckers' rose with the initials 'H.R.' on soundboard of both virginals.
STRINGING: spinet: single-strung, 8'; octave spinet: single-strung, 4'-pitch.
MEASUREMENT: length 172 cm, depth 48 cm.
IN BRUSSELS, Musée instrumental du Conservatoire Royal de Musique. Cat. No. 275.

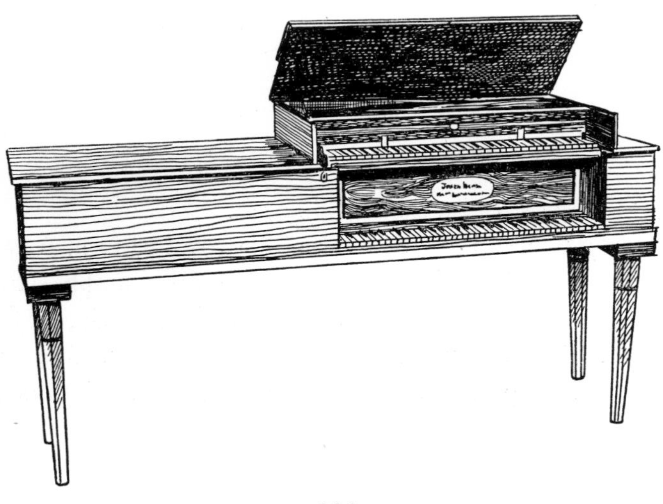

DOUBLE KEYBOARD SPINET

Italy (first half of 18th century)

UNSIGNED.
SHAPE: case pentagonal, wing-shaped, is colored a yellow brown with bronzed painted edges. The nameboard and upper edge of case are painted (modern) with bronze-colored leaf ornamentation.
KEYBOARD: two manuals. Compass of upper manual G_1, C to c‴ (one fourth below lower C, and four octaves).
Compass of lower manual G, c to c⁗. Split keys: D♯ on both manuals. Naturals covered with dark stained cedar-wood, the key-faces decorated with embossed paper, ivory sharps.
INTERIOR: jackrail ornamented with bronze-colored leaves.
STRINGING: triple stringing 8′, 8′, 4′. Upper manual 8′, 8′; lower manual 4′.
ACTION: leather plectra. There are no dampers.
MEASUREMENT: length 91 cm, depth 110 cm, height 91 cm.
IN LEIPZIG, Instrumentenmuseum der Universität. Heyer Cat. No. 56.

DOUBLE VIRGINAL

Ludovic Grovvelus—Flemish (about 1600)

SIGNATURE: the initials 'L. G.' in the roses on the soundboards.
SHAPE: case rectangular, richly gilded and ornamented with a scroll pattern. A well-preserved painting inside the cover represents David's battle with Goliath and David's triumph. The front bears the inscription: 'SCIENCIA NON HABET INIMICUM NISI IGNORANTEM.' Inscribed on the similar front of the octave virginal built to the right of player are the following words: 'ARS USU JUVANDI.' The original virginal—which is made to pull out—was damaged; the present one is a reconstruction on the model of the larger instrument by Arnold Dolmetsch.

ARS·VSV·IVVANDA
SCIENCIA·NON HABET·

SALTATVR
ME
CANENTE

KEYBOARD: compass of spinet G_1 to c''' (four octaves and a fourth). Short bass-octave. Compass of virginal C to c''' (four octaves). Ivory naturals, black sharps with fine inlay.
INTERIOR: soundboards of both instruments decorated with painted flowers and fruit. In each soundboard is a rose representing Pan playing the flute and the initials 'L. G.'
ACTION: quill plectra.
MEASUREMENT: length 6 ft 3 in., width 1 ft 8 in.
IN NEW YORK, Metropolitan Museum of Art. Cat. No. 1196.

Double spinets are very rare. Two other such instruments are in Nürnberg, Germanisches Museum (Martin van der Biest, 1580), and at Holyoke, The Belle Skinner Collection (H. Ruckers, 1591).

PEDAL SPINET

France or Italy (16th century)

UNSIGNED.
SHAPE: the instrument is in a case whose outside walls and inside of lid are painted brown-gold. The crimson panels are green and gold-bordered with flower arabesques of gold and darker green. The top of lid still retains original hinges. An irregularly shaped panel encloses two charming young figures holding a coat of arms surrounded by a scroll design of flowers. Painted on inside of cover are two angels with golden wings: one is in crimson, the other in golden-brown garments on a dark blue ground. Between the figures is a tree entwined with a scrolled motto: 'SALTATUR ME CANENTE.'
KEYBOARD: recessed compass E/C to c''' (four octaves). Short bass-octave. Naturals of boxwood with carved key-faces, sharps of reddish brown beech-wood. The nine lowest keys were originally connected to pedal-boards: the nine holes are still to be seen in the bottom of the case, six under the naturals and three under the sharps. On each side of the keyboard is a small box with lid.
INTERIOR: soundboard ornamented with flowers (roses and marguerites) and has a very beautiful Gothic rose in parchment.
MEASUREMENT: width 3 ft $2^{1}/_{2}$ in., depth 1 ft 4 in., height 6 in., height of stand 2 ft 4 in.
AT HOLYOKE, The Belle Skinner Collection. Cat. No. 15.

According to inscription behind nameboard this instrument was restored in 1921 by N. Masson, in Paris.

PEDAL SPINET

Italy, Florence (16th century)

UNSIGNED.
SHAPE: the instrument itself is pentagonal in shape, made of cedar-wood and enclosed in a square outer case painted dark brown, the stand of which, of recent date, is of boxwood. On removing the brown coloring the inside of the lid revealed an old painting of a beautiful young woman in pearls in a purple dress, her hair in long curls, playing on a small organ. On each side of the portrait are irregular dark brown panels with arabesques in reddish yellow and crimson. The little nameboard above the keys still shows traces of several different dates and inscriptions in Italian which have become illegible.
KEYBOARD: projected. Compass E/C to f‴ (four octaves and a fourth). Short bass-octave. Black sharps, naturals of boxwood with carved key-facings. Holes bored in the bottom of key-bed under the fourteen lowest keys and in corresponding position in outer case denote the original presence of pedal-boards for the bass notes.
INTERIOR: the cedar-wood soundboard possesses an unusually beautiful rose of the Irish knot pattern.
MEASUREMENT: extreme width 5 ft 7 in., depth 1 ft 8 1/2 in., extreme height 2 ft 9 in.
AT HOLYOKE, The Belle Skinner Collection. Cat. No. 14.

This beautiful instrument has a mellow, resonant tone.

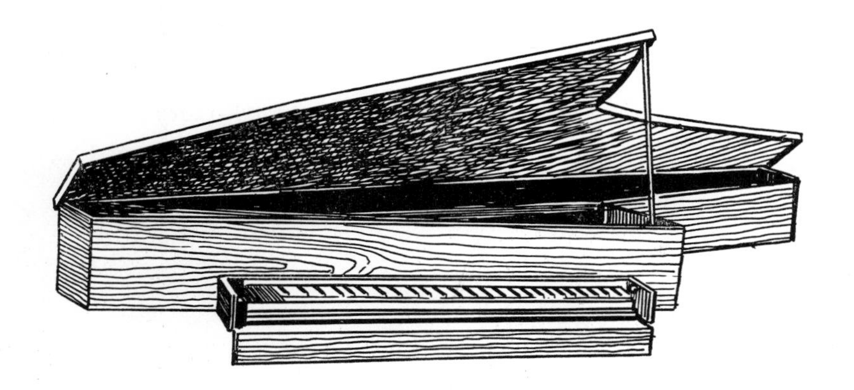

DOUBLE STRING PEDAL SPINET

(Bartolomeo Cristofori)—Italy, Florence (about 1725)

UNSIGNED.
SHAPE: the plain, undecorated case of irregular hexagonal form is on a plain stand with six legs connected by a rail. The dark brown coloring is modern.
KEYBOARD: projected. Compass F_1 to f‴ (five octaves). F♯ and G♯ nonexistent. Boxwood naturals, sharps with ebony covering. Below the keys of lowest octave, the floor of case is bored with holes for connecting with pedal-boards.
INTERIOR: charming rose on soundboard composed of seven smaller roses set together.
STRINGING: double stringing 8′, 4′.
ACTION: by pulling out the keyboard, using the two levers at the side of the keys, the 4′ jacks are disconnected. The 8′ jacks are similarly disconnected by pushing in the levers. Leather plectra are used.
MEASUREMENT: length 80 cm, depth 246 cm, height 92 cm.
IN LEIPZIG, Instrumentenmuseum der Universität. Heyer Cat. No. 86.

Bartolomeo Cristofori

1655–1731

after the original picture now in Charlottenburg

PAINTED LID

Dance of Apollo with the Muses, by Giulio Romano (1492–1546) Florence, Uffizi

HARPSICHORD

Hieronymus da Bologna—Italy, Rome 1521

SIGNATURE: 'Hieronymus Bononiensis faciebat Romae MDXXI.'
SHAPE: the instrument rests in an outer case, the outside walls of which are covered with gold embossed leather and the inside with green velvet. It bears the following inscription: 'Aspicite ut trahitur suavi modulamine vocis / Quicquid habent aer sider a terra fretum.'
KEYBOARD: compass E/(C) to d''' (four octaves and a second). Originally probably short bass-octave. The light-colored naturals in boxwood have arcaded fronts.
STRINGING: double stringing 8', 8'.
STOPS: none.
MEASUREMENT: width 2 ft 7 1/2 in., length 6 ft 3 in.
IN LONDON, Victoria and Albert Museum. Cat. No. 226–1879.

Earliest surviving dated harpsichord.

ΚΑΛΛΙΟΠΗ
ΚΛΕΩ ΕΡΑΤΩ
ΜΕΛΠΟΜΕΝΗ ΤΕΡΨΙΧΟΡΗ
ΠΟΛΥΜΝΙΑ ΕΥΤΕΡΠΕΙ
ΘΑΛΕΙΑ ΟΥΡΑΝΙΑ

HARPSICHORD

Dominicus Pisaurensis—Italy, Venice 1553

SIGNATURE: inscription on nameboard: 'DOMINICUS PISAUR[ENS]IS/A. MDLIII.'
SHAPE: the case in which the instrument itself rests is of about 100 years more recent date. The painting inside the lid represents Comedy, Tragedy, Music and Poetry. The walls of the instrument are of cedar-wood ornately carved. Nameboard and jackrail decorated with arabesques.
KEYBOARD: compass E/C to d''' (four octaves and a second). Short bass-octave.
STRINGING: double stringing.
STOPS: two hand stops, to connect and disconnect the jacks.
IN PARIS, Musée instrumental du Conservatoire National de Musique. Cesbr. Cat. No. 109.

HARPSICHORD

Johannes Antonio Baffo—Italy, Venice 1574

SIGNATURE: inscription on nameboard: 'JOHANNES ANTONIUS BAFFO VENETUS MDLXXIIII.'
SHAPE: the instrument rests in an ornately decorated outer case, painted with garlands of flowers. On the treble side are the protective outer rails so typical of Italian instruments. The inside of lid is covered in Renaissance ornamentation and a representation of Apollo with the Muses. The side walls of the instrument itself are decorated with a running inlay pattern and with gilded arabesques: on the jackrail and round all the outer edges are little ivory buttons.
KEYBOARD: compass C to f''' (four octaves and a fourth). Short bass-octave.
STRINGING: double stringing: 8', 8'.
ACTION: leather plectra.
STOPS: none.
MEASUREMENT: length 7 ft 4 in., width 3 ft, depth 9 1/2 in.
IN LONDON, Victoria and Albert Museum. 6007–1859.

HARPSICHORDS

Johannes Celestini—Italy, Venice 1596

SIGNATURE: inscription on nameboard: 'JOHANNIS CELESTINI VENETI MDXCVI.'
KEYBOARD: compass E/C to f''' (four octaves and a fourth). Short bass-octave.
STRINGING: double stringing 8', 8'.
STOPS: two side stops.
IN TORONTO, Royal Ontario Museum. T. 127.

Johannes Celestini—Italy, Venice 1608 (on p. 220)

SHAPE: this instrument is in an ornately decorated outer case. On the inside of the two-piece lid are beautiful paintings. Baroque stand, date about 1700.
MEASUREMENT: depth 180 cm, height 18 cm (without stand).
IN HAMBURG, Museum für Kunst und Gewerbe. Inv. No. 1704–711.

Vincentius Pratensis—Italy (Prato?) 1612 (on p. 221)

SIGNATURE: on the back of nameboard: 'VINCENTIUS PRATENSIS 1612.'
SHAPE: the case of this beautiful instrument—which formerly rested in an outer case no longer in existence—is of cypress-wood. The inside edge, jackrail, nameboard and cheekpieces are charmingly decorated with painting in gold (Renaissance ornamentation, birds, butterflies, etc.). In the center of nameboard is a coat of arms depicting a pawing lion, facing left. A beautifully carved horn of plenty adorns the cheekpieces.
KEYBOARD: compass E/C to c''' (four octaves). Short bass-octave. Boxwood naturals, sharps stained black.
INTERIOR: delicate rose.
STRINGING: double-strung 8', 8'.
ACTION: leather plectra.
STOPS: none.
MEASUREMENT: length 69 cm, depth 187 cm, height 19 1/2 cm (without stand).
IN LEIPZIG, Instrumentenmuseum der Universität. Heyer Cat. No. 69.

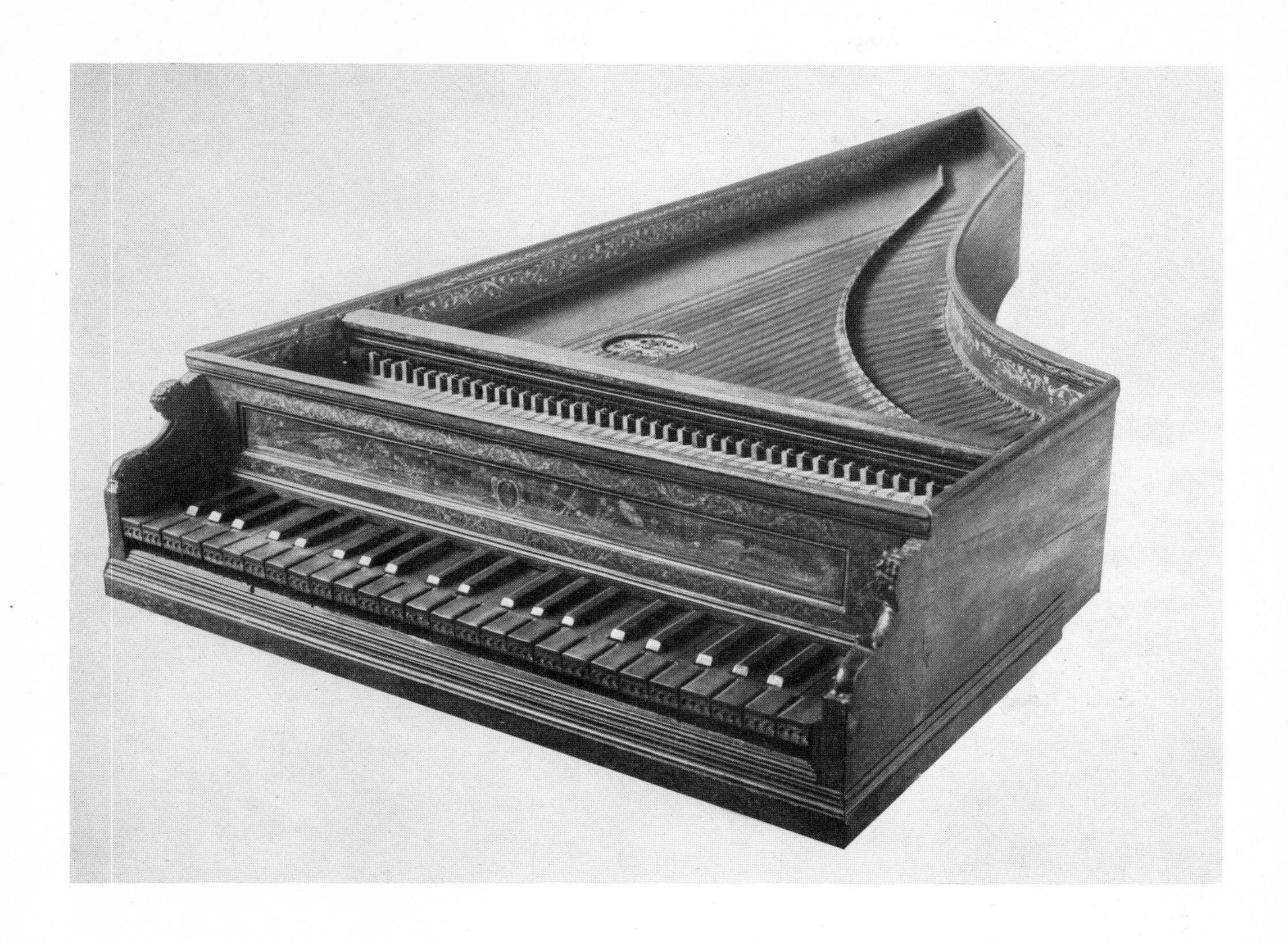

HARPSICHORD

Faby—Italy, Bologna 1677

SIGNATURE: inscription in inlaid ivory behind the nameboard, to the right of player: 'FABY BONONIENSIS OPUS'; to player's right: 'ANNO DOMINI MDCLXXVII.'

SHAPE: the outer case of this instrument is painted blue with white ornamentation, the inside of the lid with a beautiful landscape. The case of the instrument itself is of cedar-wood ornamented with magnificent inlay of finely carved ivory sculpture on ebony. Jackrail and nameboard are similarly decorated, the latter bearing a coat of arms of Hercule Pepoli, a godson of Louis XV.

KEYBOARD: compass E/C to d''' (four octaves and a second). Short bass-octave with split sharps: $\frac{F\sharp}{D}$ and $\frac{G\sharp}{E}$. Naturals with carved key-faces. Both naturals and sharps are ornamented with inlay.

INTERIOR: beautiful rose on soundboard.

STRINGING: double-strung.

ACTION: two rows of jacks.

IN PARIS, Musée instrumental du Conservatoire National de Musique. Cat. No. 328.

HARPSICHORD (Cembalone)

Giovanni Ferrini—Italy, Florence 1699

SIGNATURE: 'Giovanni Ferrini Florentinus fecit anno Domini 1699.'
SHAPE: the outer case stands on five thick, rounded legs and, except for the straight side against the wall, is decorated with colored grotesques on a white ground, mythological scenes, landscapes, figures and medallions. On the outside of lid (center), held by four putten figures is a crowned coat of arms showing three hunting horns: inside of lid a large painting depicting a scene from the Triumph of Scipio.
KEYBOARD: compass four octaves. Bone-covered naturals, black sharps.
STRINGING: double stringing 8′, 16′.
ACTION: two rows of jacks; leather plectra.
MEASUREMENT: length 87.5 cm, depth 242.5 cm, height 102 cm.
IN STUTTGART, Landesmuseum. Inv. No. 7816.

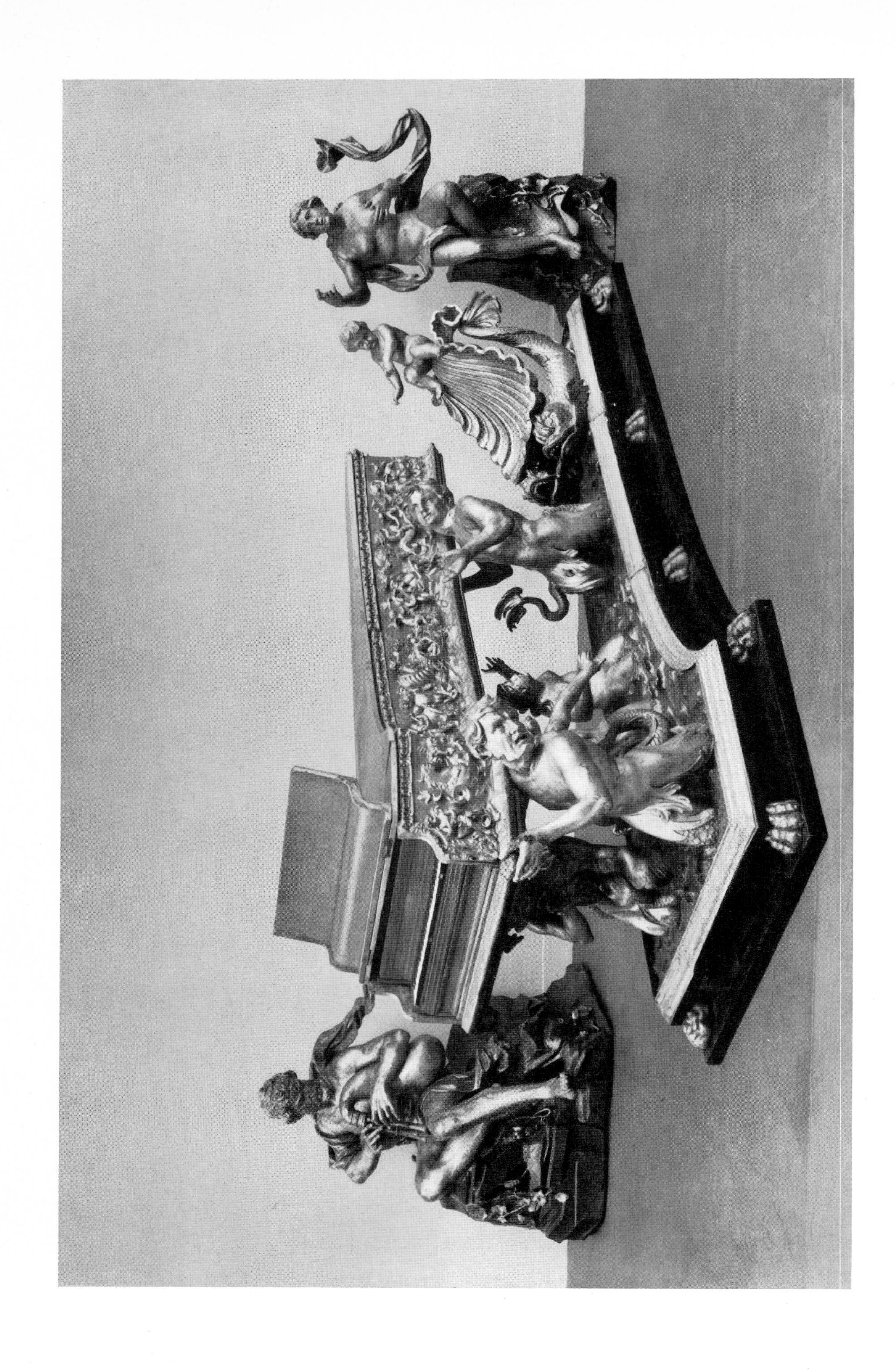

HARPSICHORD

Italy—at the turn of 17th/18th century

UNSIGNED.
SHAPE: the over-ornately decorated lid is covered with carving showing Neptune in his chariot surrounded by attendants. The stand, on ten claw-feet, consists of a platform on which is a group of large sculptured figures, sea nymphs and satyrs, of whom two carry the instrument on upraised arms. To the right, two dolphins bear a shell upon which sits a child. To the left by the keyboard sits a satyr playing the pipes and further beyond, the figure of a mermaid. The whole is richly gilded.
KEYBOARD: compass F_1 to f''' (five octaves). F♯ is missing. Ivory naturals, black sharps.
INTERIOR: the soundboard has a sunken rose.
MEASUREMENT: length 8 ft 9 in., width 2 ft 9 in.
IN NEW YORK, Metropolitan Museum of Art. Cat. No. 2929.

HARPSICHORD

Italy—Venice—Baroque style

UNSIGNED.

SHAPE: the outer case of this instrument is magnificently decorated, divided into sections each with a finely finished painting in the French style: cupids playing different musical instruments. The top surface of lid has a beautiful painting of a young couple surrounded by maidens in a lake-shore garden. On the inside of lid the painting is from the Orpheus Saga. The instrument is borne by two carved, gilded putten figures. The base platform bears a pair of love-birds, a lyre with Thyrsus wand and a pair of cymbals. The unusual height of the keyboard above the ground presupposes the instrument having been played standing.

KEYBOARD: compass four octaves. Naturals of yellow wood, black sharps.

INTERIOR: parchment rose on soundboard.

STRINGING: double-strung.

ACTION: two rows of jacks.

MEASUREMENT: length 74 cm, depth 186 cm, height 105 cm.

IN COPENHAGEN, Claudius Collection. Cat. No. 62.

A most unusual and magnificently finished instrument.

PAINTED LID

Italy, Venice—Baroque style

COPENHAGEN, Claudius Collection, Cat. No. 62.

HARPSICHORD

Italian, mid-17th century

UNSIGNED: the maker of the instrument is unknown.
SHAPE: this harpsichord is of typical Italian make, with the instrument itself removable from an outer case. Its exquisite decoration surpasses the regular instruments. The body rests on three gilded columns; between the front columns is a mermaid holding one of them—the device of the Colonna family. The case is painted in sepia with beautiful flora scrolls in the free-flowing, majestic forms of the High-Baroque.
On the inside of the lid are two landscapes with figures in tempera. The front section shows, in an opulent setting of trees, Tobias and the Angel; the larger section shows an equally lush landscape with a duck hunter. The conventionalized foliage and the aerial perspective have the flavor of the work of Gaspard Dughet, Poussin's brother-in-law, who painted chiefly in Rome.
The instrument is in a miraculous state of preservation, as if it had been made only yesterday.
KEYBOARD: compass A_1 to c'''. Ivory naturals, ebony sharps, the ebony ones having an inset strip of ivory. At each end of the keyboard there is a satyr of carved wood.
STRINGING: three sets of strings: 4′, 8′, 8′.
MEASUREMENT: length 242 cm, width 90 cm, depth 31 cm.
IN NEW YORK, Metropolitan Museum of Art, No. 4541.

For the above details, I am indebted to kind information from Mr. Emanuel Winternitz, Curator of Musical Instruments. See also Winternitz, Emanuel: Musical Instruments of the Western World, London 1966.

HARPSICHORD

Italy (middle of 18th century)

SIGNATURE: (doubtful?): 'DOMINICUS PISAURENSIS.'
SHAPE: the unusually beautiful Rococo case is painted red. Lid and sides are divided into ten sections framed in embossed gold each containing a charming flower painting. On the long side the three sections, or panels, are similarly ornamented, except that the gold framing is not embossed. Stand decorated in the same style. Inside the lid, besides flowers there are also two landscapes painted on canvas. The instrument stands on five legs.
KEYBOARD: compass four octaves. Short bass-octave. Yellow wood naturals, black sharps.
INTERIOR: beautiful rose over soundhole.
STRINGING: double-strung.
ACTION: two rows of jacks.
MEASUREMENT: length 75 cm, depth 198 cm, height 99 cm.
IN COPENHAGEN, Claudius Collection. Cat. No. 63.

HARPSICHORD

(Dominicus Pisaurensis?)—Italy (middle of 18th century)

In Copenhagen, Claudius Collection. Cat. No. 63.

HARPSICHORD

Bartolomeo Cristofori—Italy, Florence 1726

Signature: inscription on nameboard: 'Bartholomaeus de Christophoris Patavinus faciebat Florentiae M.DCC.XXVI.'
Shape: case made of cypress-wood.
Keyboard: compass C to c''' (four octaves). Boxwood naturals, ebony covered sharps.
Stringing: triple-strung 4', 8', 16'.
Action: quill plectra.
Stops: two stops, one on each side above the keyboard, connect and disconnect the jacks with the strings.
Measurement: length 94 cm, depth 257 cm, height 108 cm.
In Leipzig, Instrumentenmuseum der Universität. Heyer Cat. No. 85.

In the Heyer Catalogue the illustration of the instrument is described as follows: "This instrument stands in a bright red lacquered outer case, the edges of which are gilded and decorated in Rococo style with pretty gilt paintings of Chinese subjects. The inside is pale blue. The outer case stands on there pillar-shaped legs, richly carved and painted, the two front legs connected by a piece of gilt carving."

CHRISTOPHORIS PATAVINUS FACIEBAT FLORENTIAE M.DCCXXVI

HARPSICHORD

Italy (middle of 18th century)

UNSIGNED.
SHAPE: gorgeous outer case in Rococo style. Heavily carved stand with three Putto figures playing musical instruments upon the rail connecting the legs of the stand. Inside lid: a painting of figures playing games in the open air.
KEYBOARD: compass C to c‴ (four octaves). Short bass-octave.
INTERIOR: cypress-wood soundboard: parchment rose.
STRINGING: double stringing 8′, 8′.
MEASUREMENT: length 77 cm, depth 184 cm, height 26 cm, with stand 88 cm.
IN BAMBERG, Neupert Collection. Cat. No. 54.

HARPSICHORD

Italy (end of 18th century)

UNSIGNED.
SHAPE: the outer case of this instrument stands on five legs of classical shape. The general coloring is off-white with gold ornamentation. Landscape painted inside the lid. The inner case of the instrument itself is of cypress-wood decorated with inlay in ivory and ebony.
KEYBOARD: compass G_1 to f''' (four octaves and a seventh). Ebony keys with ivory inlay.
INTERIOR: elaborately carved rose in soundboard.
STRINGING: triple-strung 8′, 8′, 4′.
ACTION: leather plectra. 'Laute' stop.
MEASUREMENT: length 100 cm, depth 252 cm, height 94 cm.
IN HAMBURG, Museum für Hamburgische Geschichte. Inv. No. 1925, 115.

HARPSICHORD

Italy (about 1700)

SIGNATURE: the inscription on the nameboard is a modern *forged* signature written in ink: 'Johannes Antonio Baffo, Venetus. MDLXXXI.'
SHAPE: case white, with painted Baroque ornaments in red. Italian landscape on inside of lid. Three feet, in Baroque style. In front, on the locked cover of keyboard, is a coat of arms; a little tree with few leaves crossed by a rainbow.
KEYBOARD: compass G_1 to c''' (four octaves and a fourth). The lowest semitone—G♯—is missing. Yellow naturals, black sharps.
INTERIOR: soundboard of spruce.
STRINGING: double-strung 8′, 8′.
ACTION: leather plectra.
MEASUREMENT: length 95 cm, depth 250 cm.
IN BASEL, Historisches Museum. Cat. No. 221.

TRIPLE MANUAL HARPSICHORD

(Bartolomeo Cristofori?)—Italy, Florence 1703

SIGNATURE: on the nameboard (doubtful): 'Bartholomaeo Christofori Patavinus fecit Florentiae 1703.'
SHAPE: case standing on five carved, gilded legs, the case itself plentifully ornamented with Renaissance grotesques on a white ground. On the front lid, the coat of arms of the Medici: the top lid having a painting representing the triumphant progress of the Medici.
KEYBOARD: three manuals. Compass of each F_I to f''' (five octaves).
STRINGING: triple stringing 8', 8', 4'. The lower manual 8', 8'; middle manual 8', 4'; for the upper manual 4'.
MEASUREMENT: length 96 cm, depth 228 cm, height 68 cm.
IN BAMBERG, Neupert Collection. Cat. No. 122.

MVSICA · MAGNORVM

HARPSICHORD

Hans Ruckers the Elder—Flemish, Antwerp 1573

SIGNATURE: inscription on jackrail: 'HANS RUCKERS ME FECIT ANTVERPIAE, 1573.'
SHAPE: ivory-colored case in spruce. A painting adorns the inside of lid. Gilt and blue painted nameboard bearing the motto: 'MUSICA MAGNORUM SOLAMEN DULCE LABORUM.' Five curved, square legs.
KEYBOARD: compass C to c''' (four octaves). C# missing. Ebony naturals, ivory sharps.
INTERIOR: pinewood soundboard decorated with scattered flowers. Ruckers' rose with the initials 'H.R.'
STRINGING: triple stringing 8', 8', 4'.
ACTION: three rows of jacks. Raven quills.
STOPS: three side stops.
MEASUREMENT: length 89 cm, depth 182 cm, height 99 cm.
IN MUNICH, Deutsches Museum. Inv. No. 37587.

DOUBLE MANUAL HARPSICHORD

Hans Ruckers the Elder—Flemish, Antwerp 1599

SIGNATURE: inscriptions on jackrail and on a rail screwed to the nameboard, each in black Indian ink on a gold ground: 'HANS RUCKERS ME FECIT ANTVERPIAE ANNO 1599.'
SHAPE: the whole right side of the originally beige-colored case of pinewood is decorated with bronzed ornaments in relief, made of some other wood (two birds, latticework with climbing vines). These being in the reticent, almost classical late-Rococo style, have been added in the 18th century. Similar ornaments (vines, in separate panels framed in gold) are found on the lower part of the stand, spreading to the upper, thicker part of the curved and tapered four-sided legs (four in front, two behind). These are firmly fixed into the stand and being identical, classical, late-Rococo style can be presumed to have been added to the instrument after 1750 or so. The three-part lid which includes keyboard-lid, is painted plain beige, ornamented with forked brass hinges fastened with brass nails. Inside of lid is a painting (probably of later date): an English landscape with a castle by the lake-side. The keyboard lid inside bears the following motto in Indian ink on a red ground. 'MUSICA MAGNORUM SOLAMEN DULCE LABORUM.' In the front of the stand, occupying the whole space under the keyboard is a drawer. Nameboard in spruce, firmly fixed, and screwed to it a gilt rail with maker's name. Cheekpieces plain (horizontal), slightly fluted and bronzed.
KEYBOARD: compass of both manuals F_1 to f''' (five full octaves). Ivory naturals, ebony-covered sharps.
INTERIOR: fluted and bronzed jackrail. The pinewood soundboard (original) is decorated with scattered flowers in gouache-colors. Ruckers' rose in bronzed lead of an angel playing on a harp in half kneeling posture on a rock or a meadow, and the initials 'H. R.'
STRINGING: material: the bass of the 8′ from F_1 to G are of brass, all the remainder are steel strings. Triple stringing 8′, 8′, 4′; to the lower manual 8′, 8′, 4′; to the upper manual the weaker 8′.
ACTION: three rows of jacks; these are the originals. Quill plectra.
STOPS: originally probably side stops, today three front stops; to right of player 4′.
MEASUREMENT: length 95 cm, depth 228 cm, extreme height 98 cm.
IN HALLE AN DER SAALE, Museum in Händel's Birthplace.

+MVSICA + MAGNORVM +
+SOLAMEN + DVLCE +
+ LABORVM +

DOUBLE MANUAL HARPSICHORD

Johannes Ruckers—Flemish, Antwerp 1628

SIGNATURE: Ruckers' rose with the initials 'J. R.'
SHAPE: on the outside of this magnificent instrument are paintings on a gold background representing groups of children, allegorical figures, arabesques, grotesques and groups of monkeys, attributed to Claude III Audran (1658–1734). Inside the lid is an oil-painting: concert in an Italian landscape. The stand richly carved and gilded on eight balustrade-shaped legs all connected by a rail.
KEYBOARD: compass of both manuals G_1 to d''' (four octaves and a fifth). Black naturals.
INTERIOR: soundboard covered with flowers and a Ruckers' rose over soundhole.
STRINGING: triple-strung 8', 8', 4'.
ACTION: two hand stops; manual coupler.
MEASUREMENT: depth 229 cm, height 94 cm.
IN VERSAILLES, Château.

HARPSICHORD

Johannes Ruckers—Flemish, Antwerp 162[7]

SIGNATURE: inscription on nameboard: 'JOHANNES RUCKERS ME FECIT ANTVERPIAE 162[7].'
SHAPE: gold vine-leaves, flowers and fruit adorn the outside of this beautiful instrument, all in relief on brown groundwork. The back wall of the case is colored grey-green, as also is the stand. The instrument stands on seven slender legs decorated with gilt leaves and shells in flat relief. The painting in soft, restrained colors on inside of front lid is of a country scene: in the foreground on the bank of a little river a shepherd with his flock is approaching, whilst a young peasant woman in a red bodice sits on the ground with a little barefoot child resting against her. To the right, in the background, stand peaceful farms half hidden in high trees. To the left of the river's curve a little town with walls and towers is seen, at the foot of snow-covered hills. Another such beautiful painting with a similar motif adorns the inside of the lid over the soundboard: groups of laughing shepherds and shepherdesses on meadows beside a little river shaded by trees, and above, a tender blue sky with a few clouds. These paintings are attributed to Boucher (1703–70). The nameboard has flower-motifs: under the Ruckers' signature is inscribed: 'REFAIT PAR BLANCHET FACTEUR DU ROI A PARIS C. 1756.' The wrestplank bears the words: 'Restored by Chickering and Sons under the direction of Arnold Dolmetsch, Boston U.S.A. 1908.'
KEYBOARD: compass of both manuals F_1 to e''' (four octaves and a seventh). Ebony naturals with gilded faces, ebony sharps with ivory tops.
INTERIOR: soundboard with pattern of scattered flowers and Ruckers' rose with the initials 'J.R.' On the jackrail the date 162[7] (last number illegible).
STRINGING: triple-strung 8′, 8′, 4′. To the lower manual 8′, 4′; upper manual 8′.
ACTION: three rows of jacks. The jacks of one 8′ have leather plectra, whilst those of the second 8′ and the 4′ have quill plectra.
STOPS: two front stops; coupler (through drawing out and pushing in of the upper manual).
MEASUREMENT: extreme length 7 ft 8 in., width 3 ft, extreme height 3 ft 2 in. (with stand); height of case $10^1/_4$ in. (without stand).
AT HOLYOKE, The Belle Skinner Collection. Cat. No. 18.

This instrument possesses the typical 'sweet, silvery tome' of Ruckers' harpsichords.

DOUBLE MANUAL HARPSICHORD

Johannes Ruckers—Flemish—Antwerp 1632 (see pp. 254, 255, 256)

SIGNATURE: inscription on decorated rail of the nameboard: 'IOANNES RUCKERS ME FECIT ANTVERPIAE.' On one of the keys is the date 1632.
SHAPE: the outside and the nameboard of this gorgeous instrument are covered with delicate paintings on a yellow ground in the style of Watteau, representing La Fontaine's Fables. A beautiful landscape adorns the inner side of the lid. The stands is of a later date, with elaborate gilt carving in Louis XV style and has seven curved legs.

IOANNES RVCKERS ME FECIT

KEYBOARD: compass (later extended) of both manuals G_1 to c''' (four octaves and a fourth). Black naturals with arcading, sharps covered in bone.
INTERIOR: soundboard decorated with flowers and Ruckers' rose and an ornamented jackrail.
STRINGING: triple-strung 8', 8', 4'. Lower manual 8', 4'; upper manual 8'.
ACTION: three rows of jacks.
STOPS: two front stops, coupler (by pushing in upper manual).
IN NEUCHÂTEL. Musée d'Histoire.

According to tradition this instrument was a present from Marie-Antoinette, Queen of France, to Mademoiselle de Tremauville, fiancée of the Lieutenant de Montmollin of Swiss Guards, who fell at the storming of the Tuileries on 10th August 1792 (see details in catalogue of Historisches Museum in Neuchâtel). I am indebted to Monsieur Roger de Montmollin at Colombier for drawing my attention to the justifiable doubts concerning this tradition, for a careful examination of the family archives and business papers of that time yielded no supporting evidence.

DOUBLE MANUAL HARPSICHORD

Jean Couchet—Flemish, Antwerp (about 1650)

SIGNATURE: inscription on nameboard: 'IOANNES COUCHET FECIT ANTVERPIAE.'
SHAPE: outside of trapeze-shaped case decorated with flowers and ornaments on a gold background. Inside painted in black scroll on gold. The stand, elaborately carved and gilded, on seven legs.
KEYBOARD: compass of both manuals F_1 to c''' (four octaves and a fifth). Naturals in ivory with gilt arcading; black sharps.
INTERIOR: rose over soundhole on soundboard.
STRINGING: triple-strung 8', 8', 4'. Lower manual 8', 8', 4'; upper manual 8' and lute stop.
ACTION: four rows of jacks. Quill plectra.
STOPS: four; lute stop.
MEASUREMENT: length 7 ft 6 in., width 2 ft 10 in., depth 10 1/2 in.
IN NEW YORK, Metropolitan Museum of Art. Cat. No. 2363.
Originally only one manual (Boalch).

IOANNES COUCHET FECIT ANTV

DOUBLE MANUAL HARPSICHORD

John Daniel Dulcken—Flemish, Antwerp 1745

SIGNATURE: 'JOHANNES DULCKEN ME FECIT ANTVERPIAE AO 1745.'
KEYBOARD: compass of both manuals F_1 to f''' (five octaves). Black naturals, white sharps.
STOPS: three front stops.
IN WASHINGTON, Smithsonian Institution, United States National Museum. Cat. No. 315,758.

PAINTED LIDS

Belshazzar's Banquet by Franz Francke (b. 1581, d. 1643, Antwerp)

Munich, Bayerisches Nationalmuseum. Cat. No. 174

The painting represents the banquet, according to the Bible, which Belshazzar, the last King of Babylon, gave to the thousand most distinguished persons of his court. In his drunkenness he ordered the priceless gold and silver vessels to be brought in which his father, Nebuchadnezzar, had looted from the Temple in Jerusalem. The King, with his toadies, his wives and his concubines drank from these vessels in praise of their idols. Then appeared upon the illuminated wall of the banquet-hall, written by an unseen hand, the words 'mene, mene, tekel, upharsin', 'numbered, numbered, weighed, divided', meaning that God has numbered thy Kingdom; thou art weighed in the balance and found wanting; and they Kingdom shall be divided and brought to an end. Thus the prophet Daniel, one of the Jewish prisoners, interpreted to the terrified King the ghostly writing, warning him of his approaching fall which followed soon after.
This picture crowded with figures covers the whole expanse of the harpsichord lid. The long banquet table, loaded with costly plates and dishes and crowded with guests stretches right into the background of the picture, ending before a kind of altar supported by columns. The orgy continues. No one notices the fateful words written on the wall. The old King, and the Queen with bared breast, sit in the center of the long table, surrounded by guests and toadying courtiers amongst whom sit blonde, half-clothed concubines drinking from the golden goblets. In the (left) foreground is the orchestra composed only of women, singing and playing on the lute, violin, double-bass, trombone and a keyboard instrument. Above their heads one glimpses a serving-maid at a side-table covered with gorgeous golden dishes. At the right, on the narrow end of the harpsichord lid, serving men are seen approaching up some steps preceded by the master of Ceremonies with his wand of office bringing in, one after another, the different dishes. From all sides branched wall- and table candelabra lend their countless lights to the scene.

Banquet beside a river, by Phil. Schey. 1626.

Amsterdam, Rijksmuseum. Inv. NM. 3331. Cat. No. 2158

The painting bears the signature (right side): 'Phil. Schey Ao 1626.'

PAINTED LIDS

Landscape with Nymph, Satyr and musical instruments

Unsigned, 17th century

Amsterdam, Rijksmuseum. Inv. No. NM 8431.

Landscape with figures

Unsigned, Dutch School, 18th century

Amsterdam, Rijksmuseum. Inv. No. NM 8638.

HARPSICHORD

John Haward—England, London, 1622

SIGNATURE: 'JOHANNES (H)A(W)ARD.'
SHAPE: oak case with beautiful Renaissance stand. The lid and the greater part of the action are all missing.
MEASUREMENT: length 8 ft 4 in., width 2 ft 10 in.
PRIVATE PROPERTY.

The earliest remaining English harpsichord.

HARPSICHORD

Jakob Kirkman—England, London (middle 18th century)

SIGNATURE: initials 'I. K.' in the rose.
SHAPE: case veneered with satine-wood in Hepplewhite style.
KEYBOARD: compass F_1 to f''' (five octaves). F♯ missing. White naturals, black sharps.
INTERIOR: the rose over soundhole in soundboard represents King David with his harp, the maker's initials being placed one on each side.
STRINGING: triple-strung 8′, 8′, 4′.
ACTION: three rows of jacks.
STOPS: three front stops, 'Venetian swell', worked by a pedal which is missing.
MEASUREMENT: length 7 ft 3 in.
IN TORONTO, Royal Ontario Museum. T. 128.

DOUBLE MANUAL HARPSICHORD

Thomas Hitchcock—England, London (second half 17th century)

SIGNATURE: on the nameboard 'THOMAS HITCHCOCK FECIT LONDINI.'
SHAPE: walnut case. Four beautifully chased brass hinges on the lid.
KEYBOARD: the sharps were originally ornamented with ivory inlay.
MEASUREMENT: length 7 ft 8 in., width 3 ft 1 in., height 2 ft 10 in.
IN LONDON, Victoria and Albert Museum. 126–126. A–1890.

DOUBLE MANUAL HARPSICHORD

Burkat Shudi (Tschudi)—England, London 1747

SIGNATURE: 'BURKAT SHUDI (NO. 190) FECIT LONDINI 1747.'
KEYBOARD: compass F_1 to f''' (five octaves, without F♯).
IN WASHINGTON, Smithsonian Institution. United States National Museum. Cat. No. 314, 524.

IOANNES · GOERMANS · ME · FECIT · PARISIS

DOUBLE MANUAL HARPSICHORD

Jakob Kirkman—England, London 1761

SIGNATURE: inscription on nameboard: 'IACOBUS KIRKMAN LONDINI FECIT 1761.'
SHAPE: the inner as well as the straight side of case are profusely decorated with inlay work. Four-legged stand; claw feet, holding a ball.
KEYBOARD: compass of both manuals F_1 to f''' (five octaves). Ivory naturals, ebony sharps.
STRINGING: triple-strung 8′, 8′, 4′.
STOPS: four front stops, to left of player lute, 4′; right of player 8′, 8′.
MEASUREMENT: length 7 ft 8 1/2 in., width 3 ft 1 in.
PRIVATE PROPERTY.

HARPSICHORD (CONVERTED INTO PIANO)

Joannes Goermans—France, Paris 1754

SIGNATURE: inscription on nameboard: 'JOANNES GOERMANS ME FECIT PARISIIS 1754.'
SHAPE: inside of lid has chinoiserie in black and gold tray stand with cabriole legs.
INTERIOR: pewter rose in Ruckers' style with initials 'J. G.'
IN NEW YORK, Metropolitan Museum of Art. Acc. No. 44156–80–e.

HARPSICHORD

Pascal Taskin—France, Paris 1786

SIGNATURE: inscription on nameboard: 'FAIT PAR PASCAL TASKIN A PARIS 1786.'
SHAPE: the elegant case, on an elaborately carved stand in Louis XVI style, is decorated with Chinese lacquer paintings.
KEYBOARD: compass E_1 to f''' (five octaves and a second). Black naturals, white sharps.
INTERIOR: soundboard scattered with flower-paintings.
STRINGING: double-strung 8′, 8′-buff stop.
ACTION: the leather plectra, so typical of Taskin's instruments, have been unfortunately replaced with quill plectra on being restored by Charles Fleury in 1856.
STOPS: three.
MEASUREMENT: length 6 ft 1 in., width 2 ft 7 in., height 2 ft 9 1/2 in.
IN LONDON, Victoria and Albert Museum. 1121–1869.

DOUBLE MANUAL HARPSICHORD

Vincent Tibaut—France, Toulouse 1679

SIGNATURE: inscription on nameboard: 'Fait par moy Vincent Tibaut à Toulouse, 1679.'
SHAPE: the case of this magnificent instrument, especially the inside of the lid, is profusely inlaid with different kinds of woods. The cheekpieces on both manuals are ornamented with carved lions. The stand has eight (turned) legs.
KEYBOARD: compass of both manuals G_1 to c''' (four octaves and a fourth). Short basso-octave. C# and D# split keys.
INTERIOR: soundboard beautifully decorated with scattered flowers; over the soundhole is a gilded rose.
STRINGING: triple-strung 8′, 8′, 4′. Lower manual 8′, 8′, 4′; upper manual one of the 8′ of the lower manual.
ACTION: three rows of jacks. Leather plectra.
STOPS: two stops to work the 8′ and the 4′.
MEASUREMENT: length 77 cm, depth 207 cm, height 91 cm.
IN BRUSSELS, Musée instrumental du Conservatoire Royal de Musique. Cat. No. 553.

DOUBLE MANUAL HARPSICHORD

Marius Richard—France, Paris 1752

SIGNATURE: label under the strings bearing the initials: 'M.R.'
SHAPE: the instrument is of veneered mahogany, decorated with inlay and stands on five fluted, round legs. Painted ornamentation in various styles is used.
KEYBOARD: compass of both manuals F_1 to f''' (five octaves). Black naturals with arcaded face, white sharps.
STRINGING: triple-strung 8′, 8′, 4′.
ACTION: four rows of jacks.
STOPS: four pedals: 1. jacks with leather plectra ('Grand jeu de buffle'); 2. jacks with quill plectra ('Grand jeu de plumes'); 3. 8′ ('octave'); 4. 4′ ('petit clavier'). Pedals probably added later.
MEASUREMENT: length 90 cm, depth 219 cm, height 97 $^1/_2$ cm.
IN PARIS, Conservatoire des Arts et Métiers. Inv. No. 1597.

DOUBLE MANUAL HARPSICHORD

Johannes A. Hass—Germany, Hamburg 1710 (?)
"The true date must be much later, e.g. 1770" (Boalch)

SIGNATURE: inscription on soundboard near the jackrail: 'J. A. Hass/Hamb. Anno 1710.'
SHAPE: unusually long case, painted to imitate tortoise shell, on eight four-sided tapering legs. Inside the lid are Chinese decorations in gold on a bright red lacquer background. The nameboard and sides of keyboard are inlaid with laburnum wood in fish-bone pattern.
KEYBOARD: two manuals. Compass of both manuals F_1 to f''' (five octaves). Naturals covered in tortoise shell with ivory facing; ebony sharps with ivory inlay.
INTERIOR: the same brilliant red lacquer adorns the jackrail; the soundboard is ornamented with flowers painted in tempera-colors.
STRINGING: quintuple-strung 16′, 8′, 8′, 4′, 2′.
STOPS: eight stops: five to the respective unison; one lute, one buff 8′, II. Manual; one buff 16′, I. Manual. Coupler (by pushing in lower manual).
MEASUREMENT: length 9 ft 1 1/4 in., width 3 ft 4 in., extreme height 3 ft 2 in.
AT HOLYOKE, The Belle Skinner Collection. Cat. No. 21.

In his 'Reminiscences' Morris Steinert describes this instrument (pp. 216–220) praising its wonderful tone, the capacity of the instrument ranging from the soft and tender timbre of the 2′-register right up to the rich fullness of an organ.

DOUBLE MANUAL HARPSICHORD

SIGNATURE: the rose shows the master's mark—an 'S' in a triangle.
SHAPE: an oak case with panelled lid standing on four strong square legs. Late-Rococo decoration.
KEYBOARD: two manuals. Compass of both manuals F_1 to f''' (five octaves). Ebony naturals, ivory sharps.
INTERIOR: complicated parchment rose on soundhole (see above).
STRINGING: triple-strung 8', 8', 4'.
STOPS: two front stops; coupler (by pushing lower manual inwards).
MEASUREMENT: length 98 cm, depth 264 cm, height 86 cm.
IN BERLIN, Institut für Musikforschung. Cat. No. 5.

The Harpsichord was formerly with some justification attributed to Gottfried Silbermann. But Ernst Flade in his biography of Silbermann (2nd ed., 1952, p. 238) refers to the dissertation of E. Ursula Kropp, Berlin, 'Das Zupfklavier', in which she mentions finding the date 1776 in this harpsichord when the instrument was being restored. Therefore it cannot have been built by Gottfried Silbermann.

DOUBLE MANUAL HARPSICHORD

attributed to Gottfried Silbermann—Germany, Freiberg (about 1740)

SHAPE: a magnificent instrument. The case, colored pale green with beautiful Rococo ornamentation in gold is on a stand with six curved legs richly carved and gilded. A fragment, which survived, of one foot served as pattern for the whole stand, for it, as well as the music-stand—which bears the initials 'G. S.' in gold—are both of later date.
KEYBOARD: compass of both manuals F_1 to f‴ (five octaves).
INTERIOR: rose on soundboard (new).
STRINGING: triple-strung 16′, 8′, 4′; lower manual 16′, 4′; upper manual 8′, buff.
STOPS: three front stops to work the rows of jacks; buff stop 8′ (damping of strings with little strips of felt). Manual coupler.
MEASUREMENT: length 99.7 cm, depth 262.5 cm, height 99 cm.
IN EISENACH, Bachmuseum. Cat. No. 69.

This instrument was built by Silbermann shortly before his death (1753).

DOUBLE MANUAL HARPSICHORD

Johann Heinrich Gräbner (the Jounger?)—Germany, Dresden 1774

SIGNATURE: inscription on soundboard: "Johann Heinrich Gräbner Fecit in Dresden 1774."
SHAPE: case made of dark brown stained pinewood, otherwise simple and undecorated except for beautifully chased brass hinges and handles. The stand is plain, with six curved legs.
KEYBOARD: compass of both manuals F_1 to f‴ (five octaves). Naturals covered with ebony, sharps covered with ivory.
INTERIOR: delicate rose on soundboard.
STRINGING: triple-strung 16′, 8′, 4′; lower manual 16′, 8′; upper manual 4′.
ACTION: three rows of jacks; quills.
STOPS: three front stops, buff stop 8′. Coupler.
MEASUREMENT: length 99 cm, depth 257 cm, height 95 1/2 cm.
IN LEIPZIG, Instrumentenmuseum der Universität. Heyer Cat. No. 91.

DOUBLE MANUAL HARPSICHORD

Karl August Gräbner—Germany, Dresden 1782

SIGNATURE: inscription on a divided nameboard: 'Carl August Gräbner / Instrumentenmacher in / Dresden anno 1782.'
SHAPE: walnut case with panelled lid. The stand has six bent legs joined by a curved rail.
KEYBOARD: compass of both manuals F_1 to f‴ (five octaves). Black naturals, sharps covered with bone.
STRINGING: triple-strung 8′, 8′, 4′; lower manual 8′, 4′; upper manual 8′.
STOPS: front stops. Buff stops. Side stop. Push coupler.
MEASUREMENT: length 90 cm, depth 242 cm.
IN ERLANGEN, Rück Collection, Musikinstrumentensammlung der Universität.

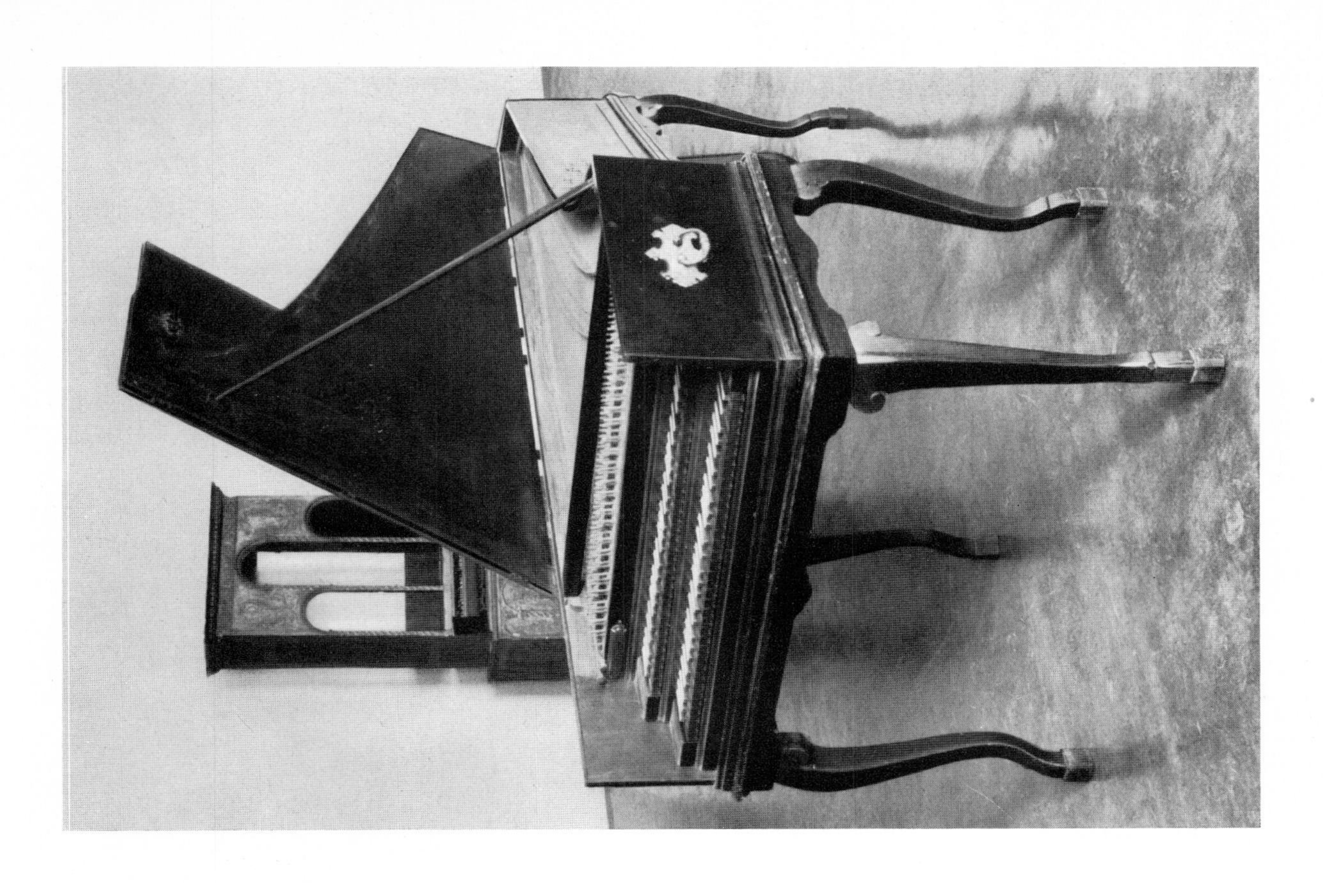

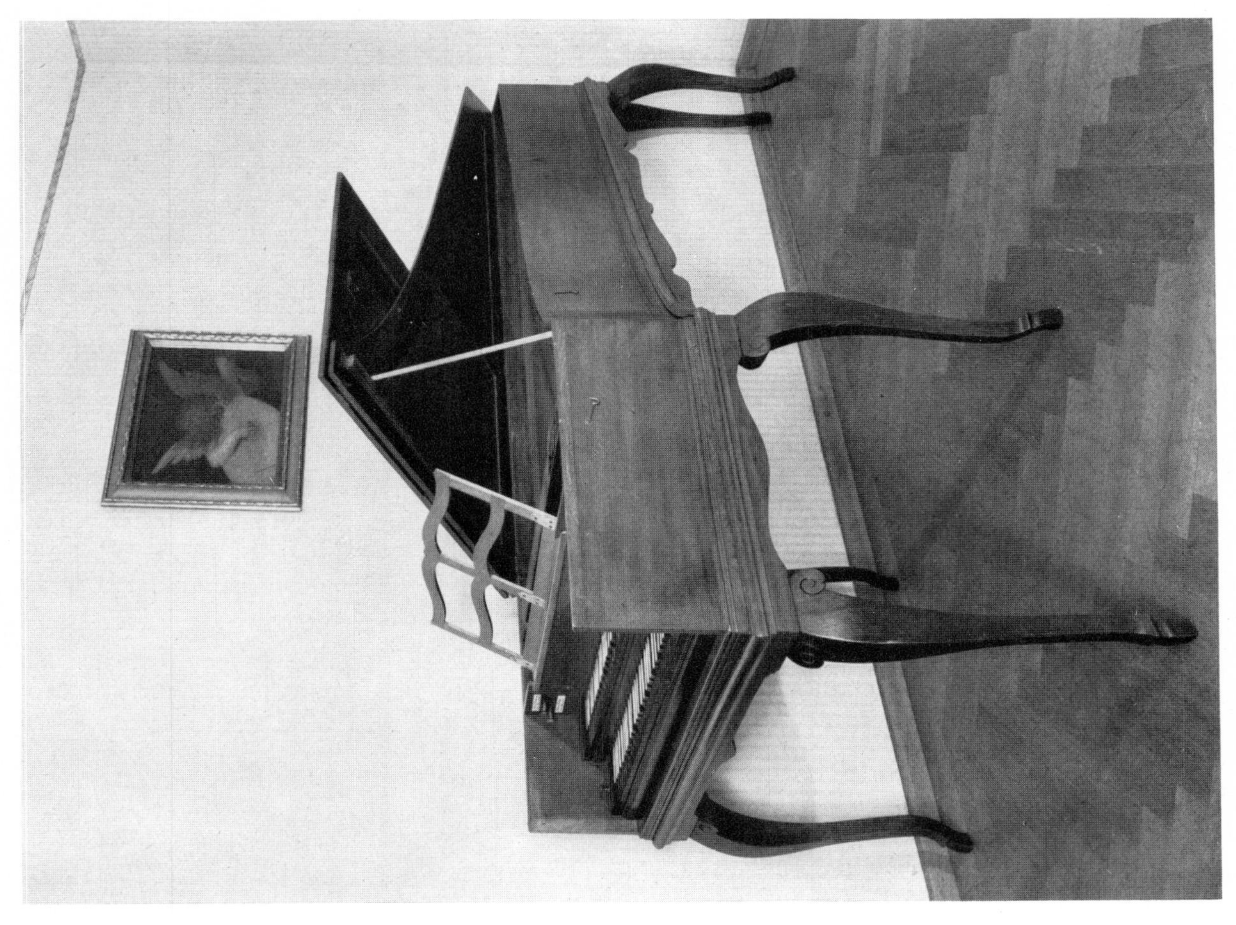

TRIPLE MANUAL HARPSICHORD

Hieronymus Albrecht Hass—Germany, Hamburg 1740

This instrument was shown at the Paris Exhibition in 1900.

DOUBLE MANUAL HARPSICHORD

Gottlieb Rosenau—Sweden, Stockholm 1786

SIGNATURE: 'Forfärdigat af Gottlieb Rosenau, Instrumentmakare i Stockholm. 1786.'
SHAPE: the instrument is colored red and stands on eight legs. The inside of the lid is painted with angels in gold, playing musical instruments, on a blue background.
KEYBOARD: compass of both manuals F_1 to f''' (five octaves). Black naturals, white sharps.
STRINGING: triple-strung 8′, 8′, 4′.
ACTION: three rows of jacks.
STOPS: three. Coupler.
MEASUREMENT: length 105 ½ cm, depth 276 cm.
IN COPENHAGEN, Claudius Collection. Cat. No. 64.

HARPSICHORD-VIRGINAL

Johann Ruckers—Flemish, Antwerp, 1619

SIGNATURE: Ruckers' rose with the initials 'J.H.' Inscription on the nameboard: 'JOANNES RUCKERS ME FECIT ANTVERPIAE 1619.'
SHAPE: the outer and inner walls of the case are stuck with a bordered paper. On the inside of the lid is a beautiful painting by Martin de Vos, of a group of women playing instruments. The instrument is a combination of a double manual harpsichord and an octave virginal in bent side.
KEYBOARD: compass of both harpsichord manuals G_1 to c''' (four octaves and a fourth). Compass of octave virginal E/C to c''' (four octaves) 4'-pitch. Octave spinet and harpsichord have a short bass-octave. The keyboard of the octave virginal is placed on the bent side.
INTERIOR: the rose on the harpsichord soundboard represents a harp-playing genius whose face is turned to the left, whilst the octave virginal rose has the same figure turned to the right. Both roses are of gilded lead and include, as mentioned above, the maker's initials.
STRINGING: harpsichord triple-strung 8', 8', 4'. Octave virginal single-strung 4'.
MEASUREMENT: length 220 cm, depth 82 cm, height 102.5 cm.
IN BRUSSELS, Musée instrumental du Conservatoire Royal de Musique. Cat. No. 2935.

A similar instrument also by J. Ruckers, is in the Berlin Collection (Sachs Cat. No. 2232).

CLAVECIN BRISÉ OU DE VOYAGE

Jean Marius—France, Paris 1709

SIGNATURE: 'Marius 1709.'
SHAPE: this instrument is in three parts which can be taken apart. When it is assembled it has the form of an oblong rectangular case. The keyboard is pushed in and comes to rest under the wrestplank.
KEYBOARD: compass B_1/G_1 to e''' (four octaves and a sixth). Short bass-octave. Naturals covered with ebony, sharps with ivory.
INTERIOR: the soundboard is decorated with artistic ornamentation and flower-paintings. Beautiful roses on the two soundholes.
STRINGING: triple-strung 8', 8', 4'.
MEASUREMENT: length 75 cm, depth 130 cm.
IN BRUSSELS, Musée instrumental du Conservatoire Royal de Musique. Cat. No. 555.

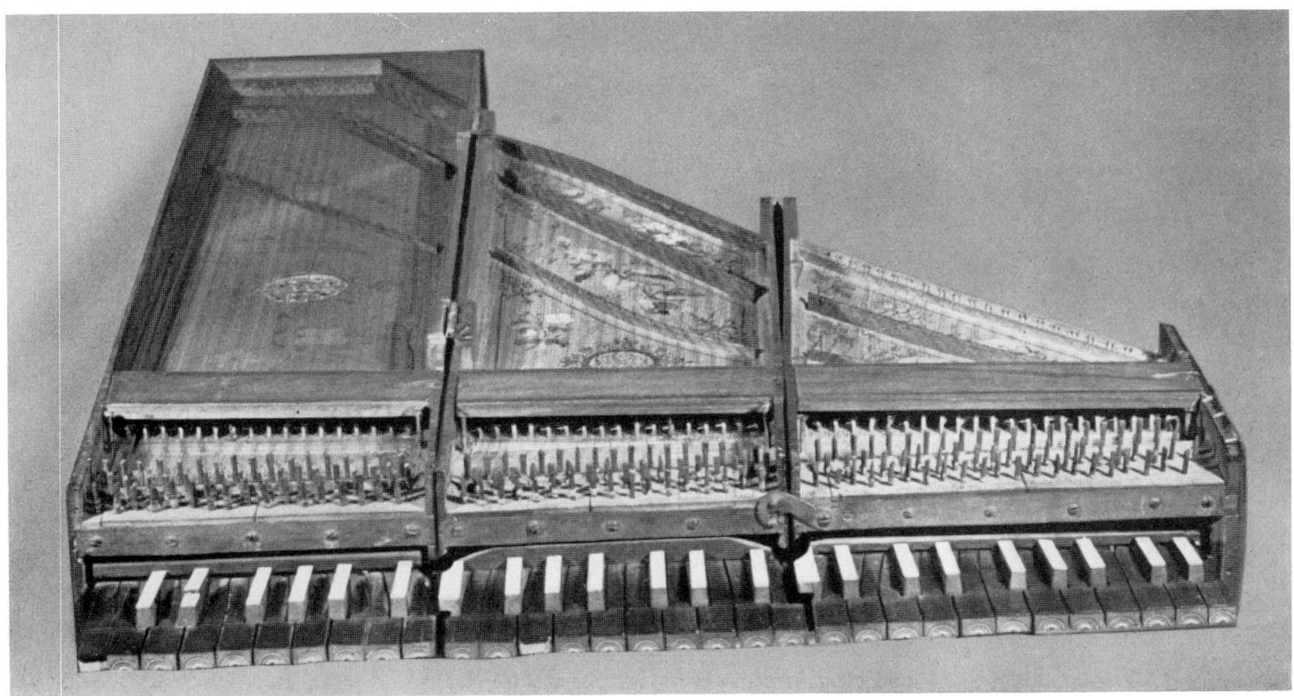

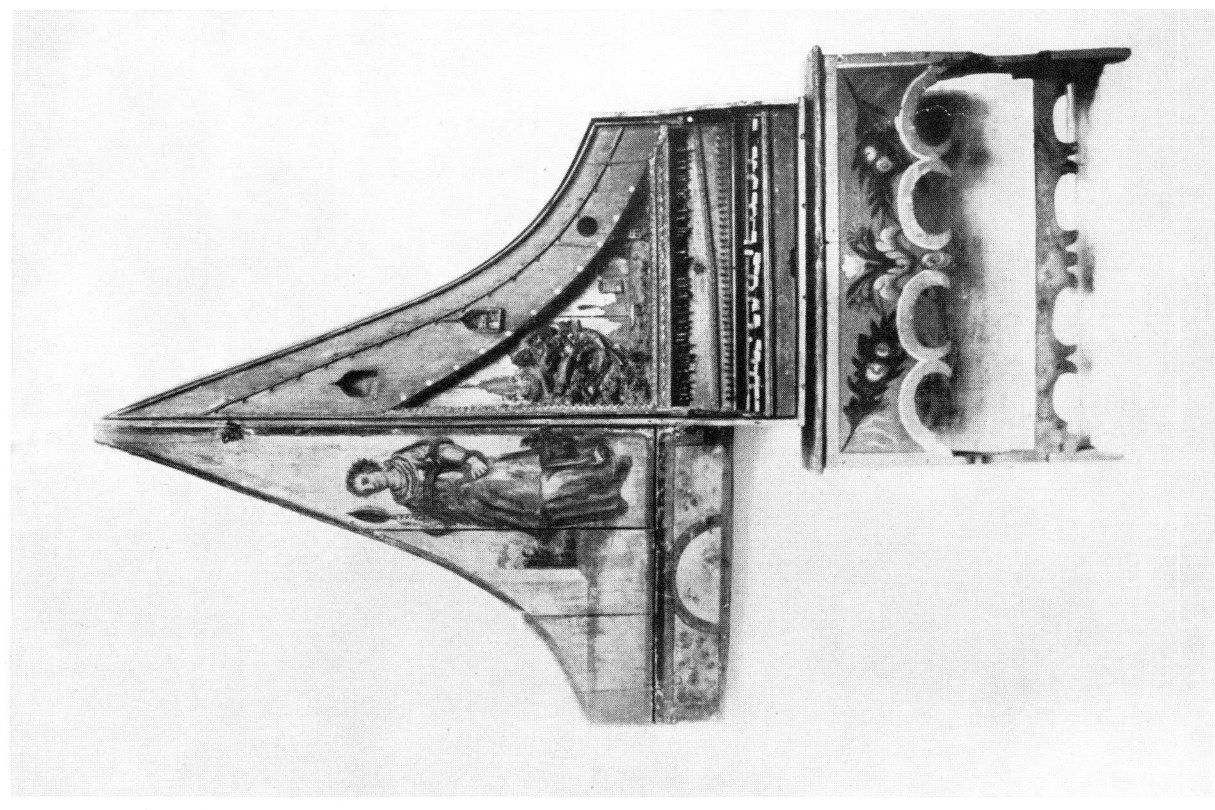

PEDAL-HARPSICHORD

Giovanni Baptista Giusti—Italy, Lucca 1667

SIGNATURE: inscription in Indian ink on the side of jackrail: 'Johannes Paptista Giusti Lucen. faciebat.'
SHAPE: the inner case is of very thin cedar-wood resting in an outer case colored blue, on the right side of which there are ornaments in gold and a landscape in a medallion (the same motif as the painting inside the lid). The lid, which is in two parts, is richly ornamented: on the outside similar ornaments are repeated, coupled with a medallion showing a nobleman playing the violin, whilst on the inside lid there is another medallion of a landscape with a shepherd blowing his horn. Outside, on the keyboard-lid is a coat of arms with trumpeting angels and scrolled motto, and inside the Pipes of Pan and two crossed wind-instruments. At the right is an iron lock. On the sliding front board there is also a landscape medallion surrounded by ornament. To right and left of the inner case near the keyboard sides are two metal holders for candles. The edges of the instrument are adorned with a shaped rail, as also the corners of the nameboard: the cheekpieces are slender and fluted. The stand of the instrument is heavy and awkward, having the feet heavily gilded in Baroque style and connected by a rail.
KEYBOARD: compass E/C to c''' (four octaves). Short bass-octave. Naturals in boxwood, sharps blackened and covered with ebony. Hooks under the key-bed indicate the presence formerly of a suspended pedal.
INTERIOR: soundboard without a rose.
STRINGING: steel- and brass-strings in the bass. Double-strung 8′, 8′.
ACTION: the jacks of the loud (forte) 8′ have leather plectra, those of the weaker 8′, quills.
STOPS: two inner stops to work the jacks in and out.
MEASUREMENT: outer case: length 82 cm, depth 214 cm, height 28 cm. Inner case: length 76 cm, depth 206 cm, height 23.5 cm. Extreme height 97.5 cm.
IN HALLE AN DER SAALE, Museum in Händel's Birthplace.

UPRIGHT HARPSICHORD (Clavicytherium)

North Italy (second half 15th century)

UNSIGNED.
SHAPE: the painting inside the doors represents Truth and is of a later date, as also the stand.
KEYBOARD: compass E/C to g''' (three octave and a fifth). Short bass-octave. Boxwood keys.
INTERIOR: on the soundboard is a painting: a rock with an upward-winding path. The fragments surviving of this painting leave it doubtful whether it represents the hill of Calvary or whether it is a background for St. George and the dragon. A Gothic window covers one soundhole on the soundboard.
ACTION: metal plectra.
MEASUREMENT: (without stand) height 4 ft 10 1/2 in., width 2 ft 3 in., depth 11 in. (base).
IN LONDON, Donaldson Museum (Royal College of Music).

CLAVICYTHERIUM

Italy (first half 16th century?)

UNSIGNED.

SHAPE: this primitive instrument is contained in an outer case colored green outside and brick-red inside: the stand is modern. The lid of the pentagonal outer case shows traces of the green color and has a bronzed ornamental outer edge. The pentagonal inner case and the jackrail have bronzed edges, also the nameboard. The sides of keyboard are cut in steps, colored dark green. All the coloring dates from the 18th century. Inside the keyboard lid is a primitive landscape painting. There are two 'Hackbretter' or Salterios, one above the other, which can be removed.

KEYBOARD: two manuals. Compass of both E/C to e‴ (each, four octaves and a third). Short bass-octave. Boxwood-covered naturals, sharps covered with ebony and veined with inlaid boxwood.

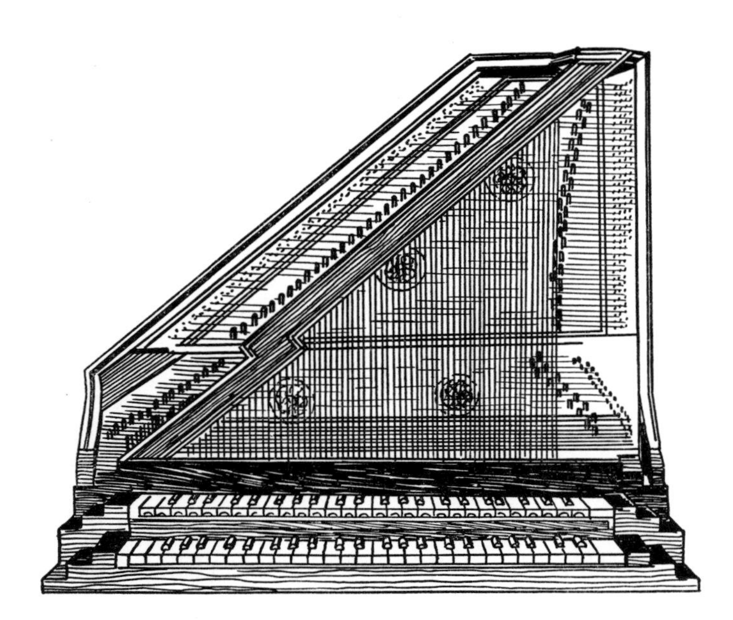

INTERIOR: in the soundholes there are two parchment roses with Moorish motifs. The jack guide-rail runs obliquely above the soundboard, so that the jacks stand at right angles, in front of the strings: the latter run level and parallel to the keyboard; each set of strings has its own two small bridges.

STRINGING: material: brass. Method: double- to quadruple-strung: the lower Hackbrett having fifteen double strings for the bass-notes (C to f♯¹), the upper Hackbrett twelve double strings for the middle register (g to f♯), and the treble (g′ to e‴) twenty-two quadruple strings.

ACTION: two rows of jacks. The jacks of the lower manual pluck the respective strings and those of the upper manual pluck only *one* string.
MEASUREMENT (without outer case): length 97 cm, depth 38 1/2 cm, height 88 1/2 cm. (With outer case) length 103 cm, depth 43 cm, height 165 cm (with stand).
IN LEIPZIG, Instrumentenmuseum der Universität. Heyer Cat. No. 66.

UPRIGHT HARPSICHORD (Clavicytherium)

Italy (early 17th century)

UNSIGNED.
SHAPE: rectangular outer case on four legs, the folding doors and the keyboard lid painted with sacred and musical subjects, the lid bearing a coat of arms.
KEYBOARD: compass E/C to c''' (four octaves). Short bass-octave. Ebony naturals, black sharps with ivory inlay.
INTERIOR: the soundboard, which has a rose, is typically trapezoid in shape. It reaches right down the instrument forming its back wall and is decorated with a painting of David playing on the harp.
STRINGING: double-strung 8', 8'.
ACTION: two rows of jacks. Leather plectra.
STOPS: two push stops.
MEASUREMENT: height 7 ft 5 in., width 2 ft 4 in.
IN NEW YORK, Metropolitan Museum of Art. Cat. No. 1224.

UPRIGHT HARPSICHORD (Clavicytherium)

Albert Delin—Belgium, Tournai (about 1750)

SIGNATURE: rose, with the initials 'A.D.'
SHAPE: white painted case with elaborate gilded carving. Double, very beautiful lid. Four slightly curved legs.
KEYBOARD: compass A_1 to f''' (four octaves and a sixth). Naturals ebony-covered with arcaded faces, sharps covered with bone (nineteen keys were covered with ivory at a later date).
INTERIOR: scattered flowers decorate the soundboard. The rose shows the figure of an angel playing the harp with the maker's initials interwoven.
STRINGING: double-strung 8′, 8′.
STOPS: two side stops and divided buff stop.
MEASUREMENT: length 89 cm, depth 51 cm, height 288 cm.
AT THE HAGUE, Gemeente Museum. No. 848.

On the right hand: view of instrument opened.

REGAL-SPINET

Anton Meidling—Germany, Augsburg 1587

SIGNATURE: 'Anthonius Meidling Augustanus fecit anno dom. 1587 mensae Decembrij.'
SHAPE: this instrument is shaped like a chessboard, opening out into two parts, with very beautiful stained wood inlay. The upper part is decorated like a chessboard, the lower part like a morris-board, whilst inside there is the so-called 'Lange Puff' (or 'trictrac'). The left half is given over to a small Regal-organ worked by two bellows, and the right half contains an octave spinet.
KEYBOARD: compass F to a″ (without F♯, G♯, g♯). Short bass-octave. Similar keyboards in both Regal and octave spinet. The keys are protected by a removable cover.
INTERIOR: very beautiful, delicately carved and painted rose on soundboard. The jackrail of the octave spinet lies across the strings and bears the following words in metal lettering: 'SIC TRANSIT GLORIA MUNDI.' The pipes of the Regal-organ are mostly missing; they are placed directly under the keyboard, and are made of brass, very short, the longest being about 5 cm long.
MEASUREMENT: (when closed) 45.3 cm square, height 15.6 cm.
IN VIENNA, Kunsthistorisches Museum; Collection of old musical instruments. Inv. No. 3930 (126).

ORGAN-SPINET

South Germany, Tirol (second half 16th century)

UNSIGNED.
SHAPE: the instrument combines a spinet, a Regal-organ and a Positive. Case is rectangular, decorated with flower ornaments on a blue-green ground; above are two bellows (with lead weights) which are painted in colorful grotesques in the Italian style. Immediately below these are the spinet strings.
KEYBOARD: compass E/C to c‴ (four octaves). 4′-pitch. Short bass-octave. White and brown keys. The covering of ivory is probably the result of some restoring done at a later date. The keyboard is on the long side of the instrument.
INTERIOR: the jackrail of the spinet bears the words: 'SIC TRANSIT GLORIA MUNDI.' Directly underneath the keys lie the reed-pipes of the Regal: the labial-pipes of the Positive are placed at the back in two rows, with gold ornamentation on a red background.
STOPS: on the right and left sides, as well as in front, there are quite a number of stops (amongst others a coupler, tremolo and sliding-register, besides other 'trick stops' such as 'frogs' dance' and 'bird song').
MEASUREMENT: length 100 cm, depth 48.5 cm, height 25 cm.
IN VIENNA, Kunsthistorisches Museum, Collection of old musical instruments. A. 132.

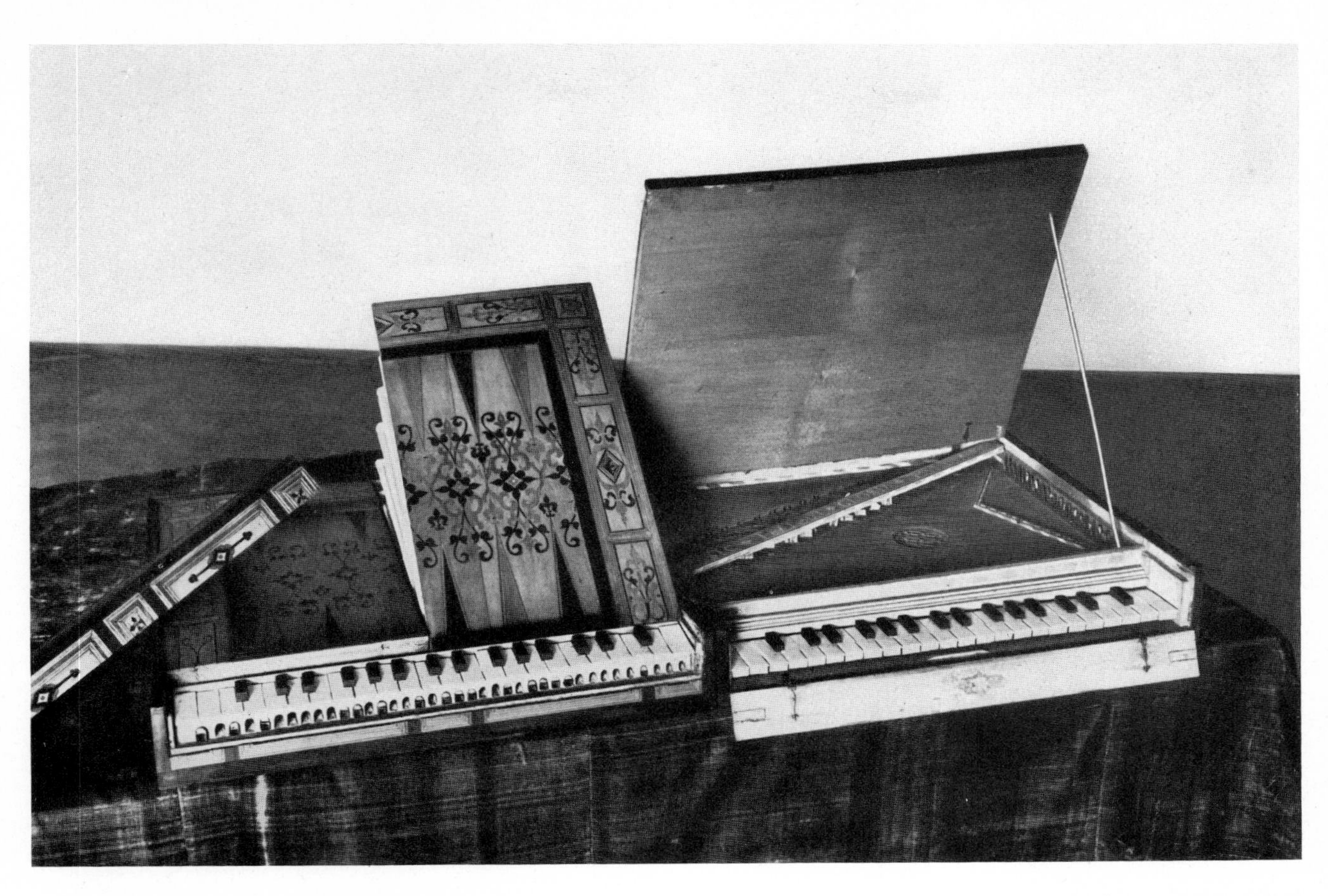

ORGAN-HARPSICHORD (Claviorganum)

Ludovic Theewes—Flemish, Antwerp, built in England 1579

SIGNATURE: 'Ludovicus Theewes me fecit.'
SHAPE: the panelled organ-case is painted with ornaments; on the long side appears the coat of arms of the family Hoby and Carey. The instrument itself has an oak case, which was originally covered with gold embossed leather. The painting inside the lid of the harpsichord represents Orpheus, charming the beasts.
KEYBOARD: only one single key remains.
INTERIOR: originally the organ had five registers, but today only one single oaken pipe remains.
STRINGING: harpsichord triple-strung: 8′, 8′, 4′.
MEASUREMENT: harpsichord: length 7 ft, width 2 ft 11 in., depth 9 in. Organ: length 7 ft 7 in., width 3 ft 4 in., height 3 ft 5 in.
IN LONDON, Victoria and Albert Museum. 125–1890.

Earliest claviorganum in existence.

HARPSICHORD / PIANOFORTE

Josephus Merlin—England, London 1780

SIGNATURE: inscription on nameboard: 'Josephus Merlin, Privilegarius Novi Forte-Piano Nr. 80. Londini 1780.'
SHAPE: mahogany case inlaid with cherry-wood. The stand has four square legs on brass castors.
KEYBOARD: compass F_1 to f''' (five octaves). Ivory naturals, ebony sharps.
INTERIOR: pinewood soundboard.
STRINGING: quadruple-strung 16′, 8′, 8′, 4′.
ACTION: three rows of jacks. Plucking- and hammer action. It was in this instrument, which was later bought from him by Prince Galizin, that Merlin constructed his 'Phantasier' or music copying machine. The music manuscript paper was stretched between two cylinders, passing from the back cylinder at the far end of the piano by means of spring clockwork to the front of the instrument to be rolled onto the revolving main-cylinder just behind the jacks. Connected to the back cylinder were as many pointed pencils as the number of keys. Pressure on the key brought the respective pencil against the paper, the paper meanwhile, whilst playing, rolling slowly off the back on to the front cylinder. The first attempt to construct such a copying machine was made in the year 1745.
STOPS: four stops in nameboard, to be pushed from left to right. Left of player: 1. octave (4′); 2. unison (8′); right of player: 3. celestial harp; 4. Welsh harp (buff stop). Three pedals: one for the 16′; two pedals to connect and disconnect the hammer action. One of these played the 8′-strings, permitting the use of the instrument either as a plucked keyboard instrument or as a pianoforte, or even as both at once.
MEASUREMENT: length 99 cm, depth 260 cm, height 101 cm.
IN MUNICH, Deutsches Museum. Inv. No. 43872.

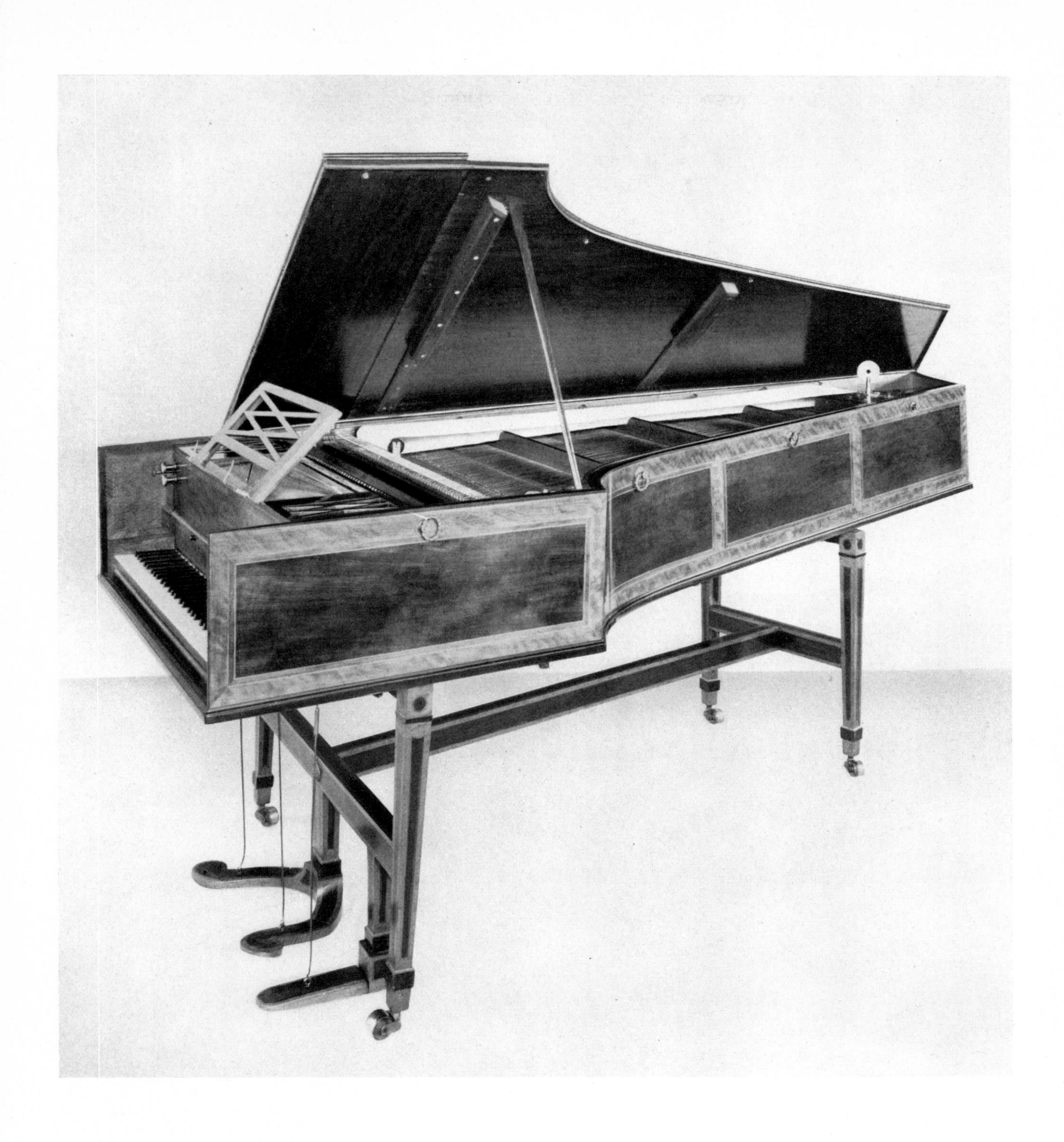

HARPSICHORD / PIANOFORTE (vis-à-vis Flügel)

Johann Andreas Stein—Germany, Augsburg 1777

SHAPE: oblong-square case into which two wing-shaped instruments have been fitted together.
KEYBOARD: four manuals; on one short side there are three, and another on the opposite short side. The one isolated manual and the lowest one of the three opposite, all belong to the pianoforte: the middle and the top manuals, to the harpsichord. Compass of all four F_1 to f‴ (five octaves).
STRINGING: pianoforte: double-strung throughout; harpsichord: quadruple-strung 16′, 8′, 8′, 4′.
ACTION: plucking and German action.
STOPS: on the harpsichord side of the instrument are two stops. One of these pushes a little wooden rail between hammers and strings so that the hammer action is dumb and only the harpsichord sounds. The second stop works the damping (also of the hammer action) consisting of a little wooden rail covered with a strip of parchment.
IN VERONA, Museo civico.

This kind of piano can be played by two players at once. The above details are taken almost word for word from the excellent work by Eva Hertz on 'Johann Andreas Stein, A Contribution to the History of Piano-Building', pp. 46–47.

AUTOMATIC SPINET

Samuel Bidermann—Germany, Augsburg (second half 16th century)

SIGNATURE: on a label: 'Samuel Bidermann, Instrumentenmacher in Augsburg.'
SHAPE: case ornamented with veneer and inlay work. To left and right are two little boxes. The stand, which is quite separate, has a table-top which can be pulled forward and several shelves. The instrument itself is built into a large cupboard of the same period (not seen in the picture).
KEYBOARD: compass C to c‴ (four octaves). Bass-octave presumably short. The fronts of the keys are ornamented in the usual way with gilded arcading. The ivory covering is probably modern.
INTERIOR: the upper part of the soundboard is decorated with scattered, naturalistic flowers. The pretty rose is made of pierced parchment.
STRINGING: fourty-five brass strings.
ACTION: the spinet can be played either by hand or automatically by a cylinder set with pins. By means of a winder the latter is started, being connected to clockwork. The position of the cylinder can be altered by a lever on a removable peg. The keys themselves are set in motion by pressure on a lever. The cylinder plays six pieces.
MEASUREMENT: length 92.5 cm, depth 45.5 cm, height 41 (or 29.5) cm.
IN VIENNA, Kunsthistorisches Museum, Collection of old musical instruments. Inv. No. 3480 (120).

FRETTED CLAVICHORD

This instrument, attributed to Alexander Trasuntinus, Italy 1537, has prooved to be a forgery.

IN COPENHAGEN, Claudius Collection, Cat. No. 45.

FRETTED CLAVICHORD

Dominicus Pisaurensis—Italy, Venice 1543

SIGNATURE: inscription on nameboard: 'Dominicus Pisaurensis. MDXXXXIII.'
SHAPE: case made of cypress-wood in irregular hexagonal shape.
KEYBOARD: compass E/C to c''' (four octaves). Short bass-octave. Naturals with carved faces and covered with boxwood, sharps stained dark.
INTERIOR: Italian bridge-work ('Italian Mensur').
STRINGING: double-strung, twenty-two strings.
MEASUREMENT: length 131 cm, depth 43 cm, height 20 1/2 cm.
IN LEIPZIG, Instrumentenmuseum der Universität. Heyer Cat. No. 1.

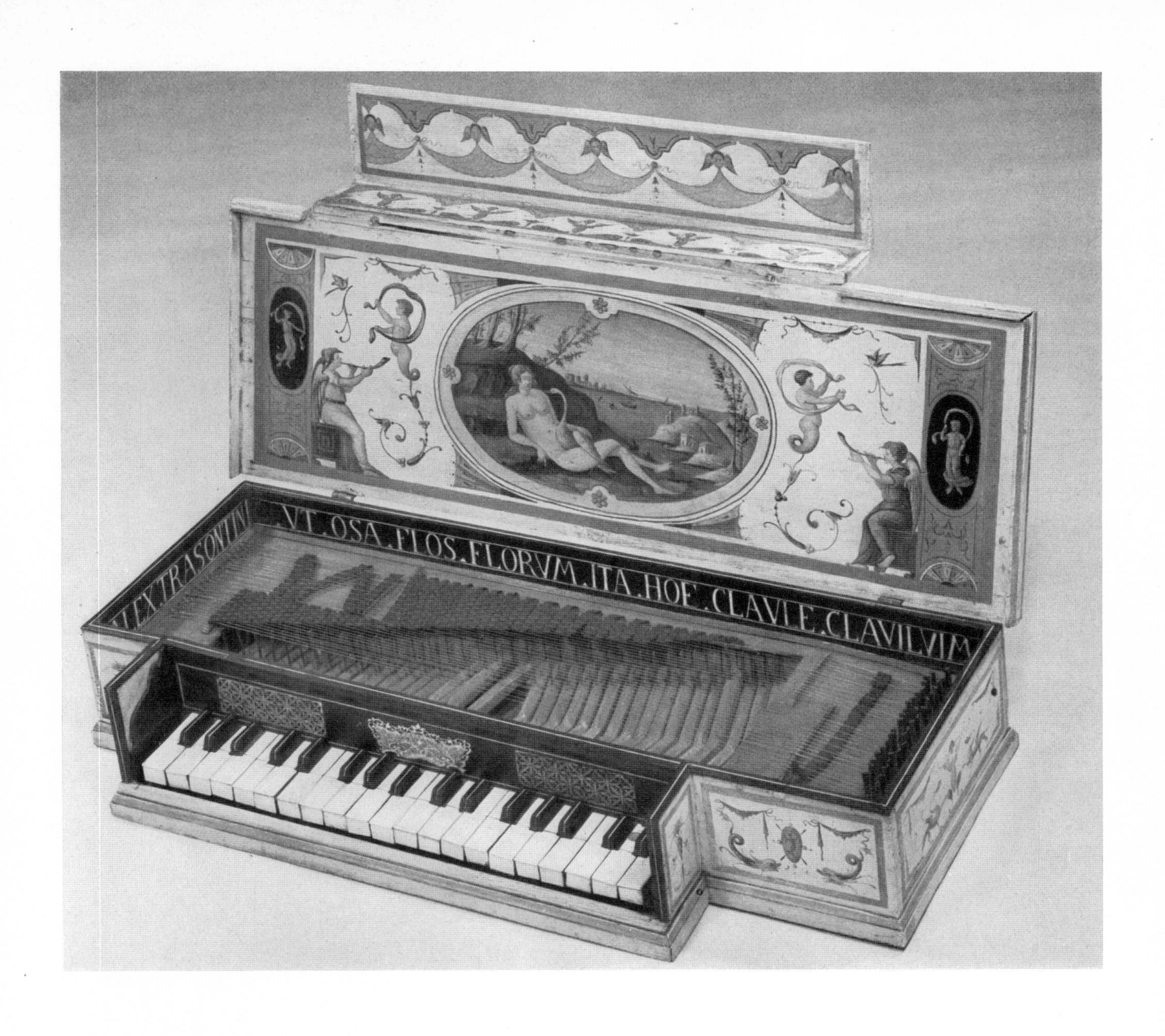
VT.OSA.FLOS.FLORVM.ITA.HOE.CLAVLE.CLAVILVIM

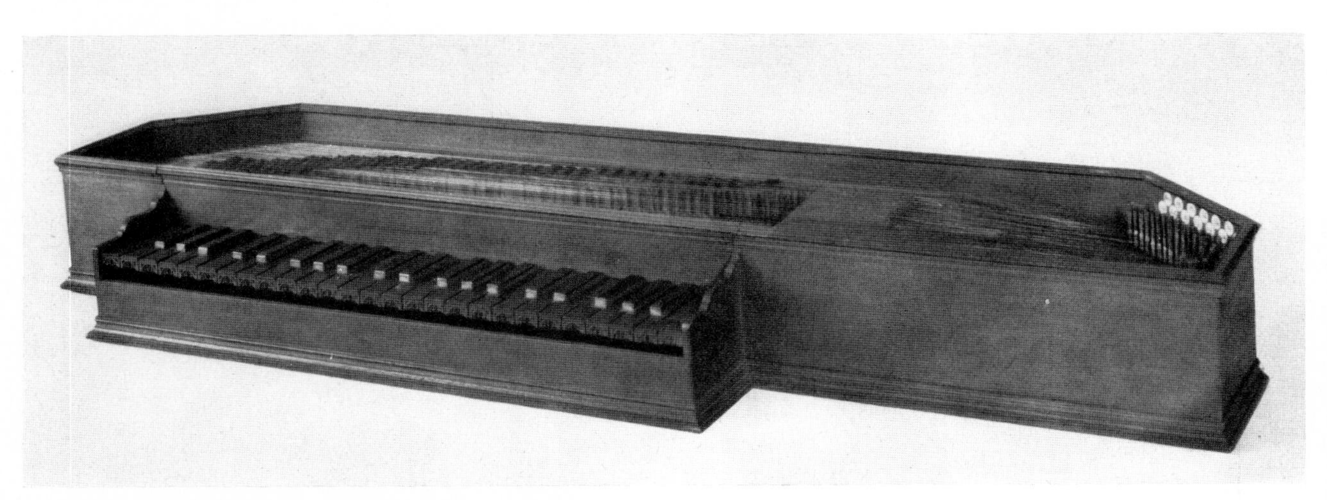

LIDS OF CLAVICHORDS

Dutch School—first half 17th century

View of a harbor (Venice?)

MEASUREMENT of picture 50 × 170 cm.
IN AMSTERDAM, Rijksmuseum. Inv. No. A 1441. Cat. No. 95.

Painting: P. Meulener—Flemish, Antwerp 1645

Landscape with figures

SIGNATURE: on the left 'P. Meulener.'
MEASUREMENT of picture 49 × 170 cm.
IN AMSTERDAM, Rijksmuseum. Inv. No. A 803. Cat. No. 1563.

Meulener, P., born Antwerp 1602, died Antwerp 1654.

FRETTED CLAVICHORD

Flemish, 17th century

UNSIGNED.
SHAPE: painting on an instrument lid by Dirck Stoop: Walk in the Forest.
MEASUREMENT: 18 × 72.5 cm.
IN AMSTERDAM, Rijksmuseum. Inv. No. NM 9487. Cat. No. 2261 a.

Stoop, Dirk, born 1610, died 1686.

FRET-FREE CLAVICHORD

Gaspare Assalone—Italy, Rome 1732

SIGNATURE: 'Gaspare Assalone fecit Romae Anno MDCCXXXII.'
SHAPE: this beautiful picture on the inside of the lid represents Adam and Eve in Paradise.
KEYBOARD: projected; compass E/C to b″ (three octaves and a seventh). Short bass-octave.
STRINGING: double-strung.
IN LISBON, Musical Instrument Collection (Conservatory of Music).

FRETTED CLAVICHORDS

(second half 18th century)

UNSIGNED.
SHAPE: case made of pinewood painted green outside, brick-red inside. A pretty painting decorates the inside of lid representing a Southern harbor surrounded by mountains and with many ships in sight.
KEYBOARD: compass C to f''' (four octaves and a fourth). Naturals covered in boxwood with red and white painted fronts; sharps covered in bone.
MEASUREMENT: length 112 1/2 cm, depth 38 cm, height 12 1/2 cm.
IN LEIPZIG, Instrumentenmuseum der Universität. Heyer Cat. No. 19.

Christian Gottlob Hubert—Germany, Ansbach 1782

SIGNATURE: on a label, inside, left: 'Christian, Gottlob, Hubert. Hochfürst (illegible) scher Hof. Instrumentenmacher. Fecit Ao 1782.'
SHAPE: case and stand in oak, shaped in Louis XV style.
KEYBOARD: compass C to g''' (four octaves and a fifth). Black naturals, white sharps.
STRINGING: double-strung from C to e, fret-free. From 'f' onwards, always a pair of strings for two neighboring semitones.
MEASUREMENT: length 140 cm, depth 36 cm, height 82 cm.
IN BASLE, Historisches Museum. Cat. No. 211 (1905.86).

FRETTED CLAVICHORD

Peter Hicks—England (about 1720)

SIGNATURE: inscription on nameboard: 'Peter Hicks fecit.'
SHAPE: mahogany case.
KEYBOARD: compass C to d''' (four octaves and a tone). Black naturals, white sharps.
MEASUREMENT: width 4 ft 1 in., depth 14 in., height 4 1/2 in.
IN LONDON, Victoria and Albert Museum. W 7–1917.

The only known existent English clavichord.

FRET-FREE CLAVICHORDS

Gottfried Silbermann—Germany, Freiberg 1723

SIGNATURE: written on a label attached to a strengthening strut inside: 'Gebaut von Gottfried Silbermann 1723.'
SHAPE: case in dark green painted fir-wood standing on four feet.
KEYBOARD: compass C to e''' (four octaves and a third). Ebony naturals, sharps ivory-covered.
STRINGING: material brass; double-strung.
MEASUREMENT: length 140 cm, depth 45 cm, height 16 cm.
IN MARKNEUKIRCHEN, Städtisches Gewerbemuseum.

Hieronymus Albrecht Hass—Germany, Hamburg 1747

SHAPE: oak case on a stand with four curved legs. Inside the lid a painting of Apollo with the nine Muses.
KEYBOARD: compass F_1 to f''' (five octaves). White naturals, black sharps.
INTERIOR: flower paintings on soundboard.
MEASUREMENT: length 145 cm, depth 55 cm.
IN OSLO, Norsk Folke Museum. Cat. No. 950–97.

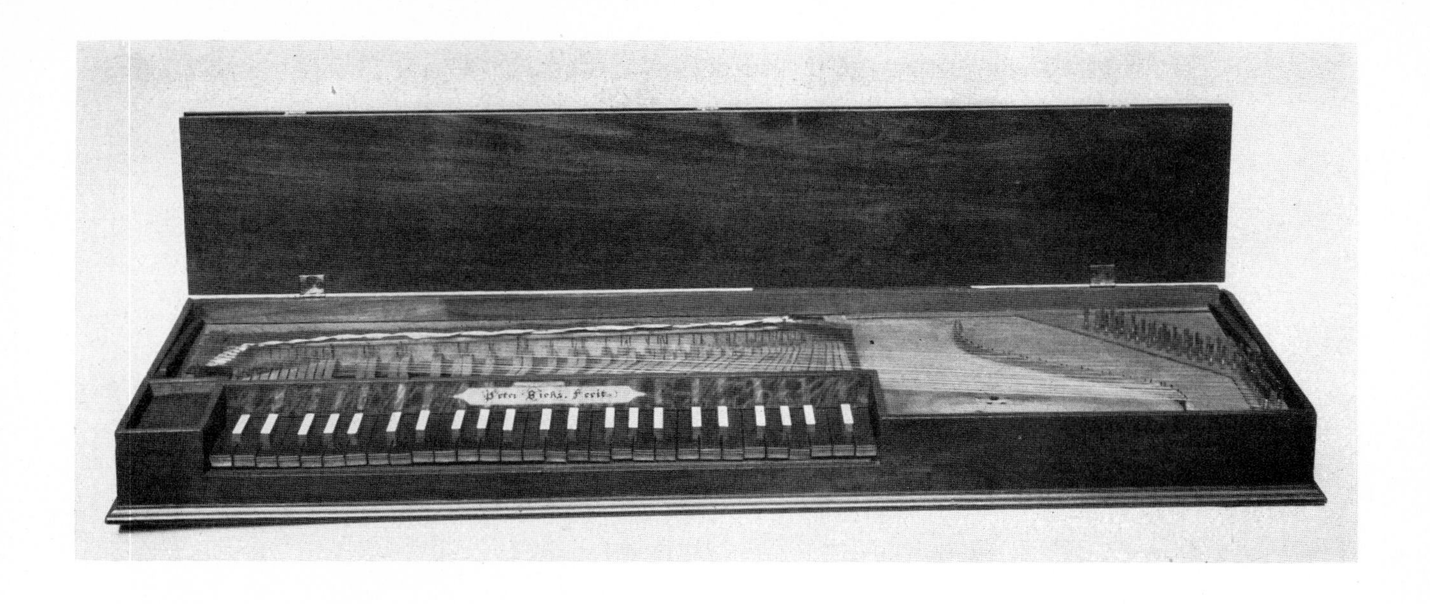
Peter Hicks. Fecit.

FRET-FREE CLAVICHORDS

J. A. Hass—Germany, Hamburg 1755

SIGNATURE: 'J. A. Hass, Hamb(urg) Anno 1755.'
SHAPE: beautiful red-lacquered case in Rococo style. Lacquer painting in Chinese style decorates the inside of lid. Stand of later date.
KEYBOARD: compass F_1 to f''' (five octaves). Naturals ivory-covered: sharps covered in tortoise shell with ivory inlay.
INTERIOR: flowers painted on soundboard.
STRINGING: triple-strung in the bass, otherwise double-strung.
MEASUREMENT: length 171 cm, depth 53 cm.
IN COPENHAGEN, Museum of the History of Music. Cat. No. 462.

Barthold Fritz—Germany, Braunschweig 1751

SIGNATURE: inscription on soundboard: 'Barthold Fritz fecit Braunschweig Anno 1751 Mens. Febr.'
SHAPE: the green painted case rests on four fluted legs. Inside the lid is a painting of a stag-hunt done entirely in blue.
KEYBOARD: recessed. Compass F_1 to a''' (five octaves and a third). Ebony naturals, ivory sharps.
STRINGING: double- and triple-strung. Lowest thirty-two notes have octave string.
MEASUREMENT: height 2 ft 7 in., length 5 ft 10 1/2 in., width 1 ft 10 1/2 in., depth 5 5/8 in.
IN LONDON, Victoria and Albert Museum. 339–1882.

FRET-FREE CLAVICHORDS

Barthold Fritz—Germany, Braunschweig 1756

SIGNATURE: written in ink above the treble wrest-pins on wrestplank: 'Barthold Fritz, fecit Braunschweig, 1756.'
SHAPE: rectangular case painted grey and decorated with gold ornament standing on four curved legs. Fastened by eyed hinges, the double lid is adorned to two thirds of its surface with roses on a grey ground, the remainder with gold ornament to match the sides. The keyboard has its own downward-opening flap cover cut out of the top lid. No cheekpieces, but to left of player a little built-in box for spare material. On the walnut lid is also a small inlaid ivory picture of an old-fashioned well-head and a tree (said to have stood before Fritz' house). In the middle front is a drawer with two knob-handles.
KEYBOARD: recessed. Compass F_1 to f''' (five octaves). Naturals veneered with rosewood, the key-faces painted green, originally having been superficially carved; sharps covered with thin ivory chased in black.
INTERIOR: soundboard devoid of rose.
STRINGING: material brass; double-strung.
MEASUREMENT: length 175 cm, depth 49 cm, height 18 cm.
IN BRAUNSCHWEIG, Städtisches Museum.

UNSIGNED.
SHAPE: a very beautifully finished instrument in Rococo style. On the lid, inside, is a painting framed in flowers of a lady playing the zither (?) being watched by her rather naïve-looking lover. A little box at the left of the keyboard has an oaken lid, veneered and decorated with pretty ivory and ebony inlay.
KEYBOARD: compass F_1 to f''' (five octaves). Ebony naturals, faces ornamented with embossed parchment; sharps ivory-covered.
STRINGING: double-strung.
MEASUREMENT: length 168 cm, depth 58 cm, height 82 cm.
IN LEIPZIG, Instrumentenmuseum der Universität. Heyer Cat. No. 25.

In the Heyer Catalogue the instrument is shown with its stand which is described as follows: "The instrument has a stand with four curved legs, the whole profusely decorated with carvings and paintings in gold. In the upper part there are two drawers."

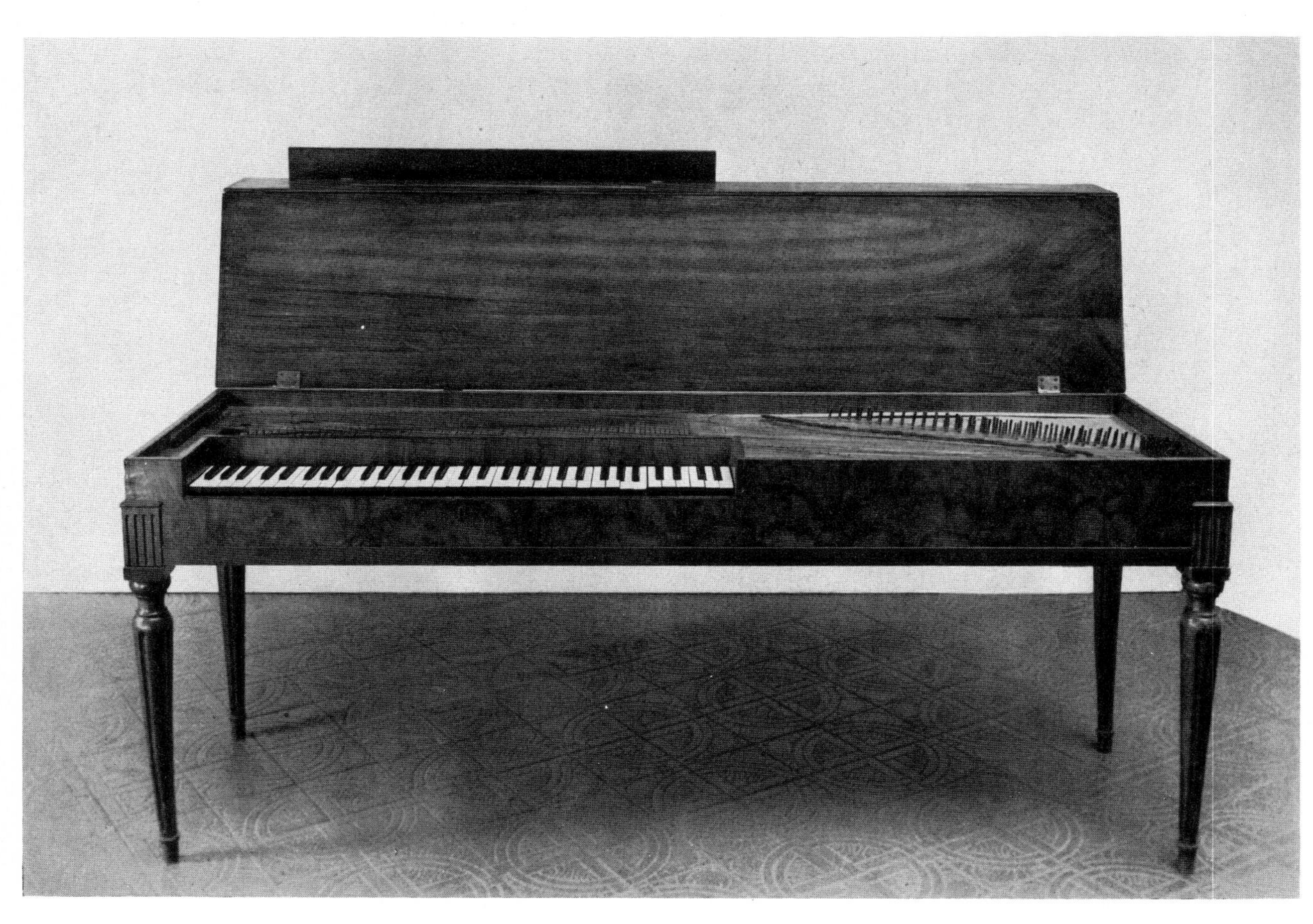

FRET-FREE CLAVICHORDS

Karl Lemme—Germany, Braunschweig 1787

SIGNATURE: inscription written on the soundboard: 'Carl Lemme Organist / in Braunschweig / Anno 1787.' N 20 802 sorte 14.
SHAPE: the case is in veneered mahogany and has the oval form invented by Lemme.
KEYBOARD: compass F_1 to a''' (five octaves and a third). Tortoise shell covered naturals, with mother-of-pearl facings, sharps of ebony and mother-of-pearl.
INTERIOR: drawn in black on the soundboard is the Braunschweig coat-of-arms.
STRINGING: triple- and also double-strung; the lowest 1 $^1/_4$ octave has a third string which vibrates sympathetically with the upper-octave and passes over a special bridge.
MEASUREMENT: length 180 cm, depth 45 cm, height 77 cm.
IN LEIPZIG, Instrumentenmuseum der Universität. Heyer Cat. No. 28.

Details in the Heyer Catalogue as follows, showing the piano on its stand: "The instrument rests on four tapering squared legs which are ornamentally carved."

Johann Paul Kraemer & Söhne—Germany, Göttingen 1801
(see p. 372, below)

SIGNATURE: inscription in handwriting, 'Sorte 7, Nr. 509 / Verfertiget / von Joh. Paul Kraemer und Söhnen / Instrumentenmacher / in / Göttingen / im Oktober 1801.'
SHAPE: mahogany case with walnut and ash veneer, standing on four round, fluted legs.
KEYBOARD: compass F_1 to a''' (five octaves and a third). Ivory naturals with arcaded faces, ebony sharps.
MEASUREMENT: length 171 cm, depth 55 cm, height 74 cm.
IN BRAUNSCHWEIG, Städtisches Museum. Cat. No. 19.

FRET-FREE CLAVICHORD

Johann Heinrich Silbermann—France, Strasbourg (about 1776)

Shape: polished walnut case with panelled lid, on a stand.
Keyboard: compass F_1 to f‴ (five octaves). Bone sharps.
Interior: parchment rose.
Measurement: length 138 cm, depth 50 1/2 cm, height 76 cm.
In Berlin. Institut für Musikforschung. Cat. No. 598.

FRET-FREE ORGAN-CLAVICHORD

Pehr Lundborg—Sweden, Stockholm 1772

Signature: printed label, right hand, back, on soundboard: "Förfärdigat af Pehr Lundborg / Kongl. Hof-Instrument Makare / Stockholm 1772 / No. 37.' Date and number of instrument added in ink.
Shape: case in pinewood painted pale green with gilt paintings, on four legs slightly curved outwards. Both the lid and soundboard are also of pinewood. Nameboard and cheekpieces outlined with an edge inlaid with different colored woods (elm, walnut, jacaranda) with which the lid of the little box on the keyboard (left) is also decorated. In the box is an old tuning-key. The same ornament occurs on the space to the right of the keyboard.
Keyboard: recessed. Compass C to f‴ (four octaves and a fourth). Ebony naturals, bone-covered sharps.
Interior: small organ. Under the soundboard the pipes ('gedackt'-flute 8′) are built in. The square pinewood pipes lie some across and some lengthways under the soundboard, where they can be locked away under an upward lifting lid.
Stringing: double-strung.
Action: organ: the air-valves open, on pressing down the key, by means of pins. The bellows is obviously of later date and is worked by foot. The connection between bellows and wind-box, through a tube made of box-calf leather, is found under the keyboard.
Measurement: length 177 cm, depth 52 cm, height 78 cm.
In Stockholm, Museum of the History of Music. Inv. No. 1440.

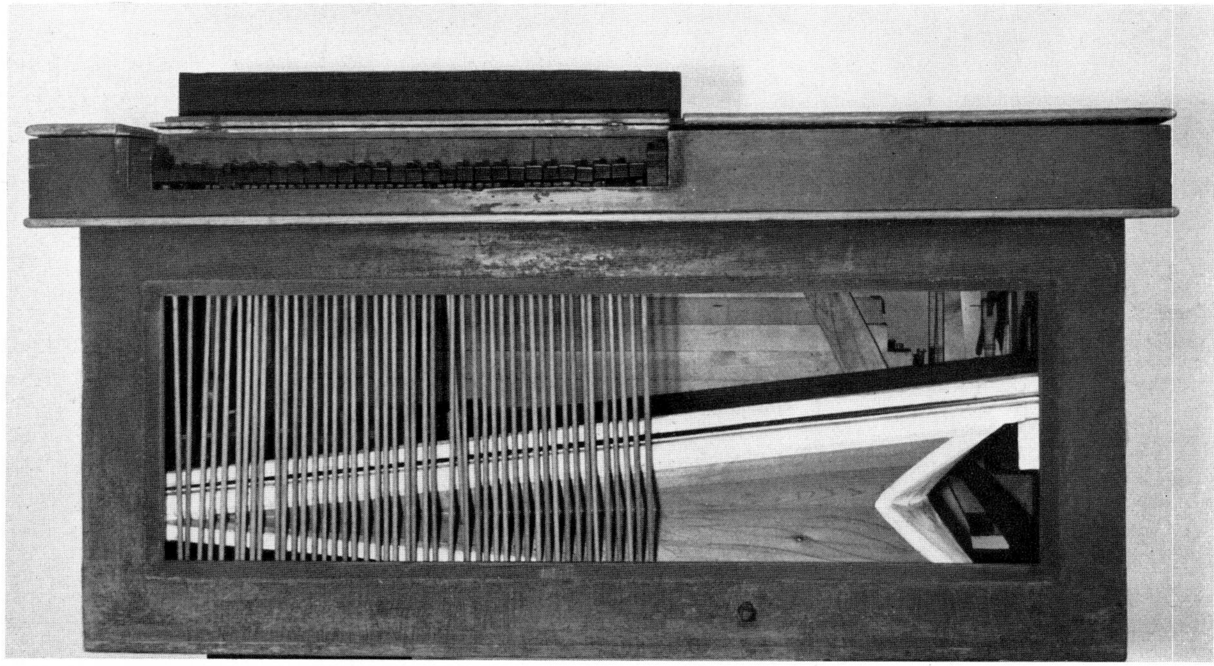

FRET-FREE ORGAN-CLAVICHORD WITH AUTOMATON

(B. Ilsaas)—Norway (about 1800)

View of front of organ—open
In Oslo, Norsk Folke Museum. Cat. No. 37–04

(B. Ilsaas)—Norway (about 1800)

SHAPE: pinewood case.
KEYBOARD: compass C to c''' (four octaves). Black naturals, white sharps.
INTERIOR: organ: under the soundboard the pipes, consisting of thirty-two wooden and one hundred fifty-six of a lead and tin alloy, have been built in.
ACTION: organ: pressure on the keys opens the air-valve by means of wooden angle-levers.
STOPS: four.
MEASUREMENT: length 159 cm, depth 83.5 cm, height 77.5 cm.
IN OSLO, Norsk Folke Museum. Cat. No. 37–04.

FRET-FREE PEDAL-CLAVICHORD

Germany, Ostheim (about 1800)

UNSIGNED.
SHAPE: the whole keyboard can be lifted out and placed on feet which are screwed in.
KEYBOARD: compass of manual F_1 to f'''' (six octaves). Black naturals, white sharps. Compass of pedal-manual C_1 to d (two octaves and an augmented second).
INTERIOR: rose over soundhole in soundboard.
STRINGING: double-strung.
MEASUREMENT: length above (keyboard) 170,5 cm, depth 56,3 cm; length below (pedal-box) 233 cm, depth 49 cm; extreme height 94 cm.
IN EISENACH, Bachmuseum. Cat. No. 68.

Michael Todini—Italy, Rome 1655

After a reproduction in Athanasius Kircher's 'Phonurgia nova'. Appendix, p. 168

"Autor igitur Symphoniarcha in machina specimina daturus artis suae, se accingit ad Archiclavicymbalum A. Registra accommodans modo omnibus incognito, incipit sonare concertum à se tanta & tam suavi, & concinna Symphonia compositum, ut aures omnium Auditorium statim dulcedine harmoniae raptas arrigat: Post haec cymbalum B. suavissimè consonat, quod sequitur cymbalum D. concertans cum cymbalo B. & tandem instrumentum C. & deinde omnia simul clavicymbala plenum & absolutissimum sonu & concentum efficiunt; in quod illud Auditores veluti attonitos reddit, quod in tribus clavicymbalis BCD. marculi, quos tastos vocant, nunc in cymbalo B. modò in C. jam in omnibus tribus per intervalla certatim sine ullo manus vestigio, nulla abditorum filorum ope, nullo per vicinum murum, aut pavimentum artificioso chordarum ductu moveri, & alternatim subsultare videantur; Symphonia verò, quam exhibent, est mirum in modum concinna, & summo ingenio ab Authore composita, non solum aures Auditorium mirum in modum soliciat, sed & marculorum subsultatu occulos veluti attonitos reddit; magicum incantamentum jure diceres."

"Wann nun der Herr und Author dieses Wunder-Music-Wercks eine Kurtzweil machen / und sich hören lassen will / so geht Er zu seinem grössten Instrument oder Clavicymbel A. ziehet und ordnet daselbsten seine Register / auf eine gantz geheime und verborgene Weise / und fahet an so lieblich und anmuthig zu spihlen / dass Er darmit gleichsam aller Zuhörer Ohren bezaubert und ent-zücket: Nach diesem fahet auch das Clavicymbel B. überauss lieblich an zu klingen / darauf das Clavicymbel D. folget / so dem Clavicymbel B. an Lieblichkeit nichts nachgibt / und Letzlich folget das Instrument oder Clavicymbel C. endlich fallen alle drey Clavicymbel in einen lieblichen Music-Thon zusammen; worbey dieses die Zuhörer am meisten verwundern / und gleichsam erstaunen machet / dass an den dreyen Clavicymbel BCD. die Döcklein / bald in dem Instrument B. bald in C. bald in allen dreyen nacheinander und Wexelweise / sich bewegen und aufspringen, da sie doch mit keiner Hand angerühret / durch keine heimliche und verborgene Fäden / Draht / oder dergleichen verborgenen Künsten / gezogen oder beweget werden; der Klang aber und Thon / so sie von sich geben / ist über die Massen lieblich und wohl-lautend / mit sonderbahrem Fleiss und Kunst von dem Authore gesetzet / so nicht allein die Ohren der Zuhörer an sich ziehet; sondern auch die Augen mit dem aufspringenden und hupffenden Instrument-Döcklein gantz bestürtzt machet; so dass man fast schwören sollte / es wäre Zauberey."
(From the German translation of Kircher's Phonurgia nova = Neue Hall- und Thonkunst, translated by Agatho Carione. Nördlingen 1684. Book L, Part VII, Appendix, p. 121.)
Rosamund Harding remarks on this: "It may be noticed in passing that in the Appendix of Kircher's Phonurgia (1673) in his description of Todini's mechanical combinations of instruments he uses the words 'marculi, quos tastos vocant', springing up without the aid of hands in first one 'Cymbalo' and then in another; but Printz, describing the same thing in his 'Historische Beschreibung der edelen Sing- und Klingkunst' (1690), deriving his informations from Kircher, calls them 'Döcklein'. We cannot therefore claim a hammer invention here."
(From the article 'Pianoforte', Grove's Dictionary, London 1954, vol. VI.)
We may point out that the description of the Todini instrument by W.C. Printz, mentioned by Rosamund Harding, is merely a litteral quotation from a former translation by Carione.
Carione was wrong in translating the term 'marculi' of the original Latin text with 'Döcklein', i.e. jack; for 'marculi', the plural of 'marculus', means small hammers, 'marculus' being the diminutive of 'marcus', a hammer. Kircher, a musicologist of comprehensive technical knowledge, can hardly have been mistaken about the designation of the tone generator in the three above mentioned *Cymbali* B, C, D. Moreover the description that the 'marculi, quos tastos vocant...' suggests the action of a hammer mechanism (possibly a tangent hammer mechanism?). It is also quite conceivable that the tone contrast between a plucked and a struck string should have been due to the distance between the *Clavicytherium* A and the *Cymbali* B, C, D. The assumption that the *Cymbali* in question were instruments with a hammer mechanism is, to my mind, quite justifiable.

A
B
C

GRAND PIANOFORTE

Bartolomeo Cristofori—Italy, Florence 1720

SIGNATURE: 'BARTHOLOMAEUS DE CHRISTOPHORIS PATAVINUS INVENTOR FACIEBAT FLORENTIAE MDCCXX.'
SHAPE: trapeze-shaped case of cedar standing on three legs; outside of case painted black.
KEYBOARD: compass C to f''' (four octaves and a fourth). White naturals, black sharps.
INTERIOR: the original jackrail has been retained.
STRINGING: double-strung.
ACTION: hoppers are used. The original hammers no longer present.
STOPS: keyboard shift ('una corda'). Worked by ivory buttons on the cheekpieces.
MEASUREMENT: length 7 ft 7 1/2 in., width 3 ft 3 in., depth 9 1/2 in.
IN NEW YORK, Metropolitan Museum of Art. Cat. No. 1219.

Earliest surviving Grand Pianoforte.

GRAND PIANOFORTES

Bartolomeo Cristofori—Italy, Florence 1726

SIGNATURE: on the nameboard: 'BARTHOLOMAEUS DE CHRISTOPHORIS PATAVINUS INVENTOR FACIEBAT FLORENTIAE MDCCXXVI.'
SHAPE: cypress-wood case. Cheekpieces veneered with ebony: at each side is an ivory button.
KEYBOARD: compass C to c''' (four octaves). Naturals covered in boxwood; shaped facing, bevelled ebony; sharps covered with rosewood.
STRINGING: double-strung.
INTERIOR: instead of the soundhole usually found on harpsichord soundboards, this instrument has four round holes pierced in the board below the soundboard.
ACTION: hoppers are used.
STOPS: keyboard shift. By means of the ivory buttons on the cheekpieces the keys are shifted towards the bass; so that the hammers strike only *one* string.
MEASUREMENT: length 91 1/2 cm, depth 250 cm, height 97 1/2 cm.
IN LEIPZIG, Instrumentenmuseum der Universität. Heyer Cat. No. 170.

The Heyer Catalogue gives a picture of the instrument and its outer case with details as follows: "The outer case of this instrument is almost identical with that of the harpsichord of the same date: outside bright red, inside pale blue with gilded edges. The right-hand side as well as the keyboard lid are lacquered and decorated with pretty Chinese gold painting. The stand is on three painted and elaborately carved legs in Baroque style, the two in front being connected by a piece of gilded carving."

Johann Andreas Stein—Germany, Augsburg 1773

SIGNATURE: inscription engraved on a label stuck on the left side of the soundboard: 'Jean André Stein / Faiseur d'Orgues, des Clavecins / et Organiste à l'Eglise des Minorittes, à Augsbourg / 1773.'
SHAPE: case made of cherry-wood on five turned and fluted legs. Like those of Silbermann, the lid is panelled.
KEYBOARD: compass F_1 to f''' (five octaves). Ebony-covered naturals, ivory-covered sharps.
STRINGING: double-strung.
ACTION: developed German action.
STOPS: knee levers (damping).
MEASUREMENT: length 95 cm, depth 216 cm, height 88 1/2 cm.
IN LEIPZIG, Instrumentenmuseum der Universität. Heyer Cat. No. 171.

This instrument is the oldest known piano fitted with Stein's invention, i.e. the developed German action or 'Prellzungenmechanik'.

GRAND PIANOFORTES

Geschwister Stein—Austria, Vienna

SIGNATURE: maker's name on nameboard: 'Frère et Sœur / Stein / d'Augsbourg / à Vienne.'
SHAPE: case made of cherry. Four tapering legs.
KEYBOARD: compass F_1 to g''' (five octaves and a second). Black naturals, sharps covered with bone.
STRINGING: double-strung.
ACTION: Viennese action.
STOPS: two knee levers (divided damping).
MEASUREMENT: length 97 cm, depth 214.5 cm, height 82 cm.
IN BASEL, Historisches Museum. Inv. No. 86,1913.

Nannette Streicher—Austria, Vienna 1819

SIGNATURE: inscribed on lozenge-shaped etiquette on nameboard: 'Streicher / à Vienne.' Written in ink on the soundboard is the following: 'Nr. 1415 / Nannette Streicher, née Stein / Vienna 1819.'
SHAPE: this beautiful instrument is numbered 1415. The case is elaborately veneered in walnut and shaped like the old harpsichords, standing on four square, slender tapering legs, of which the two in front are connected by the curved pedal-rail. Side walls and keyboard lid are ornamented all-round by a narrow strip of inlaid maple; the nameboard has bronze ornaments in the form of bunches of grapes.
KEYBOARD: recessed. Compass F_1 to f'''' (six octaves). Ivory-covered naturals, ebony-covered sharps.
INTERIOR: the damper guide-rail is backed with yellow silk and decorated with fretwork. Above the soundboard and halfway between the strings and the piano lid is an extra cover to present the accumulation of dust, built in and supported on little blocks of wood glued to the inside walls.
STRINGING: material from F_1 to D brass, the remainder steel. F_1 to B_1 double-strung, the remaining octaves triple-strung.
ACTION: Viennese action. Hammer heads leather-covered.
STOPS: four wooden pedals, left to right: 1. keyboard shift; 2. bassoon (pressure against string of a yellow silk-padded rail); 3. pianissimo (insertion of felt between hammers and strings); 4. damping. On the back edge in the center of pedal-rail on opening has been cut lengthways corresponding to a prism-shaped piece of wood dove-tailed into the floor of the case, a sign of the original presence of a lyre, which is now missing.
MEASUREMENT: length 118 cm, depth 235 cm, height 92 cm.
SCHLOSS OBERHOFEN, Historisches Museum, Bern. Inv. Nr. 33174.

GRAND PIANOFORTE

André Stein—Austria, Vienna, first half of 19th century

SIGNATURE: inscription on a porcelain plate on nameboard: 'André Stein / d'Augsbourg / à Vienne.'
SHAPE: case in mahogany with bronze mounts, on three legs.
KEYBOARD: compass F_1 to f'''' (six octaves). Ivory naturals, ebony sharps.
INTERIOR: two iron wrestplank braces.
STRINGING: triple-strung.
ACTION: Viennese action.
STOPS: two wooden pedals: keyboard shift and damping.
MEASUREMENT: length 124.5 cm, depth 226 cm, height 88 cm.
IN VIENNA, Kunsthistorisches Museum, Collection of old musical instruments. Inv. No. 569.

GRAND PIANOFORTE

Carl Stein—Austria, Vienna

SIGNATURE: lithographed on paper, in black, under glass, with a brass edge: 'Carl Stein in Wien / Landstrasse Nr. 94'; also on a label on soundboard: 'Nr. 290 / Carl Stein in Wien / Landstrasse Nr. 94.'
SHAPE: the instrument is numbered 290. It stands on three eight-sided pear-shaped legs with heavy brass castors. To judge by its dimensions, this is a concert grand.
KEYBOARD: compass C_I to g'''' (six octaves and a fifth). Ivory-covered naturals, black sharps.
INTERIOR: an iron brace between e' and f'.
STRINGING: C_I to E_I, double-strung, brass; F_I to g'''' triple-strung, thirteen of which are brass; the remainder triple-strung in steel.
ACTION: Viennese action.
STOPS: three pedals on a loosely hanging lyre. Left to right: keyboard shift onto two strings (due corde); the middle pedal slides onto that space on the hammer leather lying between the grooves made in it by the strings' impact; on the right: damping.
MEASUREMENT: length 127 cm, depth 242 cm, height 36 (without stand). These measurements do not include the lid.
IN NÜRNBERG, Rück Collection.

GRAND PIANOFORTE

Johann Baptist Streicher—Austria, Vienna 1834

SIGNATURE: inscription on a brass plate in front: 'Patent pianoforte / erfunden und verfertigt von J. B. Streicher in Wien.' Also on the soundboard: 'No. 2657 Nannette STREICHER geb. Stein und / SOHN / Wien 1834, 261.'
SHAPE: the number of this instrument is 2657. It is made of walnut and stands on three square legs.
KEYBOARD: compass C_1 to f'''' (six octaves and a fourth). Ivory naturals, ebony sharps.
INTERIOR: pinewood soundboard. Wooden framework.
STRINGING: double- and triple-strung.
ACTION: Streicher's down-striking action ('Zugmechanik').
STOPS: three pedals: damping, piano, pianissimo, the two latter by double keyboard shift.
IN MUNICH, Deutsches Museum. Inv. No. 32962.

GRAND PIANOFORTES

Anton Walter—Austria, Vienna, before 1780

Signature: written in black on an oval porcelain plate with brass edge: 'Anton Walter / in Wien.'
Shape: the case is of German walnut with panelled cover, standing on five legs. The long sides are covered with the original lining-paper. Nameboard inlaid and veneered, the legs inlaid in squares. The instrument is numbered '7' on one of the dampers.
Keyboard: compass F_1 to f''' (five octaves). Black naturals with four grooves; sharps stained black with covering of bone.
Stringing: F_1 to a' double-strung, from b' to f''' triple stringing.
Action: Viennese action. Leather-covered hammers.
Stops: the dampers are lifted by means of levers placed to right and left of the wrestplank (hand levers). A pull-button above the keyboard works the moderator-stop. That this is the earliest of all the Anton Walter pianos known of till now is shown by the presence of hand levers for the damping.
In Nürnberg, Rück Collection.

Anton Walter—Austria, Vienna (about 1785)

Signature: inscription on porcelain plate: 'Anton Walter / in Wien.'
Shape: walnut case on five legs.
Keyboard: recessed. Compass F_1 to g''' (five octaves and a second). Ebony naturals, bone-covered sharps.
Interior: small iron wrestplank brace.
Stringing: double- and triple-strung.
Action: Viennese action.
Stops: three knee levers: damping, piano, bassoon.
Measurement: length 103 cm, depth 220 cm, height 83 cm.
In Vienna, Kunsthistorisches Museum; Collection of old musical instruments. Inv. No. 453.

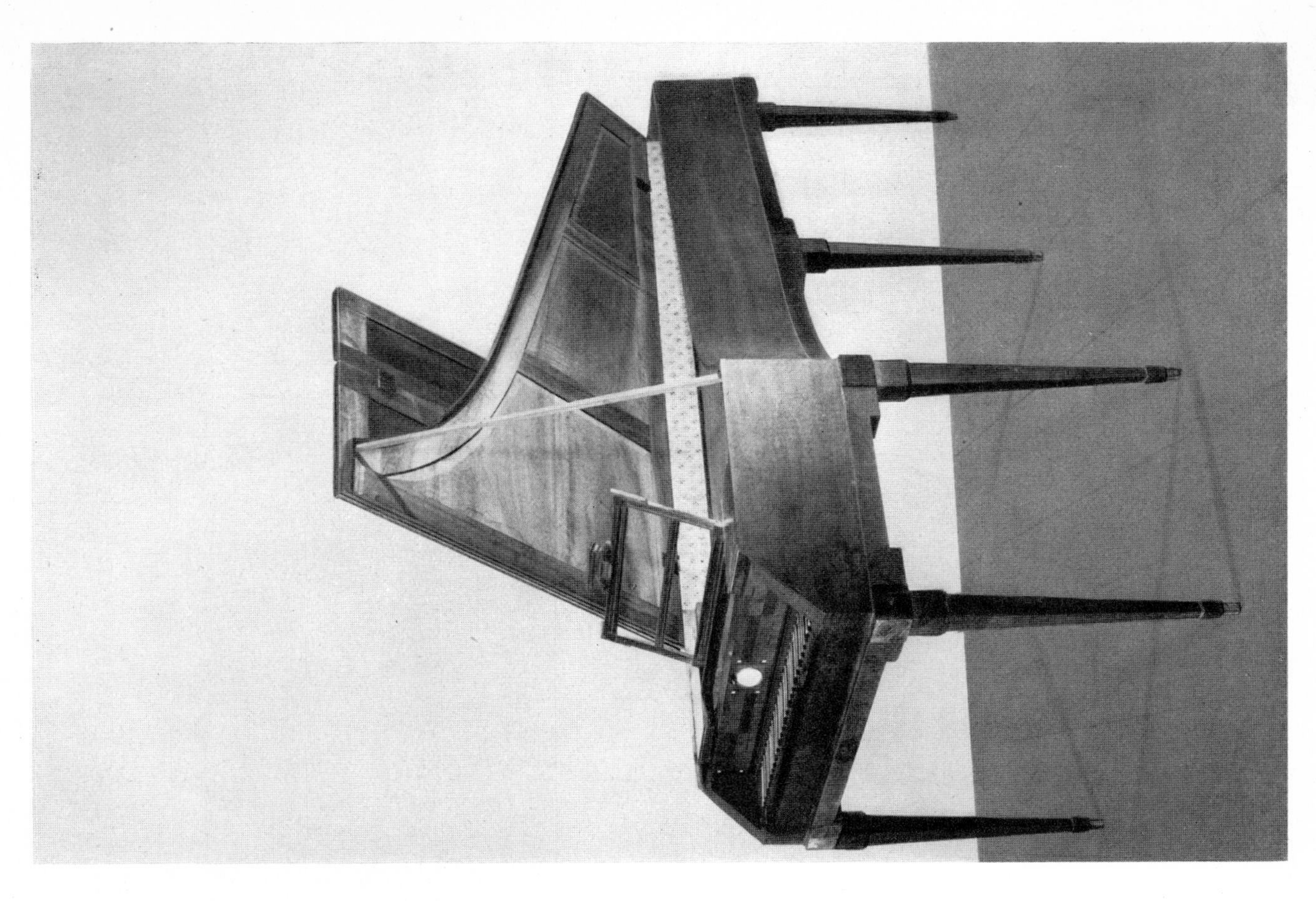

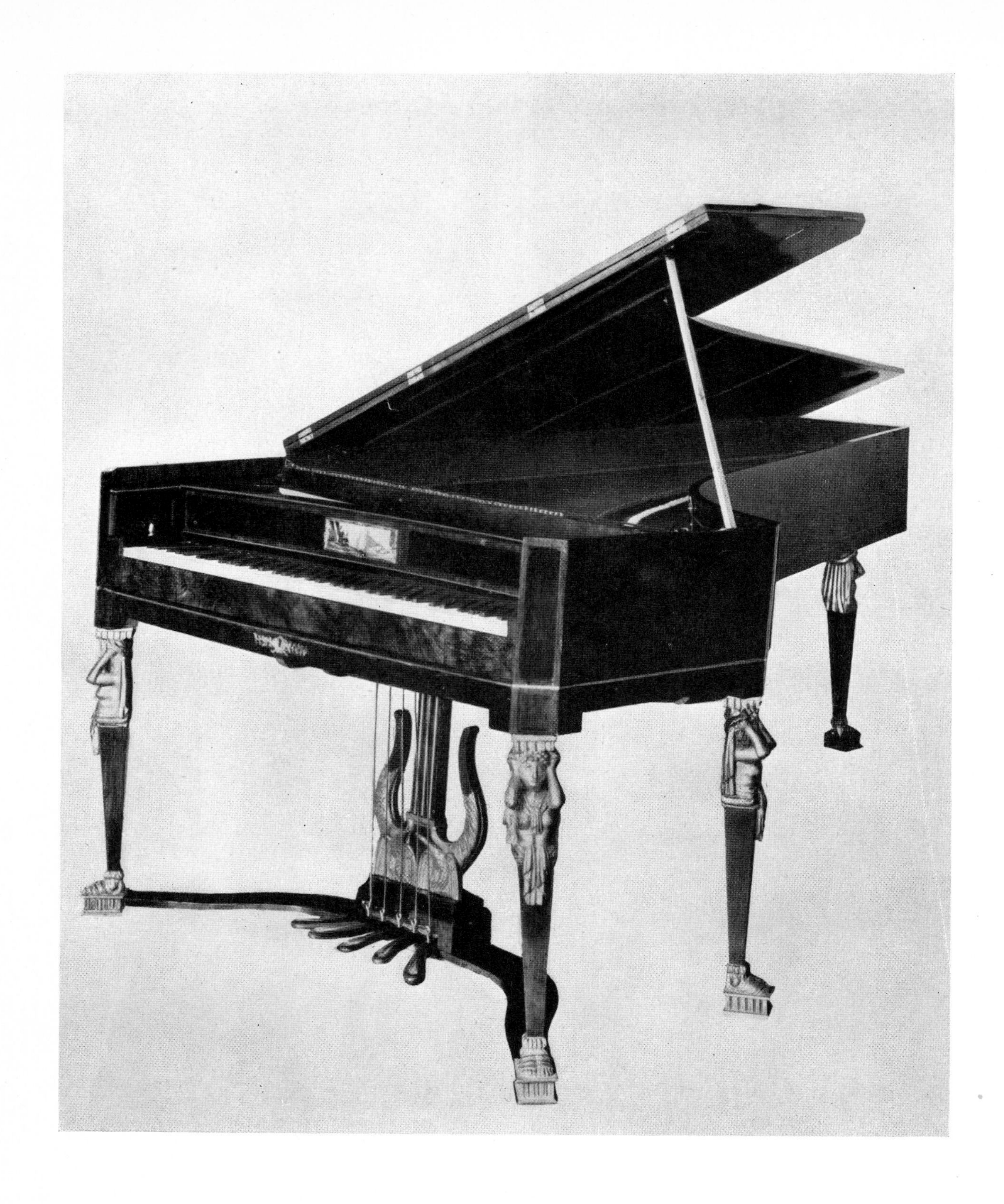

GRAND PIANOFORTE

Conrad Graf—Austria, Vienna 1811

SIGNATURE: firm-label, colored, on nameboard: 'Conrad Graf in Wien.'
SHAPE: grained walnut case. Five legs with caryatides. Gilt lyre, richly carved.
KEYBOARD: recessed. Compass C_1 to f'''' (six octaves and a fourth).
ACTION: Viennese action.
STOPS: five pedals: keyboard shift, piano, bassoon, mandoline, damping.
MEASUREMENT: length 126 cm, depth 223 cm, height 86 cm.
IN BAMBERG, Neupert Collection. Cat. No. 88.

GRAND PIANOFORTES

Ludwig Bösendorfer—Austria, Vienna (about 1870)

Signature: 'Bösendorfer / Wien.'
Shape: the design for the case of this magnificent piano, which was specially constructed by order of the Emperor Franz Joseph, was by Theophil Hansen. It is in maple and ebony, with elaborate marquetry, bronze mounts and sculpture.
Keyboard: compass A_2 to a'''' (seven octaves). Ivory naturals, ebony sharps.
Interior: string-plate strengthened with iron stays.
Stringing: single-, double- and triple-strung.
Action: Viennese action.
Stops: lyre with two pedals: keyboard shift and damping.
Measurement: length 147 cm, depth 245 cm, height 97 cm.
In Vienna, Kunsthistorisches Museum, Collection of old musical instruments. Inv. No. 387 (8962).

Louis Dulcken—Germany, Munich (about 1810)

Signature: inscription painted to resemble inlay, above keyboard: 'Louis Dulcken / à Munic.'
Shape: the case is in polished mahogany, with painted inlay around the edges, above the keyboard and to right and left of the sloping corners of the case. The instrument stands on four legs with bronze feet and gilded, hand-carved caryatides. A rail connects the two front legs, upon which is fixed the lyre in the shape of two dolphins.
Keyboard: compass F_1 to f'''' (six octaves). White naturals, sharps stained black.
Interior: originally the piano had an extra soundboard above the strings.
Stringing: F_1 to e'' double-strung, from f'' to f'''' triple stringing.
Action: Viennese action.
Stops: four pedals: left to right: bassoon, keyboard shift, moderator with cloth rail, and damping.
Measurement: length 116.3 cm, depth 230 cm, height 29 cm (without base platform).
In Nürnberg, Rück Collection.

GRAND PIANOFORTE

Johann Heinrich Silbermann—France, Strasbourg 1776

SIGNATURE: inscription on pierced parchment label on front of the action: 'Jean Henry Silbermann/Facteur de Forté-Piano &/de Clavecins 1776/A Strasbourg.'
SHAPE: the instrument, which is made of solid walnut, rests on a stand having six slender, curved legs ('pieds de biche').
KEYBOARD: compass F_1 to f''' (five octaves). Ebony naturals, bone sharps (Alsace!).
INTERIOR: the parchment rose sunk into the soundboard shows a triangle with an 'S' at every side. The wrest-plank is placed, strangely enough, above the stringing, to the underneath of which the strings are fixed. The wrest-pins pierce through and tuning is done from above.
STRINGING: double-strung.
ACTION: English action with under-hammer; 'Einzel-Oberdämpfung' (single over-damping) with two guide-wires. The whole layout is almost exactly similar to that of Cristofori's piano, dated 1720.
STOPS: two front stops: damping, keyboard shift.
MEASUREMENT: length 103 cm, depth 240 cm, height 85 cm.
IN BERLIN, Institut für Musikforschung. Cat. No. 12.

GRAND PIANOFORTE

Pascal Taskin—France, Paris 1790

SIGNATURE: signed on the rose: 'Pascal Taskin 1790.'
SHAPE: case in Louis XVI style, inside decoration Louis XV. Inlaid borders in lemon-wood. Nameboard decorated with garlands. Six round, fluted legs.
KEYBOARD: compass F_1 to f''' (five octaves). Ebony naturals, bone- or ivory-covered sharps.
INTERIOR: elaborately painted soundboard, beautiful rose.
ACTION: 'Stossmechanik'.
STOPS: two knee levers: piano, damping.
AT VERSAILLES, Petit Trianon.

The tradition that this instrument belonged to Marie-Antoinette cannot be true, for Marie-Antoinette left Versailles in October 1789, never more to return, and the instrument was only finished in the year 1790.

PASCAL
1790

GRAND PIANOFORTE

John Broadwood & Sons—England, London (about 1860)

SIGNATURE: 'John Broadwood & Sons, London.'
KEYBOARD: compass A_2 to a'''' (seven octaves). Covering of keys is modern.
STRINGING: single- to triple-strung.
IN PARIS, private property.

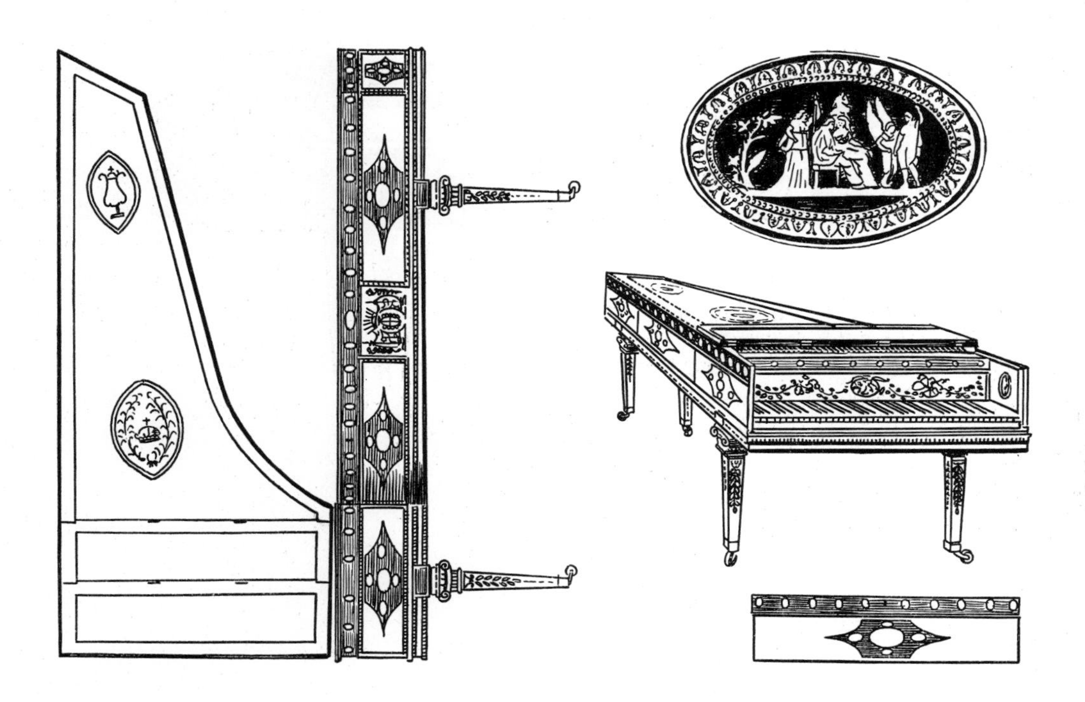

Engravings by Thomas Sheraton (1751–1806)

Designs for John Broadwood by the famous furniture designer for the piano ordered by Don Manuel de Godoy.
IN LONDON, the property of John Broadwood & Sons.

GRAND PIANOFORTE

John Broadwood & Sons—England, London (about 1796)

SHAPE: after a design by Thomas Sheraton (1751–1806).
IN TROY, NEW YORK, Private property.

This instrument was ordered by Don Manuel de Godoy, Prime Minister of Spain, for presentation to the Queen of Spain.

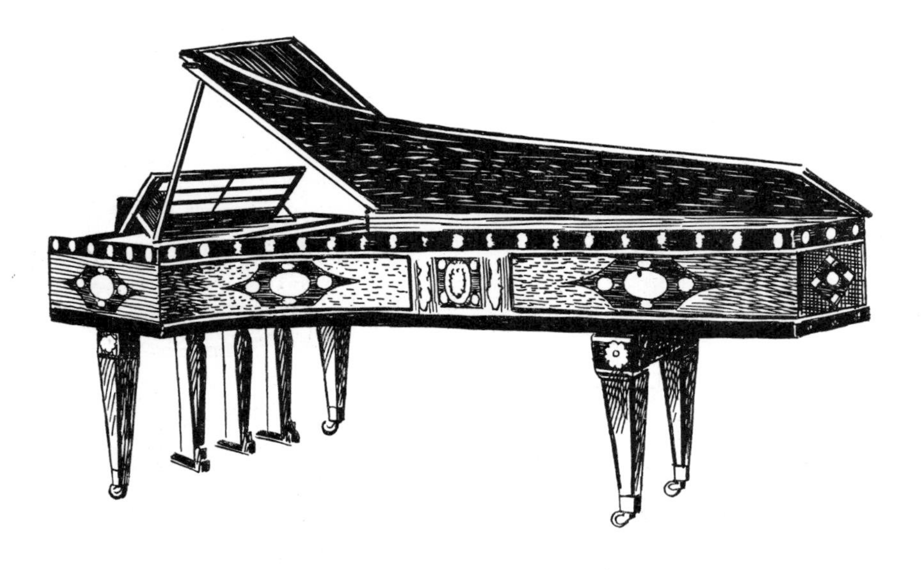

John Broadwood & Sons—England, London (about 1860)

IN PARIS, private property.

PEDAL PIANOFORTE

UNSIGNED.
SHAPE: not only does this instrument stand on a pedal-base, but also on two feet, turned in wood, in a winding thread pattern.
KEYBOARD: compass: manual F_1 to a‴ (five octaves and the third); pedal E_1/C_1 to A (octave and a sixth); short bass-octave. The pedal keyboard is arranged as follows:
E_1, F_1, $F\sharp_1$, G_1, $G\sharp_1$, A_1, $B\flat_1$, B_1, C, C♯, D, D♯, E, F, F♯, G, G♯, A. The sound, as follows: C_1, F_1, D_1, G_1, E_1, A_1, $B\flat_1$, B_1, C, $C\sharp_1$, D, $D\sharp_1$, E, F, $F\sharp_1$, G, $G\sharp_1$, A.
The pedal sounds accordingly, chromatically from C_1 to $B\flat_1$, and diatonically from C to A. This arrangement was usual in 1770, when the organ-builders retained the short octave on the pedal-keys because organists were accustomed to it, replacing the missing semitones of the contra-octave between the whole tones of the great-octave.
INTERIOR: two soundboards: one lying under the manual-strings. The usual base board of these pianos has been eliminated and in its place is a second soundboard with a straight bridge over which the separate stringing for the pedal-keyboard runs. The wrest-pins for the pedal-stringing lie under the manual: in this way there are two quite separate wrest-pin units.
STRINGING: manual: double-strung. Pedal: triple-strung.
ACTION: manual: Prellzungen; pedal: down-striking Viennese action with under-damping.
STOPS: two knee levers, damping and piano.
MEASUREMENT: length 97 cm, depth 208.5 cm, height 26.5 cm.
IN NÜRNBERG, Rück Collection.

This instrument is unsigned, but the type of work and the unusual form of the brass hammer sheath seems to point to its being made by Leopold Mozart's piano-builder Johannes Schmid, born in Wangen in the Principality of Stühlingen, died 1804 in Salzburg.
In Dr. Rück's Collection in Nürnberg there is a pianoforte signed in pencil on the base board under the soundboard which has very characteristic brass hammer sheaths (Kapseln) similar to those of this pedal-pianoforte. Besides that, this instrument is finished in the same way as the pedal-pianoforte, Cat. No. 70 in the Carolino-Augusteum Museum in Salzburg. As the pedals to this piano were missing, they have been added in strict historical accordance with those of the Salzburg pedal-pianoforte.

SQUARE PIANO

Land of origin and date unknown

UNSIGNED.
SHAPE: the whole case is ornamented in flat reliefs made of plaster; bunches of grapes, trails of vine-leaves in old-gold on a grey-green ground. The sides are ornamented throughout with conventional bordering, the painting inside the lid, of a pair of dancers in colorful clothing, being framed in stucco. The stand is of later date.
KEYBOARD: compass C to f''' (four octaves and a fourth).
ACTION: primitive German action. No dampers.
MEASUREMENT: width 4 ft 4 in., depth 1 ft 6 in., height 2 ft 8 1/2 in., height of case 5 1/2 in. (without stand).
AT HOLYOKE, The Belle Skinner Collection. Cat. No. 85.

SQUARE PIANOS

Johann Söcher—Germany, Sonthofen (Allgäu) 1742

SIGNATURE: label in the piano: 'Johann Söcher im Obern Sonthofen, Allgäu 1742.'
SHAPE: case in soft wood, painted brown. Lid decorated with painting of an Italian harbor with the figure of St. Cecilia.
KEYBOARD: compass C to f''' (four octaves and a fourth).
INTERIOR: tunable from the side.
ACTION: 'Stossmechanik' with under-damping.
STOPS: hand lever for damping.
MEASUREMENT: length 138 cm, depth 20 cm, height 50 cm.
IN BAMBERG, Neupert Collection. Cat. No. 124.

Gottfried Silbermann—Germany, Freiberg 1749

SIGNATURE: handwritten label, half torn off, inside back wall: '(Got)tfried Silbermann me Fecit 1749.'
SHAPE: case in walnut and rosewood.
KEYBOARD: compass C to e''' (four octaves and a third). Ebony naturals, bone-covered sharps.
ACTION: primitive German action.
MEASUREMENT: length 145 cm, depth 53 cm, height 76 cm.
AT THE HAGUE, Gemeente Museum.

TRANSPOSING SQUARE PIANO

(Johann Matthäus Schmahl)—Germany, Ulm, about 1792

UNSIGNED.
SHAPE: the case is shaped like a lying harp, in walnut and with pretty brass hinges. The instrument reasts on a table-shaped walnut stand, its sides curved to correspond with those of the case. The four legs are fluted, curved and tapering. There is panelling on the lid and to the right of the keyboard is an oblong drawer.
KEYBOARD: compass: F_1 to g''' (five octaves and a second). Ebony-covered naturals, bone-covered sharps. The faces of naturals have an appliqué of embossed parchment. By pushing in the keyboard, transposition of two semitones higher takes place.
INTERIOR: the string-plate is decorated in Rococo style with fretwork. The rose over the soundhole on the soundboard is in the shape of a bronzed pierced star. The maker's handwritten naming of the wrest-pins, in black and red ink, is also to be found on those instruments in Heyer's Catalogue numbered 102 and 105, both built by Schmahl.
STRINGING: single-strung.
ACTION: 'primitive Anglo-German action without escapement. The little hammers, all lying in special wooden grooves are threaded on a string which serves as an axis. The whole action can be lifted out from the back wall of the case.
STOPS: five front stops in nameboard. Left to right: 1. piano (insertion of a silk strip between hammer and strings); 2. pianissimo (insertion of a toothed leather strip between strings and hammer); 3. damping; 4. harp (pressure from the right of wooden rail covered with wool fringe against the strings); 5. missing (probably the drum, knocking of a rail against the soundboard).
MEASUREMENT: length 131 cm, depth 56.5 cm, height 85.4 cm (with stand).
IN ZÜRICH, Schweizerisches Landesmuseum. L.M. 16777.

This instrument came from the Maria Hilf Convent at Altstätten (St. Gallen).

TRANSPOSING SQUARE PIANO

(Johannes Matthäus Schmahl)—Germany, Ulm, about 1792

IN ZÜRICH, Schweizerisches Landesmuseum. L.M. 16177.

TRANSPOSING SQUARE PIANO

(Johannes Matthäus Schmahl)—Germany, Ulm, about 1792

IN ZÜRICH, Schweizerisches Landesmuseum. L.M. 16177.

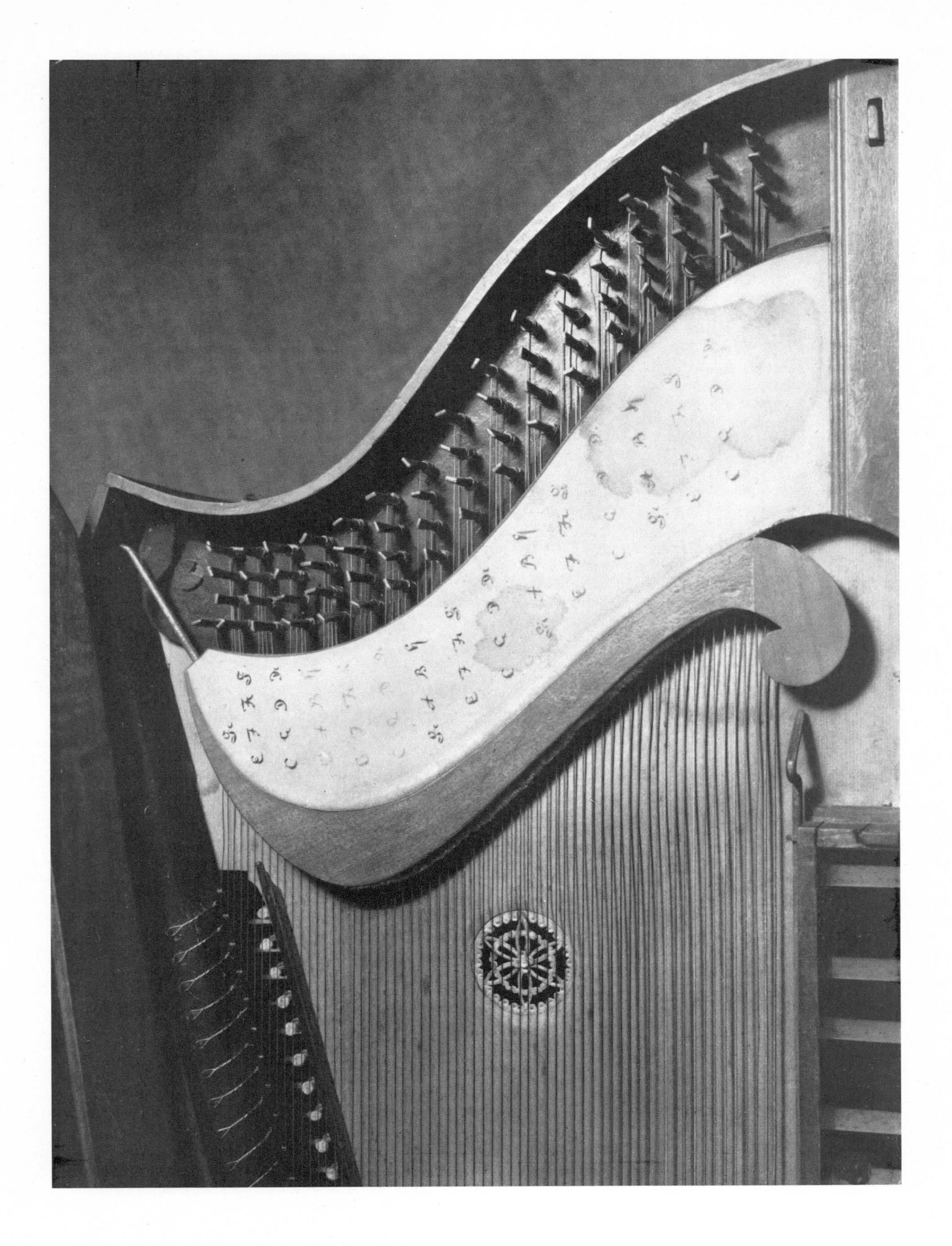

Johannes Zumpe Londini Fecit 1767

SQUARE PIANOS

Johannes Zumpe—England, London 1767

SIGNATURE: on the nameboard: 'Johannes Zumpe Londini Fecit 1767.'
KEYBOARD: compass G_1 to f''' (four octaves and a seventh). White naturals, black sharps.
ACTION: 'Stossmechanik'.
STOPS: two stops, left of player: divided damping.
MEASUREMENT: length 4 ft 3 in., width 1 ft 6 1/2 in., depth 6 1/2 in.
IN LONDON, Victoria and Albert Museum. W. 27–1928.

Goulding, D'Almaine, Potter & Company—England, London after 1811

SIGNATURE: on nameboard: 'Patent/GOULDING, D'ALMAINE, POTTER & CO. Music Sellers to Their/Royal Highnesses the Prince and Princess of Wales/20 SOHO SQUARE LONDON AND 7 WESTMORLAND STREET/DUBLIN.'
SHAPE: this beautiful case in Hepplewhite style is made of satin-wood with rosewood edges, inlaid with strips of ebony and holly-wood. Classical portraits in medallions, in oil-color, with cupids playing on instruments, rose-garlands and arabesques adorn the outside. Inside the lid is a picture of classically-clothed figure sitting under a pergola with landscape background. On both sides are medallions of musical emblems. Garlands of roses on latticework decorate the nameboard with an oval in the center containing maker's name. The instrument rests on six square, tapering legs carved with Ionic capitals and similarly decorated as the case.
KEYBOARD: compass F_1 to c'''' (five octaves and a fifth).
MEASUREMENT: width 5 ft 5 in., depth 2 ft 2 in., height 2 ft 10 1/2 in.
AT HOLYOKE, The Belle Skinner Collection. Cat. No. 89.

SQUARE PIANO

Adam Beyer—England, London 1777

SIGNATURE: on nameboard 'Adam Beyer Londini fecit 1777 / Compton Street St. Ann's Soho.'
SHAPE: rosewood case on a stand.
KEYBOARD: compass F_1 to f''' (five octaves). F_1# missing.
INTERIOR: to be tuned at one side.
ACTION: 'Stossmechanik'.
STOPS: four pedals: divided damping, lute, swell (lid, the large pedal at the right).
IN BAMBERG, Neupert Collection. Cat. No. 67.

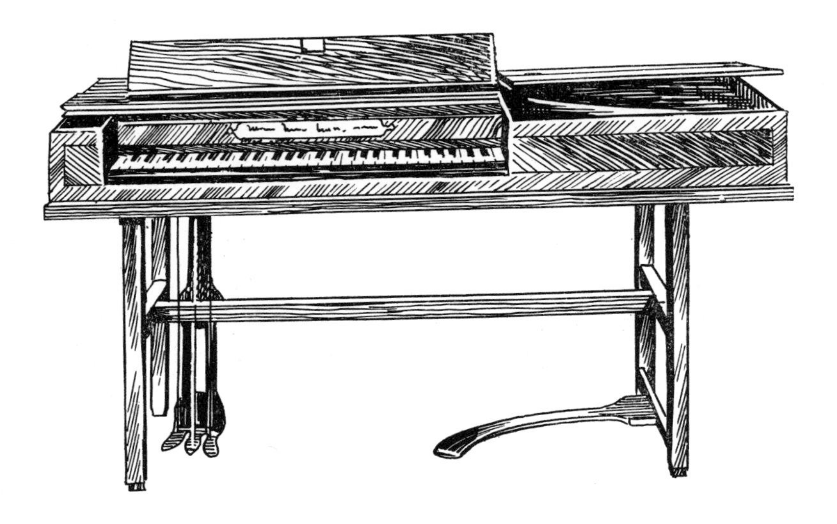

SQUARE PIANO

Alpheus Babcock—U.S.A., Boston (between 1810/29)

SIGNATURE: maker's name on nameboard: 'Made by / BABCOCK / FOR R. MACKAY / BOSTON.'
SHAPE: this beautiful old instrument, which is in perfect condition, is built of mahogany and rosewood with inlaid brass strips. It has three drawers with brass handles and stands on six legs decorated with brass inlay on brass castors. Nameboard and sides made of rosewood with brass lines. The instrument is numbered 252.
KEYBOARD: compass F_1 to f'''' (six octaves).
STOPS: two pedals.
MEASUREMENT: width 5 ft 7 1/2 in., depth 2 ft 2 3/4 in., height 2 ft 9 3/4 in.
AT HOLYOKE, The Belle Skinner Collection. Cat. No. 88.

Johannes

SQUARE PIANOS

(Johann Andreas Silbermann? France, Strasbourg)
middle of 18th century

UNSIGNED.
SHAPE: strongly reminiscent of a clavichord, this case is veneered with walnut. Inside the lid is an oil-painting on canvas of an alpine landscape.
KEYBOARD: compass C to e''' (four octaves and a third). Ebony-covered naturals, ivory-covered sharps. The key-faces of the naturals are adorned with gold embossed leather.
INTERIOR: scattered flowers painted on soundboard.
STRINGING: single- and double-strung.
ACTION: German action. The upper part of the hammers consists of parchment rings.
STOPS: left of soundboard: piano insertion of a cloth-covered rail, and damping.
MEASUREMENT: length 96 cm, depth 39 cm, height 83 cm.
IN LEIPZIG, Instrumentenmuseum der Universität. Heyer Cat. No. 97.

The picture in the Heyer Catalogue of the above instrument includes the stand and is described as follows: "The stand of this instrument is in walnut with four slightly curved legs; in the upper part there is a drawer papered inside with old wallpaper."

Johann Kilian Mercken—France, Paris, 1770

SIGNATURE: on nameboard: 'Johannes Kilianus Mercken / Paris Fecit 1770.'
KEYBOARD: compass F_1 to f''' (five octaves). Black naturals, white sharps.
STOPS: two inside stops, left of player: divided damping.
MEASUREMENT: length $152\frac{1}{2}$ cm, depth $50\frac{1}{2}$ cm, height 80 cm.
IN PARIS, Conservatoire des Arts et Métiers. No. 10960.

SQUARE PIANO

Balthazar Péronard—France, Paris 1779

SIGNATURE: on nameboard: 'Fait par Balthazar Péronard / rue Melé aux Concerts des trois frères à Paris En 1779.'
SHAPE: mahogany case profusely inlaid with colored woods. On the lid, in an oval framing, are inlaid musical instruments.
KEYBOARD: compass F_1 to f''' (five octaves). Ebony naturals, sharps covered in ivory.
INTERIOR: colorfully painted soundboard: scattered flowers, scenes in French style, Putto-figures and dogs.
STRINGING: double-strung.
MEASUREMENT: length 143.2 cm, depth 56 cm, height 76 cm.
IN FRANKFURT AM MAIN, Historisches Museum. Inv. No. 1942/8.

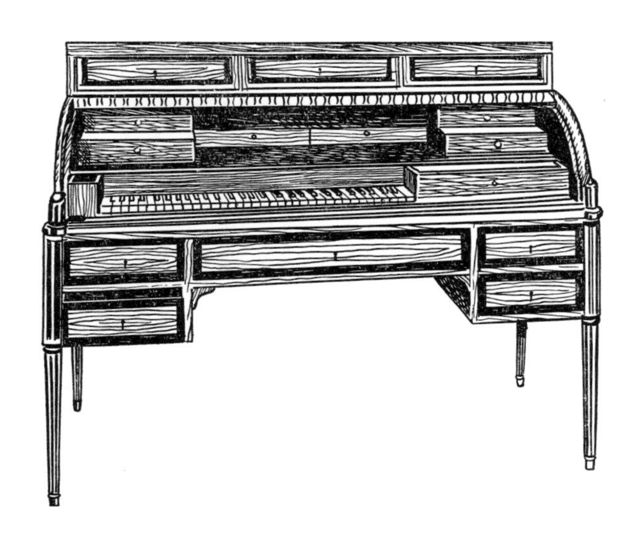

PIANO-SECRÉTAIRE

Beginning 19th century

UNSIGNED.
SHAPE: this unusual instrument is in veneered mahogany on four turned and fluted legs. It forms a complete rolltop desk with the rolltop, the drawers, the shelves and the pullout writing-flap under which lies the keyboard. All-round the case stands a pierced brass gallery.
KEYBOARD: compass F_1 to f''' (five octaves). Ivory-covered naturals, ebony-covered sharps.
STRINGING: double-strung.
ACTION: 'Prellmechanik'.
STOPS: left side of keyboard: piano and damping.
MEASUREMENT: length 142 cm, depth 65 cm, height 118 cm.
IN LEIPZIG, Instrumentenmuseum der Universität. Heyer Cat. No. 131.

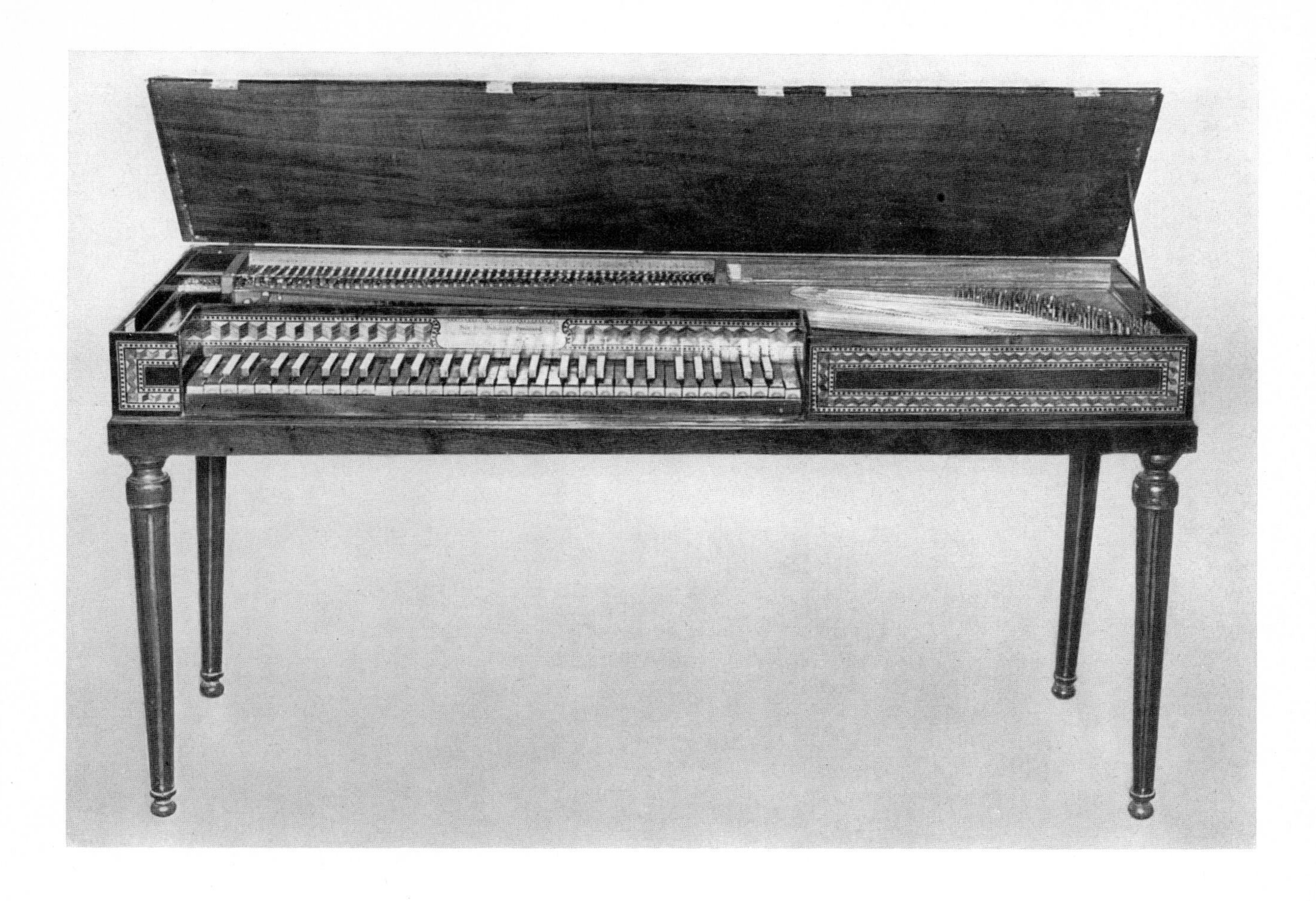

SQUARE PIANO

Henri Pape—France, Paris 1840

SIGNATURE: 'Pape, Paris et Londres.'
SHAPE: this lovely case in rosewood inlaid with mother-of-pearl stands on four curved, carved legs, joined in couples by rails.
KEYBOARD: compass C_1 to g'''' (six octaves and a fifth).
INTERIOR: bass to be tuned at the back, treble at the side.
ACTION: Down-striking.
STOPS: lyre with two pedals: piano and damping.
MEASUREMENT: length 170 cm, depth 57 cm, height 107 cm.
IN BAMBERG, Neupert Collection. Cat. No. 109.

SQUARE PIANO IN THE FORM OF A CHEST OF DRAWERS

C. G. Friederici—Germany, Gera (1804 or 1805)

SIGNATURE: written inscription on a milk-glass plate above keys: 'C. G. Friederici / Fürstl. Kammerrath / u. Klavierbauer / in / Gera.'
SHAPE: this beautiful instrument is in red polished pear-wood on four short feet on brass castors. Below, it is constructed like a chest of drawers with four large drawers, handles and ornamental keyholes of the period. Nameboard and cheekpieces decorated with veneer in ash-wood. The maker's plate is framed in a beautiful bronze mount.
KEYBOARD: compass F_1 to f'''' (six octaves). Ebony-covered naturals, bone-covered sharps.
STRINGING: single- and double-strung.
ACTION: developed German action. No checks used.
STOPS: two knee levers: damping.
MEASUREMENT: length 162 cm, depth 65 cm, height 82 cm.
IN LEIPZIG, Instrumentenmuseum der Universität. Heyer Cat. No. 130.

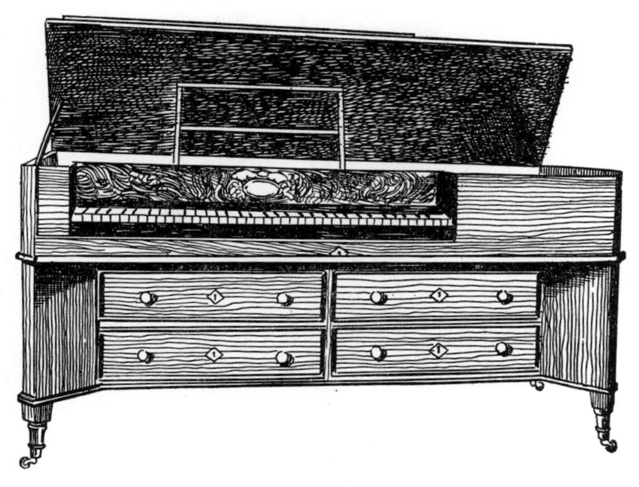

SQUARE PIANO IN THE FORM OF A TEA-TABLE

F. Mathuscheck—Germany, Worms 1840 (see p. 377)

SIGNATURE: inscription in gold-bronze on nameboard: 'F. Mathuscheck / in / Worms.'
SHAPE: when closed, this instrument looks exactly like an octagonal table. It is veneered with mahogany on a heavy, elaborately carved pillar-shaped stand which ends in four twisted feet. Around the whole outside edge of the table runs a pierced gilt rail. Table edges and front part of lid ornamented with mother-of-pearl and veins of maple-wood. The cheekpieces are carved. On opening the lid which forms half of the table, the keyboard automatically runs forward; on closing the lid it returns to its original position.
KEYBOARD: compass F_1 to g'''' (six octaves and a second). Ivory-covered naturals, ebony-covered sharps.
INTERIOR: the iron framework is further strengthened by four iron stays above the soundboard. The soundboard lies *above* the strings.
ACTION: Viennese action.
STOPS: damping pedal.
MEASUREMENT: length 130 cm, depth 123 cm, height 82 cm.
IN LEIPZIG, Instrumentenmuseum der Universität. Heyer Cat. No. 158.

This was the first instrument built by Mathuscheck.

SQUARE PIANO

William Stodart & Sons—England, London (after 1820)

With iron parallel tubes similar to Thom & Allen's Patent (1820).
IN CAMBRIDGE, private property (W. Moore).

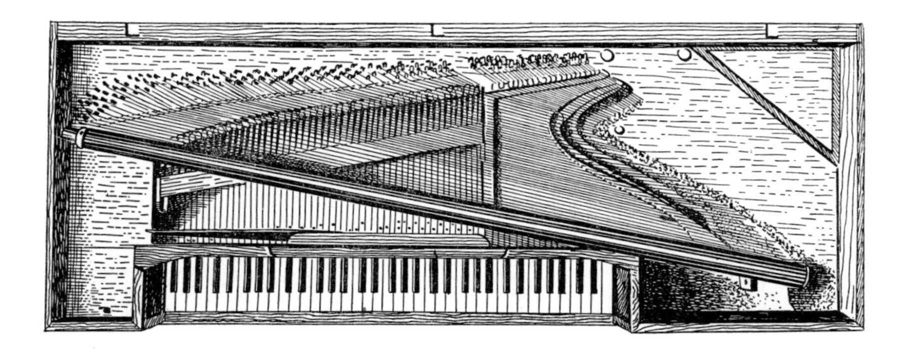

HARP-SHAPED PIANOFORTE

Christian Gottlob Hubert—Germany, Ansbach 1785

SIGNATURE: on the nameboard: 'Christian Gottlob / Hubert / Hochfürstlich Anspachischer / Hof-Instrumenten- / Bauer / fecit Anno 1785.'

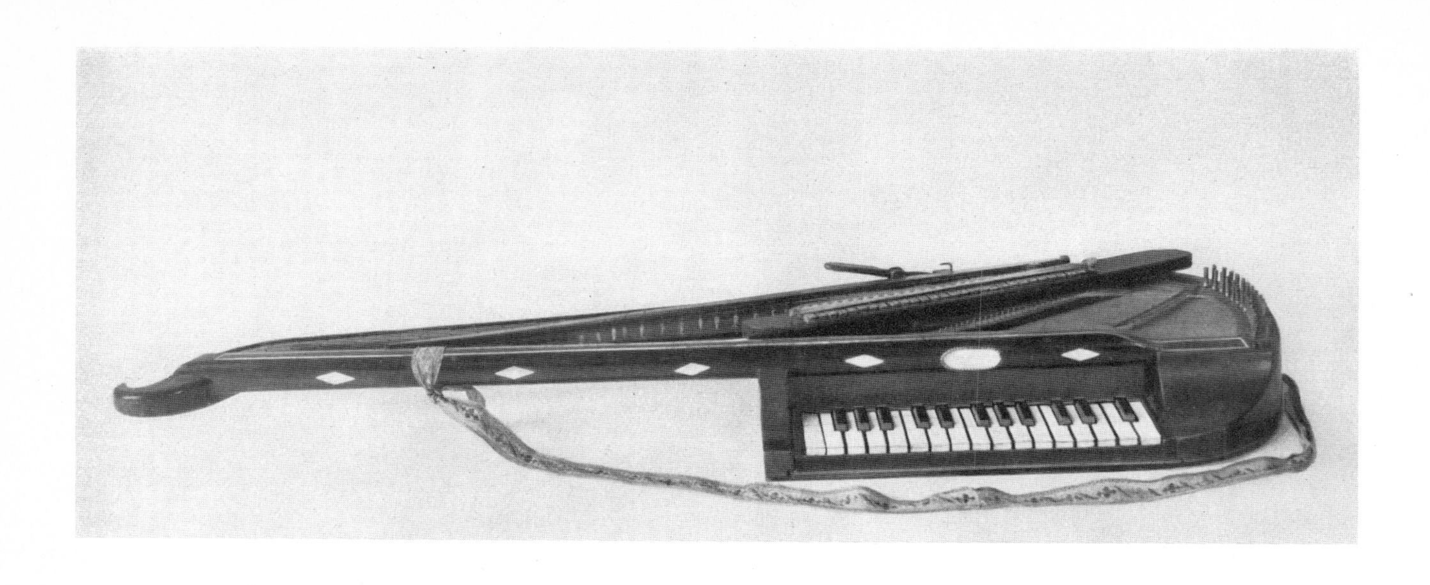

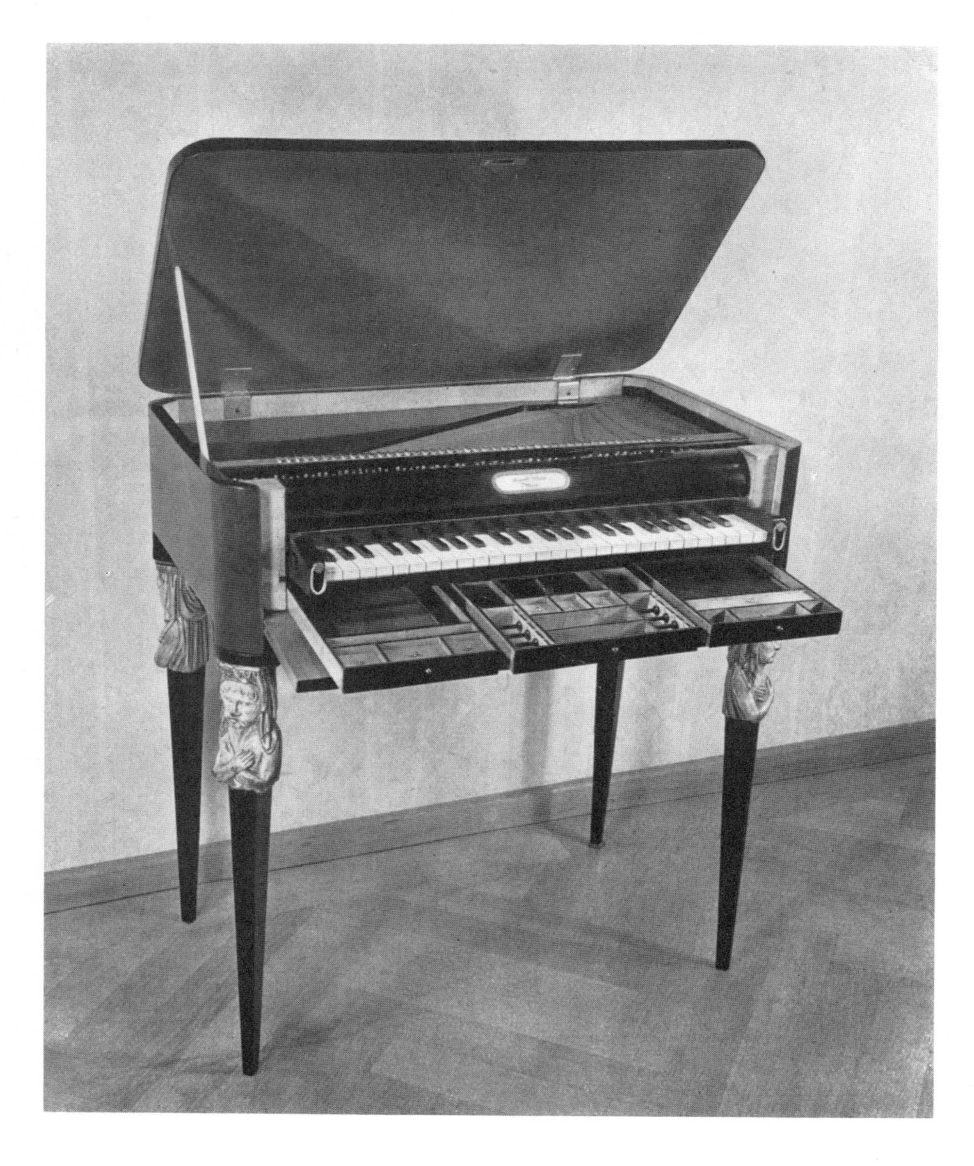

SHAPE: case in veneered walnut. As in Silbermann's instruments, the lid is panelled and constructed in three parts by which means certain modulations in the tone-volume can be achieved. The outside is decorated with beautiful ornamental inlay and poker-work. Particularly elaborate are the right side, the keyboard lid and the nameboard. There are three curved legs, carved and with bronze mounts.
KEYBOARD: C to f''' (four octaves and a fourth). Ebony-covered naturals, ivory-covered sharps.
STRINGING: double-strung.
ACTION: primitive English action without escapement.
STOPS: on right cheekpiece, two stops with ivory buttons: piano (insertion of felt-covered rail), and damping.
MEASUREMENT: length 62 cm, depth 162 cm, height 86 cm.
IN ERLANGEN, Rück Collection.

ORPHICA

Carl Leopold Röllig—Austria, Vienna, beginning 19th century

SIGNATURE: engraved signature on a little ivory disc: 'Clem. (sic!) Röllig / Invent.'
SHAPE: this lovely instrument is in veneered mahogany. The front edge of the case is inlaid with ivory veining and lozenge-shaped pieces of ivory. The name-plate is framed in brass beading and a maple-wood edging inlays the base of the outer case.
KEYBOARD: compass e to g'' (two octaves and a third). Bone-covered naturals, ebony sharps.
STRINGING: single-strung.
ACTION: Viennese action (a little rail, worked with the left hand, by slight pressure of a pointed piece of felt on the middle of the string, produces the higher octave of that particular note).
MEASUREMENT: length 102 cm, depth 24 cm, height 8 1/2 cm.
IN LEIPZIG, Instrumentenmuseum der Universität. Heyer Cat. No. 168.

SEWING TABLE PIANO

Joseph Klein—Austria, Vienna, about 1820

SIGNATURE: inscription on porcelain plate on nameboard: 'Joseph Klein / in / Wien.'
SHAPE: lid and sides of case veneered with thuya-wood, the curved edges being probably of stained maple; polished black feet ending above in many-colored heads.
KEYBOARD: compass f to f'''' (four octaves). Bone-covered naturals, black sharps.
STRINGING: double-strung.
ACTION: Viennese action.
MEASUREMENT: length 44.5 cm, depth 74.6 to 75 cm, height 17.3 cm (without pediment).
IN NÜRNBERG, Rück Collection.

UPRIGHT GRAND PIANOFORTE

Domenico del Mela—Italy, Galliano (Mugello) 1739

SIGNATURE: on nameboard: 'D. Dominicus Del Mela inventor fecit anno 1739.'
SHAPE: the discant-side of this instrument ends in a whorl. It has a four-legged, table-shaped stand from which it can be lifted by two handles.
KEYBOARD: fourty-five keys.
INTERIOR: rose on the soundboard.
STRINGING: triple-strung.
ACTION: 'Gelenkmechanik' without escapement. It is placed behind the soundboard and can be taken in and out through an opening at the back of the instrument. The checks are missing. The hammers strike from behind.
IN FLORENCE, Instrument Collection of the Conservatory of Music 'Luigi Cherubini'.

Oldest remaining upright pianoforte with definite date. An upright pianoforte from Thüringen (in Leipzig, Kinsky Cat. No. 106) bears a still earlier date (1735) but the authenticity is contested.

PYRAMID

Christian Ernst Friederici—Germany, Gera 1745

SIGNATURE: inside the case: 'Dieze Pyramyte hat gefertiget und erfunden Christian Ernst Friederici Orgelbauer in Gera in Monats 7 tr Anno 1745.'
SHAPE: the pyramid-shaped case is elaborately inlaid with flowers, ornaments and dancers. It stands on a table with four pillar-shaped legs (probably added later).
KEYBOARD: compass F_1 to d''' (four octaves and a sixth). White naturals, black sharps.
INTERIOR: soundboard rose.
ACTION: 'Stossmechanik'.
STOPS: 1. sordine (insertion of leather strip between hammer and string). 2. damping.
MEASUREMENT: length 99 cm, height including table 221 cm.
IN BRUSSELS, Musée instrumental du Conservatoire Royal de Musique. Cat. No. 1631.

Oldest remaining pyramid pianoforte.

MUSIC ROOM
IN THE GOETHEHAUS IN FRANCFORT ON THE MAIN

with the pyramid piano by Christian Ernst Friederici, Gera (1745)

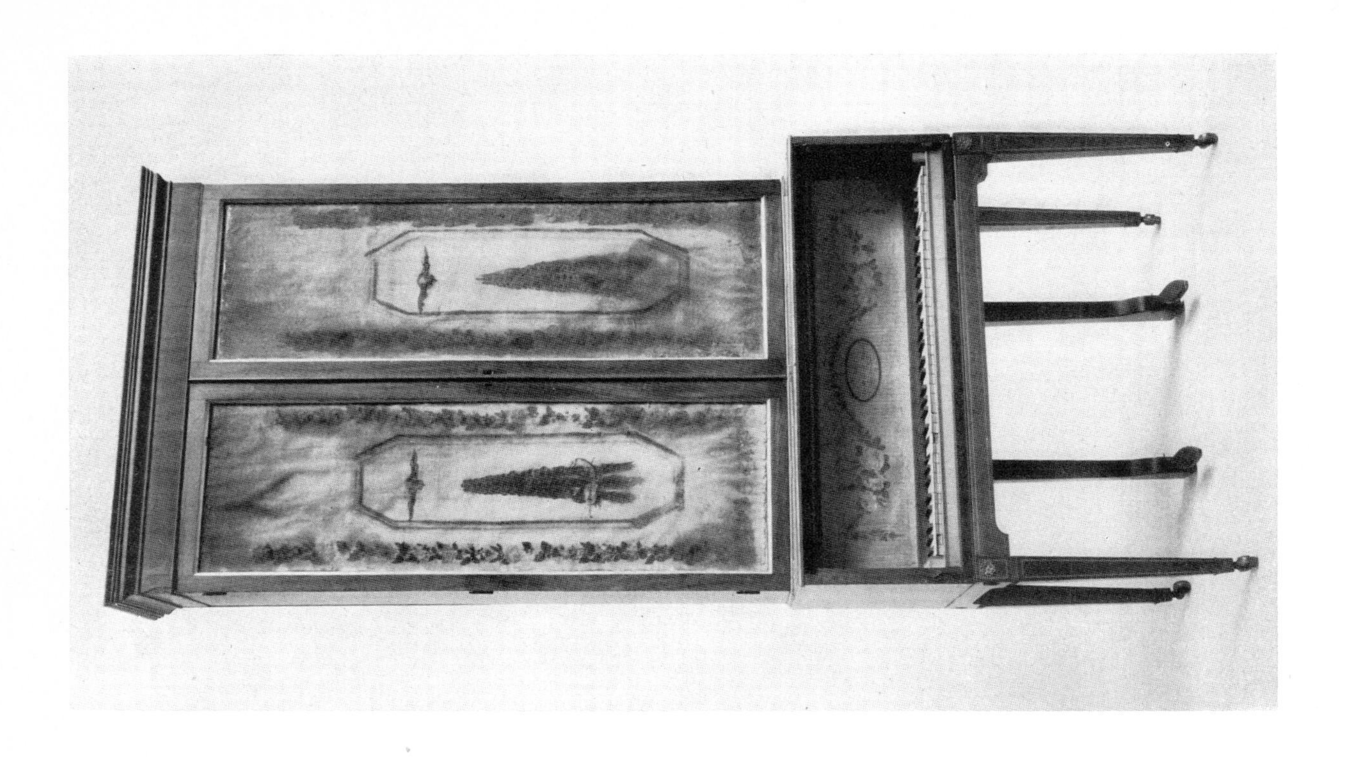

UPRIGHT GRAND PIANOFORTES

William W. Stodart—England, London 1810

SIGNATURE: on nameboard: 'Patent / W. W. Stodart, Makers / Golden Square London.'
SHAPE: the case is in veneered mahogany on four, square tapering legs decorated with brass ornaments. The upper part in cabinet form consists of double doors stretched with old white velvet decorated with faded paintings of musical instruments. The nameboard is also adorned with garlands. Two music- or book-shelves fill the right side of case, whilst the left contains the actual instrument.
KEYBOARD: compass F_1 to c'''' (five octaves and a fifth). Ivory-covered naturals, ebony-covered sharps.
STRINGING: triple-strung (straight).
ACTION: English action ('Upright Grand Pianoforte action'), placed behind the soundboard. The hammers strike from behind through an opening.
STOPS: two pedals.
MEASUREMENT: height 8 ft 8 in., width 3 ft 7 1/2 in., depth 1 ft 10 in.
IN NEW YORK, Metropolitan Museum of Art. Cat. No. 2804.

Wachtl and Bleyer—Austria, Vienna about 1812

SIGNATURE: 'Erfunden von Wachtl und Bleyer in Wien.'
SHAPE: mahogany case.
KEYBOARD: compass F_1 to g'''' (six octaves and a second). White naturals, black sharps.
ACTION: suspended Viennese action.
STOPS: five pedals: bassoon, damping, piano, keyboard shift, drum.
MEASUREMENT: length 117 cm, depth 54 cm, height 203 cm.
IN BAMBERG, Neupert Collection. Cat. No. 95.

UPRIGHT GRAND PIANOFORTE

C. Ehrlich—Germany, Bamberg, about 1820?

SIGNATURE: inscription in black letters sunk into the soundboard: 'C. EHRLICH / BAMBERG.'
SHAPE: case in polished cherry-wood with black rails. Upper part of case lined with gold-colored silk, formerly with sky-blue. The two pillars supporting the keyboard are topped by black sphinx-like heads with golden tresses and end in black feet.
KEYBOARD: compass F_1 to f'''' (six octaves). Black naturals, ivory-covered sharps.
STRINGING: double and triple stringing.
ACTION: suspended Viennese action.
STOPS: six pedals; left to right: bassoon, damping, pianissimo, piano, keyboard shift, drum and bells.
MEASUREMENT: length 118 cm, depth 61 cm, height 196.3 cm.
IN NÜRNBERG, Rück Collection.

View of instrument closed and open

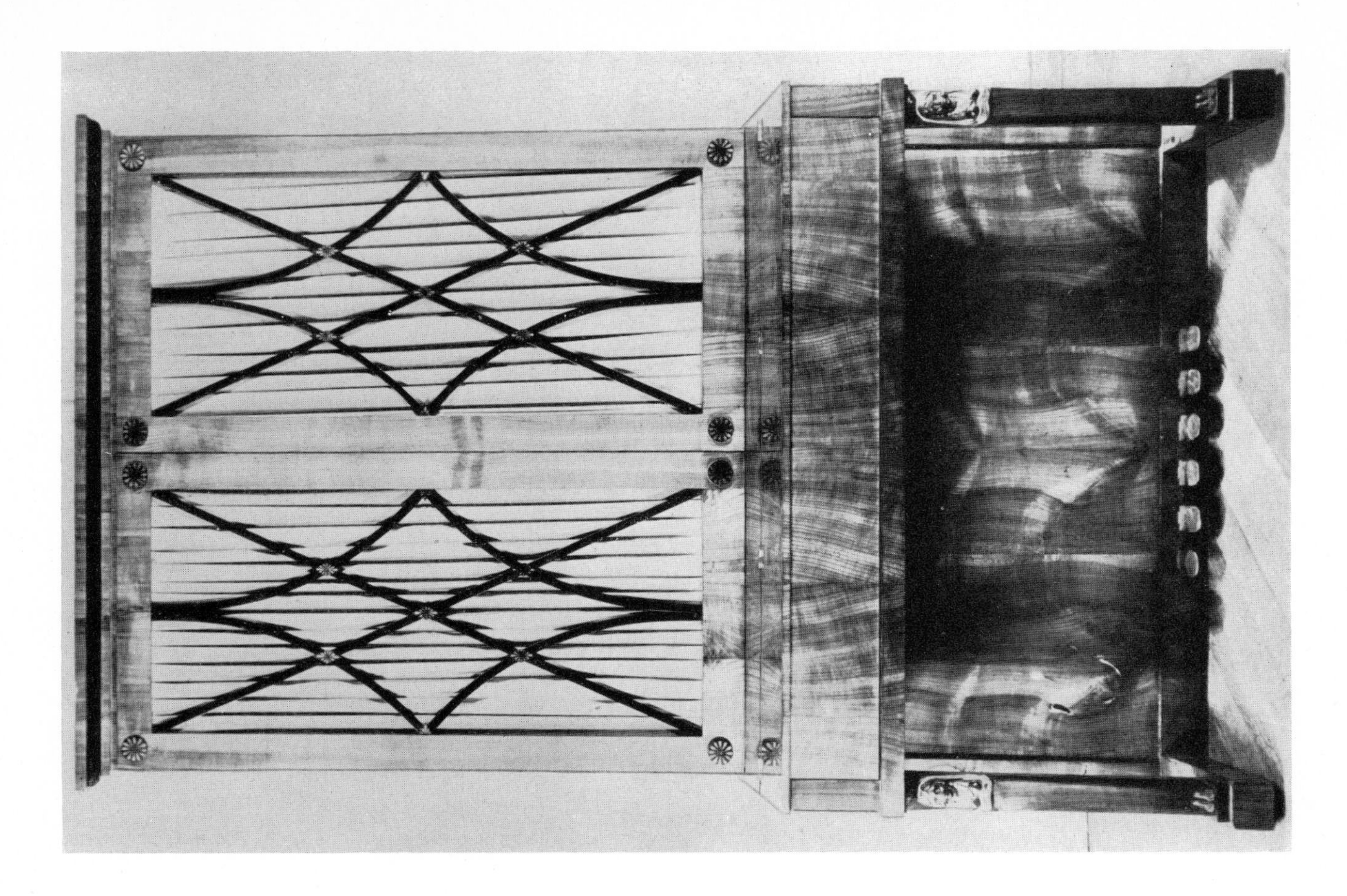

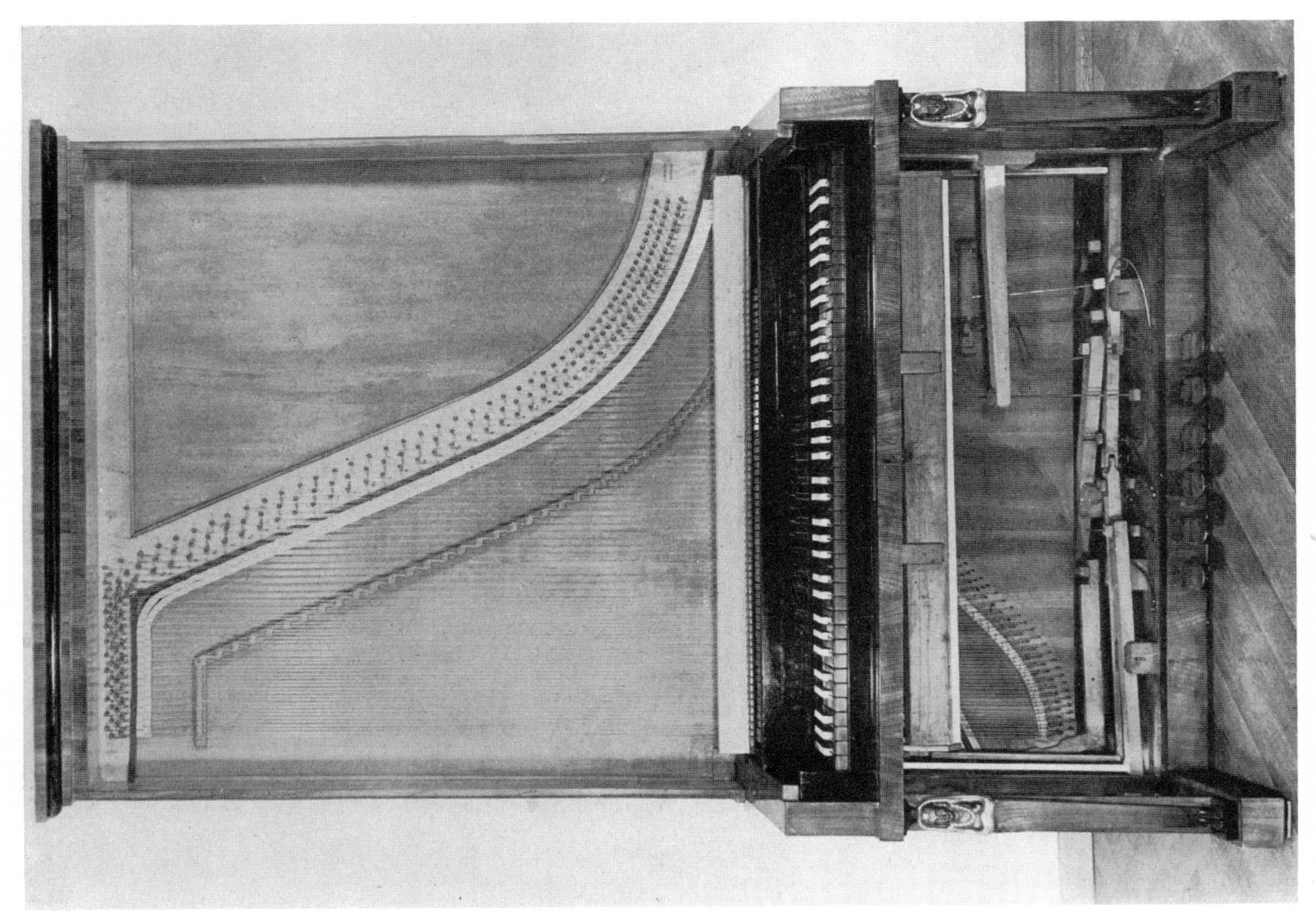

PYRAMID

Conrad Graf—Austria, Vienna, about 1829

SIGNATURE: inscription behind a glass plate in center of nameboard: 'CONRAD GRAF / Kaiserl. Kön. Hof-Fortepianomacher / WIEN / nächst der Carls-Kirche im Mondschein Nr. 102.'
SHAPE: this magnificent instrument in mahogany is finished in Empire style. The open-work upper case shows a carved double eagle with gilded crown, the whole backed with pale-green silk. The five-stringed lyre below is also partly gilded. The outside of case and nameboard decorated with bronze mounts. Two Wedgwood porcelain plates of women playing instruments also adorn the nameboard. The lower framework, formed like a fan, is also backed with green silk. Two gilded caryatids with bronze mounts bear up the keyboard. On both sides of the case stand two carved and partly gilded figures of Moorish women bearing candelabra. A gold vase crowns the whole and the instrument stands on four brass castors.
KEYBOARD: compass F_1 to f'''' (six octaves). Mother-of-pearl covered naturals, sharps ebony-covered.
STRINGING: bass octave double-, the remainder triple-strung.
ACTION: Viennese action.
STOPS: four pedals (out of order): damping, piano, keyboard shift, bassoon.
MEASUREMENT: length 116 cm, depth 64 cm, height 268 cm.
AT THE HAGUE, Gemeente Museum. No. 1502.

In 1829 this instrument was ordered from Conrad Graf by a Hungarian magnate. The piano "should be something quite original, above all things a decorative piece. He did not wish to spoil his room by having in it a great long tripod. Graf should somehow manage to combine the practical side (in this case, of secondary importance) with the demands of a magnificent piece of furniture, which was what he really wanted." Later on the owner presented it to a departing employee, after which it fell into the hands of the village schoolmaster, ending up in the lumber room. From here it was rescued and restored by Seyffarth, in whose salon in Empire style it looked decorative.

PYRAMID

Conrad Graf—Austria, Vienna, about 1829

WIEN

'GIRAFFE'

Christoph Ehrlich—Germany, Bamberg about 1830

SIGNATURE: 'Christoph Ehrlich zu Bamberg.'
SHAPE: case of polished mahogany, the straight formation cut in steps, with three open-work panels in the upper front framework. On the left: vine-leaves with Pan-pipes and fan-shaped palm leaves. In the middle panel is a half-circular landscape in lacquer from which fan-shaped scrolls emerge. In the right-hand part is an ornamented bronze lyre. The keyboard stands on the feet of two genii. On the lowest step (right) is a clock encased in a lyre. The nameboard and sides of keyboard are decorated with gilt-bronze mounts.
KEYBOARD: compass F_1 to f'''' (six octaves). White naturals, black sharps.
STRINGING: triple stringing (straight).
ACTION: Viennese action.
STOPS: six pedals: damping, piano, drum, bells, bassoon, and the last is out of order (?).
MEASUREMENT: length 116 cm, heitht 236 cm.
IN STUTTGART, Landesgewerbemuseum.

'GIRAFFE'

Van der Hoef—Netherlands, Amsterdam (about 1810)

SIGNATURE: inscription on nameboard: 'Van der Hoef / Amsterdam.'
SHAPE: mahogany case. On the bass side is a Corinthian column with gilt socle and capital. Gilt lions' heads support the keyboard: the nameboard is decorated with painted flowers.
KEYBOARD: compass F_1 to f'''' (six octaves). White naturals, black sharps.
STOPS: six pedals, left to right: bassoon, drum, celeste, bells, keyboard shift, damper.
MEASUREMENT: height 7 ft, width 4 ft 8 in., depth 2 ft 3 in.
IN LONDON, Bethnal Green Museum. 461–1907.

This instrument formerly belonged to the painter Sir William Q. Orchardson and appears in his picture 'Music, when soft voices die, vibrates in the memory.'

CABINET PIANOFORTE (Double Giraffe)

C. J. Nordquist—Sweden, Stockholm 1826

SIGNATURE: maker's name on nameboard: 'C. J. Nordquist, Stockholm 1826.'
SHAPE: mahogany case, the upper part decorated with bronze mounts and backed with green silk. At the right a music-cupboard with four open shelves and a little drawer for accessories has been built in. Two round pillars veneered in ebony and ornamented above and below with bronze rings, support the keyboard. Above the pedals there is a large five-stringed gilt lyre made of wood. Cheekpieces and the nameboard veneered in ebony and edged with small round ivory buttons.
KEYBOARD: compass F_1 to a'''' (six octaves and a third). Ivory-covered naturals, ebony-covered sharps.
STRINGING: double- and triple-strung (straight).
ACTION: suspended German action.
STOPS: five wooden pedals covered with brass. Left to right: keyboard shift, damping, piano, coupled piano, Janissary music, drum (drum at the right above; three bells at the right below).
MEASUREMENT: length 123 cm, depth 58 cm, height 232 cm.
In STOCKHOLM, Museum of the History of Music. Cat. No. 402.

Instrument closed—upper part open

'LYRAFLÜGEL'

J. A. Westermann—Germany, Berlin (about 1830)

SIGNATURE: maker's name on nameboard: 'J. A. Westermann / Akademischer Künstler / in Berlin.'
SHAPE: mahogany case backed with cloth (or silk) standing on lions' feet. Maple-wood nameboard inlaid with rosewood and green stained maple.
KEYBOARD: compass E_1 to f'''' (six octaves and one tone). Naturals covered with ivory.
STRINGING: double and triple stringing.
ACTION: German action (suspended) with over-damping.
STOPS: four wooden pedals: keyboard shift piano, coupled piano and damping.
MEASUREMENT: length 127 cm, depth 59 cm, height 215 cm.
ORIGINALLY IN BERLIN, Institut für Musikforschung.

The instrument was destroyed in World War II.

'LIEGENDER GIRAFFENFLÜGEL'

P.C. Uldahl—Denmark, Copenhagen
(first quarter of 19th century)

SIGNATURE: maker's name on nameboard: 'P.C. Uldahl / I Kobenhavn.'
SHAPE: mahogany case.
KEYBOARD: compass F_1 to f'''' (six octaves).
MEASUREMENT: length 121 1/2 cm, depth 52 cm, height 164 cm.
IN COPENHAGEN, Claudius Collection. Cat. No. 72.

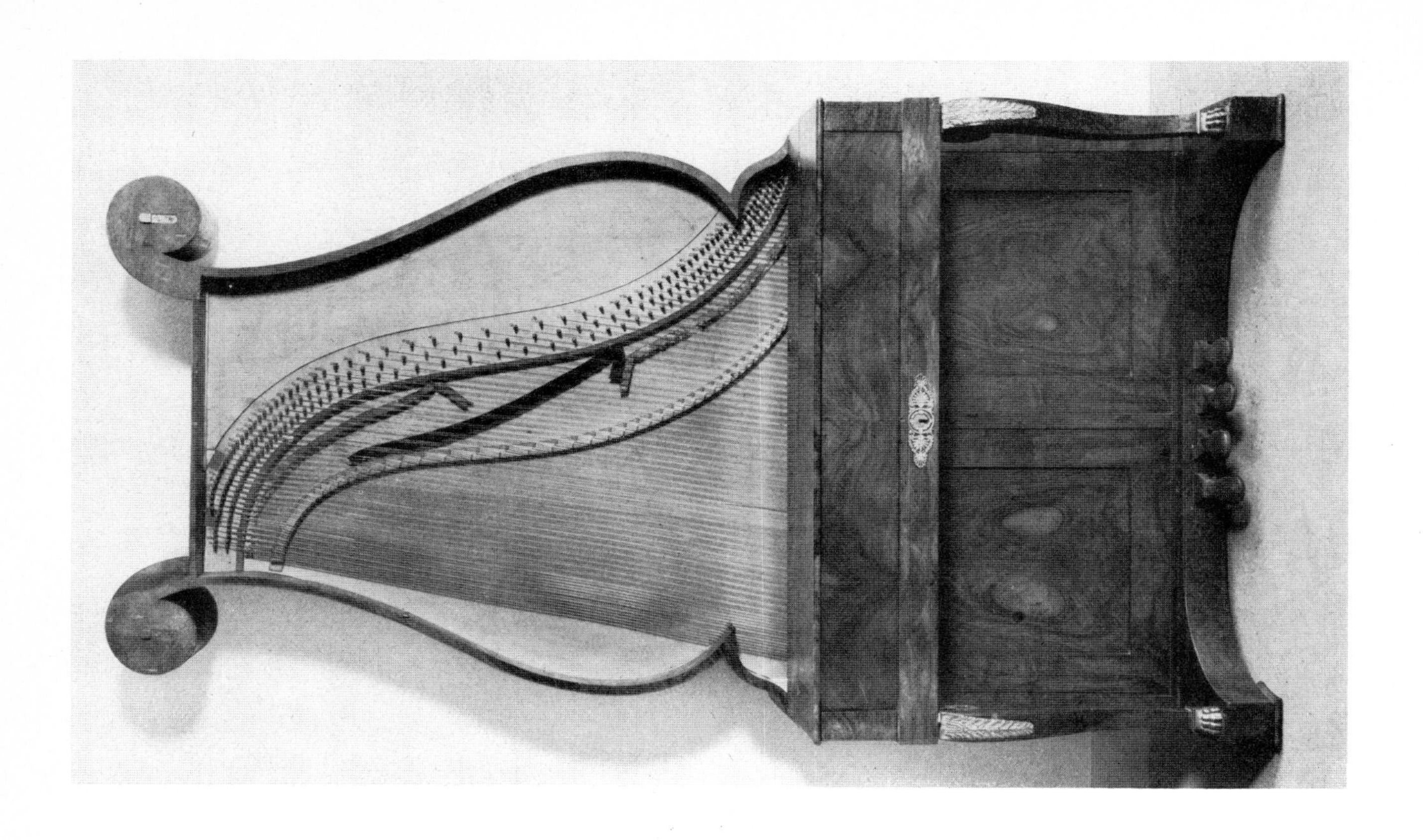

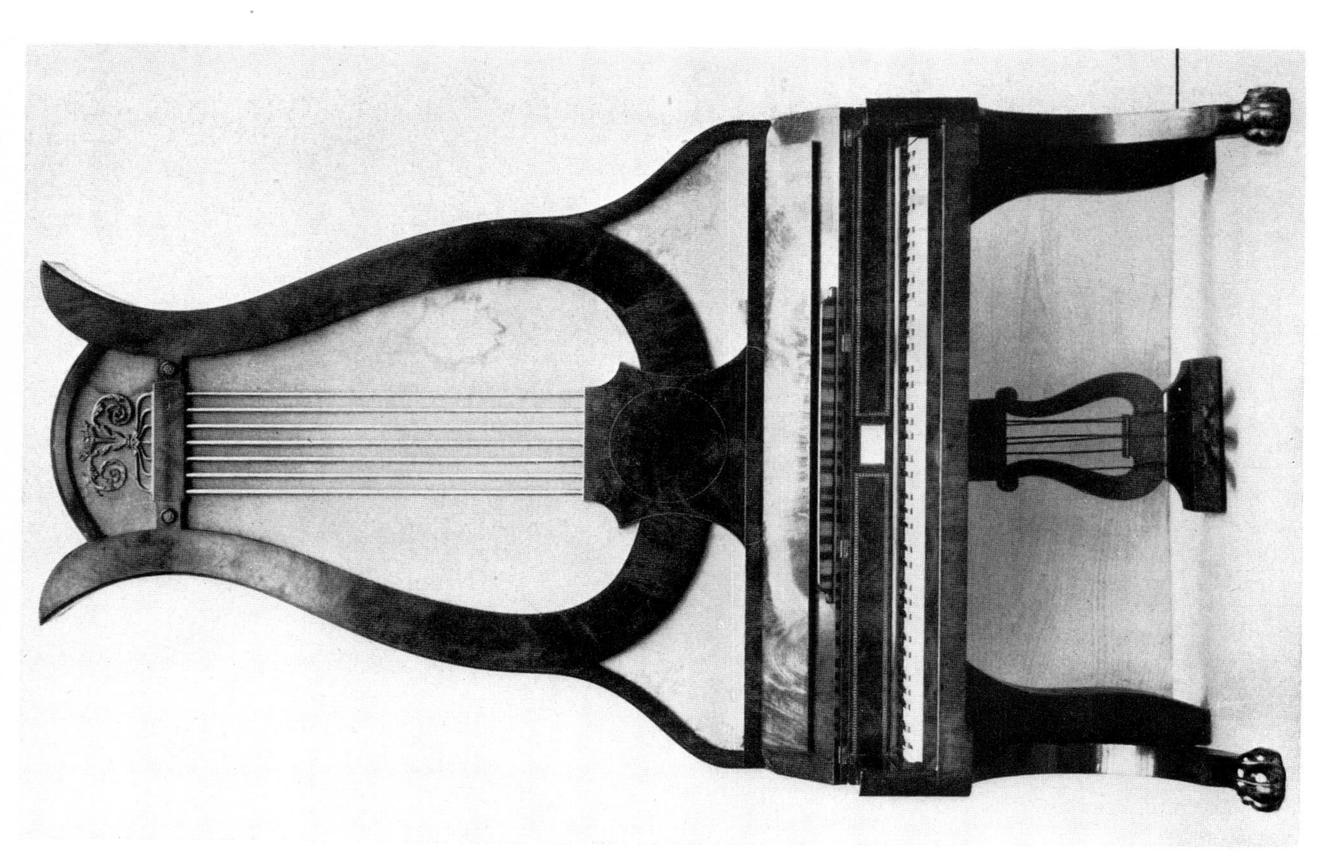

A. Flohr—Switzerland, Bern 1830

with the upper part of framework open.
IN BERN, Museum of History. Inv. No. 6111.

In 1830 this instrument was exhibited at the Bern Exhibition. "Herr Andreas Flohr, Instrument maker in Bern, exhibited an upright Piano-Forte with compass of six octaves. The case of the instrument was shaped like a colossal antique lyre with a great deal of gilding.
The strength of this instrument is remarkable. The entire construction is simple and plain, the finish of the woodwork, both inside and out, being unusually beautiful. Possibly, if the case had been a trifle longer it would not have been detrimental neither to the dimensions of the lyre, nor to the length of the strings, and that would not have harmed the tone. The latter is somewhat uniform. There is a keyboard shift and the pedals allow of three different tone-registers. Flohr received a gold medal woth 8 ducats.» (Karl Brunner, Report, Bern 1830, p. 77.)

J.C. Schleip—Germany, Berlin
(first quarter of 19th century)

SIGNATURE: 'J.C. Schleip, Berlin.'
SHAPE: case in jacaranda-wood inlaid with veins of cherry.
KEYBOARD: compass C_1 to a'''' (six octaves and a sixth). White naturals, black sharps.
ACTION: English (upright) action.
STOPS: three pedals: keyboard shift, bassoon, damping.
MEASUREMENT: length 124 cm, depth 60 cm, height 124 cm.
IN BAMBERG, Neupert Collection.

CABINET-PIANOFORTE

John Broadwood & Sons—England, London
(first quarter of 19th century)

SIGNATURE: on a piece of inlaid maple on the nameboard: 'John Broadwood & Sons . . . . London.'
SHAPE: case veneered with mahogany: upper framework backed with cloth. The lower half has two doors. The keyboard stands on two turned legs ending in brass castors.
KEYBOARD: compass F_1 to f'''' (six octaves). Modern covering to keys.
STRINGING: double-strung (straight).
ACTION: English action.
STOPS: two pedals, piano and damping.
MEASUREMENT: length 115.5 cm, depth 61 cm, height 184.3 cm.
AT THE HAGUE, Gemeente Museum. No. 1423.

CABINET-PIANOFORTE

Wilkinson—England, London (no date)

upper and lower part of case standing open.

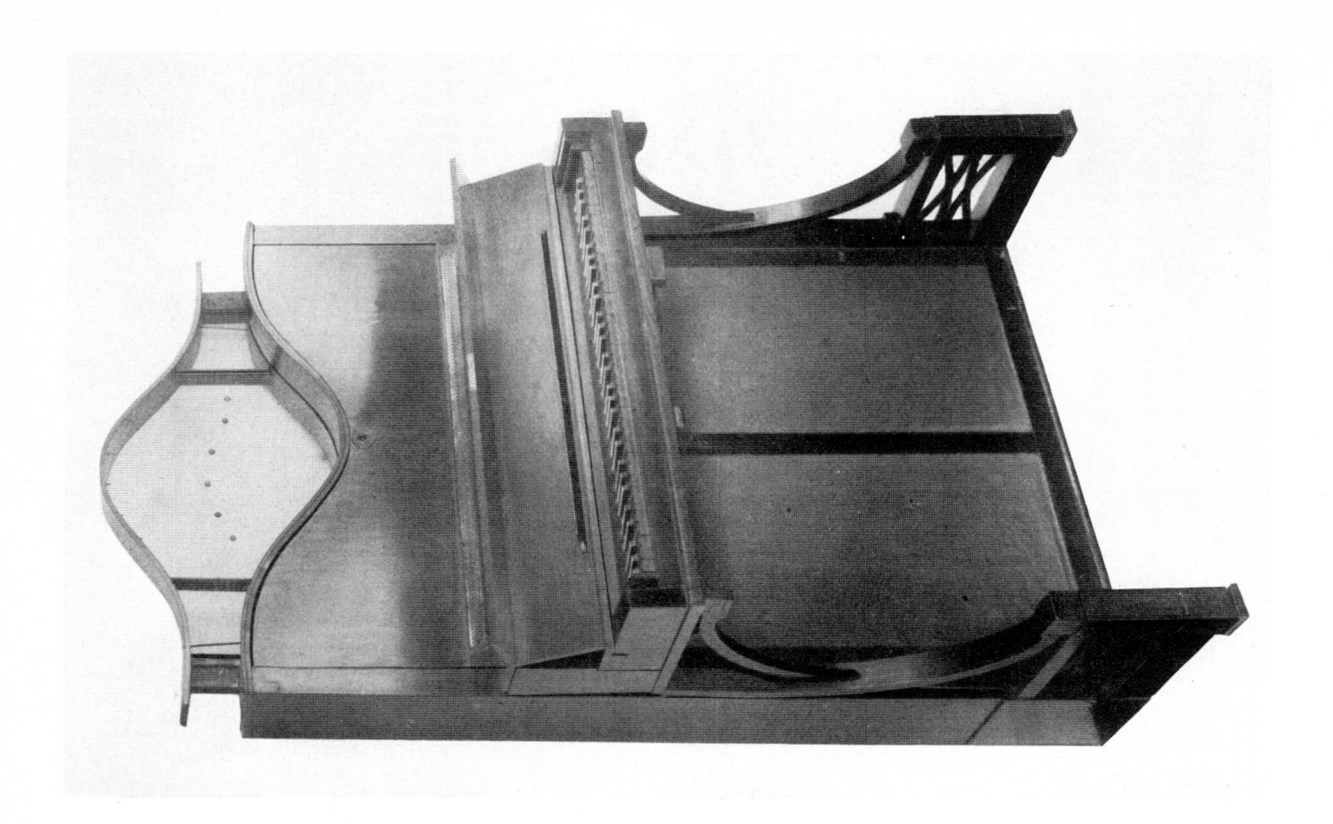

UPRIGHT PIANO (Ditanaklasis)

Matthias Müller—Austria, Vienna 1800

SIGNATURE: 'Matthias Müller, Wien.'
SHAPE: cherry-wood case.
KEYBOARD: compass F_1 to c''' (five octaves and a fifth).
STRINGING: vertical.
ACTION: Viennese action.
STOPS: two knee levers: damping and piano.
MEASUREMENT: length 107 cm, depth 57 cm, height 156 cm.
IN BAMBERG, Neupert Collection. Cat. No. 126.

Oldest upright piano in Europe.

PORTABLE GRAND PIANOFORTE

John Isaak Hawkins—U.S.A., Philadelphia 1800

SHAPE: pianino.
KEYBOARD: can be folded back. Compass F_1 to c'''' (five octaves and a fifth). White naturals, black sharps.
INTERIOR: full cast iron frame.
STRINGING: vertical.
IN LONDON, Broadwood Collection. Cat. No. 17.

The inventions in this piano are astonishingly premature, anticipating the development of pianino manufacture by about fifty years. Only lack of experience and the ignorance of the demand for well-constructed pianino can have caused Hawkins to fail to develop his promising invention.

PIANINOS

Anton Biber—Germany, Munich, about 1860
(on p. 411)

SIGNATURE: on a rectangular ebony shield attached to wrestplank (left upper side) is the inscription in inlaid bone letters: 'Anton Biber / München.'
SHAPE: rectangular cabinet shape. Lower and upper parts of this instrument strongly recessed. The oak case stands on four iron castors, has a carved upper half in open-work with case-shaped upper corners. Sides and front elaborate with panelling and carving, oblique, with fluted edges and two wooden knobs to draw out the keyboard. The main lid, half of which opens upwards, has a lock and to the right, a little supporting rail to keep it open. The iron pedal is enclosed in carved woodwork with shell-shaped edge and comes automatically forward with the drawing out of the keyboard. Keyboard lid in red mahogany: on each side adjustable velvet-covered wooden plates to hold candlesticks.
KEYBOARD: compass A_2 to a'''' (seven octaves). Bone-covered naturals, sharps of solid ebony.
STRINGING: cross stringing from A_2 to G_1 single (steel with copper wrapping); from B_1 to B double (steel with copper); from c to a'''' triple stringing (steel).
ACTION: English action with under-damping.
STOPS: one pedal, damping.
MEASUREMENT: length 127 cm, depth 39 cm, height 133 cm.
IN HALLE AN DER SAALE, Museum in Händel's Birthplace.

Anton Biber—Germany, Munich (about 1860)

with keyboard opened downwards (opposite page top right)

Henri Pape—France, Paris 1850
(on p. 411)

SIGNATURE: 'H. Pape / Facteur de Pianos du Roi / rue des ... (?) enfants, ex rue de Valois / Paris.'
SHAPE: elaborately decorated rosewood case with beautiful bronze mounts and five enamelled Sèvres porcelain medallions.
KEYBOARD: compass seven octaves. Ivory-covered naturals, ebony-covered sharps.
STRINGING: from single to triple stringing.
ACTION: English action (upright or 'stehende').
STOPS: two pedals, piano and damping.
MEASUREMENT: length 162 cm, depth 48 cm, height 113 cm.
IN GENEVA, Musée d'Art et d'Histoire. Inv. No. 19062.

COTTAGE PIANO

Wilkinson & Wornum—England, London 1811

SHAPE: mahogany case.
KEYBOARD: compass F_1 to c'''' (five octaves and a fifth).
STRINGING: oblique stringing.
ACTION: English action (upright or 'stehende').
STOPS: two pedals. 'Buff'; damping.
MEASUREMENT: width 4 ft 4 in., depth 1 ft 8 1/2 in., height 3 ft 5 in.
IN LONDON, London Museum. No. A 10689.

This is said to be the fifth 'Cottage Piano' built by Wornum with oblique stringing. The instrument was presented to the museum by the maker's grand-daughter, Mrs. A. Mongredien.

PICCOLO PIANOFORTE

Robert Wornum—England, London

SIGNATURE: 'Royal Patent Equal Tension. Piccolo Piano Forte, Invented and Manufactured by ROBERT WORNUM, Music Hall, Store Street, Bedford Square, London.'
SHAPE: small upright piano.
KEYBOARD: compass F_1 to f'''' (six octaves). Ivory naturals, black sharps.
STRINGING: double-strung throughout.
ACTION: 'stehende' English action ('English double action').
STOPS: two pedals: keyboard shift (towards the bass!) and damping.
MEASUREMENT: length 113.2 cm, depth 45 cm (including keyboard), height 113.5 cm.
IN NEW HAVEN (Conn.), Musical Instrument Collection, University. Cat. No. 47.

This instrument has no iron framework.

'PIANO DROIT'

A. Flohr—Switzerland, Bern (about 1840)

SIGNATURE: maker's name: 'A. Flohr.'
SHAPE: the case is low, with lyre-shaped curved sides in light walnut. Two curved legs on lions' feet support the keyboard.
KEYBOARD: compass F_1 to f'''' (six octaves). Ivory-covered naturals, ebony-covered sharps.
STRINGING: single- to triple-strung. Oblique stringing.
ACTION: English action with checks.
STOPS: two pedals: left, damping; right, piano.
MEASUREMENT: length 155 cm, depth 54 cm, height 98 cm.
IN BERN, Museum of History. Inv. No. 24773.

PIANINO

Andreas Marschall—Denmark, Copenhagen (first half of 19th century)

SIGNATURE: 'A. Marschall / Copenhagen.'
SHAPE: Case in mahogany.
KEYBOARD: Compass F_1 to f'''' (six octaves).
STOPS: two pedals: damping, piano.
MEASUREMENT: length 140 cm, depth 52 cm, height 101 cm.
IN OSLO, Norsk Folke Museum. Cat. No. 88.

PIANO-CONSOLE

Henri Pape—France, Paris 1844

SIGNATURE: maker's name: 'Pape / Paris & Londres / Piano Console-Brevet d'invention.'
SHAPE: the rosewood case shaped like a side-table is particularly beautiful both in form and finish. The stringing is all placed below so that an upper framework is lacking. The table-top has a little gallery running along each side; in front of the lower part stand four turned console-legs. The whole instrument is inlaid with mother-of-pearl.
KEYBOARD: compass C_I to g'''' (six octaves and a fifth). Ivory-covered naturals, ebony-covered sharps.
INTERIOR: iron framework.
STRINGING: cross stringing.
ACTION: 'stehende' English action with under-damping.
STOPS: two pedals: keyboard shift and damping.
IN BAMBERG, Neupert Collection. Cat. No. 107.

UPRIGHT SQUARE PIANOFORTES

William Southwell—England, London 1798
(From the sketch for the patent)

It is clear from the sketch that the interior disposition of this piano resembles that of the square piano, i.e. wrestplank and wrest-pins placed to the right of player, the hitch-pin block above, to the left.

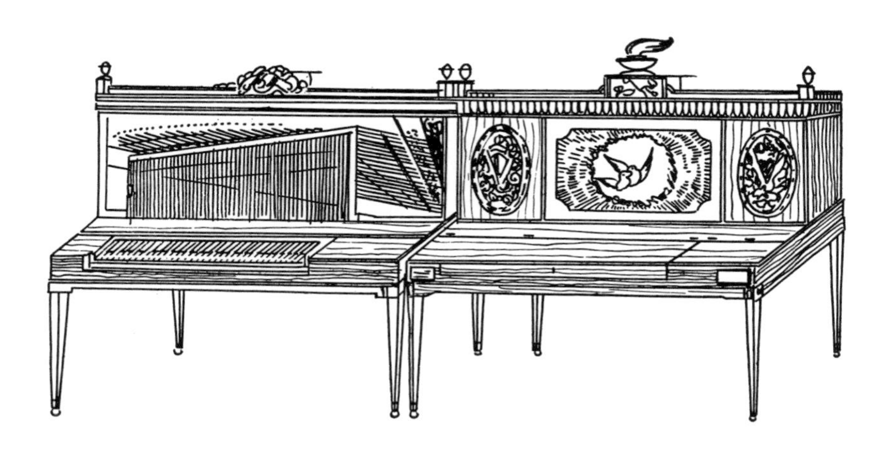

Clementi & Co.—England, London
(first third of 19th century)

SIGNATURE: inscription on a burnt-in stamp on soundboard: 'CLEMENTI & CO. 356'; also on an inlaid maple square under the keyboard: 'CLEMENTI & CO. / 16 LONDON 20.'
SHAPE: the outside of mahogany case decorated with rails and mounts of gilded bronze, stands on five fluted legs. The upper part of case is backed with green cloth.
KEYBOARD: compass F_1 to f'''' (six octaves). Ivory-covered naturals, ebony-covered sharps.
STRINGING: oblique, single and double.
MEASUREMENT: length 144.5 cm, depth 50.5 cm, height 150 cm.
IN GÖTEBORG'S MUSEUM. Cat. No. 152.

William Southwell—England, London 1811
(From the sketch for the patent)

For description, see 'Upright square pianos', p. 147.

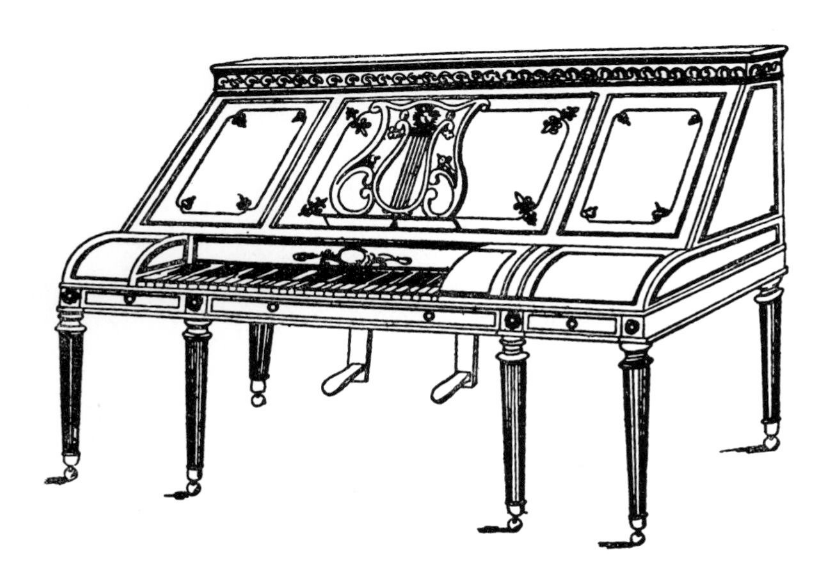

ORGAN-PIANOFORTE

Johann Andreas Stein—Germany, Augsburg 1770

SIGNATURE: printed inscription: 'Jean André Stein, faiseur d'Orgues, des Clavecins et organiste à l'Eglise des Minorittes, à Augsbourg, 177(0).' ('0' added in handwriting.)
SHAPE: walnut case.
KEYBOARD: compass F_1 to f''' (five octaves). Black naturals, white sharps. Two manuals: the upper manual works the piano hammer action, the lower manual the organ, consisting of wooden 'gedackt' pipes.
MEASUREMENT: length 88.5 cm, depth 193 cm, height 98 cm.
IN GÖTEBORG'S MUSEUM. Inv. No. 4478.

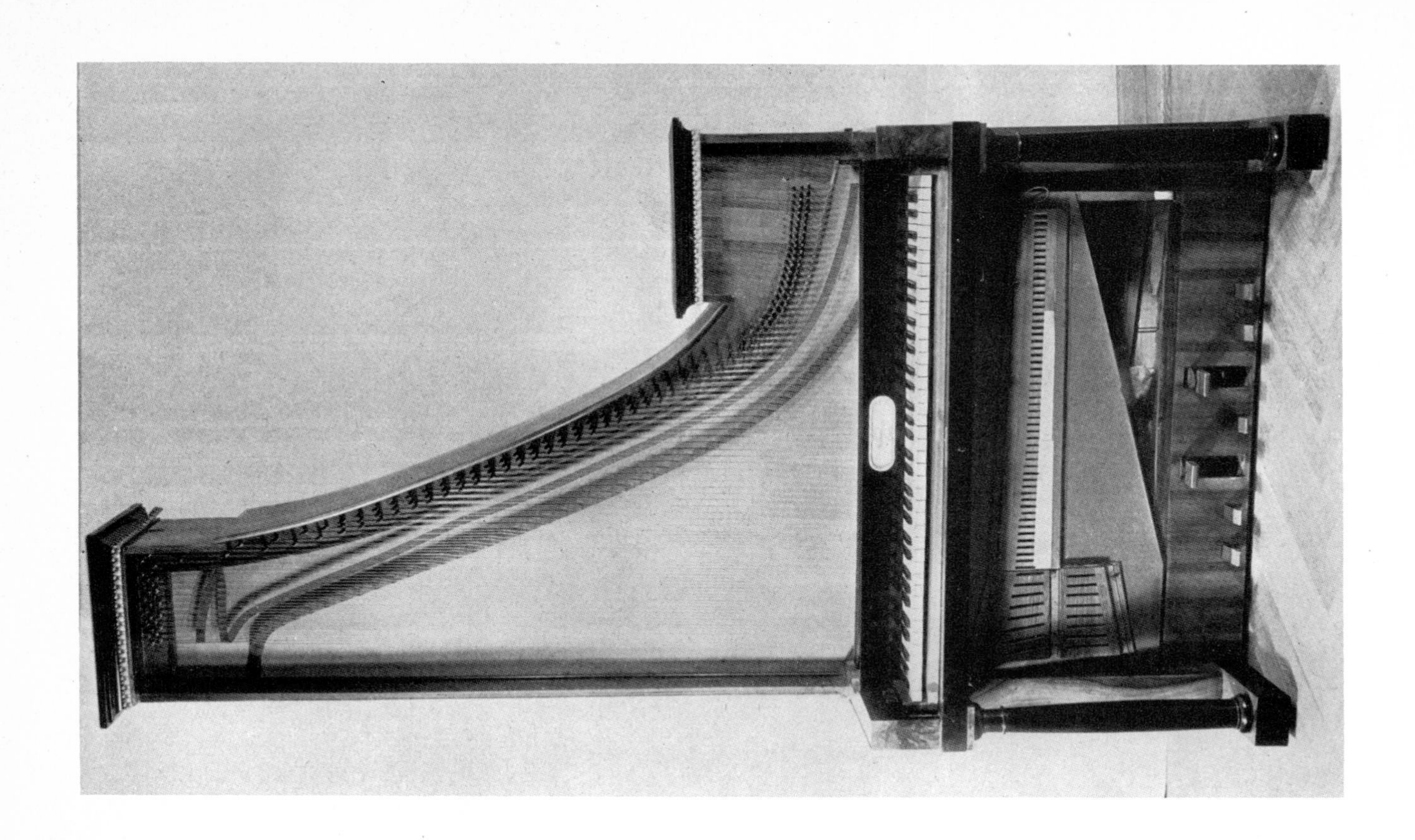

GIRAFFE-HARMONIUM

Caspar Schlimbach—Germany, Königshofen
between 1810–1835

SIGNATURE: signed in Indian ink on an elliptical factory-label framed in ribbed brass and protected by glass on the nameboard: 'Caspar / Schlimbach / in / Königshofen.'
SHAPE: walnut case, the front being divided into several panels. The frame is backed with green silk; the middle division has black stained carving: ornamentation above taking the form of a crown made in brass. The keyboard lies on a rounded console, the whole supported on a rectangular base.
KEYBOARD: compass F_1 to f'''' (six octaves). Bone-covered naturals, sharps stained black.
STRINGING: F_1 to B double-strung afterward triple stringing. Brass and steel strings.
ACTION: German action.
STOPS: pedals arranged in two layers, one above another: two larger pedals of a different shape from those below work the air-supply for the aeoline. The five pedals below have the following functions (left to right); basson; moderator (partial damping); moderator (more complete damping); and damping. Besides this there are push couplers; left, on bass side: front stop, disconnects piano; back stop, connects piano; to the right on treble side: front stop, disconnects harmonium; back stop, connects harmonium.
AEOLINE: the aeoline built into the lower part is worked by hand.
MEASUREMENT: length 109 cm, extreme height 221 cm.
IN NÜRNBERG; Rück Collection.

According to Curt Sachs ('Reallexikon der Musikinstrumente', p. 15) Eschenbach, a cousin of C. Schlimbach, was the inventor of the aeoline (1810). Probably Eschenbach and Schlimbach built instruments together.

GRAND PIANOFORTE-HARMONIUM

Erard & Alexandre—France, Paris

SIGNATURE: on nameboard: 'Alexandre, Père et Fils, Paris / Piano d'Erard.'
SHAPE: pianoforte combined with an organ.
KEYBOARD: compass of piano A_2 to a'''' (seven octaves). Compass of harmonium C to c'''' (five octaves). Two manuals: pedal.
INTERIOR OF PIANO: iron string-plate with six iron stays.
STRINGING: single- to triple-strung.
ACTION: Erard's double escapement action with under-damping.
STOPS: Pianoforte: two pedals: keyboard shift and damping. Harmonium: ten stops left, six on the right of the manuals. Two bellows-pedals, two knee levers.
MEASUREMENT: Pianoforte: depth 246 cm, height 34 cm. Harmonium: depth 270 cm, height 104 cm, extreme length 139 cm, extreme height 138 cm.
IN VIENNA, Kunsthistorisches Museum. Collection of old musical instruments. Loaned by the Gesellschaft der Musikfreunde, Vienna.

Our illustration is taken by kind permission of the author Robert Bory, from his book entitled 'The Life of Franz Liszt'. It is a contemporary engraving showing the music room at the Altenburg near Weimar. This instrument was once the property of Franz Liszt.

PYRAMID-HARMONIUM

Caspar Schlimbach—Germany, Königshofen
middle of 19th century

SIGNATURE: maker's label: 'C. Schlimbach / in Königshofen.'
SHAPE: walnut case, the front in open-work backed with cloth.
KEYBOARD: compass F_1 to f'''' (six octaves). Ivory-covered naturals, ebony sharps.
INTERIOR: frame constructed of wood, the lower half of instrument contains a built-in harmonium.
STRINGING: oblique, from F_1 to F double-, the remainder in triple stringing.
ACTION: German action (suspended) with over-damping.
STOPS: piano: six pedals: Janissary music, two lute stops, keyboard shift, damping, drum and triangle. Harmonium: stop to connect and disconnect harmonium; two pedals for wind.
MEASUREMENT: length 118 cm, depth 67 cm, height 240 cm.
IN MUNICH, Deutsches Museum. Inv. No. 45880.

CLAVIHARP

Johann Christian Dietz—France, Paris 1814

SHAPE: "This instrument is formed rather similar to a giraffe-piano but with no outer case and above the keyboard there is no soundboard. The straight bass side of the string-frame forms a column with bronze capital and socle, the whole standing on two sickle-shaped supports. All the wood employed is mahogany." [1]
KEYBOARD: compass F_1 to f'''' (six octaves). Ivory naturals, ebony sharps.
ACTION: Dietz' Claviharp Action.
STOPS: one damping pedal.
IN BRUSSELS, Musée instrumental du Conservatoire Royal de Musique. Cat. No. 2513.

[1] *Sachs*, Curt, Catalogue of the Collection of Musical Instruments in Berlin.

TANGENT-PIANOFORTE

Späth & Schmahl—Germany, Regensburg (about 1790)

SIGNATURE: on the right of wrestplank written in ink: 'J. Späth u. Schmahl Regenspurg.'
SHAPE: This instrument is of tapering pianoforte shape without projected keyboard. Walnut case with panelled three-fold lid (front lid broken off short), old stamped brass hinges, brass lock and five round tapering legs. The bottom of case is finished with an appliqué rail. A music stand is glued to keyboard lid, with two places to hold candles. On outside edge (right) of inner case is a brass hook to hold lid: inside nameboard decorated with sloping rectangular surfaces of darker walnut with maple-wood inlay. Similar ornamentation on sloping keyboard side, which have recesses for candlesticks.
KEYBOARD: compass F_1 to f''' (five octaves). Ebony-covered naturals, the faces ornamented with carved half-moons, bone-covered sharps.
INTERIOR: pinewood soundboard.
STRINGING: steel strings, double-strung.
ACTION: tangent action.
STOPS: two knee levers: left, keyboard shift: right, damping. Besides this, on wrestplank two wooden inside stops to left and right: one presses a fringe-covered rail on the treble strings, the other on the bass (lute). When these stops are drawn out, the contrivance is disconnected.
MEASUREMENT: length 99 cm, depth 220 cm, height 86 cm.
IN HALLE AN DER SAALE, Museum in Händel's Birthplace.

TANGENT-PIANOFORTE WITH ORGAN

(Späth & Schmahl?)—(Germany), Regensburg (?)
End of 18th century

UNSIGNED.
KEYBOARD: compass F_1 to f''' (five octaves). Black naturals, white sharps. Compass of coupler-pedals: C to a.
STRINGING: double-strung.
ACTION: Schmahl's tangent action.
STOPS: two damping stops above soundboard can be used singly or together for bass and treble. Another stop (left, above keyboard) cuts off the pianoforte. Organ: three stops: 'gedackt' 8'; 'gedackt' 4'; flute 4', bass and treble divided. The stops to cut off the organ also work separately.
MEASUREMENT: length 180.5 cm, depth 64.5 cm, height 99 cm.
IN EISENACH, Bach's House. Cat. No. 158.

Index of Museums and Private Collections of Musical Instruments in Alphabetical Order

Salzburg	Museum Carolino-Augusteum
	Mozarteum
Stockholm	Museum of the History of Music
Stuttgart	Württembergisches Landesgewerbemuseum
Taunton	Somerset County Museum
Torino	Museo civico
Toronto	Royal Ontario Museum
Verona	Museo civico
Versailles	Château
Warrington	Municipal Museum
Washington	United States National Museum
Weimar	Goethehaus
	Lisztmuseum
Wien	Gesellschaft der Musikfreunde
	Historisches Museum der Stadt Wien
	Kunsthistorisches Museum, Sammlung alter Musikinstrumente
	Österreichisches Museum für angewandte Kunst
York	York Castle Museum

Stringed keyboard instruments are also found in the following Swiss Museums:

Aarau	Museum Alt-Aarau, Schlössli
Aarburg	Museum der Historischen Vereinigung Alt-Aarburg
Altstätten	Historisches Museum
Arbon	Historisches Museum
Arenenberg	Napoleonmuseum, Schloss
Basel	Historisches Museum
	Schola Cantorum Basiliensis, Collection of musical instruments
Bern	Historisches Museum
Bischofszell	Ortsmuseum, Schloss
Bulle	Musée Gruyérien
Chur	Rätisches Museum
Delémont	Musée jurassien
Frauenfeld	Thurgauisches Museum
Fribourg	Musée d'Art et d'Histoire
Genève	Musée d'Art et d'Histoire
Lausanne	Musée du Vieux Lausanne et Musée de Mon-Repos
Lichtensteig	Toggenburger Heimatmuseum
Le Locle	Musée historique
Luzern	Wagnermuseum, Tribschen
	Städt. Sammlung alter Musikinstrumente, Tribschen
Neuchâtel	Musée historique
Oberhofen	Schloss, Historisches Museum Bern
Olten	Historisches Museum
Rapperswil	Heimatmuseum
Sarnen	Heimatmuseum
Solothurn	Historisches Museum
Thun	Historisches Museum, Schloss
Yverdon	Musée du Vieil-Yverdon
Zürich	Schweizerisches Landesmuseum

PART V

CHRONOLOGICAL LIST OF LEADING INTERNATIONAL STRINGED KEYBOARD INSTRUMENT BUILDERS UNTIL 1880

Belgium	Ernest *Closson*, La facture des instruments de musique en Belgique. Bruxelles 1935.
England	a) Clavichord and Harpsichord Makers:
	Donald H. *Boalch*, Makers of the Harpsichord and Clavichord. 1440 to 1848. London 1956.
	b) Pianoforte Makers:
	Rosamond *Harding*, A History of the Pianoforte. Cambridge 1933. pp. 385–409.
France	Constant *Pierre*, Les facteurs d'instruments de musique. Paris 1893.
United States of America	Alfred *Dolge*, Pianos and their Makers. Covina 1911.
	Daniel *Spillane*, The History of the American Pianoforte. New York 1890.

The following factors have determined our chronological list of leading international stringed keyboard instrument builders:

1. The various countries and cities have been quoted in alphabetical order.
2. Our list does not pretend to be complete. We have intentionally given much more information about the instrument builders prior to 1800 because later on factory production has considerably eliminated the personal part and influence of the masters on the form and musical quality of each particular instrument.
3. In cities like Paris, Berlin, Leipzig, Dresden, London, Philadelphia, Boston and New York, which are great centers of keyboard instrument production, only the most outstanding producers have been listed. In provincial towns, on the contrary, we have felt it necessary to mention the lesser masters so as not to give a false and one-sided picture of instrument production in the various countries.
4. Dating. As far as possible, we have quoted the dates of the founding and ceasing of the business, together with the most important dates referring to collaborators, change of owners, mergers, etc. These latter indications are sometimes important for establishing the chronology of undated instruments. Where exact dates were missing, we have tried by reference to existing instruments and on the basis of contemporary documents, where they exist, to fix the period when the instrument makers were working. Such methods of dating, however, are fluctuating and uncertain, and may have to be revised in the light of new data. They can therefore only have the value of approximate points of reference in dating. Where these indications are missing, we have given the years of birth and death of the instrument makers, or in the absence even of such data, general indications of a more or less precise character.
5. We have used the following special signs with reference to the different kinds of keyboard instruments which have been built by such and such instrument makers:

○ = 'Streichklaviere'
÷ = 'Bogenflügel'
⊥ = 'Klaviergamba'
∞ = 'Geigen-Clavicymbel'
> = 'Lauten-Clavicymbel'
§ = Virginals, Spinets, Harpsichords
+ = Clavichords
♀ = Tangent Pianos
⋆ = Pianofortes
△ = Harpsichords with Organs
⌀ = Pianofortes with Organs
□ = Spinet regal
— = Claviharps

The following abbreviations have also been used:

chr. = christened
E. = the Elder
Y. = the Younger
c. = circa

AUSTRIA

LINZ

Valentius *Zeiss*, § recorded in 1639.

Frenzel... * recorded in 1837.

SALZBURG

Johann *Schmidt*, * pupil of J. A. Stein, recorded 1785–1804 (year of death).

Johann *Dumel*, * second quarter of 19th century.

Ludwig *Mooser*, * third quarter of 19th century.

VIENNA

Johann *Moyse*, + recorded in 1765.

J. Chr. *Heyne*, * recorded in 1777.

C. *Müller*, * recorded in 1780.

Anton *Walter*, * after 1780 he was recorded in Vienna 'Anton Walter in Wien'.

Joseph *Walter*, * his adopted son, joined the firm, then called 'Anton Walter & Son', at the turn of the century. A. Walter d. in 1826.

Christoph *Bock*, § * recorded in 1804.

Ferdinand *Hofmann*, * b. 1760 in Vienna, d. 1829.

Johann Jakob *Könnicke*, * worked in Vienna c. 1790–1811 (year of death).

Johann *Jakesch*, * recorded c. 1790–1800.

Ignatz *Kober*, * b. 1755 in Olmütz, d. 1813 in Vienna.

Wenzel *Ledezki*, * end of 18th century.

Joseph *Klein*, § recorded c. 1800.

Nannette *Streicher* and Matthäus Andreas, * were in Vienna after 1794 and called their business 'Frère et sœur Stein'. In 1802 Matthäus Andreas retired.

Nannette *Streicher*, * 1802–18 she called the business 'Nannette Streicher, née Stein'.

Johann Baptist *Streicher*, * 1823–1833 the business was called 'Nannette Streicher geb. Stein und Sohn', 1833–1859 'Johann Baptist Streicher'.

Emil *Streicher*, * 1859–1896 'J. B. Streicher & Sohn'. In 1871 he took over the business; in 1896 the firm was liquidated.

Johann Andreas *Streicher*, * cooperated after 1802, d. 1863.

Matthäus Andreas *Stein*, * set up a business of his own in 1802–1842, called it 'André Stein'; d. 1842.

Karl Andreas *Stein*, * founded a business in 1829, d. 1863.

Ferdinand *Stein*, * first half of 19th century.

Wenzel *Schantz*, * worked in Vienna after c. 1780 (?), d. 1790.

Johann *Schantz*, * succeeded the former, d. 1828.

Carl Leopold *Röllig* invented the Orphica in 1795.

J. *Schieder*, * c. 1800.

Johann *Schiebe*, * recorded 1817–1821.

Franz *Lauterer*, * first third of 19th century.

J. A. *Knam*, * first half of 19th century.

Joseph *Dohnal*, * b. 1759 in Dub, d. 1829 in Vienna.

Joseph *Dohnal* (Y.) * pupil of Brodmann, in 1829 he took over the business, d. towards 1850.

Johann *Fritz*, * recorded 1799–1820.

Joseph *Brodmann*, * recorded 1800–1820.

Caspar *Katholnik*, * recorded after 1800.

Mathias *Müller*, * recorded in Vienna after 1800, d. 1844.

Michael *Rosenberger*, * beginning of 19th century. Pupil of A. Walter.

Wilhelm *Leschen*, * pupil of Könnicke and of Brodmann. Worked in Vienna after 1805.

Johann *Promberger*, * pupil of Mathias Müller. Recorded in Vienna after 1809, d. 1834.

Josef *Promberger*, * in 1834?, he called his firm 'Josef Promberger, Sohn', after...? 'Promberger & Sohn'.

Franz Martin *Seuffert*, * pupil of Anton Walter; he founded a business in 1801, first together with Joseph Wachtl and Bleyer, calling it 'Wachtl & Co', later on alone.

Eduard *Seuffert*, * 1830–1857 'Seuffert Sohn & Seidler'.

Friedrich *Ehrbar*, * pupil of Seuffert; succeeded him in 1857.

Joseph *Wachtl*, * business founded in 1801, called 'Wachtl & Co.' (see above), in 1802 'Wachtl & Bleyer'; he worked alone in the end; in 1832(?) the firm was liquidated. He was a pupil of A. Walter.

Conrad *Graf*, * business founded in 1804 (took it over from Schelke); d. 1851.

Friedrich *Hoxa*, * recorded 1817–1851.

Ignaz *Bösendorfer*, * business founded in 1828. Pupil and successor of Brodmann.

Ludwig *Bösendorfer*, * took over the business in 1859.

Johann Michael *Schweighofer*, * business founded in 1832. 1852–1867 it was called 'Schweighofers Witwe' (widow), after 1867 'Schweighofer & Söhne'.

Johann *Heitzmann*, * business founded in 1867.

Karl *Kutschera*, * recorded after 1873.

Josef *Schneider*, * recorded after 1873.

Jakob *Czapka*, * recorded after 1873.

BELGIUM

AERSCHOT

Johannes Franciscus *Matheus*, § recorded 1770–1783.

ANTWERP

Hans van *Ceulen*, § recorded 1512–1557.
Antonius *Moors*, + recorded 1514–1562.
Joost *Kareest*, + § recorded in Antwerp in 1516, d. 1556/57 (Boalch).
Goosen *Kareest*, + § recorded 1519–1568.
Peter *Matthys*, + recorded in 1519.
Jakob *Theeuwes*, § recorded 1533–1557.
Ludovic *Theeuwes*, § ∅ recorded in 1557.
Marten *Blomsteen*, § recorded 1535–1562.
Christoffel *Blomsteen*, § recorded 1550–1558.
Jakob *Aelbrechts*, + § recorded after February 13, 1542, d. 1585.
Lukas *Aelbrechts*, § recorded 1585–1589.
Pieter *Vornenberch* or *Vorenbergh*, + recorded 1542–1552.
Albrecht van *Meer*, § + recorded 1542–1560.
Pieter de *Lyen*, + recorded in 1543.
Hans *Bos*, § recorded 1543–1572.
Simon *Moens*, § recorded 1552–1557.
Hans van *Peborgh*, § recorded in 1557.
Ghijsbrecht van den *Bogaerde*, § recorded 1557–1559.
Jan *Diercks*, § b. 1531, recorded until 1574.
Wilhelm *Herremans*, § recorded in 1557.
Marten van der *Biest*, § recorded 1557–1584.
Lodewijk van *Diepenrijck*, § recorded 1558–1589.
Willem *Gompaerts*, § recorded 1560–1610.
Johan de *Hevilez*, § recorded in 1561.
Willem *Leest*, + § recorded 1561–1569.
Hans *Moermans*, § recorded 1570–1610.
Hans *Ruckers* I (E.), + §, b.c. 1550, d. after 1623.
Hans *Ruckers* II (Y.), § chr. January 15, 1578, d. 1643.
Andreas *Ruckers* I (E.), § chr. August 20, 1579, recorded until 1644 (Boalch).
Andreas *Ruckers* II (Y.), § b. 1607, recorded until 1651.
Christoph *Ruckers*, § c. 1620.
Aert van den *Elst*, § recorded 1576–1579.
Jan *Grouwels*, § recorded 1579–1580.
Lodewijk *Grouwels*, § recorded in 1600.
Merten *Verbiest*, § recorded in 1580.
Jan van *Eesbroeck*, § recorded in 1583.
Edward or Eevout *Wolfaert*, § recorded in 1589.
Daniel *Bader*, § recorded 1600–1607.
Franz van *Uffel*, § recorded 1609–1620.
Reynier *Leunis or Leums*, recorded 1610–1626.
Michael *Immenraet*, § recorded in 1610.
Melchior *Ykens*, recorded in 1613.
Joris *Britsen* I (Georg), § recorded 1613–1681.
Joris *Britsen* II, § recorded 1655/56.
Joris *Britsen* III, § recorded 1658–1675.
Alexander *Britsen*, § recorded in 1717. Note: a virginal by Georg Britsen (which of the three?) is dated 1686 (Brussels, No. 631).
Cornelius *Haquaerts* or Haghens, § recorded after 1626, d. 1641.
Simon *Haquaerts* or Haghens, § recorded in 1642.
Antoni *Joannes*, § recorded in 1627.
Dirk de *Vries*, § d. 1628/29.
Jan *Couchet* I, § recorded in Antwerp after 1642, d. 1655.
Joseph *Couchet*, § recorded 1666–1679.
Abraham *Couchet*, § recorded 1666/67.
Jan *Couchet* II (E.), § recorded 1655–1680.
Peter *Verheyden*, § recorded 1643–1655.
Gonnar van *Everbroeck*, § recorded 1655/56.
Thomas *Watson*, § recorded 1658/59.
Christian *Pelle*, § recorded 1658–59.
Jacobus van der *Elsche*, § recorded 1707–1767.
Anton *Dulcken*, § lived in Antwerp after c. 1740, d. 1763.
Johann Daniel *Dulcken*, § recorded 1745–1769.
Johannes Petrus *Dull*, § recorded 1776–1789.
Johann *Heinemann*, § recorded in 1793.

BRUSSELS

Jérôme *Mahieu*, § recorded in 1732, d. 1737.
Johann Daniel *Dulcken*, § recorded 1741–1769.
Henricus van *Casteel*, ♀ ⋆ recorded 1763–1784.
J. B. *Winands*, ⋆ recorded in 1789.
Daniel frères, ⋆ at the turn of 18th to 19th cent.
J. P. J. *Ermel*, ⋆ recorded 1807–1818.
François *Berden* & Co., ⋆ business founded in 1815.
Grotaers frères, ⋆ recorded 1820–1841 (after 1841 'Veuve P. Grotaers').
Jean Chrétien *Dietz* I (E.), — recorded after 1820, d.c. 1845 in Holland.
Jean Chrétien *Dietz* II (Y.), — b. 1801 or 1804, lived in Paris until 1886.
Christian *Dietz*, — b. 1851 in Paris.
Edouard *Hoeberechts*, ⋆ recorded 1825–1847. After 1841 'Lambert Hoeberechts et fils'.
François *Vogelsangs*, ⋆ business founded in 1829, recorded until 1867.
Jacques *Vogelsangs*, ⋆ after 1847.
H. H. *Lichtenthal*, ⋆ recorded after 1830. Moved to St. Petersburg (Leningrad) in 1851.
C. *Hortsman*, ⋆ recorded 1835–1847.
Guillaume *Stadeler*, ⋆ recorded 1835–1847.
Patin & Co, ⋆ recorded in 1841.
Louis *Sternberg* & Co., ⋆ recorded 1841–1867.
Jacques *Günther*, ⋆ business founded 1845.
F. *Jastrzébsky*, ⋆ recorded 1847–1851.

GENT

Symphorien *Ermel*, ⋆ recorded in 1802.
Damekens, ⋆ recorded 1805–1845.

LIÈGE

Marc *Moors*, + recorded in 1508.
F.J. *Dumoulin*, * recorded 1830–1847.

MECHELN

Franz *Ruckers*, (§?) b.c. 1520; year of death unknown.
Frans de *Vries*, § recorded 1550–1570.
Dagoneau, § recorded in 1773.

MONS

J.J. *Ermel*, § △ recorded 1780–1785.
Eugène *Ermel*, § * recorded in 1779.
Louis Fétis, * recorded 1797–1804.

NAMUR

Frein & Co., * recorded in 1837.
Joseph *Florence*, * business founded in 1835; recorded until 1875. Name changed to 'Florence et Vauclair' after 1835, with Florence as sole owner after 1837.

TOURNAI

Albert *Delin*, § recorded 1750–1770.

CANADA

TORONTO

Theodore A. *Heintzmann*, * business founded in 1860.

CZECHOSLOVAKIA

JAROMĚŘ

Ignaz *Kunz*, + recorded in 1821.

PILSEN

Leicht, * b. 1790.

PRAGUE

Johann Joseph *Muschel*, * second half of 18th century, d. 1789 or 1800.
Simon Joseph *Truska*, + recorded 1734–1809.
Kalb, * c. 1796.
Johann and Thomas *Still*, * recorded c. 1796.
Johann *Zelenka*, + § * 18th century.
Michael *Weiss*, * recorded in 1807.
Leicht, * beginning of 19th century.
Meiners, * first quarter of 19th century.

TACHAU (BOHEMIA)

Gärtner, * recorded in 1763.

DENMARK

COPENHAGEN

M. *Christensen*, + recorded in 1759.
Müller, + middle of 18th century.
Moritz Georg *Moshack*, + * recorded in 1768; probably identical with Mosbach.
Peter Christian *Uldahl*, * pupil of Wachtl in Vienna. Business founded in 1809, d. 1820.
Andreas *Marschall*, * pupil of Uldahl. Business founded in 1813.
Sören *Hjorth*, * 1842–1847 successor of Marschall.
A. *Richter-Bechmann*, * business founded in 1814.
J.N. *Gade* (E.), * recorded c. 1820.
Conrad Christian *Hornung*, * settled in Copenhagen in 1842.
H.P. *Möller*, * collaborated many years (1851–1859) with Hornung whom he succeeded; business then being called 'Hornung & Möller'. After Möller's death in 1859, his widow and eldest son took over the firm. In 1869 the son, first alone, later on together with his brother, took the business in hand.
Hermann N. *Petersen* & Sohn, * business founded in 1849.
Carl *Alpers*, * business founded middle of 19th century.
Ludwig *Wulff* & Co., * business founded in 1853.
Harald *Hindsberg*, * succeeded Wulff in 1878.
J. *Larsen* & Sohn, * business founded in 1855.
A.C. *Sundahl*, * pupil of Hornung. Business founded c. 1860.
C. *Landschultz*, * business founded in 1866.
I.H. *Ehlert*, * business founded in 1870.
A. *Arvesen* & Co., * business founded c. 1870.

ODENSE

Johann Jesper *Jørgensen*, + recorded in 1777.

SKELSKOER

Conrad Christian *Hornung*, ★ business founded in 1827; in 1834 transferred to Slagelse.

SLAGELSE

Conrad Christian *Hornung*, ★ worked there 1834–1842; moved to Copenhagen in 1842.

FRANCE

BORDEAUX

Thévenard, § recorded in 1727.

CLERMONT-FERRAND

Laussedat fils, ★ recorded 1844–1853.

LE HAVRE

Pfeffel, △ recorded in 1797.

LYON

Nicolas *Bontemps*, + § recorded 1506–1523.
Honoré de *Loeuvre*, § recorded after 1523, d.c. 1551.
Stirnemann, ∅ ★ recorded in 1783.

MARSEILLE

J. *Bas*, § recorded 1737–1781.
Jean Louis *Boisselot*, ★ business founded in 1830; d. May 1847.
Louis Constantin *Boisselot*, ★ successor 1847–1850, d. June 1850.
Dominique-François-Xavier *Boisselot*, ★ successor, d. April 8, 1893.

NANCY

N. *Marchal*, § recorded in 1726.
Pierre Hyacinthe *Mangeot*, ★ business founded in 1830.
Alfred and Edouard Joseph *Mangeot*, ★ successors after 1859.

NANTES

Louis *Gairoud*, § recorded in 1854 and 1855.

PARIS

Antoine *Potin*, § second half of 16th century.
d'Emery, § at the turn of the 16th to 17th century.
Richard, § recorded 1623–1672.
Jean *Jacquart*, § first half of 17th century.
Jean *Denis*, § recorded 1636–1653.
Le Breton, § recorded 1603–1656.
Nicolas *Dumont*, § recorded 1680–1697.
Philippe *Denis*, § recorded 1663–1691.
Faby, § recorded 1677–1691.
Jean *Marius*, § ★ recorded 1700–1715.
Cuisinier, § ○ recorded 1708–1734.
François-Etienne *Blanchet*, § ★ recorded 1709–1774.
Armand-François *Blanchet*, § ★ b. 1763, d. 1818; pupil of Taskin.
Nicolas *Blanchet*, § ★ in 1818 successor, together with Johannes *Roller*, until 1851.
P. A. C. *Blanchet*, ★ 1855–1867 recorded as successor of Nicolas Blanchet and Blanchet & Roller.
Antoine *Valter*, § recorded 1715–1755.
Louis *Bellot*, § recorded 1732–1753.
Le Voir, ○ § recorded in 1742.
Pascal *Taskin*, § ★ pupil of François-Etienne Blanchet; b. 1723, d. 1793.
Renaud, § recorded in 1745.
Jean-Henri *Hemsch*, § recorded 1747–1775.
Baillon, § 18th century.
Rigault, § 18th century (17th century, Boalch).
Weltmann, § middle of 18th century.
Gai, § second half of 18th century.
Jacques *Bourdet*, § recorded 1750/51.
Joseph *Treyer*, called 'L'Empereur', recorded 1756–1789.
Treyer, called 'Le Tourneur', § recorded 1750–1779.
Pierre *Ruelle*, § recorded in 1754.
Joachim *Ruelle*, § recorded 1775–1789.
Munier, § recorded in 1754.
Balthasar *Péronard*, § ★ recorded 1760–1789.
Virbès, ★ recorded 1768–1771.
Jean *Leisert*, § recorded in 1769.
Benoît *Stelle*, § recorded 1769–1777.
Jacques *Tourode*, § recorded in 1769.
Jean *Gérard*, § recorded in 1769.
Jean-Henri *Moers*, § recorded 1769–1789.
Johann Kilian *Mercken*, ★ recorded from 1770 until c. 1825.
Beckers, ★ after 1825 successor of Mercken.
Jean-Pierre *Leclerc*, § recorded 1777–1800.
Pierre-Charles *Simonneau*, § recorded 1775–1779.
Malade, § recorded after 1775–1779. His wife succeeded him after his death.
Jean *Hermès*, § recorded 1740–1788.
Jacques *Goermans*, § recorded 1775–1789.
Jean-Marie *Debedan*, § ★ recorded 1775–1789.
Louis *Benard*, § recorded 1776–1789.
Jean *Naulot*, § recorded 1777–1783.
Jean *Goermans*, § recorded 1748–1777.
Morel, § recorded 1777–1783.
Johann Jakob *Schnell*, § recorded 1777–1809.
Nicolas *Hoffmann*, § recorded 1777–1800.
Sébastien *Erard*, § ★ business founded in 1777; d. 1831.
Pierre *Erard*, ★ succeded the former in 1831–1855, d. 1855. His wife, together with M. *Schœffer* took over the business in 1855. In 1873, after Schœffer's death, Mrs. Erard handed the business over to Albert-Louis *Blondel*.
Pierre *Grenot*, § recorded 1778–1789.
Pierre *Dubois*, § recorded 1778–1799.

J.-J. *Nesle*, § recorded in 1780.
Jean *Schwerr*, * recorded in 1783.
Pierre-Jacques *Godelart*, § recorded 1783–1789.
Jacques *Klein*, * recorded 1783–1789.
Pierre *Gateaux*, § recorded 1783–1793.
Louis *Dulcken*, § recorded 1783–1789.
Jacques *Barberini*, § * recorded 1783–1791.
Hillebrand, * recorded in 1783 until c. 1800.
Léonard *Systermans*, * end of 18th century.
Joachim *Swanen*, § recorded 1783–1816.
Franz *Hopkinson*, § recorded in 1788.
Eberhard, * recorded in 1788.
Daujard, * recorded 1788/89.
Wolber, * recorded 1788–1799.
Schmidt, * recorded 1788–1799.
Daickviller, * recorded 1788–1799.
Bosch, * recorded 1788–1800.
Johann Wilhelm *Freudenthaler*, recorded prior to 1789. In 1824 his sons took over the business, but soon abandoned it.
Wolff, * recorded 1797–1799.
Charles *Lemmé*, * business founded in 1799; d. 1832.
Dupoirier, * recorded in 1806.
Guillaume Leberecht *Petzold*, * 1806–1814 partner of Pfeiffer.
J. *Pfeiffer*, * 1806–1814 partner of Petzold. After 1814 sole owner; d. 1838.
Ignaz *Pleyel*, * business founded in 1807.
Camille *Pleyel*, * succeeded the former in 1824, d. 1855.
A.D.B. *Wolff*, * succeeded the former in 1852.
Johannes *Roller*, * recorded after 1808. After 1818 partner of Nicolas Blanchet; they called the business 'Blanchet & Roller'.
Jean-Henri *Pape*, * business founded in 1815; d. 1875. From c. 1855 till 1872 his son managed the business, and 1872–1885 'Mme Pape et Delouche'.
Gaidon frères, * business founded in 1820. Each brother had his own workshop.
Henri *Herz*, * in 1825 partner of *Klepfer*, but soon after on his own; d. 1888.
Rinaldi-Usse, * recorded 1827–1867.
François *Souffleto*, * business founded in 1828; d. 1872.
Charles-Etienne *Souffleto*, * succeeded the former in 1872.
Sébastien *Mercier*, * business founded in 1830; recorded until 1851.
Jean-Georges *Kriegelstein*, * business founded in 1831; d. 1865.
Charles *Kriegelstein*, * succeeded the former in 1858.
Alexandre-François *Debain*, * business founded in 1834; d. 1877.
Claude *Montal*, * business founded in 1836; d. 1865.
Tesserau, * succeeded the former in 1865.
Wölfel, * business founded in 1837; recorded until 1862.
Alphonse-Philippe *Blondel*, * business founded in 1839; d. 1893.
Alexandre *Blondel*, * the former's partner in 1869.
Amédé-Benoît *Thibout*, * business founded in 1840; d. 1877.
Antoine-Jean-Denise *Bord*, * business founded in 1843; d. 1888.
Jean *Schwander*, * business founded in 1844; d. 1882. In 1865 he associated with Herrburger.
Frédéric *Elcke*, * business founded in 1846.
Joseph-Gabriel *Gaveau*, * business founded in 1847; d. 1903.
Charles-Louis *Franche*, * recorded 1849–1878.
Henri-Joseph *Pruvost*, * business founded in 1850.
Henri *Pruvost*, * took over the business in 1880.
Victor *Pruvost*, * business founded in 1852.
Edmond-Victor *Pruvost*, * took over the business in 1890.
J. *Jaulin*, * recorded in 1851.
Joseph *Herrburger*, * worked in Paris after 1853, with Schwander after 1855; in 1865 partner of Schwander.
Limonaire, * recorded in 1855.
M. *Ruch*, * business founded in 1869.

ROUEN

Nicolas *Lefèbvre* I, § recorded 1630–1640.
Nicolas *Lefèbvre* II, § recorded 1733–1772.

STRASBOURG

Friederich *Ring*, § recorded in 1700.
Johann Andreas *Silbermann*, * b. 1712, d. 1783.
Johann Josias *Silbermann*, succeeded the former in 1783, d. 1786.
Johann Heinrich *Silbermann*, + § * b. 1727, d. 1799.
Johann Friedrich *Silbermann*, ?? *, b. 1762, d. 1817.
A.F. *Erhart*, + recorded in 1782.
G.L. *Allinger*, * recorded in 1867.

TOULOUSE

Vincent *Tibaut*, § recorded in 1679.
Martin, * business founded c. 1840.

GERMANY

WITH UNKNOWN DOMICILE

Martinus *Kaiser* (also Kayser) (E.), § recorded in 1698.

AALEN

Heinrich *Haegele*, business founded in 1846.

ADLERSRUH

Johann Samuel *Puchert*, + b. 1741, d. 1794.

ALTENBURG

Elias *Schlegel*, + § recorded in 1730.

ALTONA

Lorenz Rudolph *Wohlien*, * b. 1789, d. 1834.

ALTZEN

Brettschneider, * recorded in 1813.

ANSBACH

Johann Chr. *Wiclef* or *Wigleb*, § recorded 1724–1740.
Christian Gottlob *Hubert*, + * b. 1714, d. 1793.
Johann Wilhelm *Hoffmann*, * succeeded Hubert after his death.

ARNSTADT

Ludwig Wilhelm *Hänert*, * recorded after 1785 until 1797.

AUGSBURG

Samuel *Biedermann*, § recorded in Augsburg c. 1570–1622.
Anton *Meidling*, □ recorded in Augsburg in 1587.
Johann Christoph *Leo* (E.), + § settled in Augsburg after 1685.
David Jakob *Weidner*, + recorded in 1697.
Johann Andreas *Stein*, + § worked in Augsburg after 1750; d. 1792.
Nannette and Mathäus Andreas *Stein*, * took over the business in 1792; moved to Vienna in 1794.
Mathäus *Schautz*, + § * worked in Augsburg after 1793. Pupil of J. A. Stein.
Ignaz Joseph *Senft*, * last third of 18th century.

BAMBERG

Martin *Steinbacher*, * recorded in 1793.
Christoph *Ehrlich*, * recorded after 1816 until c. 1850.
J. C. *Neupert*, * business founded in 1868.

BARMEN

Johannes Adolph *Ibach*, * business founded in 1794; d. 1848.
Carl Rudolf *Ibach*, * recorded in 1834 as 'A. Ibach & Sohn' (d. 1863).
Richard *Ibach*, * in 1839 'A. Ibach & Soehne'.
Gustav Adolf *Ibach*, * joined the business in 1844; left in 1862 to work on his own.
Rudolf *Ibach*, * joined the firm, then called 'Carl Rudolf & Richard Ibach', in 1862; after 1869, the name changed to 'Rudolf Ibach Sohn'.
Gustav Adolf *Ibach* (see above), * business founded in 1862.

BAUTZEN

Georg *Haase*, + b. 1650, d. 1712.
Johann Gottfried *Augustin*, + recorded 1762–1806.

BAYREUTH

Eduard *Steingräber*, * business founded in 1852.

BERLIN and CHARLOTTENBURG

Michael *Mietke*, § recorded 1680–1719.
Johann *Hohlfeld*, ÷ b. 1711, d. 1771.
Johann Augustin *Straube*, + § * b. 1725, d. 1802.
Rost, § recorded in 1760.
Johann Christian *Schramm*, + § * recorded after 1768 until 1806.
Johann Christian *Oesterlein*, ♀ recorded 1773–1792 (1794, Boalch).
Kalix, * recorded in 1786.
J. A. *Westermann*, * business founded in 1790; recorded until 1850.
Heinrich Adam *Siegmü ler*, * recorded in 1793.
Johann Martin *Bothe*, * recorded 1794–1800.
Carl Ludwig *Steibelt*, + * recorded 1797–1798.
Johann Friedrich *Bode*, + * recorded in 1798.
Heinrich Christian *Kisting*, * business founded in 1799 in Potsdam, later on he moved to Berlin.
Eduard *Kisting*, * in 1828 'Kisting & Sohn'; 1832 Eduard Kisting sole manager.
Hunn, * recorded 1799–1812.
Conrad, + c. 1800.
Karl Ludwig *Schramm*, * recorded 1800–1806.
Johann *Müller*, * recorded 1804–1850.
J. F. *Schwarzlose*, * beginning of 19th century.
Johann *Kruse* & Co., * recorded beginning of 19th century.
Johann *Schneider*, * recorded 1812–1836.
J. C. *Schleip*, * recorded 1820–1844.
J. L. *Schultz*, * first half of 19th century.
Friedrich *Kaselitz*, * recorded 1824–1839.
Josef *Zattlasch*, * recorded 1826–1830.
W. *Bohme*, * recorded in 1830.
J. C. *Andrée*, * recorded 1830–1844.
Theodor *Stöcker*, * business founded in 1836.
F. B. *Voigt*, * recorded after 1839, in 1840 'F. B. Voigt & Sohn'.
H. *Kolwes*, * recorded c. 1840.
H. G. *Ostermann*, * recorded after 1844.
Heinrich *Schwechten*, * business founded in 1841.
Georg *Schwechten*, * took over the business in 1853.
Carl *Bechstein*, * business founded in 1853.
W. *Spangenberg*, * recorded after 1854.
Duysen, * business founded in 1859.

BIELEFELD

Th. *Mann*, * business founded in 1836.
C. W. *Volkening*, * business founded in 1836, abandoned in 1856.

KLOSTER BILDHAUSEN

Friedrich Wilhelm *Pfrang*, * recorded in 1778.

BOCKENHEIM near FRANKFORT

G. W. *Kuper* & Co., * middle of 19th century.
André *Greiner*, * middle of 19th century.

BONN

Gottlieb Friedrich *Riedlen*, § * recorded 1749–1782.

BORNA (SAXONY)

Johann Rudolph *Greifenhagen*, ? recorded 1756–1806 (year of death).

BRAUNSCHWEIG

Barthold *Fritz*, + 1697–1766 (year of death).
Carl Friedrich Wilhelm *Lemme*, + * b. 1747, d. 1808.

Johann *Kruse*, * beginning of 19th century.
Zeitter & Winkelmann, * business founded in 1837.
Theodor *Steinweg*, * business founded in Braunschweig in 1859.
Friedrich *Grotrian, Helfferich & Schulz*, * after 1865, when Theodor Steinweg left for America, they took over his business and called the joint business 'Grotrian, Helfferich & Schulz, Th. Steinweg's Nachfolger'.

CLEVE

Johann Friedrich *Hoffmann*, ? 18th century.

COLOGNE ON THE RHINE

C. *Kareest*, + § recorded 1500–1556.
Johann *Loth*, § recorded c. 1647.
Wilhelm Konstantin *Schiffer*, * recorded 1779–1797.
Johann Jakob *Eck* & Co., * business founded in 1838; abandoned and transferred to Zurich (Switzerland) in 1844.

CRAILSHEIM

Daniel Tobias *Faber*, + recorded in 1725.

DARMSTADT

Johann *Schweinz*, + § * beginning of 19th century.
Heinrich *Welcker* von Gontershausen, * b. 1811, d. 1873.
Karl *Arnold*, * business founded in 1830.

DRESDEN

Georg *Kretzschmar*, + recorded in 1565, d. after 1623.
Hans *Dietz*, recorded in 1605.
Johann Christoph *Gräbner*, + recorded 1678–1692.
Johann Christian *Gräbner*, ? recorded 1678–1704.
Johann Heinrich *Gräbner* (E.), + § b. 1665, d. 1739.
Johann Heinrich *Gräbner* (Y.), + § recorded 1735–1774.
Ernst Gottlob *Gräbner*, ? b. 1734, d. 1759.
Johann Gottfried *Gräbner*, + § * b. 1736, d. 1808.
Johann Wilhelm *Gräbner*, § * b. 1737, d. 1798.
Karl August *Gräbner*, + § * b. 1749, in 1796 still recorded.
Johann Gotthelf *Gräbner*, * recorded until 1840.
Johann Christian *Heydenreich*, + recorded in 1729.
Zacharias *Hildebrand*, > * d. 1757.
Schwarze, + recorded in 1748, d. c. 1770. Pupil of A. Silbermann.
Tobias *Schramm*, § recorded 1742–1791 (year of death).
David *Schubert*, * recorded 1765–1769 (year of death). Pupil of Silbermann.
Gottfried *Hildebrand*, ∅ d. 1775.
Gottfried Joseph *Horn*, + * business founded in 1772; d. 1797.
Johann Gottlob *Horn*, + § * business founded in 1779; d. 1796.
Heinrich Rudolph *Mack*, + after 1792 assistant to Horn. In 1796 successor of J. G. Horn. After 1799 firm of his own. d. 1807.
Karl Ernst Fürchtegott *Rentsch*, + * after 1792 he worked with J. G. Horn; on his own after 1797.
Johann Gottlob and Christian Salomon *Wagner*, + § * pupils of Gottfried Silbermann. After 1773 collaborators. When Johann Gottlob died, Christian Salomon continued the business alone (presumably 1812–1816) until he died.
Carl Gottlob *Sauer*, * business founded in 1780. Worked in Dresden until 1825.
Johann Heinrich Ernst *Fessel*, + b. 1764. After 1785 pupil of Horn, worked on his own after 1791; recorded until 1796 (Boalch).
Gotthelf David *Lehmann*, + * recorded until 1790.
Carl Gottfried *Bellmann*, * 1796 settled in Dresden.
Ernst Philipp *Rosenkranz*, * business founded in 1797.
Friedrich Wilhelm *Rosenkranz*, * 1828–1856 successor of E. Ph. Rosenkranz.
Ernst Adolph *Rosenkranz*, * 1856–1873 successor. In 1873 the factory was taken over by the lawyer Hippe and the trader Cyriacus. In 1877 Wilhelm August Voigt occupied the post of Cyriacus.
Carl Rudolph August *Venzky*, + * b. 1767, recorded in 1804.
Karl *Rönisch*, * business founded in 1845.
Ernst *Kaps*, * business founded in 1859.

DÜSSELDORF

J. B. *Klems*, * recorded in 1854.

EISENACH

Johann *Hasert*, + b. 1680, recorded until 1709.

EISLEBEN

Samuel *Kühlewein*, ∅ * recorded 1800–1810.

ERFURT

Jakob *Adlung*, + § worked in Erfurt 1727–1762 (year of death).
Joseph *Heilmann*, * recorded after 1798.
G. *Möller*, * recorded in 1800.

ERLANGEN

Balthasar *Schiedmayer*, business founded in 1735.
Adam Achatius *Schiedmayer*, * recorded in 1777.
Johann David *Schiedmayer*, * business founded in 1781, transferred to Nürnberg in 1797.
Johann Erhard *Schiedmayer*, d. 1821.
J. C. *Bulla*, * business founded in 1789; d. 1790.

FRANKFORT ON THE MAIN

Israel *Gellinger*, + § recorded 1639–1677.
C. A. *André*, * recorded 1828–1839.

FREIBERG (SAXONY)

Gottfried *Silbermann*, + § * worked in Freiberg 1710–1753.
Georg *Schoene*, * pupil of Silbermann, b. 1707; left for England c. 1764 (?).
Adam Gottfried *Oehme*, * pupil of Silbermann; recorded 1718–1789.

FREIBURG (BREISGAU)

M. *Welte,* * business founded in 1833.

FÜSSEN

Martinus *Kaiser,* § recorded in 1698.

GEHREN

Johann Michael *Bach,* + recorded 1673–1694.

GERA

Christian Ernst *Friederici,* § * pupil of Silbermann. Business founded c. 1744; d. 1780.
Christian Gottfried *Friederici,* § * collaborated with Christian Ernst Friederici; d. 1777.
Christian Gottlob *Friederici,* + * in 1780 successor of Chr. Gottfried; d. 1805.
Ernst Ludwig *Friederici,* * successor; d. 1883.

GERINGSWALDE (SAXONY)

Johann David *Gerstenberg,* + b. 1716, d. 1796.

GÖTTINGEN

Daniel *Meyer,* § recorded in 1575.
Johann Paul *Kraemer,* + * 1772–1819.
Johann Christian Friedrich and Georg Adam *Kraemer,* + * founded their own business in 1806.
Siegmund Theodor *Kraemer,* + * b. 1750, d. 1828.
Gottlieb Wilhelm *Ritmüller,* + * business founded in 1795.
Johann Wilhelm and Johann Martin *Ritmüller,* + * successors of the former after 1829.

GOTHA

Hofmann, § recorded in 1779.
Johann August *Böttiger,* * recorded after 1800.

GROSS-BREITENBACH near ARNSTADT

Johann Nicolaus *Deckert,* + * b. 1772, d. 1844.

HALBERSTADT

Johann Christop *Jesse,* + recorded in 1765.

HALLE

Weikhart, § 18th century.
Gotthilf *Honigmann,* * recorded 1818–1869.
C. Richard *Ritter,* * business founded in 1828.

HAMBURG

Johann Christoph *Fleischer,* + § > b. 1676, d. after 1732.
Carl Konrad *Fleischer,* recorded in 1720, d. 1737.
Johann A. *Hass,* + § recorded 1740–1768.
Hieronymus Albrecht *Hass,* + § recorded until 1744.
Johann Christian *Gerlach,* + § recorded 1744–1790.
Voigt, ? recorded in 1793.
Johann Peter *Hinrichs,* * recorded in 1796.
Meinke *Meyer,* * first quarter of 19th century.
Pieter *Meyer,* * first quarter of 19th century.
Andreas *Meyer,* * first half of 19th century.
Gustav Adolf *Buschmann,* * business founded in 1805.
J.C. *Humrich,* * recorded c. 1830.
Mathias Ferdinand *Rachals,* * business founded in 1832.
Ferdinand *Rachals,* * recorded after 1844.
Steinway & Sons, * business founded in 1880.

HANNOVER

Hermans Willen *Brock,* + △ recorded in 1712.
W.H. *Baethmann,* + recorded in 1799.
Ernst *Haake,* * business founded in 1836.

HEILBRONN

G. *Nagel,* * business founded in 1831.

HEUTINGSHEIM (SCHWABEN)

Johann Michael *Schwingstein,* * recorded in 1799; pupil of J.A. Stein.

ILMENAU (THÜRINGER WALD)

Johann Georg *Gleichmann,* + ⊥ recorded 1698–1770 (year of death)

JENA

Johann Nikolaus *Bach,* § recorded 1695–1753.
Schmuhl, * recorded in 1802.
C. *Weidig,* * business founded in 1843.

KASSEL

Wilhelmi, + § * recorded in 1784.
Carl *Scheel,* * pupil of Erard. Business founded in 1846.
Riese & Feurich, * business founded in 1825; abandoned in 1850 (?).

KIRCHHEIM

Franz *Kaim,* * business founded in 1819; in 1845 'Kaim & Günther'.

KISSINGEN

Rüth, * first half of 19th century.

KOBLENZ

Carl *Mand,* * business founded in 1832.

KÖNIGSBERG

Gabrecht, § second half of 16th century.
J.F. *Marty,* * recorded in 1800.
C.J. *Gebauhr,* * business founded in 1834.

KÖNIGSHOFEN (WÜRZBURG)

Johann Kaspar *Schlimbach*, ★ business founded in 1806; d. 1861.

LEIPZIG

Johann Jakob *Donat*, + recorded in 1700.
Christian Immanuel *Schweinefleisch*, + recorded 1731–1782.
Breitkopf & Härtel, ★ pianoforte builders 1807–1874.
Gottfried Christoph *Härtel*, ★ 1808–1874.
Johann Christian Gottlob *Irmler*, ★ business founded in 1818.
Otto and Oswald *Irmler*, ★ successors 1857; Otto d. 1861.
Schambach & Merhaut, ★ recorded in 1844.
Ernst *Irmler*, ★ successor c. 1854.
Julius *Feurich*, ★ business founded in 1851.
Julius *Blüthner*, ★ business founded in 1853.

LIEGNITZ

Eduard *Seiler*, ★ business founded in 1849.
J. *Gerstenberger*, ★ business founded in 1864.
Eduard *Sponnagel*, ★ business founded in 1866.

LÖBAU (SAXONY)

Friedrich August *Förster*, ★ business founded in 1859.

LÜBECK

Timotheus *Schaar*, ? recorded 1647–1650.
Martin *Siercks*, § recorded in 1712.
Ludwig *Franck*, ★ b.c. 1700, d. 1763.
Winter & Meyers, ? recorded in 1781.
Johann Friedrich Nölck, ? recorded 1799–1802.

LUDWIGSBURG

Karl Heinrich *Kaeferle*, ♀★ worked in Ludwigsburg after 1797.
Friedrich *Kaeferle*, ★ successor 1834.
Ferdinand *Kaeferle*.

MAINZ

Heilmann, ? second half of 18th century.
Edmund Ignaz *Quernbach*, ? recorded 1780–1790.
B. *Schott's Söhne*, ★ pianoforte factory founded in 1827, abandoned in 1842 (?).

MARBURG

Michael *Müller*, + ★ b. 1758.

MEISSEN

Ferdinand *Thürner*, ★ business founded in 1834.

MERSEBURG

Scherzer, ? recorded in 1780.

MÜHLHAUSEN (THÜRINGEN)

Gebrüder *Selle*, ★ business founded in 1828.

MÜNCHEN

Wolfgang *Faber*, + § recorded 1555–1563.
Joseph *Glonner*, + § ★ recorded 1753–1772.
Johann Ludwig *Dulcken*, ★ recorded 1779–1781 until 1835.
Gregor *Deifs*, *Deiff* or *Deiss*, ★ recorded 1818–1822.
J. *Mayer*, ★ business founded in 1826.
Aloys *Biber*, ★ business founded in 1833.
V. *Berdux*, ★ business founded in 1871.

MÜNSTER

B. *Knake*, ★ business founded in 1808.

MÜNSTERBERG (SCHLESIEN) (Silesia)

Zacharias *Hildebrand*, > ★ b. 1688, d. 1757 in Dresden.

MUSBACH near NEUSTADT AN DER HARDT

Johann Georg Michael *Guth*, ★ second half of 18th century.

NEU-BRANDENBURG

H. *Roloff*, ★ recorded in 1840 until end of 19th century.

NEUSTADT AN DER AISCH

Johann Christoph Georg *Schiedmeyer*, + b. 1740 recorded 1770–1796.

NÜRNBERG

Johann *Hayden*, ∞ b.c. 1540, d. 1631.
Johann Friedrich *Schneider*, ? recorded c. 1750.
Johann Georg *Kuppler*, ★ pupil of Stein, business founded in 1781.
Johann David *Schiedmayer*, ★ business founded in 1798; d. 1805.
Carl *Lang*, ★ beginning of 19th century.
Anton *Biber*, ★ recorded 1835–1840.

OSNABRÜCK

Gebrüder *Rohlfing*, ★ business founded in 1790.

PEISSENBERG (BAVARIA)

Bernhard *Smid*, + § recorded in 1433.

PLAUEN

Vogel & Sohn, ★ business founded in 1828.

REGENSBURG

Franz Jakob *Späth* (Y.), ♀★ b. 1714, d. 1786.
Christoph Friedrich *Schmahl*, ♀ ★ after 1774 partner of Späth; from 1774–1793 'Späth & Schmahl'; after 1794–1812 'Ch. Friedrich Schmahl'.
Jakob Friedrich and Christian Carl *Schmahl*, ♀★ in 1812 business called 'Chr. Friedrich Schmahl & Soehne'; 1813–1815 'Gebrüder Schmahl', also 'C.F. Schmahls Soehne'; in 1815 abandoned.
Albrecht *Ziegler*, ★ recorded in 1821.

RENDSBURG

Markus Gabriel *Sondermann*, + recorded in 1796.

RONNEBURG (SAXONY)

Christian Gotthelf *Hoffmann*, ? recorded 1763–1784.

ROTHENBURG

Georg Martin *Gessinger*, * recorded 1760–1780.

RUDOLSTADT

Christoph Michael *Lenker*, * recorded in 1765; in 1790 no longer alive.

SAARBRÜCKEN

Julius *Deesz*, * business founded in 1820.

SATRUP

Chr. *Hansen*, + recorded in 1799.

SEESEN

Heinrich Engelhardt *Steinweg*, * business founded in 1835; emigrated to New York in 1850.
Carl Friedrich Theodor *Steinweg*, successor; in 1855 business transferred to Wolfenbüttel.

SONDERSHAUSEN

Johann Georg *Schirmer*, + * pupil of Friederici; recorded in 1782, d. 1790.
Carl Conrad *Büchner*, * b. 1778 in Hameln; lived in Sondershausen.

SONTHOFEN (ALLGÄU)

Johann *Socher*, * recorded in 1742.

SCHLESWIG

Johann Christoph *Jürgensen*, + * business founded in 1780; d. 1815.

SCHMIEDEFELD

Michael and Johann *Wagner*, ? recorded in 1764 and 1770.

SCHWEINFURTH

F. *Kiedolps*, + recorded in 1751.
Michael *Voit* + * recorded 1804–1812.

STUTTGART

F. C. *Haug*, § * recorded in 1797.
F. B. *Wegmann*, * recorded in 1800 and 1802.
Johann Lorenz *Schiedmayer* and Carl *Dieudonné*, * business founded in 1809; called 'Dieudonné & Schiedmayer'.
Adolph (Y.) and Hermann (Y.) *Schiedmayer*, * entered the business as partners in 1875.
Julius and Paul *Schiedmayer*, * business founded in 1853; called 'Schiedmayer, Pianofortefabrik'.
F. *Dörner*, * business founded in 1830.
Richard *Lipp*, * business founded in 1831.
Bernhard Klinckerfuss, * business founded in 1832.
Carl *Hardt*, * business founded in 1855.
Joseph Anton *Pfeiffer*, * business founded in 1862.

TANGERMÜNDE

Gottfried Wilhelm *Zabel*, + pupil of Hildebrand; recorded previous to 1792 until 1803.

ULM

Georg Friedrich *Schmahl* (E.), + recorded after 1726; d. 1773.
Johann Matthäus *Schmahl*, * pupil of Georg Friedrich Schmahl (E.); b. 1734, d. 1793.
Georg Friedrich *Schmahl*, (Y.) + * b. 1748, d. 1827.

UNTERTÜRKHEIM (WÜRTTEMBERG)

Philipp Jakob *Warth*, * recorded 1788–1800.

VAIHINGEN AN DER ENZ (WÜRTTEMBERG)

Johann Michael *Bühler*, + * recorded in 1791.

VOLKSTEDT

Samuel *Kühlewind*, ∅ recorded in 1791.

WEIGANDSTHAL

Johann Christoph *Maywaldt*, + recorded in 1729.

WEIMAR

Johann Andreas *Ziegler*, + § b. 1658, d. 1737.
Adam *Eylenstein*, + § b. 1705, recorded until 1731.
Johann Georg *Schenk*, + * b. 1760 in Ostheim, settled in Weimar c. 1790, d. c. 1830. Pupil of J. A. Stein.

WESEL

Gerhard *Adam*, * business founded in 1828.

WIESBADEN

Johann Andreas and Johann Gottfried *Mahr*, * recorded 1774–1814.

WOLFENBÜTTEL

Theodor *Steinweg*, * business founded in 1855, transferred to Braunschweig in 1859.

WORMS

Johann Christoph *Jeckel*, * recorded in 1783.
Ferdinand *Mathuscheck*, * business founded in 1840. He left for New York in 1849.

WÜRZBURG

Michael *Joneck,* ★ b. 1748; recorded until 1812.
Joseph *Joneck,* ★ first quarter of 19th century.
Joseph *Klein,* ★ b. 1766 in Münsterberg; worked in Würzburg.
Jakob *Pfister,* ★ business founded in 1800.

ZITTAU

Johann Gottlieb (E.) *Tamitius,* + recorded after 1716–1754.
Johann Gottlieb (Y.) *Tamitius,* + ★ in c. 1840 the Tamitius family were still well-known in Zittau as clavichord and pianoforte builders.

ZWEIBRÜCKEN

Christian *Baumann,* ★ recorded 1766–1816 (year of death).
Johann Christoph *Schnell,* ★ recorded c. 1788.

ZWINGENBERG

G. *Dietz,* ∅ recorded in 1792.

GREAT BRITAIN

DOMICILE UNKNOWN

John *James,* § recorded in 1571.
John *Davidson,* § about 1652.
Peter *Hicks,* + recorded in 1720.
John *Woolfinden,* § recorded c. 1725.
John *Relfe,* § recorded c. 1740.
John *Hitchcock,* § recorded 1743–1774.
Schrader & Hartz, ★ recorded 1768–1780.
William *Gerber,* § recorded in 1775.
Skeene, § recorded in 1779.
Redpath & Davidson, ★ recorded in 1787.
Doug'ld *Gilchrist,* § recorded in 1793.
Alex. *Fairn,* § recorded in 1793.
John *Donner,* § recorded in 1793.

ALDGATE

Jasper *Blanchart,* § recorded 1566–1582.

BATH

Thomas *Underwood,* § recorded 1746–1760.

BRISTOL

John *Kemys,* § recorded in 1752.
Brice *Seede,* § recorded 1753–1772.
John *Smith,* § recorded in 1775.
Maddey, § recorded in 1785.
William *Eitkem,* ★ first half of 19th century.

CHESTER

W. *Goodman,* § middle of 16th century.

EDINBURGH

Neil *Stewart,* § recorded 1759–1805.
John Smith, § recorded in 1760.
Andrew *Rochead* & Son, § recorded 1793–1821.
Robertus *Marr,* ★ recorded in 1794.
John and Archibald *Watson,* ★ (early 19th century).

EXETER

John *Loosemoore,* § b. 1613, d. 1681.
Charles *Rewallin,* § recorded 1657–1697 (year of death).

GLOUCESTER

Thomas *Warn,* § recorded c. 1740.

LEEDS

John *Hopkinson,* ★ business founded in 1835; in 1846 transferred to London.

LIVERPOOL

Ruive, § recorded in 1790.
Joseph *Wrenshall,* ★ recorded 1793–1795.
Rushworth & Dreaper, ★ business founded in 1828.

LONDON

Sir Michael *Mercator,* recorded 1491–1544.
William *Treasorer,* § recorded 1521–1576.
William *Lewes,* § recorded in 1530.
Ludovic *Theeuwes,* § △ recorded 1568–1579.
Richard *Luxton,* § recorded in 1611.
Thomas *White,* § recorded 1621–1660 (year of death).
John *Haward,* § recorded 1622–1667 (year of death).
Gabriel *Townsend,* § recorded 1624–1662 (?).
Adam *Leversidge,* § recorded 1649–1670.
John *Player,* § recorded 1650–1705 or 1708.
Stephen *Keene,* § recorded 1655–1719.
Thomas *Haward,* § recorded 1656–1663.
James *White,* § recorded 1656–1676.
Andrea *Testa,* § recorded 1658–1700.
Philip *Jones,* § recorded 1658–1671.
Benjamin *Sison,* § recorded 1658–1710.
Alexander *Adam,* § recorded in 1659.
Charles *Haward,* § recorded 1660–1687.
Thomas *Hitchcock* (E.), § recorded 1660–1700.
Benjamin *Slade,* § b.c. 1669, recorded until 1698.
Edward *Blunt,* § b.c. 1678, d. prior to December 1718.
Thomas *Barton,* § recorded 1685–1735.
Thomas *Hitchcock* (Y.), § b.c. 1685, d. after 1733 (?).

Fenton, § recorded c. 1700.
Joseph *Tisseran*, § recorded c. 1700.
Thomas *Hancock*, § recorded c. 1700–1720.
Charles *Brackley*, § recorded 1703–1719.
Hermann *Tabel*, § recorded 1716–1738 (year of death).
Joseph *Baudin*, § recorded in 1723.
Burkhardt (Burkat) *Tschudy (Shudi)* (E.), § business founded in 1728; d. 1773.
Burkhardt *Tschudy* (Y.), * successor of the former, together with John Broadwood, 1773–1793.
Joshua *Tschudi*, ? b. 1739, d. 1774.
John *Broadwood*, § * 1770–1773 Tschudi E.'s pupil and assistant; 1773–1793 Tschudi Y.'s partner; they called the firm 'Shudi & Broadwood'.
James Shudi *Broadwood*, * in 1795 partner; firm called 'Broadwood & Son' (until 1807).
Thomas *Broadwood*, * in 1807 also partner; firm called 'John Broadwood & Sons'. John Broadwood d. in 1812, Thomas Broadwood d. in 1851.
Henry Fowler *Broadwood*, * successor in 1851, d. 1893.
Aston, § recorded 1693–1730.
John *Harris*, § recorded 1730–1768 when he left for Boston.
Hans Balthasar *Zopfi*, + § recorded 1747–1750 (year of death).
Joseph *Mahoon*, § recorded 1735–1771.
Jacob *Kirkman*, § * business founded in 1739; d. 1778? of 1792.
Abraham *Kirkman*, § * after 1773 partner; firm called 'Jakob & Abraham Kirkman'. Abraham Kirkman d. in 1794.
Joseph *Kirkman* (E.), § * in 1789 partner; 1794–1832 director; he called the firm 'Josephus Kirkman'.
Joseph *Kirkman* (Y.) and Henry John, * 1822–1896; business abandoned in 1896. Successors: 'Collard & Collard'.
Baker *Harris*, § recorded 1740–1780.
Roger *Plenius*, ○ § recorded 1741–1763.
Crang, § △ recorded 1745–1792 (year of death).
Heming *Hopton*, § recorded 1739–1752.
John *Hitchcock*, § * recorded 1743–1774.
Francis *Child*, § recorded in 1749.
Sells, § recorded in 1750.
Frederick *Neubauer*, § recorded 1763–1774.
Ephraim *Celson*, § recorded in 1778.
Samuel *Blumer*, § recorded 1749–1788.
John *Harrison*, § recorded 1743–1781.
Joseph *Harris*, § recorded 1750–1765.
John Joseph *Merlin*, § * business founded in 1760; d. 1804.
Faulkner, § recorded 1760–1773.
Johann *Zumpe*, * recorded 1761–1784. After a short partnership with Buntebart (1769–1778) Zumpe returned to Germany (1784).
Schoene and Co., * 1783–1820 successors of Zumpe.
James *Scouler* (E.), § recorded 1762–1782 (year of death).
George *Downing*, § recorded 1763–1783.
Charles, Samuel, Anne and Peter *Thompson*, § recorded 1764–1802.
John *Plenius*, § recorded 1765–1793.
William *Harris*, § recorded 1766–1793.
Americus *Backers*, § * 1763–1781.
Johannes *Pohlmann*, § * 1767–1793.
Adam *Beyer*, * business founded in 1774; recorded until 1790.
James *Longman*, § △ * 1767–1769.
Lukey, § * 1769–1776; firm called 'Longman, Lukey & Co.'.
Francis *Broderip*, § * 1769–1776; firm called 'Longman, Lukey & Broderip'; when Lukey left in 1776, they called it 'Longman & Broderip' (1776–1798); in 1798 bankrupt. John Longman associated with Clementi, and Broderip with Wilkinson.
Broderip & Wilkinson, * 1798–1810.
John *Longman*, * in 1801 John Longman left the firm Clementi; set up a new business in 1802. In 1805 firm called 'Longman & Co', in 1806 'J. Longman'.
Giles *Longman*, * in 1816 business called 'Longman & Heron'; in 1820 liquidation; 1824–1833 'G. Longman & T.C. Bates'.
Muzio *Clementi*, § * 1799–1805 partner of J. Longman; 1805–32 business called 'Clementi and Co.'.
F.W. and W.P. *Collard*, * after 1809 partners; in 1832, after Clementi's death, owners; called the business 'Collard & Collard'.
Samuel *Gillespy*, § recorded 1769–1774.
Gabriel *Buntebart*, * 1769–1795.
Adam D. and J. *Walker*, § recorded 1772–1781.
Newbane, § recorded in 1773.
Frederick *Beck*, * 1774–1794.
Christopher *Ganer*, * 1774–1807.
T. *Garbutt*, * 1775–1793.
George *Pether*, * 1775–1794.
Robert (E.), William, Matthew and *Stodart*, * 1775–1861.
John *Preston*, * 1777–1825.
John Crang *Hancock*, * 1779–1799.
William *Le Bond*, * 1780–1792 (according to Harding 1730–1792).
Charles *Trute*, § * recorded 1782–1808.
George *Garcia*, * 1783–1792.
Henry *Holland*, * 1783–1798.
George *Goulding*, *d'Almaine* and *Potter*, * in 1785 they founded the business, calling it 'Goulding, d'Almaine and Potter'; after 1835 '*D'Almaine & Co.*'.
Rolfe, William and Davies, * 1785–1888.
John *Geib* (I), * 1786–1798; in 1798 he emigrated to America.
John *Landreth*, * 1787.
Humphrey *Walton*, * 1787.
Samuel Bury & Co., * 1787–1794.
George *Froeschle*, * 1788–1800.
Joseph Smith, * recorded in 1790.
Augustus *Lenkfield*, * 1790–1796.
James Ball, * 1790–1834.
Pringle, * 1792.
Joseph *Dale*, * 1792–1809.
Joshua *Done*, * 1792–1814.
John *Lincoln*, * recorded in 1793.
Robert and William *Gray*, * recorded in 1793.
John *Adlam*, * 1793.
Joseph Buckinger, * 1793–1809.
Monrow and May, * 1793–1839.
Elwick, * recorded in 1794.
Corrie, * 1794.

George *Astor*, * 1794–1815 'George Astor & Co.'
Horwood, * 1815–1822 'Astor & Horwood', 1822–1824 'Astor & Co.'.
C. *Gerock*, * 1824–1837 'Gerock, Astor & Co.', in 1837 'C. Gerock & Co.'.
William *Southwell* (E.), * 1794–1842 (year of death).
William *Southwell* (Y.), * the former's successor 1844–1857.
Bland and Weller, * 1795–1817.
George *Wilkinson*, * 1798–1810 'Broderip & Wilkinson'.
Bell, * 1800.
John F. and John Thomas *Bell*, * 1844–1850.
Henry *Lawson* & Co., * 1800–1824.
Thomas *Tomkinson*, * 1800–1854.
Scott & Co, * 1801–1828.
Thomas *Loud* (E.), * 1802–1825, when he left for New York.
John Isaac *Hawkins*, * 1803–1845.
William *Dettmar*, * 1805–1848.
George *Dettmar*, * 1848–1849 the former's successor.
Charles *Dierkes*, * 1810–1835.
Robert *Wornum*, * 1811–1813 'Wilkinson & Wornum'; 1813–1835 'George Wilkinson'.
Thomas *Butcher*, * 1811–1837.
William *Challen*, * succeeded the former 1838–1862.
C. *Challen*, * William Challen's successor in 1862.
C. H. *Challen*, * in 1873 partnership, 'Challen & Son'.
Robert *Wornum* (E.), * 1811–1813 'Wilkinson & Wornum' in 1813 he set up a business of his own.
Robert *Wornum* (Y.) after 1815; in 1861 'Robert Wornum & Sons'.
John *Price*, * 1814–1840.
Evenden and Sons, * 1820.
J. H. R. and J. C. *Mott* & Co., * 1820–1863.
James *Stewart*, * 1827–1843.
J. *Strohmenger* * 1830–1870; in 1870 'J. Strohmenger & Son'.
William *Jenkins*, * 1835–1838; 1838–1842 'William Jenkins & Son'; 1842–1862 'William Jenkins & Sons'; business abandoned in 1862.
F. *Greiner*, * business founded in 1837.
Charles *Cadby*, * 1839–1867; 1867–1885 'Charles Cadby & Son'.
John *Brinsmead*, * business founded in 1836.
Thomas James and Edgar William *Brinsmead*, * entered into partnership in 1870.
Oetzmann and Plumb, * business founded in 1846; after 1861 'F. Oetzmann & Sons'.
John and James *Hopkinson*, business founded in 1846; John Hopkinson left in 1869.
J. *Harrison and Co.*, * 1850–1864.
Ralph *Allison*, * business founded in 1850.
Arthur *Allison*, * in 1879 'Arthur Allison & Co' (?).
F. *Hund* and Son, * 1851–1880.
Chas. *Holdernesse*, * business founded in 1851; in 1856 'Holdernesse & Holdernesse'.
Chappell & Co., * after 1860 they also built pianos.
Cramer & Co., * after c. 1862 also piano makers.

MANCHESTER

John *Kirshaw*, § recorded 1740–1773.
Joseph *Kirshaw*, § recorded in 1773.

NORWICH

James *Holmes*, * recorded in 1795.

OXFORD

Henry *Hardy*, * recorded in 1800.

WESTMINSTER

George *Glanville*, § recorded in 1749.

YORK

John *Watson*, § recorded in 1762.
Thomas *Haxby*, § recorded 1737–1798.

HUNGARY

BUDAPEST

Chmel & Son, * business founded in 1835.
Ludwig *Beregsgâszy*, * recorded 1845–1873.

IRELAND

DUBLIN

Adrian *Strong*, § recorded 1639–1655.
Thomas *Hollister*, § recorded 1728–1775.
John and Robert *Woffington*, § * recorded 1728–1836.
Ferdinand *Weber*, § recorded 1739–1784 (year of death).
William *Gibson*, § recorded 1764–1778.
William *Hollister*, § recorded 1766–1784.
Thomas *Hollister*, § recorded 1728–1775.
Henry *Rother*, § recorded 1774–1782.
John Bernard *Logier*, * b. 1780, d. 1846.
Rice, § recorded in 1790.
John and Edward *Lee*, § recorded 1790–1800.
Alexander, James and Daniel *MacDonnel*, § recorded 1790–1804.
Samuel *Morland*, * recorded in 1807.

ITALY

DOMICILE UNKNOWN

Marcus *Siculus*, § recorded in 1540.
Markus *Jadra*, § recorded 1552–1568.
Franciscus *Bonafinis*, § recorded in 1585.
Gaetanus *Giannini*, § recorded in 1628.
Joannes Fiammengo *Tollenari*, § recorded in 1670.
Bartholomæus *Stephanini*, § recorded in 1694.
Joseph Maria *Gozzini*, § recorded 1725, 1726.
Luigi *Rasori*, § 18th century.
Giovanni Francesco *Tronco*, § recorded in 1757.
Antonio *Brunelli*, § recorded in 1798.

AREZZO

A. *Santini*, § recorded in 1570.
Antonio *Bati*, § recorded in 1691.

BERGAMO

Donatus *Undeus*, § recorded 1592–1623.
Alessandro *Riva*, § b. 1803, d. 1868.

BOLOGNA

Bononiensis *Antonius*, § recorded in 1592.
Joannes *Baptista*, § recorded in 1602.
Faby, § recorded 1677–1691; later on he lived in France.

BOLZANO

Johann *Baumgartner*, + recorded in 1683.

BRESCIA

Giovanni *Antegnati*, § (?) recorded 1533-1537.
Francesco da Brescia, § recorded in 1564.
Matteo *Benti*, § b. 1580, d. after 1653.

COMO

Carlo Antonio *Somigliana*, § recorded in 1737.

CORTONA

Giovanni Baptista *Boni*, § recorded 1619–1675.

CREMONA

Antonio *Anelli*, * business founded in 1836.

FERRARA

Alfonso *Cricca*, § recorded in 1591.
Ippolito *Cricca*, called Paliarino, § recorded in 1598.

FIRENZE (FLORENCE)

Giovanni *Cellini*, § b. c. 1460, d. 1527 or 1528.
Christophorus *Rigunini*, § recorded in 1602.
Pasuinius *Quercius*, § recorded 1610–1615.
Nicolaus de *Quoco*, § recorded 1612–1694.
Rigoli, § recorded c. 1620.
Joannes de *Pertici*, § recorded 1665–1690.
Girolamo *Zenti*, § after 1666 he probably worked in Florence; still recorded in 1683.
Antonio *Migliai*, § recorded 1682–1704.
Giovanni *Carcassi*, § recorded 1688–1698; he probably lived in Florence.
Lorenzo *Magniai*, § recorded in 1689.
Giuseppe *Zolfanelli*, § recorded 1690–1709.
Bartolomeo *Cristofori*, § worked in Florence after c. 1690, d. 1731.
Franciscus *Poggio*, called Crinetus, § recorded 1586–1634 (year of death?).
Vincentius Pratensis, § recorded 1610–1612.
Giuseppe *Mendini*, § recorded 1631–1646.
Agostinus *Feroci*, § recorded in 1705.
Francesco *Nobili*, § recorded in 1693.
Giovanni *Ferrini*, § * pupil of Cristofori; recorded 1690–1755.
Gherardi da Padova, § pupil of Cristofori.
Vincenzio *Sodi*, § recorded 1779–1792.
Francesco *Spighi*, § recorded in 1790.
Brizzi & Niccolai, * business founded in 1844.

GAGLIANO (MUGELLO)

Domenico del *Mela*, * recorded in 1739.

GENOVA (GENOA)

Onesto *Tosi*, + recorded in 1568.

LUCCA

Jacobus Lucensis *Bagninius*, § recorded in 1613.
Giovanni Baptista *Giusti*, § recorded 1667–1700.
Giuseppe *Crudeli*, § recorded in 1781.

MILANO (MILAN)

Annibale dei *Rossi*, § recorded after 1550, d. between 1577–1595; identical with Annibale Mediolanensis.
Ferrante *Rossi*, § recorded 1580–1595. Identical with the spinet builder 'Ferandi de Rosis Mediolanensis'.
Antonio *Scoti*, § recorded in 1753.
Felice *Piantanida*, * recorded in 1799.

MANTOVA (MANTUA)

Giovanni Battista *Pessetti*, § recorded in 1674.

MESSINA

Carolus *Grimaldi*, § recorded in 1697.

MODENA

Sesto *Tantini*, § recorded 1461–1490.
Alexander *Pasi*, § recorded in 1493.
Martinelli, called 'il Gobbo', § 17th century.
Pietro *Termanini*, § recorded 1755–1773.

NAPOLI

Giovanni *Boccalari*, § recorded in 1717.
Fischer (E.), * end of 18th century.
Fischer (Y.), * first quarter of 19th century.
Ferdinando *Sievers*, * business founded c. 1865.

PADOVA

Patavinus *Franciscus*, § recorded 1527–1561.
Patavinus *Antonius*, § recorded in 1550.
Abbé Gregorio *Trentin*, * b. 1768 in Conselve near Padova, d. in Padova, 1854.
Nicolo *Lachin*, * business founded in 1830.

PARMA

Fratelli *Berzioli*, * business founded in 1836.

PAVIA

Lorenzo *Gusnaschi*, + § recorded in 1494, d. prior to 1539.
Paul *Belisonius*, § recorded in 1522.

RIMINI

Franciscus *Neri*, § recorded in 1695.

ROMA (ROME)

Bononiensis *Hieronymus*, § recorded in 1521.
Antonius *Irena*, § recorded in 1564.
Francesco della *Nona*, § recorded 1610–1612 (of French origin).
Valerius *Peres*, § recorded 1625–1631.
Orazio *Albana*, § recorded 1628–1645.
Hieronymus da *Zentis* (sometimes Sentis), § is recorded in Pavia 1633–1666. After 1668 he probably worked in Florence.
Michele *Todini*, § *, b. 1625 in Saluzzo; recorded in Rome until 1676.
Francesco *Nobili*, § recorded 1693–1695.
Gaspare *Assalone*, § recorded in 1732.
Johannes Paulus *Leoni*, § recorded in 1773.

SIENA

Joannes *Landi*, § recorded in 1670.

TREVISO

Joseph *Danis*, § recorded in 1570.

TRENTO

Johannes Antonius *Berera*, § recorded 1745–1761.

TRIESTE

Giovanni *Haichele*, * first half of 19th century.

TORINO

Abel *Adam*, § recorded 1657–1714.
Giovanni Francesco *Franco*, § recorded in 1757. Was probably domiciled in Torino.
Carlo *Perotti*, * end of 18th century; business founded c. 1870.
Carlo *Roeseler*, * business founded c. 1850.
Giuseppe *Mola*, business founded in 1862.

VENEZIA (VENICE)

Bernhard *Murer*, called 'Il Tedesco' (the German), § recorded in 1445.
Pisaurensis *Dominicus*, + § recorded 1533–1600.
Johannes Antonius *Baffo*, § recorded after 1523 until 1581.
Alessandro *Trasuntinus*, + § recorded 1531–1604.
Aloysius *Ventura*, § recorded in 1533.
Giovanni *Domenico*, recorded 1556–1566.
Vitus de *Trasuntinus*, § recorded 1560–1606.
Benedetto *Floriani* or Floriano, § recorded 1568–1572.
Johannes *Celestini*, § recorded 1587–1610.
Antonio *Monsuto*, § recorded in 1674.
Johannes Andreas *Menegoni*, § recorded 1690–1715.
Petrus *Centamin*, § recorded in 1711.
J. *Chianei*, § recorded 1766–1771.

VERONA

Bastiano da Verona, § lived in the 15th and 16th century.
Francesco da *Portalupi*, § recorded in 1523.

VITERBO

Toma Rossi, § recorded in 1759.

NETHERLANDS

WITH UNKNOWN DOMICILE

Artus Cheerdink, § recorded in 1605.

AMSTERDAM

Dirk van der *Lugt*, § recorded in 1770.
Meincke & Pieter *Meyer*, * recorded c. 1780; left for Hamburg at the turn of the century.
van den *Hoef*, * recorded c. 1810.
J. van *Diepen*, * first half of 19th century.
Allgäuer & Zoon, * business founded in 1830.
van Raay & Zonen, * first half of 19th century.

DEN HAAG

Bräutigam, ? recorded in 1762.
J.F. *Cuijpers*, * business founded in 1832.
Ch. F. *Rijken* & Co., *.
J.H.H. *Traut*, * beginning of 19th century.

HAARLEM

J.A. *Ban*, § recorded in 1637.

LEIDEN

A. *Leenhouwer*, § recorded in 1787.

ROERMOND

Johann Joseph *Coenen*, § recorded c. 1735.

ROTTERDAM

Rijken & de Lange, * business founded in 1852.

UTRECHT

Willem *Deckens*, △ recorded in 1627.

NORWAY

MOSS

H. *Jansen*, + recorded in 1757.

OSLO

Georg Daniel *Schoene*, + recorded in 1793.
Emanuel *Schoene*, * d. 1851. Pupil of Marschall in Copenhagen.
G.F. *Waarum*, * d. 1836.
Christopher *Thomle*, * b. 1794, d. 1857. Pupil of Marschall.
Karl Marius Anton Johann and Petter Martin Emil Nilson *Hals*, * business founded in 1848. Petter M. Hals d. in 1871, Karl Marius in 1898.
Enger, * recorded in 1854.

POLAND

CRACOW

Michael v. *Pilzna*, + 15th century.
Kasper *Hauk*, § 17th century.
Martin, + recorded in 1609.
Krzysztof *Kiejcher*, + § c. 1700.

DANZIG

Paulus *Steinicht*, § recorded 1657–1661.
Dalitz (Delitz), § * recorded 1765–1785.

GÖRLITZ

August *Rieser*, * first half of 19th century.

POZNAŃ

Mazlowski, § recorded in 1805.

WARSAW

Malecki & Schroeder and Julian *Malecki*, * second half of 19th century.
Krall & Seidler (Zeidler?), * second half of 19th century.

WROCLAW (SILESIA)

Jakob *Rohmann*, * c. 1800–1859.
Johann Wilhelm *Lunnert*, * first quarter of 19th century.
Friedrich *Kuhlboers*, * first half of 19th century.
P.F. *Welzel*, * business founded in 1835.
Traugott *Berndt*, * business founded in 1837.
Bessalié, *...

WÜSTE-GIERSDORF (SILESIA)

Friedrich *Stentzel*, ? recorded in 1775.

PORTUGAL

BEJA

Manuel Anjos *Leo*, § recorded c. 1703.

LISBON

Manuel *Antunes*, * recorded 1760–1789.
Jacintho *Ferreira*, + recorded in 1783.

PORTO

Manoel de Sa Carmo, + recorded in 1796.

SPAIN

WITH UNKNOWN DOMICILE

Fray Raymundo *Truchado*, ○ recorded in 1625.

BARCELONA

Johannes *Kyburz*, * recorded 1800–1822.
Franz Joseph *Otter*, * recorded 1800–1807.
Josef *Marti*, * recorded in 1805.
Juan *Munné*, * first quarter of 19th century.
Manuel *Bordas*, * first half of 19th century.
Raf. *Car. Pons*, * first half of 19th century.
Giacomo *Balbi*, * first half of 19th century.
Pindo de Pedro *Estela*, * business founded in 1830.
Hermanos *Guarra*, * business founded in 1860.
Louis *Izabel*, * business founded in 1860.
Chassaigne frères, business founded in 1864.
Bernareggi & Co., * recorded in 1867.

BELORADO (PROVINCE BURGOS)

Jaras, + recorded in 1809.

MADRID

Jan *Brebos*, § recorded 1567–1609.
Colmenareso, * recorded in 1822.
Fernandez, * recorded in 1828.
Montana, * business founded in 1864.

MAHON (MINORCA)

Antonio *Llado*, * first half of 19th century.

TARAZONA

José *Grabalos*, + (18th century).

SWEDEN

GÖTEBORG

Gustav Gabriel *Woltkersson*, + recorded in 1759.
J.H. *Daugh*, * recorded c. 1800.
J.G. *Högvall*, * recorded in 1811.
Johann Gustav *Malmsjö*, * business founded in 1843.

MALMÖ

G. & Co. *Ekstrem*, * business founded in 1836.

NORRKÖPING

A.F. *Sätherberg*, * (second half of 19th century), recorded in 1862.

SÖDERHAMN

Magnus *Åsell*, * recorded in 1821.

STOCKHOLM

Erik *German*, + recorded in 1736.
Philipp Jacob *Specken*, § + recorded 1737–1742.
David *Strähle*, + recorded in 1738.
Johannes *Bromann*, + § recorded in 1736 until 1750.
Gottlieb *Rosenau*, § recorded 1757–1786.
Peer *Lundborg*, + recorded 1772–1796.
Mathias Petter *Kraft*, * pupil of Lundborg. Business founded in 1778; d. 1807.

Peer *Lindholm*, + his workmanship got known after 1780 (b. 1742). 1803–1806 the business was called 'Peer Lindholm & Söderström'; d. 1813.
George Christoffer *Rackwitz*, + * recorded in 1796.
N.G. *Hultenberg*, * (beginning of 19th century).
H.J. *Söderström*, + recorded 1803–1816.
Carl Jac. *Nordquist*, + * recorded 1823–1826.
P. *Rosenvall*, * (c. 1830).
Olof *Granfeldt*, * recorded in 1828 and 1834.
Anders *Söderberg*, * business founded in 1832.
August Friedrich *Hoffmann*, * successor of Söderberg, after 1859; d. 1884.

SWITZERLAND

AARAU

Bernhard *Herzog*, * business founded in 1840; transferred to Basel in 1853.

ALT ST. JOHANN (TOGGENBURG)

Ulrich *Ammann*, * worked in St. Johann 1808–1821.

BASEL

Anton *Soumlin*, + recorded in 1490/91, 1495 and 1506.
Jeremias *Schlegel*, § b. 1730, d. 1792.
Peter Friedrich *Brosy*, § recorded 1734–1765 (year of death).
Johann Jakob *Brosy*, § * recorded c. 1750–1812.
Valentin *Krehmer* or *Kraemer*, * recorded after 1797 (in 1806 pupil of Brosy) until 1839.
Adam Georg Gottlieb *Immler*, * business founded in 1818. In 1833 or 1834 he emigrated to Ohio (in Basel's directory he is mentioned up to 1843!)
Simon *Daeschler*, * business founded in 1844.
Friedrich *Abend*, * succeeded Daeschler in 1858, recorded until 1877.
Karl Michael *Ott*, * recorded after 1854, still mentioned in 1877.
Friedrich Ernst *Hegar*, * b. 1816, mentioned in 1877, d. 1888.
Karl *Aldinger*, * business founded in 1888, in 1909 he merely dealt in pianos.

BERN

Johann Ludwig *Haehlen* or Hehlen (also Hellen), ? recorded after 1761; 1764–1772 the business was called 'Haehlen samt Bruder', 1772/73 until 1780 'Gebrueder Haehlen, Orgelmacher'; 1780–1781 'Haehlen, Claviermacher'. J. L. Haehlen d. 1781.
Johannes *Hauert* (Howard), § * recorded in 1777/78; no longer after 1783/84.
Joseph *Howard*, § * recorded 1783/84–1824 (year of death).
Karl Ludwig *Howard*, * business founded c. 1822; d. 1863.
Georg Adam *Kyburz*, * recorded in 1782, d. 1801.
Niklaus *Kaderly*, * recorded 1783–1797.
Christian *Wyss*, * recorded 1789–1830 (year of death).
Theophil *Gleiniger*, * recorded 1810–1823 (year of death).
Friedrich *Suter*, * recorded 1822–1866.
Johann *Daeppen*, * recorded in 1830.
Johann Andreas *Flohr*, * business founded in 1830, d. 1872.
August *Schmidt*, * succeeded the former 1872–1904 (year of death).
Albert *Schmidt*, * in 1889 the former's partner; 1904–1936 his successor; d. 1936.
Max & Hans *Schmidt*, * successors after 1936.
Karl Christoph *Kützing*, * business founded in 1834; d. 1862.
Rudolf *Waedenschweiler*, * business founded in 1845; he moved to Zurich in 1852.
Mathias *Vogt*, * business founded in 1860; d. 1890.
Jakob *Rindlisbacher*, * business founded in 1872; d. 1892.

BIEL (BIENNE)

Christian *Burger*, * business founded in 1876; d. 1925.
Ernst *Burger*, * d. 1934.
Hans *Burger*, * proxy in the firm Burger & Jacobi.
Hermann Emil *Jacobi*, * in 1881 partner of Burger, in 1882 firm mentioned as 'Burger & Jacobi'.
Hermann Heinrich Christian *Jacobi*, * after 1911 collaborator, after 1924 director.
Hugo Edwin Hans *Jacobi*, * worked in the firm after 1912, became member of the board of directors after 1924.
Werner Lucas Guido *Jacobi*, * after 1924 member of the board.

BURGDORF

Christian *Burger*, business founded in 1869; moved to Bienne in 1876.

EINSIEDELN (SCHWYZ)

Pius *Kreuel*, ? b. 1629, d. 1696.

FISCHINGEN (THURGAU)

Franz Jakob *Bodmer*, * b. 1753, recorded until 1797.

FRIBOURG

Jean *Dreyer*, * recorded 1766–1825 (year of death).
Aloys *Mooser*, § * pupil of Kraemer and of Anton Walter; recorded c. 1792 (?) until 1839 (year of death).
Jean *Mooser*, * 1818–1846 (year of death).
Joseph *Mooser* (III), * recorded after 1820 until 1876 (year of death).

GENEVA

Jean Guillaume *Braschoss*, called William, * business founded in 1823; d. 1871.

Georges and Adolphe *Frey*, * recorded c. 1828. In 1848 Georges F. died; 1848–1861 Adolphe Frey sole manager.

Gustave *Frey*, * succeeded the former in 1861 until c. 1870; after this date the firm ceased to exist.

Sébastien *Straub* (also Strauber), * business founded c. 1828, abandoned shortly after this date.

In this context we might mention the firm Mussard although it belongs to the Paris group.

Jacob Pierre *Mussard*, b. 1786 in Geneva; 1825–1835 he built pianos in Lausanne; moved to Paris in 1835, and became a partner in the piano factory of his brother Emile; d. 1847.

Jean Louis Emile *Mussard*, b. 1793 in Geneva; recorded in Paris after 1828. In 1835 he entered into partnership with his brother Pierre Jacob, calling the firm 'Mussard frères'; name changed into 'Mussard & Co.' after 1847. They ceased business in 1852; J. B. Frantz became successor.

HÄGGENSCHWIL

Bonifaz *Bieger*, * business founded in 1842, transferred to Rorschach in 1856.

LAUSANNE

Jean David *Dupraz*, * recorded 1823–1872 (year of death).

Pierre Jacob *Mussard*, * recorded 1825–1835. Moved to Paris in 1835.

LUCERNE

Josef Fridolin *Rütschi*, * recorded in 1790.

Anton *Bürgi*, * recorded 1835–1848.

Josef *Muth*, * recorded in 1856.

Jakob *Ritzmann*, * recorded in 1856.

J. *Weber*, * recorded in 1883.

MAMMERN

J. *Weber*, * recorded in 1850, in 1883 in Lucerne.

NEUCHATEL

Alexander *Speissegger*, § recorded 1750–1772 (year of death).

Benoît *Hauert*, * recorded 1797–1814 (year of death).

Hugo E. *Jacobi*, * recorded 1896–1907 (year of death).

RAPPERSWIL

Jakob *Bodmer*, * recorded 1813–1822 (year of death).

Heinrich *Hüni* (I), * recorded 1829–1850.

Heinrich *Hüni* (II), * recorded in 1850, moved to Zurich.

Hüni & Belmond and Jakob *Belmond*, * 1850–1860 successors (?).

Theodor *Rordorf*, * 1919–1923; transferred to Lyon in 1923.

RORSCHACH

Bonifaz *Bieger*, * after 1856 piano factory in Rorschach.

Wilhelm, Otto, Emil and Bonifaz (Y.) *Bieger*, * successors in 1870.

Lorenz *Sabel*, * successor in 1919 when Emil Bieger retired.

Franz Hugo *Jacobi*, * after 1948 proxy in the firm 'Sabel AG, Rorschach'.

SOLOTHURN

Franz Joseph *Otter*, * recorded 1772–1794 (worked in Barcelona c. 1800–1802, d. 1807).

Johannes *Kyburz*, * recorded 1822–1844 (year of death).

Philipp Heinrich *Caesar*, * recorded 1816–1843 (year of death).

Wolfgang *Strähl*, * in 1844 he succeeded Caesar.

Spörndly, partner of Strähl in the firm 'Strähl & Spörndly', recorded until 1860.

Johann *Heinzmann*, * business founded in 1851.

ST. GALL

Friedrich *Jahn*, * recorded c. 1820.

Georg Hermann *Buff*, * business founded c. 1852; moved to Tägerwilen (Thurgau) in 1890.

STÄFA

Ernst *Rordorf*, * 1911–1917 (year of death).

Theodor *Rordorf*, * 1917–1919, when he moved to Rapperswil.

THUN

Heinrich *Jacobi*, * business founded in 1842; d. 1879; business dissolved in 1880 (?).

WIL

Johann Ludwig *Türig*, + recorded in 1680.

S. *Hugentobler*, * recorded in 1883.

ZURICH

Jean Caspar *Maag*, recorded 1787–1822.

Hans Jakob *Goll*, * recorded 1815–1822, when he moved to Vienna. In 1825 back in Zurich where he worked until 1839. Business liquidated in 1839.

Heinrich *Goll*, * worked with his father in Zurich and Vienna (until 1826–1827), then again in Zurich until c. 1836–1838.

Jakob *Fäsi*, * recorded 1816–1864, when he moved to Freiburg im Breisgau.

Heinrich *Hüni* (E.), * business founded in 1825 (in Zurich?).

Heinrich *Hüni* (Y.) and Jakob *Hüni*, * in 1846 recorded as 'Heinrich Hüni & Soehne, Zurich und Rapperswyl'; in 1850 merged with firm Hübert. Heinrich Hüni (Y.) d. 1853, Heinrich Hüni (E.) d. 1867, leaving Hübert to manage the business alone.

Jean *Bourry*, * partner of Hübert in 1877.

Jean Henri *Bourry*, ⋆ joined the business as partner in 1879. In 1883 Jean Bourry sole owner of the factory which burnt down in 1885. Liquidation in 1886.

Nicolaus *Hübert*, ⋆ business founded in 1838. 1845–1847 partnership with Günzler and Gassmann, recorded as 'Nicolaus Hübert & Co.'; merged with the firm Hüni in 1850; left the firm Hüni & Hübert in 1883. Nicolaus Hübert d. 1890.

Julius *Günzler* and Jakob *Gassmann*, ⋆ 1845–1847 partner in the firm 'Nicolaus Hübert & Co', in 1847 he founded his own firm, which was liquidated in 1850. Gassmann left the firm in 1848 and in his turn founded a firm which he abandoned in 1867.

Conrad *Rordorf* (E.) and Rudolf Rordorf, ⋆ founded a business called 'Rordorf & Co.'.

Conrad *Rordorf* (Y.) and Rudolf Rordorf (Y.) successors c. 1885.

Theodor and Ernst *Rordorf*, ⋆ transferred the business to Stäfa in 1911.

Christian *Sprecher* and Johann Kaspar *Bär*, ⋆ business founded in 1850, called 'Sprecher & Bär', in 1852 'Sprecher & Co.'.

Wilhelm *Butte*, ⋆ partner 1872–1875, firm called 'Sprecher & Butte'.

Theodor and Moritz *Sprecher*, ⋆ 1875–1889 'Sprecher & Söhne'. Moritz Sprecher left in 1889 and founded his own firm 'Moritz Sprecher, vormals in Firma Sprecher & Söhne'. Business dissolved in 1911. The former firm Sprecher & Soehne was taken over by Theodor Sprecher in 1889 and continued as 'Sprecher & Wirth' until 1892 when it was abandoned.

Joseph *Ganter*, ⋆ business founded in 1855; d. 1910.

Hermann *Ganter*, ⋆ succeeded Joseph 1910–1917; abandoned in 1917.

Johannes *Kull* and Rudolf *Wädenschweiler*, ⋆ business founded in 1858 and abandoned the same year. 1859–1862 Wädenschweiler managed his own firm which he abandoned in 1862.

Heinrich *Kölliker* and Jacques *Trost*, ⋆ business founded and abandoned in 1866.

Zachäus *Grammer*, ⋆ founded in 1866 a new firm called 'Kölliker & Grammer which ceased in 1882.

Jacques *Trost* & Co. and Arnold *Hünerwadel*, ⋆ business founded in 1868, called 'J. Trost & Co.'; liquidated in 1893.

Heinrich *Hüni* and Rudolf *Rordorf*, ⋆ in 1893 'Hüni & Rordorf' (successors of Trost & Co.). In 1895 Rordorf left the firm, 1895–1908 it was merely called 'Hüni'.

Alfred *Hüni*, ⋆ 1908–1926 he continued the firm, now called 'Hüni & Co.'.

Heinrich *Escher*, ⋆ started a business in 1869.

Heinrich *Suter*, ⋆ took over Escher's firm in 1877; it lasted until 1914 when Suter died.

Heinrich and August *Martmer*, ⋆ started business in 1871; recorded in 1873 as 'A. Martmer & Co.'; cessation in 1880.

Jakob Hüni-(Koller), ⋆ business founded in 1872, abandoned in 1875.

Carl *Gaissert*, ⋆ business founded in 1873.

Carl Ludwig *Gaissert*, ⋆ succeeded the former in 1893–1923 (year of death).

UNION OF SOVIET SOCIALIST REPUBLICS

LENINGRAD

J. W. *Calix*, ⋆ at the turn of the 18th to 19th century.

Gabram, ⋆ recorded in 1783 and 1795. Pupil of Kirschnigk.

A. *Tischner*, ⋆ first half of 19th century.

Diederichs Gebrüder, ⋆ business founded in 1870.

Johann Friedrich *Schröder*, ⋆ business founded in 1818.

Karl Michael *Schröder*, ⋆ succeeded the former in 1852.

J. C. *Lüdecke*, ⋆ recorded in 1837.

Jakob *Becker*, ⋆ business founded in 1841.

Michael A. *Bietepage*, ⋆ succeeded Becker in 1871.

H. H. *Lichtenthal*, ⋆ business founded in 1851.

MOSCOW

M. *Kirschnigk*, ⋆ recorded in 1781 and 1794, lived until the beginning of the 19th century.

Johann Christoph *Hübner*, ⋆ recorded in 1801.

ODESSA

M. *Rausch*, ⋆ business founded in 1856.

RIGA

Henning *Hake*, § recorded in 1657.

Th. *Johannsohn*, ⋆ business founded in 1855.

UNITED STATES OF AMERICA

ALBANY

Harley *Hosford*, ⋆ business founded c. 1810. Probably the first to build pianos in Albany.

J. & H. *Meacham*, ⋆ business founded c. 1813.

Sylvanus *Pond*, ⋆ partner after 1825, firm called 'Meacham & Pond'; well-known until 1850.

John *Osborn*, ⋆ business founded in 1829, together with G. King; nine months later transferred to New York.

William G. *Boardman*, ⋆ business founded in 1835.

James *Gray,* * in 1836 collaborator, after 1837 partner in the firm 'Boardman & Gray'. A few years before his death (1881), Boardman retires and leaves the management to Gray alone.

William James and James Stuart *Gray,* * enter into partnership with their father in 1887.

Henry *Hazelton,* * in 1838 pupil of Boardman. In 1840 firm 'Hazelton, Lyon & Talbot'. Transferred to New York in 1841.

Myron A. *Decker,* * business founded in 1856.

BALTIMORE

John *Harper,* * recorded 1802–1812/1814.

James *Stewart,* * pupil of Harper; started a business in 1812, transferred to Boston in 1820.

Joseph *Hiskey,* * business founded in 1819, abandoned in 1848.

Henry *Hartyre,* * business founded in 1826, sinks into oblivion after 1836.

William *Knabe,* * business founded in 1837, with Henry Gaehle as partner; 1839–1854 'Knabe & Gaehle'; after 1854 'Knabe & Company' in partnership with his sons.

William *Knabe* (Y.) and Ernest Knabe, the former's sons took over the firm in 1864.

Henry *Gaehle,* * 1839–1854 partner of William Knabe. After 1854 independent firm called 'Gaehle & Company'.

Charles M. *Stieff,* * founded a business in 1842.

Frederick P. *Stieff,* * succeeded the former.

Joseph *Newman,* * founded c. 1850 a business called 'Newman & Brothers'; entered into partnership with W. R. Talbot in 1853; d. 1884.

BOSTON

John *Harris,* § recorded in 1768.

Benjamin *Crehore,* § * recorded in Milton (a suburb of Boston) after c. 1785; built spinets since c. 1791, after 1800 pianofortes of the English type; d. 1819.

William and Adam *Bent,* * in 1800 'William & Adam Bent, musical instrument makers'; after c. 1803 pianofortes. Recorded in 1807 as 'William Bent, pianoforte maker'; business dissolved in 1809.

Alpheus and Lewis *Babcock,* * pupils of Crehore; started a business in 1810. Lewis d. 1817. In 1822 Alpheus entered into partnership with Makay ('Babcock & Makay'). Moved to Philadelphia in 1829.

John *Osborn,* * pupil of Crehore; started business in 1815; moved to Albany in 1829.

James *Stewart,* * associated with Osborn 1820–1823, 1823–1826 with Jonas Chickering; left for London in 1826.

Jonas *Chickering,* * pupil of Osborn; started a business together with James Stewart in 1823; until 1826 'Chickering & Stewart'; 1829–1841 partner of Makay ('Chickering & Makay'); d. 1841.

Thomas *Chickering,* C. Frank & George H. Chickering, * partners after 1852 in the business then called 'Chickering & Sons'.

Timothy *Gilbert,* * started business in 1829; firm called 'Timothy Gilbert & Company'.

Lemanuel *Gilbert,* * founded a business in 1829, abandoned it in 1858.

Edwin *Brown,* * started a business together with Russel Hallet in 1835, called it 'Brown & Hallet'; Brown left the firm in 1843.

Russel *Hallet,* * partner of Brown 1835–1839.

George H. *Davies,* * 1839–1879 partner of Hallet in the firm 'Hallet, Davies & Company'.

William *Bourne,* * pupil of Chickering; started a business called 'William Bourne & Company' in 1837.

Charles E. *Bourne,* * in 1863 'Bourne & Son Piano Company'.

Henry F. *Miller,* * pupil of Brown & Hallet; started a business in 1863.

H. Walker, James C., Edwin C. and William T. *Miller,* * in 1884 'H.F. Miller & Sons'.

CHARLESTON

Charles *Watt,* * started business in 1791. Probably one or two piano makers had worked in Charleston before 1791.

CHICAGO

Reed & Son, * business founded in 1842.

Julius *Bauer,* * business founded in 1857.

CINCINNATI

Lucien *Wulsin,* * business founded c. 1862.

D. H. *Baldwin,* * in 1866 collaborator with the former, in 1873 Wulsin's partner in the firm 'D.H. Baldwin & Company'.

NEW HAVEN

Bernhard *Shoninger,* * business founded in 1850; d. 1910.

Ferdinand *Mathuschek,* * founded in 1866 the firm 'Mathushek Piano Company'.

NEW YORK

Tremaine, § recorded in 1759.

David *Walhaupter,* § recorded in 1773.

James *Juhan,* * recorded in 1783.

Johann Gottlob *Clemm,* § recorded 1745–1757.

Thomas *Dodds,* § * recorded in 1786.

Charles *Watt,* * business founded in 1789, transferred to Charleston in 1790.

Thomas *Gibson* and Morgan *Davies,* * firm recorded in 1801 as 'Gibson & Davies'; they separated after 1820 and started independent firms which vanished c. 1839.

John *Geib* (I) and Adam *Geib,* * recorded after 1798, c. 1802 'John Geib & Son', 1806–1809 'John & Adam Geib'.

William *Geib* and John *Geib* (II), * after 1815 'William Geib'; in 1830 'Geib & Walker'; in 1844 again 'William Geib'.

John *Firth* and William *Hall,* * recorded in 1815, in 1824 'Firth & Hall; after 1830 they also built pianos.

B. Sylvanus *Pond,* * c. 1840 recorded as 'Firth, Hall & Pond'; in 1847 Hall left to start his own business with his son James F. H., calling it 'Hall & Son'. The former firm was then called 'Firth, Pond & Company' with John Firth, his son Taddeus Firth and

Sylvanus Pond as partners. Later on, Firth likewise started a new business together with his son calling it 'Firth, Son & Company', and Pond continued the original firm then called after him in c. 1863.

Robert *Stodart* (Y.), * recorded after 1819; business founded in 1820.

William *Dubois*, * 1821–1831 partnership with Stodart, 'Stodart & Dubois'; Stodart left in 1831 and the firm continued as 'Dubois & Chamber'.

George *Bacon*, * in 1836 'Dubois, Bacon & Chamber'. Dubois left in 1841 to start his own firm 'Dubois & Company'; 1845–1851 'Dubois & Warriner'. The original firm became famous when, in 1841, Raven joined it as partner and it was named 'Bacon & Raven'; in 1871 recorded as 'Bacon & Karr'.

Thomas *Loud* (E.), * founded a business in 1825; d. 1834.

Robert *Nunns*, * business founded in 1824; 1833–1839 'Nunns, Clark & Company'; 1839–1840 partnership with J. & C. Fischer, 'Nunns & Fischer'.

William *Nunns*, * in 1840 Fischer starts an independent business calling it 'J. & C. Fischer'; Nunns in his turn starts a new enterprise called 'William Nunns Company'.

John *Osborn*, * business founded in 1830; d. 1835.

Adam *Stodart*, Horatio *Worcester* and J. B. *Dunham*, * in 1835 the firm Stodart was continued and called 'Stodart, Worcester & Dunham'; in 1840 Dunham leaves and starts his own firm 'J. B. Dunham & Company'; in 1867 'Dunham & Sons'.

Bridgeland & Jardine, * business founded in 1832; in 1838 John Jardine leaves; after 1860 'Jardine & Son'.

William *Lindeman*, * business founded in 1836.

Henry *Lindeman*, * in 1857 'Lindeman & Son'; after 1875 'Henry Lindeman & Sons'.

John and Charles *Fischer*, * business 'J. & C. Fischer' founded in 1840; in 1873 John Fischer retires and Charles Fischer and his four sons take over the factory then called 'C.S. Fischer & Sons'.

J.A. *Grovesteen*, * business founded c. 1847.

Henry and Frederik *Hazelton*, * business 'F. & H. Hazelton' founded in 1841.

John *Hazelton*, * in 1849 'Hazelton Brothers'.

Samuel *Hazelton*, * in 1881 partner.

F.C. *Lighte* and W.H. *Newtone*, * business founded in 1448.

Ferdinand *Mathuschek*, * in 1849 he started a business together with J.B. Dunham; 1857–1863 associated with Drigg; settled in New Haven and founded the firm 'Mathushek Piano Company' in 1866; in 1871 back in New York, firm called 'Mathushek & Son Piano Company'.

A. & W. *Ladd*, * business founded in c. 1850.

J. Napoleon and Francis W. *Haines*, * founded the business 'N.J. Haines & Company' in 1851.

Albert *Weber*, * business founded in 1852.

Albert *Weber* (Y.), * succeeded his father in 1879.

Heinrich Engelhardt *Steinway*, business founded in 1853.

Carl, Heinrich, Wilhelm, Albert and Theodor *Steinway*, * 'Steinway & Sons'; Theodor came to New York in 1865.

Ernest *Gabler*, * business founded in 1854.

George *Steck*, * business founded in 1857.

Myron A. *Decker*, * business founded in 1864.

Frank C. *Decker*, * after 1875 partner, 'Decker & Son'.

G. Henry *Hülskamp*, * recorded after 1866.

PHILADELPHIA

Johann Gottlob *Clemm*, § recorded in 1739.

Gustav *Hesselius*, § recorded in 1742.

John *Behrent* or *Brent*, * in 1775 he built the first pianoforte in America.

John *Adam*, * recorded after 1785.

Charles *Albrecht*, * business founded in 1789.

Christian F.L. *Albrecht*, * succeeded Charles in 1825–1842.

Charles *Taws*, * business founded prior to 1795; d. in 1833 (?)

John *Harper*, * recorded 1797–1802.

Isaak *Hawkins*, * 1800–1802. He built the first upright piano in America.

Thomas *Loud* (Y.), * business founded c. 1812.

John *Loud*, * partner after 1818.

Philologus and Joseph *Loud*, * likewise partners after 1824, firm then called 'Loud Brothers'; dissolved in 1837. 1837–1855 'Loud & Company' with Thomas (Y.), Thomas C. Loud and a son of Thomas Loud (Y.) as managers.

Alpheus *Babcock*, * in 1829 he started a business together with Klemm.

Conrad *Meyer*, * business founded in 1829; d. 1881.

John Henry *Schomacker*, in 1837 he started a business together with Bosert. 1837–1842 'Bosert & Schomacker'; after 1842 'Schomacker Piano Company'.

Henry C. *Schomacker*, * succeeded John Henry in 1875.

SALEM (MASS.)

Samuel Blythe, § recorded 1789–1795 (year of death).

TROY

G. Henry (Gustav Heinrich) *Hülskamp*, * started a business in 1850; in 1866 it was transferred to New York.

WILMINGTON (DELAWARE)

Charles *Trute*, § * recorded 1795–1807 (or 1808) (year of death).

BIBLIOGRAPHY

Works of special importance have been marked with stars: ★★★, ★★, ★.
The bibliography herewith recorded makes no claim to being complete.
Books dealing with such varied themes as

the history of the piano,
the history of piano-playing and its technique,
the history of piano-literature,

have been intentionally excluded, as their attempt to treat simultaneously of many subjects leads to confusion.
On the contrary, at this point I should like to acknowledge my indebtedness to those works which, from first to last whilst writing this book, have lain beside me for constant reference; in alphabetical order of their authors:

CLOSSON, ERNEST. Histoire du Piano. Bruxelles 1944.

HARDING, ROSAMOND. A History of the Pianoforte. Cambridge 1933.

JAMES, PHILIP. Early Keyboard Instruments. London 1930.

JOSTEN, H. H. Württembergisches Landesgewerbemuseum. Katalog der Sammlung alter Musikinstrumente. Stuttgart 1928.

KINSKY, GEORG. Das Musikhistorische Museum von W. Heyer. Vol. 1. Köln 1910.

NEUPERT, HANNS. Das Cembalo. Kassel and Basel 1951.

– Das Klavichord. Kassel and Basel 1948, 1956.

NORLIND, TOBIAS. Systematik der Saiteninstrumente, vol. 2: Geschichte des Klavieres. Hannover 1939.

PFEIFFER, WALTER. Vom Hammer. Stuttgart 1948.

SACHS, CURT. Katalog der Sammlung alter Musikinstrumente bei der Staatlichen Hochschule für Musik zu Berlin. Berlin 1922.

– Das Klavier. Berlin 1923.

– History of Musical Instruments. New York 1940; London 1942.

ABERT, HERMANN. Illustriertes Musiklexikon. Stuttgart 1927.

ADLUNG, JAKOB**. Musica mechanica Organoedi. Two volumes. Berlin 1768. New edition by Mahrenholz. Kassel 1931.

AGRICOLA, MARTIN*. Musica instrumentalis deutsch. Wittenberg 1528 and 1545. New edition by Robert Eitner. Leipzig 1896.

ALTMANN, WILHELM. See FRANK-ALTMANN.

ARNOLD, GUSTAV. Musikalische Instrumente. Fachbericht über die Gruppe 33 der Schweizerischen Landesausstellung in Zürich 1883. Luzern 1883.

ARNOLD VON ZWOLLE, HEINRICH**. See LE CERF – LABANDE.

BALFOORT, DIRK. Gemeente Museum 's Gravenhage. De Muziek-Historische Afdeeling. 's Gravenhage 1935.

Bamberg. Führer durch das Musikhistorische Museum Neupert. Nürnberg 1938.

BARGAGNA, LETO. Gli strumenti musicali raccolti nel Museo del R. Istituto Cherubini a Firenze. Undated.

BEHREND, WILLIAM. Illustreret Musik-Lexikon. In collaboration with Hortense Panum and O.M. Sandvik. Köbenhavn 1924/25.

Berlin. Staatliches Institut für Musikforschung: Führer durch das Musikinstrumentenmuseum. Berlin 1939.

BERMUDO, JUAN*. Declaración de instrumentos musicales. Ossuna 1555.

BERNER, ALFRED. Zum Klavierbau im 17. und 18. Jahrhundert. Published in the 'Kongressbericht'. Lüneburg 1950. Kassel and Basel.

– Die Berliner Musikinstrumenten-Sammlung. Einführung mit historischen und technischen Erläuterungen. Berlin 1952.

BERNSDORF, EDUARD. Neues Universallexikon der Tonkunst. Three volumes and one supplement. Dresden 1856.

BESSARABOFF, NICOLAS***. An organological Study of the Musical Instruments in the Leslie-Lindsey-Mason Collection at the Museum of Fine Arts. Boston 1941. Outstanding.

BIERDIMPFL, K. A. Die Sammlung der Musikinstrumente des Bayerischen Nationalmuseums. München 1883.

BLONDEL, SP. Histoire anecdotique du Piano. Paris 1880.

– Article 'Piano' in Lavignac 'Encyclopédie de la musique et Dictionnaire du Conservatoire'. Paris 1927.

BLÜTHNER und GRETSCHEL. Lehrbuch des Pianofortebaues, mit Atlas. First edition 1872. Fourth edition (Hannemann-Niemann) Leipzig 1920.

BLUME, FRIEDRICH. Die Musik in Geschichte und Gegenwart. Kassel and Basel 1949 ff.

BOALCH, D.H. Makers of the Clavichord and Harpsichord. 1440 to 1848. London 1956.

Bologna. Museo civico. Raccolta di antichi strumenti conservata nel Liceo musicale di Bologna. Bologna 1880.

BOLTE, TH. Die Musikerfamilien Stein und Streicher. Wien 1917.

BONAVENTURA, ARNALDO. Domenico del Mela e il primo Pianoforte verticale. Firenze 1928.

BOTTÉE DE TOULMON, AUGUSTE. Dissertation sur les instruments de musique employés au moyen-âge, in 'Mémoires de la Société royale des antiquaires de France', vol. 17. Paris 1844.

BRANCOUR, RENÉ. Histoire des instruments de Musique, Paris 1921.

Breslau. Schlesisches Museum für Kunstgewerbe und Altertümer. Guide and Catologue of the Collection of Old Musical Instruments. Breslau 1932.

BRINDSMEAD, EDGAR. The History of the Piano. London 1889.

BROADWOOD. The Broadwood Collection of Antique Instruments, Forerunners of the Modern Pianoforte. London 1903.

BRUNNER, H.*. Das Klavierklangideal Mozarts und die Klaviere seiner Zeit. Augsburg 1933.

BURBURE, LÉON DE. Recherches sur les facteurs de clavecins et les luthiers d'Anvers depuis le XVIe jusqu'au XIXe siècle. Bruxelles 1863.

BURNEY, CHARLES. The Present State of Music. London 1771.

CASELLA, ALFREDO. Il Pianoforte. Roma, Milano 1939.

CERONE. Melopeo y Maestro. Napoli 1613.

CESI, BENJAMINO. Storia del Pianoforte. Milano 1903.

CHOUQUET, G. Les instruments de musique et les éditions musicales à l'Exposition universelle... de 1878 à Paris. Paris 1880.

– Le Musée du Conservatoire National de Musique. Catalogue descriptif et raisonné... Nouvelle édition, ornée de figures. (Nos 1 à 1006.) Paris 1884. By LÉON PILLAUD following supplements have been edited: Premier supplément au catalogue 1884 (Nos 1007–1362). Paris 1894. Second supplément... (Nos 1363–1463). Paris 1899. Troisième supplément... (Nos 1464–1568). Paris 1903.

Cincinnati. Collection of the Cincinnati Art Museum. Musical Instruments (Catalogue). Cincinnati 1949. Therefrom: The Musical Instruments, pp. 10 ff.

CLEMEN, O. Andreas Streicher in Wien. Beethoven-Jahrbuch, 4th year, pp. 107 ff. Augsburg 1930.

CLOSSON, ERNEST**. Pascal Taskin*. Published in 'Sammelbände der Internationalen Musikgesellschaft', 12th year (1910/11), p. 234.

– La facture des instruments de musique en Belgique*. Bruxelles 1935.

– Histoire du Piano**. Bruxelles 1944. The best French history of the Piano. Outstanding.

CORTE, ANDREA DELLA and GATTI, GUIDO MARIA. Dizionario di Musica. Torino 1925. Third edition 1930.

COUTAGNE, HENRY. Gaspart Duiffoproucart et les Luthiers Lyonnais du XVe siècle. Paris 1893.

CRUZ, MARIA ANTONIETA DE LIMA. O Museu Instrumental. Published in 'Boletím do Conservatório Nacional, Vol. 1, No. 1. Lisboa 1947.

DALE, WILLIAM*. Tschudi, the Harpsichord Maker. London 1913.

DENSMORE, FRANCES. Handbook of the Collection of Musical Instruments in the US National Museum. Bulletin 136. Washington 1927.

DIDEROT, DENIS et D'ALEMBERT, JEAN. Encyclopédie, seventeen volumes. Therefrom vol. 3. Paris, Neuchâtel 1751–1765. Recueil des planches, eleven volumes. Therefrom vol. 5: 'Lutherie'.

DIETSCHI, HUGO. Orgel-, Klavier- und Geigenbaukunst im Kanton Solothurn. Separate print from 'Solothurnisches Sänger- und Musikblatt', Nos. 7/8, 9/10, 11/12, 17th year (1940), and Nos. 1/2, 3/4, 18th year (1941).

DOLGE, ALFRED*. Pianos and Their Makers. Covina, Calif. 1911.

DOLMETSCH, ARNOLD*. The Interpretation of the Music of the XVIIth and XVIIIth Centuries. Therefrom chapter 7: The Musical Instruments of the Period, pp. 419–436. London 1915.

DOMMER, ARREY VON. Musikalisches Lexikon (after Koch). Heidelberg 1865.

DONALDSON, SIR. G. Catalogue of the Musical Instruments at the Royal College of Music. London 1898/99.

DRECHSEL, F. A. Zur Geschichte des Klavierbaues in Dresden. Zeitschrift für Instrumentenbau. 48th year (1927/28). P. 881 to 884, 925 to 929.

DUFOURCQ, NORBERT*. Le Clavecin. Paris 1949. Concise and excellent.

DUVERNOY A. See GRATIA – DUVERNOY.

Edinburgh. Catalogue of the National Museums of Antiquities of Scotland. Edinburgh 1892.

Eisenach. Verzeichnis der Sammlung alter Musikinstrumente im Bachhaus zu Eisenach. 3rd edition. Leipzig 1939.

EISENMANN, ALEXANDER. Schiedmayer & Söhne, Hof-Pianoforte-Fabrik, Stuttgart 1809–1909. Stuttgart 1909.

EITNER, ROBERT. Biographisch-bibliographisches Quellenlexikon der Musiker und Musikgelehrten der christlichen Zeitrechnung bis zur Mitte des 19. Jahrhunderts. Ten volumes. Leipzig 1900–1904.

ENGEL, CARL. A Descriptive Catalogue of the Musical Instruments in the South Kensington Museum. First edition London 1870. Second edition London 1874.

– Art Handbooks of the South Kensington Museum. Music Instruments. London 1880.

EPSTEIN, PETER. Katalog der Musikinstrumente im Historischen Museum der Stadt Frankfurt. Frankfurt 1927.

*Erlanger Traktat**. Pro clavichordiis faciendis. Second half of 15th century. MS.

ERNST, FRITZ*. Vom Cembalo. Zürich 1950.

ESSEN, BERTHA VAN*. Bouwen Geschiedenis van het Klavier. Rotterdam 1948.

FALLET, EDOUARD-M. La vie musicale au pays de Neuchâtel. Strasbourg 1936.

FÉTIS, FRANÇOIS JOSEPH. Biographie universelle des Musiciens. Eight volumes. Paris 1835–1844. Second edition Paris 1868. Two supplements by A. POUGIN. Paris 1881.

– Fabrications des Instruments de Musique*. Paris 1856. (Official report of the Paris World Exhibition 1856, Musical Instruments.)

FETT, HARRY. Norsk Folke Museum Saerudstillning No. 2: Musikinstrumenter. Catalogue. Oslo 1904.

FISCHHOF, JOSEPH*. Versuch einer Geschichte des Klavierbaues. Wien 1853. First greater work on the history of the Piano with comprehensive description of the Piano instruments at the London World Exhibition 1851; of historical value.

FLADE, ERNST. Gottfried Silbermann. Leipzig 1953.

FLEISCHER, OSKAR. Die Musikinstrumente auf der Ausstellung. Paper in Schneider, Siegmund (see there): Die Internationale Ausstellung für Musik- und Theaterwesen, Wien 1892, pp. 57–75. Wien 1894.

– Das Bach'sche Klavicymbel und seine Neukonstruktion. Zeitschrift der Internationalen Musikgesellschaft. 1st year (1899/1900).

FRANK, P.-ALTMANN. Kurzgefasstes Tonkünstlerlexikon. First edition 1860. Fourteenth edition Regensburg 1936.

FRANZ, GOTTFRIED VON. Mozarts Klavierbauer Anton Walter. Neues Mozart-Jahrbuch. First edition. P. 211. Regensburg 1941.

FRIMMEL, TH. V. Beethoven und das Ehepaar Streicher. Alt-Wiener-kalender 1925.

GALLAY, J. Un inventaire sous la Terreur. Etat des instruments de musique relevé chez les émigrés et condamnés par A. Bruni. Paris 1890.

GALPIN, FRANCIS W.*. Old English Instruments of Music. First edition London 1910. Third edition London 1932.

GATTI, GUIDO MARIA. Dizionario di Musica, edited in collaboration with Andrea della Corte. First edition Torino 1925. Third edition Torino 1930.

GEIRINGER, KARL. Alte Musikinstrumente im Museum Carolino-Augusteum, Salzburg. Leipzig 1932.

– Musical instruments. Their history from the Stone Age to the present day. First edition London 1943. Second edition London 1945.

GÉNARD, P. Catalogue du Musée d'Antiquités. Instruments de Musique. (Nos. 1–46.) Pp. 187–190. Anvers 1894.

GERBER, ERNST LUDWIG**. Historisch-biographisches Lexikon der Tonkünstler. Fortsetzung und Ergänzung zu WALTHERS Lexikon. Two volumes. 1790/92. Neues Historisch-biographisches Lexikon der Tonkünstler**. Four volumes. Leipzig 1812–1814.

GOEBEL, J. Grundzüge des modernen Klavierbaues. Leipzig 1925.

GOEHLINGER, FR. A. Geschichte des Clavichords. Basel 1910.

Göteborg. Historiska Avdelningen Göteborgs Museum. Catalogue. Göteborg 1931.

GRATIA, L. E. et DUVERNOY, A. Le piano et sa technique. Published in Lavignac 'Encyclopédie de la musique et Dictionnaire du Conservatoire'. Paris 1927.

GROVE, GEORGE**. Dictionary of Music and Musicians. (Since 1450.) Four volumes. First edition London 1879–1883. Second edition (Fuller-Maitland), five volumes, 1904–1909. Third edition (H. C. Colles), five volumes, 1927–1928. American Supplement (Pratt). New York 1935. Fourth edition (H. C. Colles). Five volumes and one supplement, 1940 (revised third edition). Fifth edition (Blom), nine volumes, London 1954.

GUARINONI, E. Gli strumenti musicali nel Museo del Conservatorio di Milano. Milano 1909.

HAAS, ROBERT. Bach und Mozart in Wien. Wien 1951.

Hälsingborg. Hälsingborgs Museum. Utställning av Musikinstrument ur Daniel Fryklunds Samling i Hälsingborg, med förord av professor Tobias Norlind. Catalogue. Hälsingborg 1945.

HAMMERICH, ANGUL. Das Musikhistorische Museum zu Kopenhagen. Köbenhavn 1911.

Hampstead. Fenton House. London. Undated.

HANSING, SIEGFRIED. Das Pianoforte in seinen akustischen Anlagen. First edition Schwerin 1888. Second edition revised by the author 1908. Reprinted Stuttgart 1950.

HARDING, ROSAMOND***. A History of the Pianoforte. Its history traced to the Great Exhibition of 1851. Cambridge 1933. An extraordinary book. The best and most comprehensive work on the Piano history till 1851. Ought to be translated in all world languages. Out of print.

HAUTERIVE, G. M. La facture du Piano. Revue Internationale de Musique. Vol. I, Nos. 5–6, pp. 80ff. Bruxelles 1939.

HEINITZ, WILHELM*. Instrumentenkunde. Potsdam 1929.

HELLMESBERGER, JOSEPH. Musikinstrumente auf der Allgemeinen Agrikultur- und Industrieausstellung zu Paris 1855. Wien 1858.

HERRMANN, HEINRICH*. Die Regensburger Klavierbauer Späth und Schmahl und ihre Tangentenflügel. Thesis Erlangen 1928.

HERTZ, EVA**. Johann Andreas Stein. Ein Beitrag zur Geschichte des Klavierbaues. Thesis Würzburg 1937.

HIPKINS, A. J. Guide to the Loan Collection of Musical Instruments of the International Inventions Exhibition. London 1885. Old Keyboard Instruments. London 1887. A description and history of the Pianoforte and of the older keyboard stringed instruments**. London and New York 1896. The best earlier work on Piano and Piano-building.

– Musical instruments, historic, rare and unique. London 1921.

HIRT, FRANZ JOSEF. Wiener Hammerflügel von N. Streicher, 1819, in: Jahrbuch des Bernischen Historischen Museums, 18th year (1948), p. 9ff.

– Die Entwicklung der besaiteten Tasteninstrumente, in: Schweizerische Musikzeitung, year 1948, No. 2.

HUBER, HANS. Klaviere. Fachbericht über die 27. Gruppe, *Musikinstrumente*, der Schweizerischen Landesausstellung in Bern 1914. Fachberichte, vol. 6, pp. 79ff.

Innsbruck. Verzeichnis der Musikinstrumente in der Sammlung des Museums Ferdinandeum.

Instrumentenbauzeitung. Editor: Prof. Dr. H. Matzke. Konstanz, since 1946.

JAMES, PHILIP**. Early Keyboard Instruments, from their Beginnings to the Year 1820. London 1930.

JEANS, SUSI. The Pedal clavicord and other Practice Instruments of Organists. London 1950.

JEMNITZ, ALEXANDER. Klavierfabrikation als Kulturdokument. Published in 'Allgemeine Musikzeitung'. 49th year (1922). No. 39, p. 704.

JOSTEN, H. H.**. Württembergisches Landesgewerbemuseum. Katalog der Sammlung alter Musikinstrumente. Stuttgart 1928.

JUNGHANNS, H.*. Der Piano- und Flügelbau. Leipzig 1932.

KASTNER, SANTIAGO*. Contribución al estudio de la Música española y portuguesa. Lisboa 1941.

– Portugiesische und spanische Clavichorde des 18. Jahrhunderts. Published in Acta Musicologica, vol. 24, fasc, I–II. Köbenhavn 1952.

KELLER, JOACHIM. La vie musicale à Fribourg de 1750 à 1843. Fribourg 1941.

KELLEY, EDGAR STILLMAN. Musical instruments. Boston 1925.

KINKELDEY, OTTO. Orgel und Klavier in der Musik des 16. Jahrhunderts. Leipzig 1910.

KINSKY, GEORG**. Das Musikhistorische Museum von W. Heyer. Vol. I. Köln 1910.

– Kurze Oktaven auf besaiteten Tasteninstrumenten. Ein Beitrag zur Geschichte des Klaviers**. Zeitschrift für Musikwissenschaft, 2nd year (1919/20), pp. 65ff.

– Geschichte der Musik in Bildern*. Leipzig 1929.

– Die Flügel Friedrichs des Grossen*. Zeitschrift für Instrumentenbau, 54th year (1933/34), pp. 195–197, 254.

– Beethoven und das Hammerklavier*. Zeitschrift für Instrumentenbau, 56th year (1935/36), pp. 36ff.

– Der Streicherflügel im Weimarer Goethehaus und andere Musikinstrumente aus dem Goethekreise.

– Mozart-Instrumente*. Published in Acta Musicologica. Vol. 12, fasc. I–IV. Köbenhavn 1940.

KIRCHER, ATHANASIUS**. Musurgia universalis sive ars magna consoni et dissoni. Two volumes. Roma 1650. Therefrom Tomus I, Liber VI: De musica instrumentalis.

– **Phonurgia nova. Campidonae 1673. Therefrom Appendix, pp. 168/69. German edition: Neue Hall- und Tonkunst. Nördlingen 1684, pp. 120/21: Appendix: Von dem berühmten und höchst verwunderlichen Orgelwerk Michaelis Todini von Savoyen.

Köbenhavn. Carl Claudius Samling af Gamle Musik-Instrumenter*. Catalogue. Köbenhavn 1931.

KREBS, KARL. Die besaiteten Klavierinstrumente bis zum Anfang des 17. Jahrhunderts. Separate print from 'Vierteljahresschrift für Musikwissenschaft'. Leipzig 1892.

KÜPPERS, PAUL. Ein Beitrag zur Geschichte des Musikinstrumentenmacher-Gewerbes mit besonderer Rücksicht auf Leipzig. Thesis Leipzig 1886.

KÜTZING, CHARLES. Beiträge zur praktischen Akustik. Bern, Chur. Leipzig 1838.

– Das Wissenschaftliche der Pianoforte Baukunst*. Bern 1844.

Kunst- und Gewerbeblatt des Polytechnischen Vereins im Königreich Bayern. 4th year (1818). 6th year (1820). 7th year (1821). 8th year (1822).

LAURENCIE, LIONEL DE LA*. See LAVIGNAC.

LAVIGNAC, ALBERT et LAURENCIE, LIONEL DE LA*. Encyclopédie de la musique et Dictionnaire du Conservatoire. Fourth edition Paris 1930.

LE CERF, G. et LABANDE, E.-R.**. Les traités d'Henri Arnaut de Zwolle et de divers anonymes. (MS. Bibliothèque Nationale, Latin 7295.) Paris 1932. The first description of the stringed keyboard instruments, about 1440.

LECOMTE, EUGÈNE. Catalogue des instruments anciens de musique de l'Exposition universelle de Paris 1878. Paris 1878.

Linz. Führer durch das Museum Francisco-Carolinum. Catalogue. Linz 1910. Pp. 41–43.

LIPOWSKY, FELIX. Musiklexikon. München 1811.

Loan Exhibition, London 1904. An illustrated Catalogue of the Music Loan Exhibition at Fishmongers Hall. London 1909. Pp. 165–173.

LOCARD, PAUL*. Le piano. Paris 1948. Concise and excellent.

London. Victoria & Albert Museum. A. Picture Book of Keyboard Musical Instruments. London 1929.

– Musical Instruments and Memorials of Musicians, being the catalogue to the International Loan Exhibition, Crystal Palace. London 1900.

LÜTGE, W. Andreas und Annette Streicher, in: Der Bär (Breitkopf & Härtel), Leipzig 1927.

MAHILLON, V. C. Catalogue du musée instrumental du Conservatoire. Vol. I (Nos. 1–576), 1893. Vol. 2 (Nos. 577–1321), 1909; Second edition. Vol. 3 (Nos. 1322–2055), 1900. Vol. 4 (Nos. 2056 to 2961), 1912. Vol. 5 (Nos. 2962–3300), 1922. Gand.

MANDYCZEWSKY, EUSEBIUS. Geschichte der Gesellschaft der Musikfreunde in Wien. Supplement. Wien 1912. With Addenda.

MARCUSE, SYBIL. Transposing Keyboards on extant flemish Harpsichords. Published in 'The Musical Quarterly'. July 1952, vol. 38, No. 3. New York.

MATTHESON, JOHANN. Das neu eröffnete Orchester. Hamburg 1713.

MENDEL, HERMANN and REISSMANN, AUGUST. Musiklexikon. Eleven volumes. Berlin 1870–79. Supplement Berlin 1883.

MERSENNE, P. MARIN. Harmonie universelle. Vol. 2: De instrumentis harmonicis. Liber Primus. Paris 1636.

MEYER, ERWIN and BUCHMANN, GERHARD. Die Klangspektren der Musikinstrumente. In: Year 1913 of 'Sitzungsberichte der Preussischen Akademien der Wissenschaften'. Berlin 1931.

MOOSER, R. ALOYS. L'Orchestre-Instrument d'Aloys Mooser. Published in 'Dissonances', April 1934. Genève.

– Aloys Mooser, facteur d'orgues à Fribourg. (1770–1839.) Tirage à part des Etrennes Fribourgeoises, 1935.

MORRIS, FRANCES. The Crosby Brown Collection of musical instruments of all nations. Catalogue of Keyboard Instruments. Metropolitan Museum New York. New York 1903.

MOSER, HANS JOACHIM. Musiklexikon. Berlin 1935. New edition Hamburg 1951, with Addenda 1953.

MURIS, JOHANN VON. Musica speculativa (1323). Published in Gerbert Martin. Scriptores ecclesiastici de Musica sacra. 1784. Vol. 3, pp. 249–255.

MUSALEWSKY, W. I. Russian Piano Music. (In Russian.) Leningrad, Moscow 1949.

NALDER, LAWRENCE. The Modern Piano. London 1927.

NASARRE, FRAY PABLO*. Escuela Música. Therefrom Liber IV, Cap. XVI, pp. 465 ff. Saragossa 1723–24.

NEF, KARL. Klavicymbel und Klavichord. Separate print from 'Jahrbuch der Musikbibliothek Peters'. 10th year (1903).

– Katalog Nr. 4 des Historischen Museums Basel: Musikinstrumente. Basel 1906.

– Geschichte unserer Musikinstrumente. Leipzig 1926. New edition by F. Schneider. Basel 1949.

Neuchâtel. Musée Historique. Notice et Guide Sommaire. Undated.

NEUMANN, ADOLF. Die Musikinstrumentenindustrie Deutschlands. Thesis Leipzig 1925.

NEUPERT, HANNS. Vom Musikstab zum modernen Klavier. Bamberg 1926.

– Das Cembalo**. Eine geschichtliche und technische Betrachtung der Kielinstrumente. Second edition, Kassel and Basel 1951.

– Das Klavichord**. Kassel and Basel 1948, 1956.

NORLIND, TOBIAS. Allmänt Musik-Lexikon. First edition 1916. Second edition 1927/29.

– Systematik der Saiteninstrumente. Vol. 2: Geschichte des Klavieres**. Musikhistorisches Museum Stockholm. Verlag für musikalische Kultur, Hannover 1939.

– En bok om musikinstrument. Deras utvecklingshistoria. Stockholm 1928.

PAHISSA, J. Diccionario de la música. Barcelona 1927/29.

PANUM, HORTENSE, BEHREND, WILLIAM, SANDVIK, O. M. Illustreret Musik-Lexikon. Köbenhavn 1924/25.

Paris. Musée rétrospectif... Instruments de musique, matériel, procédés et produits à l'Exposition universelle internationale de 1900 à Paris. Paris 1900.

PAUL, OSKAR*. Geschichte des Klaviers. Leipzig 1868.

– Handbuch der Tonkunst. Two volumes. Leipzig 1873.

– Musikalische Instrumente*. Amtlicher Bericht über die Wiener Weltausstellung im Jahre 1873. Braunschweig 1874.

PAULIRINUS, PAULUS**. Liber XX artium. Praha, about 1460. Manuscript parchment codex No. 257. Library of the Jagiello University, Cracow. Partly published by Josef Reiss, in: 'Zeitschrift für Musikwissenschaft', 7th year (1924).

PEDRELL, F. Organografía Musical antiqua española. Barcelona 1900.

PFEIFFER, WALTER. Von Flügel- und Klavierbezeichnungen, zugleich ein Vorschlag zur Neuordnung der heutigen Benennungen. Zeitschrift für Instrumentenbau. 59th year.

– Flügel oder Klavier? Eine alte Geschichte in neuer Beleuchtung. Stuttgart 1940.

– Vom Hammer*. Stuttgart 1948.

PIERRE, CONSTANT*. Les facteurs d'instruments de musique. Paris 1893.

PIRRO, ANDRÉ. Les clavecinistes. Paris. Undated.

PONSICCHI, C.*. Il Pianoforte, sua origine e sviluppo. Firenze 1876.

– Il primo Pianoforte Verticale. Firenze 1898.

PONTÉCOULANT, AD. DE. Organographie. Two volumes. Paris 1861.

– Voyages d'un mélomane à travers l'Exposition universelle (of London 1862). Paris 1862.

– Histoires et anecdotes. Paris 1864.

– La Musique à l'Exposition universelle de 1867. Paris 1868.

PRAETORIUS, MICHAEL**. Syntagma Musicum. Tomus secundus: De Organographia. Wolfenbüttel 1619. New edition by W. Gurlitt. Kassel 1929.

PRINTZ, WOLFGANG C. Historische Beschreibung der edelen Sing- und Klingkunst. Dresden 1690. Pp. 202 ff.

PULITI, L. Cenni storici... della origine del pianoforte. Firenze 1874.

PULVER, JEFFREY. A Dictionary of Old English Music and Musical Instruments. London 1923.

QUIRINUS VON BLANKENBURG. Elementa Musica. 's Gravenhage 1739.

RAMIS DE PAREJA, BARTOLOMEO*. Musica pratica. Therefrom: Capitulum sextum: Diversorum instrumentorum brevis notitia. Bologna 1482. New edition Leipzig 1901 (J. Wolf).

REFARDT, EDGAR*. Historisch-biographisches Musiker-Lexikon der Schweiz. Leipzig 1928.

REISSMANN, AUGUST. Musiklexikon. Edited in collaboration with Hermann Mendel. Eleven volumes. Berlin 1870–79. Supplement Berlin 1883.

Revue Internationale de Musique. Special issue on the Piano. Vol. 1, Nos. 5–6. April 1939.

RIEMANN, HUGO**. Musiklexikon. First edition 1882. Eleventh edition (Einstein) Berlin 1929.

RIMBAULT, E. F.*. The Pianoforte, its origin, progress and construction. London 1860.

– Musical instruments. London 1876. Second edition London 1878. Published in 'British manufacturing Industries'.

RUSHWORTH & DREAPER. The Rushworth & Dreaper Collection of antique musical instruments. Liverpool 1932.

SACHS, CURT. Der Berliner Instrumentenbau auf den Ausstellungen der Kgl. Preussischen Akademie der Künste 1794–1844. In: Zeitschrift für Instrumentenbau, 32th year (1911/12), pp. 1087ff., 1128ff.

- Reallexikon der Musikinstrumentenkunde**. Berlin 1913.
- Handbuch der Musikinstrumentenkunde*. First edition Leipzig 1920. Second edition Leipzig 1930.
- Sammlung alter Musikinstrumente bei der Staatlichen Hochschule für Musik zu Berlin**. A descriptive Catalogue. Berlin 1922.
- Die modernen Musikinstrumente. Berlin 1923.
- Das Klavier**. Berlin 1923.
- History of Musical Instruments***. New York 1940, London 1942.

SALINAS, FRANCISCO DE*. De Musica Libri Septem. Salamanca 1577.

Salzburg. Die Internationale Stiftung Mozarteum. Salzburg 1931.

SANDVIK, OLE MÖRK. Illustreret Musik-Lexikon. Edited in collaboration with Hortense Panum and William Behrend.

SANTAGATO, ETTORE. Il museo storico di 'S. Pietro a Majella'. Napoli 1930.

SANTOS, IVONE. Historia do Piano. Published in 'Boletím do Conservatório Nacional'. Vol. 1, No. 1. Lisboa 1947.

SCHAEFFNER, ANDRÉ*. Article 'Clavecin' in 'Encyclopédie de la musique et Dictionnaire du Conservatoire', Paris 1927.

SCHAFHÄUTL, KARL EMIL v. Die Musikinstrumente. Bericht der Beurteilungskommission bei der allgemeinen deutschen Industrie-Ausstellung in München, 1854. Sektion I v. Pp. 169–170. München 1855.

- Die Pianofortebaukunst der Deutschen, repräsentiert auf der allgemeinen deutschen Industrie-Ausstellung zu München im Jahre 1854*. München 1855.

SCHEFOLD, MAX*. Die Ulmer Orgel- und Klavierbauerfamilie Schmahl. Zeitschrift für Musikwissenschaft No. 12. Leipzig 1930.

SCHELLE, EDUARD*. Musikalische Instrumente. Gruppe XV. Wien 1873.

SCHILLING, GUSTAV. Universallexikon der Tonkunst. Six volumes. Stuttgart 1835–1840. Supplement 1842.

SCHLOSSER, JULIUS. Die Sammlung alter Musikinstrumente. Wien 1920.

- Unsere Musikinstrumente. Eine Einführung in ihre Geschichte. Wien 1922.

SCHNEIDER, SIEGMUND. Die Internationale Ausstellung für Musik- und Theaterwesen, Wien 1892, 1894.

SCHROEDER, HANS. Verzeichnis der Sammlung alter Musikinstrumente im Städtischen Museum Braunschweig. Braunschweig 1928.

- Die Sammlung alter Musikinstrumente. Museum für Hamburgische Geschichte, Hamburg. Hamburg 1930.

SCHÜNEMANN, GEORG. Die Musikinstrumente. Atlantis-Buch der Musik. Fifth edition. Zürich 1946.

SIMONI, RENATO. Catalogo del Museo teatrale alla Scala. Milano 1940.

SKINNER, WILLIAM**. The Belle Skinner Collection of Old Musical Instruments. A descriptive Catalogue compiled under the direction of William Skinner. 1933.

SPIELMANN, H. Vom Klavier. Köln, Krefeld 1951.

SPILLANE, DANIEL*. The History of the American Pianoforte. New York 1890.

STANLEY, ALBERT. Catalogue of the Stearns Collection of Musical Instruments. Ann Arbor. First edition Ann Arbor 1918. Second edition Ann Arbor 1921.

STEGLICH, RUDOLF. Mozarts Flügel klingt wieder. Nürnberg and Salzburg 1937.

- Studien an Mozarts Hammerflügel*. Separate print from 'Neues Mozart Jahrbuch', 1st year. Regensburg (after 1940).
- Vom klassischen und romantischen Klavierklang. Schweizerische Musikzeitung 1935. Pp. 297ff.
- Cembalo und Klavichord in der Gegenwart. Separate print from 'Zeitschrift für Musik'.

STEINERT, MORRIS. Die Entwicklung der Clavier-Baukunst bis auf die Gegenwart. Published in: Schneider, Siegmund: Die Internationale Ausstellung für Musik- und Theaterwesen, Wien 1892, 1894.

STELLFELD, J. A.*. Bronnen tot de geschiedeneis der antwerpsche clavicimbel en orgelbouwers in de XVIe en XVIIe eeuwen. Antwerpen 1942.

STIEHL, CARL JOHANN. Museumskatalog der Stadt Lübeck. 1893.

STÖSSEL, CHRISTOPH and JOHANN DAVID. Kurzgefasstes musikalisches Lexikon. Chemnitz 1737.

STRAETEN, EDMOND VAN DER. La musique aux Pays-Bas. Eight volumes. Bruxelles 1867–1888.

STYRON, SADE C. A Tour of Early Keyboard Instruments in the Nation's Capital. Published in 'The Etude Music Magazine', vol. LI, No. 2. February 1937. Philadelphia.

SVANBERG, JOHANNES. Musikhistoriska Museets i Stockholms Instrumentsamling. Stockholm 1902.

TAMIR, M. Les expositions internationales à travers les âges. Thesis Paris 1939.

THOMPSON, OSCAR. The International Cyclopedia of Music and Musicians. Fourth edition, New York 1946.

THON, CHR. F. G. Abhandlung über Klavier-Saiten-Instrumente. First edition Sondershausen 1817. Second edition Weimar 1836.

TRENDELENBURG, F., THIENHAUS FRANZ*. Zur Klangwirkung von Clavichord, Cembalo und Flügel. Published in 'Akustische Zeitschrift', 5th year, fasc. 6. Leipzig 1940.

Tribschen (Luzern). Wagner Museum. Catalogue, third edition Luzern 1947.

VANNES, RENÉ. Dictionnaire Universel des Luthiers. First edition Paris 1932. Second edition Bruxelles 1951.

VIRDUNG, SEBASTIAN**. Musica getutscht und ausgezogen. Basel 1511. New edition by Schrade. Kassel 1931.

WALTHER, JOHANN GOTTFRIED. Musikalisches Lexikon. Leipzig 1732. Facsimile edition by P. Schaal, Kassel 1953.

WATSON, HENRY. Catalogue of the Henry Watson Collection of musical instruments in the Royal Manchester College of Music. 1906.

WELCKER VON GONTERSHAUSEN, HEINRICH. Neu eröffnetes Magazin musikalischer Tonwerkzeuge. Frankfurt a. M. 1855.

– Der Flügel oder die Beschaffenheit des Pianos in allen Formen. New edition Frankfurt a.M. 1856.

– Der Klavierbau und seine Theorie, Technik und Geschichte. Fourth edition Frankfurt a.M. 1870.

WILLSON, THEODORE BOOTH. Historical Catalogue of the M. Steinert Collection of Musical Instruments. New Haven 1913.

WOOD, BERNHARD. Musical Instruments in York Castle Museum. York. Undated.

Zeitschrift für Instrumentenbau*. Since 1881 in Leipzig. Editor: Paul de Wit. Discontinued since 1943. The review totalled 63 volumes. Die *Instrumentenbauzeitung** (Editor: Prof. Dr. H. Matzke) can be regarded as continuation of the foregoing review. (Since 1946.)

ORIGIN OF THE PHOTOGRAPHS

The following illustrations have been reproduced by courteous consent of Her Royal Highness, Princess Wilhelmina of the Netherlands: pp. 50, 53.

We owe thanks to the various institutes and persons here listed for allowing us to reproduce the following pictures:

Archives Photographiques, Caisse Nationale des Monuments Historiques, Paris: pp. 167 bottom, 250.
Bayerisches Nationalmuseum, Munich: p. 263 top.
Beethoven-Haus, Bonn: p. 49.
Bertrand, Freddy, Geneva: p. 411 bottom right and left.
Blacha, Frankfurt/Main: pp. 61 bottom, 65 top.
Bouckaert, Albert, Bruxelles: pp. 26 top, 164 middle, 171 bottom, 179, 291 bottom.
Bussers, H., Vincennes: pp. 9, 10, 216 top, 351 top, 351 bottom.
Conservatoire des Arts et Métiers (Photos Chevojon, Paris): pp. 279, 372 bottom.
County Council, London (Photos Campbell, London): p. 187 bottom.
Deutsches Museum, Munich: pp. 192, 246, 305, 340, 427 right.
Eichgrün, Potsdam: pp. 21, 22 top.
Erard, Paris: p. 54.
Gabinetto Fotografico della Sopraintendenza alle Gallerie, Florence: p. 215 top.
Gewitz, Eisenach: pp. 284, 428 bottom.
Gemeente Museum, Den Haag: pp. 187 top, 298, 392, 395 (Photos A. Frequin), 407 right.
Göteborg Museum: pp. 203 top, 421.
Harding, Dr. Rosamond, and Cambridge University Press, London: pp. 407 left, 408 right.
Hartig, Siegfried, Frankfurt/Main: p. 387.
Held, Louis, Weimar: pp. 62, 82, 85.
Hesse, Martin, Bern: pp. 254, 255, 256.
Historisches Museum, Basel: pp. 200 top, 242, 314 bottom, 335 top.
Historisches Museum, Bern: pp. 335 bottom, 404 right, 415 top.
Historisches Museum, Frankfurt/Main: p. 375.
The Horniman Museum, London (Photos Campbell, London): p. 187 bottom.
Institut für Musikforschung, Berlin: p. 403 right.
The Belle and William Skinner Collection of Old Musical Instruments, Holyoke (Photos Paramount Commercial Studios, Springfield, Mass. U.S.A.): pp. 5, 13, 41, 180, 184, 208, 211, 253, 280, 359, 368 bottom, 371.
Knudstrup-Andresen, Anna and Th., Copenhagen: p. 237 top.
Kunsthistorisches Museum, Vienna: pp. 17, 29, 30 top, 45, 61 top, 70, 301, 306 bottom, 336, 343 left, 347 top.
Landesgewerbeamt, Stuttgart: pp. 225, 396.
Lichtbildwerkstätte 'Alpenland'. From the archives of the National Library of Austria: pp. 30 bottom, 37 top.
London Museum, London: p. 412.
Martinez, Pozal, F., Lisbon: p. 313 bottom.
Metropolitan Museum of Art, New York: pp. 204, 207, 226, 233, 259, 272, 297, 331, 388 right.
Mozarteum, Salzburg: pp. 37 bottom, 38.
Museum of Fine Arts, Boston, U.S.A.: p. 199 bottom.
Museum für Hamburgische Geschichte, Hamburg: p. 241.
Museum of the History of Music, Copenhagen: p. 318 top.
Museum of the History of Music, Stockholm: pp. 325 bottom, 400.
Museum für Kunst und Gewerbe, Hamburg: p. 220.
Museo civico, Verona: p. 306 top.
Muzeum Narodowe w Poznaniu, Poznań: p. 22 bottom.
Musikgeschichtliche Sammlung, Pianohaus Rück, Nürnberg: pp. 74, 167 top, 287 left, 339, 343 right, 347 bottom, 356, 379, 380 bottom, 391, 422.
Musikwissenschaftliches Institut und Instrumentenmuseum der Universität Leipzig: p. 221.
National Museum of Hungary, Budapest: p. 46.
Neupert, J.C. Bamberg (placed at our disposal by H. Hanns Neupert): pp. 176 top, 212, 238, 245, 249, 292 right, 344, 360 top, 376, 388 left, 408 right, 411 top, 416, 428 top.
Norsk Folke Museum, Oslo: pp. 317 bottom, 326, 415 bottom.
Petraschk, K. A., Berlin: pp. 58, 195, 196 top, 283, 325 top, 348.
Pfeifer, O., SWB, Luzern: p. 77.
Photos Jean Collas, Paris: pp. 57 top, 69.
Photos Martinotti, Milan: pp. 33 bottom, 78, 81.
Photos Pierre Pizon, Paris: pp. 33 top, 42, 57 bottom, 65 bottom, 116, 117, 118, 164 top, 168, 183, 222, 352, 355.
Photo Winter, Leipzig: pp. 18, 203 bottom, 287 right, 309 bottom, 332 top, 380 top.
Pichonnier, Paul et Jean, Bruxelles: pp. 163, 175, 276, 291 top, 384, 427 left.
Pineider, Dr. G., Florence: p. 383.
Pitt River Museum, Oxford (from the Curator): p. 164 bottom.
Pleyel, Paris: p. 73.
Rijksmuseum, Amsterdam (Photo-Commissie): pp. 115, 263 bottom, 264, 310, 313 top, 360 bottom.
Royal College of Music, London: p. 292 left.
Royal Ontario Museum of Archaeology. Toronto: pp. 219, 267.
Schubert, Vilma, Braunschweig: pp. 321 top, 322 bottom.
Schweizerisches Landesmuseum, Zurich: pp. 363, 364, 367.
Seiser, Hans, Photo-Verlag, Salzburg: p. 34 bottom.

Smithsonian Institution, Washington, United States Museum: pp. 176 bottom, 199 top, 260, 271.
Soviet Foreign Office: pp. 66, 86.
State Conservatory of Music, Prague, p. 34 top.
Teknisk Foto, Copenhagen: pp. 171 middle, 191, 200 bottom, 229, 230, 234, 288, 309 top, 403 left.
Tempo, Leipzig: pp. 237 bottom, 314 top, 321 bottom, 322 top, 332 bottom, 372 top.
Victoria and Albert Museum, London (Crown Copyright reserved): pp. VII, 6, 14, 172, 188, 196 bottom, 215 and 216 bottom, 268, 275, 302, 317 top, 318 bottom, 368 top, 399.

DESIGNS

after photographs by:

Bouckaert, Albert, Bruxelles: pp. XXIX, 205.
Gewitz, Eisenach: p. 327.
Göteborg Museum: p. 419 top.
Musikwissenschaftliches Institut und Instrumentenmuseum der Universität Leipzig: p. 295.
Neupert, Hanns, Bamberg: p. 370.
Photo Tempo, Leipzig, p. 213.
Photo Winter, Leipzig: pp. 206, 377.
Drawn by Dr. Rosamond Harding: pp. 378, 418, 419 bottom.
By courtesy of Philip James and the Windmill Press, London: pp. 265, 273, 353.
By kind permission of Städtisches Gewerbemuseum, Markneukirchen: p. 316.
From Yale University, New Haven: p. 413.
After an illustration in William Dale's book: Tschudy the Harpsichord Maker, London 1913: p. 354.
After an illustration in Norlind's History of the Piano, Hannover 1939: p. 294.

Note: 'Keyboard shift' is the right expression for which sometimes 'Keyboard glide' is used in this book. Technical circumstances made uniformity impossible.